TRANSITIONAL JUSTICE, INTERNATIONAL ASSISTANCE, AND CIVIL SOCIETY

In recent years, transitional justice has become increasingly international in its scope. Due to ongoing animosities, lack of political will, and the absence of credible governing or judicial institutions, international organizations, donors, and NGOs advocate for transitional justice initiatives like truth commissions or special tribunals – alongside national actors, like civil society and victims' groups. This book examines how international assistance affects transitional justice, and where power truly lies in making decisions about justice for victims of massive human rights abuse. The book finds that government donors typically lack strategies for transitional justice, they struggle with information deficits, and they are constrained by short-term approaches that do not give enough attention to what is often a weak and divided civil society sector. All the authors have both practical and scholarly perspectives on transitional justice. Country case studies are provided, including descriptions of the challenges in developing data on transitional justice financing.

Paige Arthur is Deputy Director of the Center on International Cooperation at New York University. She is the editor of *Identities in Transition: Challenges for Transitional Justice in Divided Societies* (Cambridge, 2011).

Christalla Yakinthou is a Birmingham Research Fellow with the Institute for Conflict, Cooperation and Security in the Department of Political Science and International Studies at the University of Birmingham, England. She is the author of *Political Settlements in Divided Societies* (2009), and the co-editor of *Conflict Management in Divided Societies: Theories and Practice* (2011).

Transitional Justice, International Assistance, and Civil Society

MISSED CONNECTIONS

Edited by
PAIGE ARTHUR
Center on International Cooperation – New York University
CHRISTALLA YAKINTHOU
University of Birmingham

CAMBRIDGE
UNIVERSITY PRESS

CAMBRIDGE
UNIVERSITY PRESS

University Printing House, Cambridge CB2 8BS, United Kingdom

One Liberty Plaza, 20th Floor, New York, NY 10006, USA

477 Williamstown Road, Port Melbourne, VIC 3207, Australia

314–321, 3rd Floor, Plot 3, Splendor Forum, Jasola District Centre, New Delhi – 110025, India

79 Anson Road, #06–04/06, Singapore 079906

Cambridge University Press is part of the University of Cambridge.

It furthers the University's mission by disseminating knowledge in the pursuit of education, learning, and research at the highest international levels of excellence.

www.cambridge.org
Information on this title: www.cambridge.org/9781107166783
DOI: 10.1017/9781316711347

First published 2018

Printed in the United Kingdom by Clays, St Ives plc

A catalogue record for this publication is available from the British Library.

Library of Congress Cataloging-in-Publication Data
NAMES: Arthur, Paige, editor. | Yakinthou, Christalla, 1980– editor.
TITLE: Transitional justice, international assistance, and civil society : missed connections / edited by Paige Arthur, New York University, Christalla Yakinthou, University of Birmingham.
DESCRIPTION: Cambridge, United Kingdom ; New York, NY : Cambridge University Press, [2018] | Includes bibliographical references and index.
IDENTIFIERS: LCCN 2017060379 | ISBN 9781107166783 (alk. paper)
SUBJECTS: LCSH: Transitional justice. | Civil society. | Human rights.
CLASSIFICATION: LCC JC571 .T6996 2018 | DDC 340/.115–dc23
LC record available at https://lccn.loc.gov/2017060379

ISBN 978-1-107-16678-3 Hardback

Contents

Tables

Contributors

Paige Arthur is Deputy Director of the Center on International Cooperation (CIC) at New York University. She is the editor of *Identities in Transition: Challenges for Transitional Justice in Divided Societies* (Cambridge, 2011).

Tania Bernath has been working in the international humanitarian aid field for more than twenty years and holds an MA in international education and development as well as a Certificate in the Advanced Study of Evaluation. She currently works as a consultant on a wide array of projects with UN agencies, donors, consulting firms, and international organizations. She has worked in more than thirty countries, including Uganda, in both the international humanitarian aid and human rights sectors in post-conflict and emergency settings. Bernath is the coauthor of *Becoming an International Aid Worker* (2016).

Anita Isaacs is the Benjamin R. Collins Professor of Social Sciences and Professor of Political Science at Haverford College. Her research and teaching focus on Latin American politics, US–Latin American relations, and the domestic and global challenges of democratization and peacebuilding. She is the author of a forthcoming book on the politics of transitional justice in postwar Guatemala.

Laura McGrew has a PhD in peace studies from Coventry University, and a master's in public policy from Johns Hopkins School of Advanced International Studies. She is the author of several articles and book chapters on transitional justice, coexistence, governance, and peacebuilding, primarily related to Cambodia. She has given numerous presentations on a variety of subjects related to peacebuilding and transitional justice. She also consults for various organizations and has worked with the United Nations and NGOs in Cambodia, the Thai–Cambodian border, Bosnia, Rwanda, Sri Lanka, Afghanistan, Nepal, West and Central Africa, the Maldives, and the United States, in the fields of development, gender, human rights, rule of law, conflict analysis, peacebuilding, and coexistence.

Rachel A. Schwartz is a PhD candidate in political science at the University of Wisconsin–Madison. Her research focuses on the legacies of armed conflict, state building, and institutional change in Central America. She was previously a program associate at the Inter-American Dialogue, where she coordinated programs on citizen security and migration in Central America and Mexico.

Christalla Yakinthou is a Birmingham Fellow with the Institute for Conflict, Cooperation and Security and the Department of Political Science and International Studies the University of Birmingham, England. She is the author of *Political Settlements in Divided Societies*, and the co-editor of *Conflict Management in Divided Societies: Theories and Practice*.

Foreword

Follow the money. Money talks. Money makes the world go 'round. Money is power.

And yet, we know very little about the money when it comes to processes of social change generally, and transitional justice processes in particular. How are such processes of dealing with the past, and especially dealing with a legacy of serious human rights violations, affected by, supported, thwarted, changed, or sustained by the presence – or absence – of funding from donor states? How does the choice to fund some things and not others change the very categories of what is known as transitional justice? While there has been some information on specific places or mechanisms, this is the first time that those working in or around processes of dealing with the past can explore the role of international donor cooperation in these processes. We have Paige Arthur and Christalla Yakinthou to thank for that.

The theory and practice of transitional justice (also referred to as post-conflict justice or dealing with the past) has evolved over the years. From a set of experiences largely designed and financed domestically to deal with the crimes of a dictatorship in South America, Eastern Europe, or South Africa, the ideas migrated to post-conflict situations with far fewer internal resources and far more international intervention. The kinds of responses, mechanisms, timetables, and scope became a matter of concern for the United Nations and for donor agencies. The "toolkit" of transitional justice measures – criminal trials, truth commissions, reparations programs, vetting, and other structural reforms – sometimes supported and made possible local responses, but sometimes operated to the detriment of local concerns and ways of rebuilding after conflict. Indeed, as the following pages show, internationalized or hybrid criminal tribunals vacuumed up the bulk of the resources, while little flowed to civil society groups despite rhetoric acknowledging their importance.

The confounding effect of introducing outside resources into complex political environments is well known to development scholars and practitioners: money skews priorities, creates new actors, and artificially inflates some sectors of the economy while starving others. But there is little consideration of how exactly outside resources do this in peacebuilding, post-conflict, or post-dictatorship contexts. Thus, the results of these studies will be important for development practitioners, especially in light of the World Bank's recent attention to issues of law, governance, and conflict as keys to long-term development, as exemplified by the Bank's 2011 *World Development Report*. In particular, people working in embassies or development cooperation agencies will appreciate the attention to support for civil society in a transitional or post-conflict setting, as well as the companion website, fundingtj.org. Such support, especially in a moment of attacks and efforts to discredit and weaken civil society groups, has become more fraught, complex, and necessary. The case studies in this volume show why.

We live in a moment of retrenchment and retreat from the internationalist impulse of the immediate post–Cold War era, with its creation of international bodies like the ad hoc and hybrid criminal tribunals and the International Criminal Court. Support for retrenchment and national security-centric politics spreads, from the United States to Turkey to Europe. As I write, the current occupant of the US White House proposes to cut the foreign aid budget by a third. Europe, with funding emergencies of its own, is less able to stay the course for the long-term needs of societies emerging from conflict. And new funders, more interested in physical infrastructure than social reconstruction, have been slow to step up.

It may be that the current illiberal moment is merely a blip, or it may be that societies emerging from dictatorship or civil conflict will largely again be left on their own. In either case, there will be a continuing need for clear thinking about how resources were well – or poorly – deployed in the wake of conflict, why civil society is important to sustainable change, how international frameworks create "friction" with domestic constructs, and how ideas, interests, and institutions combine to explain patterns of behavior in international relations. This book provides important insights into all of these, and more.

Above all, there will be a continuing need to support the survivors, advocates, and civil society organizations that emerge from situations like those described in this volume. Their heroic, under-resourced, optimistic struggles against long odds to build a better society remain at the core of a justice agenda, whether transitional or otherwise.

Naomi Roht-Arriaza
San Francisco, California
April 2017

Acknowledgments

The idea for this book came out of a set of case studies and the subsequent toolkit that we developed for the Bureau of Democracy, Human Rights and Labor (DRL) at the US Department of State from 2013 to 2015. The program officer in charge of our grant, Riva Kantowitz, was our constant interlocutor and also participated as an observer in two of our field visits (to Bosnia and Herzegovina and Cambodia). Without this grant, and especially without the encouragement of Riva and her colleagues, Katrina Fotovat and Patricia Davis, this book surely would not exist. Our other invaluable source of support was our senior advisor, Naomi Roht-Arriaza, who graciously shared her expertise as we developed our case study methodology and, later, our initial case study report for DRL in 2014. Debbie Sharnak also provided helpful research assistance in the initial phase of this project.

We thank our case study authors, Anita Isaacs, Rachel Schwartz, Laura McGrew, and Tania Bernath, all of whom made enormous efforts to transform the original case studies for DRL (which followed a specific template provided in the methodology) into the more nuanced and interesting chapters that appear in this book. We would also like to acknowledge the financial contribution of IREX for the case study that Paige Arthur conducted in Morocco.

A critical piece of work in the early phase was figuring out how we could easily access and use the immense Creditor Reporting System database on the OECD's web site, which provides grant-level data on foreign aid from all OECD countries stretching back decades. Andrew Rosenfeld, a software engineer, stepped in on a pro bono basis and built a custom research interface to help us identify, select, and code grants related to transitional justice (TJ). You will see this data referred to as the TJ International Assistance Database in this book, and it provided us with important direction about who was funding what in each of our case study countries, so that we were not flying blind.

Once the case studies were finished, we held an authors' meeting in New York to discuss key findings and to decide on the most important issues to raise in the toolkit. We thank the International Center for Transitional Justice (ICTJ) for providing space for the meeting, and the following people for their participation and feedback on our work: Ari Bassin, Ruben Carranza, Alison Davidian, Djordje Djordjevic, Eduardo González, Clara Ramirez-Barat, Laura Antonia Roberta Schurr, Elizabeth Silkes, Andrew Solomon, Nahla Valji, and Brian Williams.

Although the toolkit itself ("Funding Transitional Justice: A Guide for Supporting Civil Society Engagement") is not part of this book, we drew on it extensively in our conclusion and recommendations. We therefore wish to acknowledge those who played a role in its development. Refik Hodzic served as an external advisor on the report (alongside Riva Kantowitz and Naomi Roht-Arriaza), providing detailed comments on the final draft. We also thank the following people – many of whom were also initially interviewed as part of the case study research – for providing feedback on the draft toolkit either in writing or as part of a focus group: Ari Bassin, Sabrina Büchler, Alison Davidian, Ambassador William Longhurst, Veronica Melander, Thomas Osorio, Marcos Smith, Andrew Solomon, Lucy Turner, Nahla Valji, and Margherita Vismara.

Finally, we are truly humbled to acknowledge the civil society organizations, donors, UN agencies, and government agencies that shared with us their time, candor, and experience in the five countries where we conducted case study research. These interviews, and their experiences and reflections, were the essential foundation upon which this book was constructed. We owe them our deepest gratitude.

In Guatemala: Historical Archive of the National Police (Archivo Histórico de la Policía Nacional, AHPN); Legal Firm for Human Rights (Bufete Jurídico de Derechos Humanos); Center for Legal Action on Human Rights (Centro de Acción Legal en Derechos Humanos, CALDH); Center for Forensic Analysis and Applied Sciences (Centro de Análisis Forense y Ciencias Aplicadas, CAFCA); Guatemalan National Widows' Coordinating Committee (Coordinadora Nacional de Viudas de Guatemala, CONAVIGUA); Families of the Detained and Disappeared in Guatemala (Familiares de Detenidos y Desaparecidos en Guatemala, FAMDEGUA); Latin American Faculty for Social Sciences, Guatemala (FLACSO, Guatemala); Forensic Anthropology Foundation of Guatemala (Fundación de Antropología Forense de Guatemala, FAFG); Myrna Mack Foundation (Fundación Myrna Mack); Mutual Support Group (Grupo de Apoyo Mutuo, GAM); Institute for the Comparative Study of Legal Sciences (Instituto de Estudios Comparados en Ciencias Penales de Guatemala, ICCPG); International Institute for Learning on Social Reconciliation (Instituto Internacional del Aprendizaje para la Reconciliación Social, IIARS); Pro Justice Movement (Movimiento Pro Justicia); Norwegian Embassy; Office of the High Commissioner for Human Rights (OHCHR); Archbishop's Office on Human Rights in Guatemala (Oficina de Derechos Humanos del Arzobipado de Guatemala, ODHAG); Human Rights Ombudsman (Procuraduría de Derechos Humanos, PDH); Spanish Embassy; Swedish Embassy; Unit for the Protection of

Human Rights Defenders of Guatemala (Unidad de Protección a Defensores y Defensoras de Derechos Humanos, Guatemala, UDEFEGUA); United Nations Development Programme (UNDP); United Nations Special Rapporteur on Freedom of Expression; US Embassy; USAID.

In Bosnia and Herzegovina: Association TJ, Accountability, and Remembrance in Bosnia and Herzegovina; Association of Women from Prijedor "IZVOR"; Balkan Investigative Reporting Network (BIRN); Center for Nonviolent Action; Center for Torture Victims; Civil Society Promotion Center; EU Delegation; Helsinki Committee for Human Rights in Republika Srpska; International Commission for Missing Persons (ICMP); Missing Persons Institute (MPI); Mothers of Srebrenica and Zepa Enclaves (Pokret Majke enklava Srebrenice i Žepe); NED; Netherlands Embassy; Network for Peace Building (Mreža Mira); Republican Organization of Families of Detained Soldiers and Missing Civilians of RS (Republička organizacija porodica zarobljenih boraca i nestalih civila RS-a); Swedish International Development Cooperation Agency (Sida); Swiss Embassy; Track Impunity Always (TRIAL); UK Embassy; UNDP; Women to Women (Zene Zenama); Youth Communication Center (OKC); Youth Initiative for Human Rights (YIHR).

In Morocco: Amazigh Theater, Al Hoceima; Association ADALA; Urban Initiative Association (Association Initiative Urbaine); Moroccan Human Rights Association (Association Marocaine des Droits de l'Homme, AMDH); Medical Association for the Rehabilitation of Torture Victims (Association Médicale de Réhabilitation des Victimes de Torture, AMRVT); Avocats Sans Frontières; Casamemoire; Center for Cross-Cultural Learning; National Human Rights Council (Conseil National des Droits de l'Homme, CNDH, multiple units); Regional Human Rights Council-Al Hoceima (Conseil Régional des Droits de l'Homme-Al Hoceima, CRDH-Al Hoceima); Cultivation of Roses Project; EU Delegation; Deposit and Management Fund (Fondation Caisse de Depôt et Gestion, FCDG); Moroccan Forum for Truth and Justice (Forum Marocain pour la Justice et la Vérité, FMVJ); Human Rights Watch (HRW); ICTJ (former staff); Local Coordinating Committee of the Community Reparations Program for Hay Mohammadi (former staff); Mediterranean Youth Council for Development; National Endowment for Democracy (NED); Netherlands Embassy; Network of Development Associations of the Al Hoceima Region (RADRA); Search for Common Ground; US Ebassy.

In Uganda: African Network for the Prevention and Protection of Child Abuse and Neglect (ANPPCAN); African Youth Initiative Network (AYINET); Aid Africa; Alliance for Peacebuilding (AfP); Avocats Sans Frontières (ASF); CARE; Center for Global Health and Peacebuilding; Center for Governance, Peace, and Security; Center for Reparations and Rehabilitation (CRR); Child Voice International (CVI); Community Action Project/Uganda Youth Coalition; Democratic Governance Facility (DGF); Diakonia; Gideon Foundation; Human Rights Network Uganda

(HURINET); ICC in Uganda; ICC Trust Fund for Victims; ICTJ; Irish Embassy; Justice and Reconciliation Project (JRP); Justice Law and Order Section (JLOS); Ker Kai Acholi; MacArthur Foundation; Netherlands Development Cooperation; Northern Uganda Transitional Justice Working Group (NUTJWG); OHCHR; Refugee Law Project (RLP); Trust Africa; Uganda Fund; Uganda Victims Foundation (UVF); Uganda Women's Action Program; UNDP; UN Women; Unam; US State Department.

In Cambodia: Cambodian Human Rights and Development Association (CHRDA); Asia International Justice Initiative/East-West Center (AIJI/EWC); Cambodian Defenders Project (CDP); Cambodian Human Rights Action Committee (CHRAC); the Documentation Center of Cambodia (DCCam); Extraordinary Chambers in the Courts of Cambodia (ECCC): Civil Party Lead Co-lawyers Section, Office of the Co-prosecutors, Public Affairs Section, Victims Support Section; European Union/CEC/EDF; French Embassy; French Ministry of Foreign Affairs; German Federal Ministry for Economic Cooperation and Development (BMZ); Civil Peace Service/German Corporation for International Cooperation (GIZ); Human Rights Resource Center (former AIJI/EWC); ICTJ (former staff); Kdei Karuna; Netherlands MFA; New Zealand Embassy, Bangkok; OHCHR; Open Society Justice Initiative (OSJI); Swedish Embassy; Transcultural Psychosocial Organisation (TPO); UK Embassy; US Embassy; US State Department; USAID; Youth for Peace.

Introduction

Changing Contexts of International Assistance to Transitional Justice

Paige Arthur and Christalla Yakinthou

The field of transitional justice (TJ) began to emerge in the 1980s, as newly democratizing regimes in Latin America and elsewhere sought to create strategies both to assist victims of human rights abuses of the previous regimes and to signal their commitment to a new, rights-respecting dispensation. Generally, TJ has been associated with a specific set of state-led measures to address past systemic or massive human rights violations: truth-telling initiatives, such as the opening of archives or the establishment of a truth commission; prosecutions, often focusing on those "most responsible" for human rights crimes (usually meaning the intellectual authors of the crimes); reparations for victims, administered through a state fund rather than litigated by individuals through the courts; and institutional reforms specifically designed to prevent the recurrence of systemic or massive human rights abuses – in particular, vetting of members of the security forces who may have condoned or been responsible for abuses.

Many of the early (and paradigmatic) TJ efforts such as those in Argentina, Chile, and South Africa were primarily national efforts supported through national funds, with limited technical assistance from non-nationals. These middle-income countries were able to draw largely on their own financial and technical resources to advance a nationally conceived TJ agenda – albeit while drawing on and influenced by the experiences of other countries.

In more recent years, however, as TJ has shifted to post-conflict contexts in lower-middle- and lower-income countries (according to World Bank measures), the norm is for TJ processes to be funded largely by international donors and for international technical assistance to play a strong role in all aspects of the process. This shift, among others, has spurred a debate both in TJ practice and in the academic study of TJ concerning the "internationalization" or "globalization" of TJ, which may be viewed in a positive or a negative light. On the one hand, internationalization of TJ helps to hold recalcitrant states to account, including by bolstering national actors' capacity and standing in advocating for justice measures, and by linking them to advocacy networks outside of their own countries. On the other, however, this shift raises the concern that international actors are setting the terms for national TJ agendas, and that national actors, including civil society organizations (CSOs), may feel more accountable to international actors than to their own constituents.[1] For example, in a recent special issue of the *International Journal of Transitional Justice*, Lucy Hovil and Moses Chrispus Okello note that in northern Uganda, a network of peacebuilding CSOs that has existed for more than a decade:

> now find themselves having to forsake their experience and reframe their activities under the heading of transitional justice, a term that has become increasingly nebulous as a result. Having shifted positions to suit their international minders, many of these CSOs are under pressure to disown the amnesty process in support of international prosecutions . . . The result is a clumsy silence and an inability on the part of CSOs to engage coherently and honestly with their constituencies.[2]

This book examines the relationship between international assistance and local civil society actors working in or alongside the field of TJ. We center our research on this underexplored relationship because, although much of the attention in TJ has been on the responsibility of the state (especially with respect to the development of international norms), many observers have noted the important roles that civil society actors play.[3] Indeed, TJ is not simply a court, a truth commission, or other official institution. Rather, it is a complex social process in which both the state and civil society participate. In early experiments with TJ, for example, civil society actors in Argentina, Chile, and South Africa pushed the state to take action – either as advocates standing outside of the state in CSOs, or as new participants in government institutions, as the state moved away from autocratic rule. Yet we see in more recent, internationally financed interventions that funding and attention is

[1] See, e.g., Moses Chrispus Okello, "Interview with Piers Pigou," *International Journal of Transitional Justice* 5, no. 3 (2011): 508–18; Iavor Rangelov and Ruti Teitel, "Global Civil Society and Transitional Justice," in *Global Civil Society 2011* (London: Palgrave 2011): 172; and Michael Humphrey, "Victims, Civil Society and Transitional Justice in Bosnia and Herzegovina," *Temida* 15, no. 1 (2012): 59–76. For a dissenting and not particularly persuasive view, see Lucy Hovil, "Interview with Aryeh Neier," *International Journal of Transitional Justice* 5, no. 3 (2011): 504–08. Neier claims that international donors merely "respond" to local TJ interest (as though this interest is unproblematic and unitary), rather than shaping or "guiding" it.

[2] Lucy Hovil and Moses Chrispus Okello, "Editorial Note," *International Journal of Transitional Justice* 5, no. 3 (2011): 333–44.

[3] See the recent reports of the UN Special Rapporteur on the promotion of truth, justice, reparation, and guarantees of non-recurrence, Pablo de Greiff, including: "Report to the Human Rights Council on the Participation of Victims in Transitional Justice Measures," A/HRC/34/62 (December 27, 2016); and "Report to the General Assembly on National Consultations Concerning the Design and Implementation of Transitional Justice Measures," A/71/567 (October 25, 2016). More generally, see David Crocker, "Civil Society and Transitional Justice," in *Civil Society, Democracy, and Civic Renewal*, ed. Robert K. Fullinwider (Lanham, MD: Rowman & Littlefield, 1999), 375–401; David Backer, "Civil Society and Transitional Justice: Possibilities, Patterns and Prospects," *Journal of Human Rights* 2, no. 3 (2003): 297–313; David Crocker, "Civil Society and Transitional Justice and International Civil Society: Toward a Normative Framework," *Constellations* 5, no. 4 (1998): 492–517; and Naomi Roht-Arriaza, "Civil Society in Processes of Accountability," in *Post-Conflict Justice*, ed. Cherif Bassiouni (Ardsley, NY: Transnational, 2002), 97–114.

given primarily to state or hybrid institutions. This focus is worthy of scrutiny, because it is doubtful that any formal TJ institution has ever completed its mandate successfully without engaging with civil society actors, which play a wide variety of roles in TJ processes, including investigation, monitoring and advocacy, facilitation and consultation, service delivery, research and education, and establishing parallel (nonofficial) TJ initiatives in contexts where states fail to live up to their obligations.[4]

Outside of the TJ field, it is well known that donors and multilateral institutions have shifted their focus (and funding) to civil society actors over the past twenty to thirty years.[5] A number of factors have contributed to this shift. One is the recognition that non-state actors are often more effective local partners than states, which may be weak or corrupt. Another is the rise of the theory that a thriving civil society promotes social capital and interpersonal trust, which in turn has the potential to support sustainable, transparent democratic institutions. That is, civil society engagement is seen as important not only to enhance the effectiveness of any particular intervention – such as a TJ measure – but also in order to contribute to the broader social change goals of civic engagement and democratization.

BACKGROUND

This book was born from and partially supported by a research project commissioned by the Bureau of Democracy, Human Rights and Labor (DRL) at the US Department of State. In 2013, DRL gave a grant to Paige Arthur's consultancy, Public Action Research, to develop a "toolkit" for TJ donors, which was to be based on substantial, field-based case study research in countries with some experience of TJ. The case studies were undertaken in the spring and summer of 2014, and the toolkit, called "Funding Transitional Justice: A Guide for Supporting Civil Society Engagement," was completed and launched at the United Nations (UN) and in private meetings with donors in 2015. The case studies examined in this book are based on the research commissioned for the DRL project. After the close of the grant, the project's team leaders, Paige Arthur and Christalla Yakinthou, developed a separate set of conceptual pieces based on the case studies.

In developing the toolkit project, we noted early on that very little is actually known about international assistance to TJ measures, in spite of the fact that

4 See Crocker, "Civil Society and Transitional Justice," and David Backer, "Civil Society and Transitional Justice: Possibilities, Patterns and Prospects," *Journal of Human Rights* 2, no. 3 (2003): 297–313.

5 A UNDP report, "Donors' Civil Society Strategies and Partnership Modalities: A Resource Guide" (New York: UNDP, 2012), gives a comprehensive overview of multilateral and bilateral approaches to civil society funding – including changes in these strategies over the years. The report describes each donor's definition of civil society, its approach to civil society, and various modalities for funding civil society (e.g., individual grants, pooled funds, etc.). In some cases, the report cites statistics on the proportion of assistance devoted to civil society support; in the case of USAID, for example, more than 40 percent ($5 billion) of its assistance in 2011 (the latest year for which data was available at the time) went to international or local NGOs.

international actors have come to play a strong role in many TJ processes in recent years. Moreover, what little is known about international assistance relates to assistance to state or hybrid institutions (like courts or truth commissions), rather than assistance to critical support actions undertaken by civil society.[6]

Additionally, we observed that although the shift toward a "globalization" of TJ is widely noted, little research exists that can shed light on patterns of international assistance and its impact on TJ processes. This gap stems, in large part, from a lack of basic information that could be used for developing analysis and hypotheses for subsequent testing. For example, there is little qualitative data on how international assistance to TJ actually operates. How are decisions made on TJ funding, and who makes them, in which donor agencies? Do donors have specific strategies with respect to funding TJ? How and when do they work with national actors, especially civil society actors, in setting strategies or making decisions? How do they see the role of civil society in relation to achieving TJ-related goals? And so on. In general, donor decision-making on TJ has been a "black box"; donors do not have public records of their decision-making processes, and they are not particularly open to (or have time for) the interviews required for qualitative research.

We also saw that little is known about the civil society actors who are receiving (or not receiving) international assistance. What proportion of TJ funding in a country goes to civil society support? What types of civil society actions are being supported? How do civil society actors themselves engage with donors? And how does the professionalization of the CSO sphere – linked, in many countries, to accessing international funding – impact the pursuit both of funding and of achieving larger TJ goals? Has international assistance aimed to foster general TJ goals, such as promoting strong, networked civil society actors? These questions were particularly important to DRL, since support to civil society is part of its mandate.

INTERNATIONAL ASSISTANCE AND TRANSITIONAL JUSTICE

Scholars have conducted little research on international assistance to TJ. This gap stems, in large part, from the difficulty of obtaining data. Some TJ measures, such as international and hybrid tribunals, as well as some truth commissions, provide data on year-over-year contributions in annual or final reports. Such reporting is, however, the exception rather than the rule. Moreover, although it would theoretically be possible to pull data on TJ funding from existing grant databases, especially the online Organisation for Economic Co-operation and Development (OECD) database on overseas development assistance (ODA) and other overseas

6 See, most notably, Marieke Wierda and Anthony Triolo, "Resources," in *International Prosecutors*, ed. Luc Reydams, Jan Wouters, and Cedric Ryngaert (New York: Oxford University Press, 2012), 113–70; and William Muck and Eric Wiebelhaus-Brahm, "Patterns of Transitional Justice Assistance among the International Community," paper presented at the Sixth European Consortium for Political Research General Conference, Reykjavik, Iceland, August 25–27, 2011.

assistance, this would by no means be a straightforward task, since what counts as TJ is not always clear.[7] Even within the US government, which commissioned the toolkit, little was known about the government's own TJ funding. TJ focal points and advisors for USAID, including Naomi Roht-Arriaza and Andrew Solomon, have made efforts to identify this funding, with some limited success.

The research that does exist often does not focus on assistance to TJ as such, but rather on assistance to international/hybrid tribunals,[8] and on the broader trend toward funding justice-sector initiatives (including TJ) over the past fifteen to twenty years. Research has examined donor motivations for contributing to war crimes tribunals,[9] the "judicialization of international assistance," of which TJ and international tribunals are a part,[10] and numbers regarding funding to international and hybrid tribunals.[11]

There is thus a decisive gap in the TJ literature concerning the costs of TJ and international financing for TJ. In general, only the costs of the international and hybrid tribunals are well known. The costs for truth commissions are somewhat well known as a result of Priscilla Hayner's recent reissue of *Unspeakable Truths: Confronting State Terror and Atrocity*, which now includes budget figures for many, though not all, truth commissions.[12] Concerning reparations programs with substantial international contributions, very little data is available, with the exception of Sierra Leone, whose reparations program was funded by the UN Peacebuilding Fund. Finally, although security system reform (SSR), which may or may not include vetting processes to exclude human rights abusers from security forces, likely draws a sizable percentage of all TJ-related assistance, there is almost no

7 To access the OECD's Creditor Reporting System (CRS) database and perform simple keyword searches, see "Query Wizard for International Development Assistance" on the OECD web site, available at stats.oecd.org/qwids/. A simple query for "transitional justice" will give information on a range of TJ projects, including most of the bilateral assistance received by the International Center for Transitional Justice.

8 For the most recent published research, see Wierda and Triolo, "Resources."

9 See Sara Kendall, "Donors' Justice: Recasting International Criminal Accountability," *Leiden Journal of International Law* 24, no. 3 (2011): 585–606; and Steven D. Roper and Lillian A. Barria, "Gatekeeping versus Allocating in Foreign Assistance: Donor Motivations and Contributions to War Crimes Tribunals," *The Journal of Conflict Resolution* 51, no. 2 (2007): 285–304. Roper and Barria found that funding for tribunals correlates with higher levels of democratization and GDP in donor states. A donor's status as a former colonial power also correlates with funding for tribunals. Factors that do not correlate, however, include a donor's membership in the UN Security Council or its location in a particular region. The research concludes that funding for tribunals closely matches general patterns of foreign assistance.

10 Barbara Oomen, "Donor-Driven Justice and Its Discontents: The Case of Rwanda," *Development and Change* 36, no. 5 (2005): 887–910. Oomen describes (and criticizes) the strong growth in funding to a wide variety of justice-sector reforms in developing countries over the past fifteen to twenty years.

11 Rupert Skilbeck, "Funding Justice: The Price of War Crimes Tribunals," *Human Rights Brief* 15, no. 3 (2008): 6–10. Skilbeck generally defends their high cost.

12 Priscilla Hayner, *Unspeakable Truths: Confronting State Terror and Atrocity*, 2nd edn. (New York: Routledge, 2010), Appendix 2, Chart 4. Even in this case, however, many budgets are missing, and the data sources for the budgets given are not always clear.

data on SSR that parses international contributions to TJ-related elements such as vetting. Case studies of TJ in individual countries rarely discuss international financing.[13]

Debates on International Assistance to Transitional Justice

Although data is scarce, TJ academics and practitioners engage nonetheless in a number of debates on international assistance to TJ. A key debate concerns the "internationalization" or "globalization" of TJ, mentioned earlier, which some observers view in a negative light. Another concerns the outsized nature of funding for international and hybrid tribunals vis-à-vis all other TJ measures. This debate stems from well-known critiques of the high costs of international criminal justice in general (whether or not these tribunals are seen as related to TJ). With trials costing millions and even tens of millions of dollars per person prosecuted, often in poor and developing countries, many have suggested that the money would have been better spent on other initiatives. Those who defend these costs argue that the assessment of the worth of tribunals should be seen relative to the large numbers of people killed, the difficulties of prosecuting systemic and mass crimes, and the historical records that the tribunals will provide.[14]

Even so, the TJ literature does not appear to include anyone who defends the weighty imbalance between funding for prosecutions and all other TJ initiatives. For those who support the high costs of prosecutions, the solution for rectifying the imbalance lies in providing more support to complementary TJ initiatives, especially more "victim-centered" initiatives like reparations, rather than reducing support to prosecutions.

An additional debate concerns how much and how long the international community should be expected to support TJ initiatives. This discussion revolves largely around tribunals, since they have tended to be costly. "Donor fatigue" with the high costs of the International Criminal Tribunal for the Former Yugoslavia (ICTY) and the International Criminal Tribunal for Rwanda (ICTR) was one motivating factor behind creating national-international "hybrid" tribunals in East Timor, Sierra Leone, and elsewhere.[15] While pushing for "cheaper" justice is one consequence of donor fatigue, another is inadequate or incomplete justice, when donors largely withdraw at the end of a formal TJ initiative, leaving little funding for important follow-up activities – especially those led by civil society groups. Another consequence may be donors' loss of interest in supporting successive TJ initiatives (e.g., a reparations program after the conclusion of a truth commission) – or even

[13] A noteworthy exception is Stina Petersen, Ingrid Samset, and Vibeke Wang, "Aid to Transitional Justice in Rwanda and Guatemala 1995–2005," in *Building a Future on Peace and Justice: Studies on Transitional Justice, Peace and Development: The Nuremberg Declaration on Peace and Justice*, ed. Kai Ambos, Judith Lange, and Marieke Wierda (Berlin: Springer, 2009), 429–67.

[14] See Skilbeck, "Funding Justice," 6–10.

[15] See Wierda and Triolo, "Resources."

successive peacebuilding or rule of law initiatives in a complex context (like Sierra Leone).[16]

Other areas of debate do not appear to have filtered through to the academic literature on TJ yet. In our own experience as practitioners, we have observed discussions among TJ actors on whether donors routinely privilege some TJ actors over others, and what positive or negative consequences may result: for example, preferences for funding "known" nongovernmental organizations (NGOs) or international nongovernmental organizations (INGOs), especially those with which the donor has a preexisting relationship. Other discussions have included whether international actors (INGOs, UN agencies) monopolize the provision of technical assistance, when there are local resources or resources in nearby countries; whether donors focus too much on ad hoc institutions (courts, commissions), which are expensive and by nature short term; and perceptions of donor fickleness with respect to 1) types of initiatives supported and 2) countries where TJ may be supported.[17]

Forms and Modalities of International Assistance

International assistance can be defined in a number of ways, and it can come from many types of actors. The most obvious form of assistance is the direct transfer of money to official TJ initiatives from donors – bilateral and multilateral donors, private foundations, etc. These transfers can be critical to the very existence and operation of a TJ measure, such as a special court, a truth commission, or a reparations program. Not every TJ measure relies on such financial transfers, and transfers are obviously most important in less-developed countries where resources are stretched thin. While some TJ measures rely on a mix of contributions from the national government and international donors, the trend over the past two decades seems to be for more TJ measures to rely on international financial assistance in order to undertake and/or complete their work.

In addition to financial transfers to TJ measures, donors also contribute money to non-state actors (INGOs, NGOs, etc.) that support TJ work or initiate nonofficial TJ initiatives, such as memorials or unofficial truth commissions. Examples of such actors include the International Center for Transitional Justice (ICTJ) and Benetech in the United States, the Center for Legal and Social Studies (Centro de Estudios Legales et Sociales) and the Argentine Forensic Anthropology Team

16 The difficulties in raising funds for the Sierra Leone Truth and Reconciliation Commission may be an example of this kind of fatigue. Another factor, however, may have been donor mistrust that the truth commission process would be well handled. See International Crisis Group, "Sierra Leone's Truth and Reconciliation Commission: A Fresh Start?" (Brussels: International Crisis Group, 2002), 8–9, available at www.crisisgroup.org/~/media/Files/africa/west-africa/sierra-leone/B012%20Sierra%20Leones%20Truth%20and%20Reconciliation%20Commission%20A%20Fresh%20Start.pdf.

17 Some of these debates, however, have emerged in the related areas of development and international assistance and critiques of the liberal peacebuilding project.

(Equipo Argentino de Antropología Forense) in Argentina, the Centre for the Study of Violence and Reconciliation (CSVR) in South Africa, the Documentation Center of Cambodia (DCCam), the Humanitarian Law Center (HLC) and Documenta in the former Yugoslavia, among many others.

Another, related form of assistance is technical assistance on TJ. Such assistance is nonmonetary, and it is usually provided directly by bilateral donors, through provision or secondment of relevant experts from their countries; by UN agencies like the Office of the High Commissioner for Human Rights (OHCHR), the United National Development Programme (UNDP), and UN Women; by INGOs; and, in a few cases, by formal and informal transnational networks, such as the Latin American Association of Forensic Anthropology and the now-defunct Documentation Affinity Group. Technical assistance can be substantial, especially in contexts where TJ is an unknown concept, or where state institutions (and qualified personnel) have either been decimated by conflict or tainted by repressive policies.

Somewhat less clearly, international assistance plays a fourth role, which is shaping the TJ agenda in a particular country. Both monetary and nonmonetary assistance may contribute to such agenda setting. Although the idea that international assistance helps to shape TJ agendas is acknowledged in the field, the extent and the dynamics of that influence vary from context to context. Unfortunately, so far only a handful of case studies specifically address these dynamics in the TJ context.[18]

The primary modality for funding TJ is the direct grant from bilateral or multilateral donors (e.g., a state entity or an NGO receives a grant from a government). Assistance from the international community has often focused on financing TJ institutions (e.g., ad hoc courts or commissions). When these are administered by UN entities, they are either funded through involuntary assessments on member states or through annual appeals to donors for voluntary contributions.

In recent years, donors have used a variety of basket fund modalities to fund TJ – a modality that will be examined in detail in two of our case studies. In some instances, special instruments have been created to fund a variety of TJ projects, rather than a TJ institution per se. Recently in Guatemala and Colombia, donors have created facilities, administered by the UN, to pool resources and distribute funds to a range of state and civil society actors. In another instance, TJ has been funded through a larger basket fund, where TJ is one among a number of pillars – as has been the case with the Democratic Governance Facility in Uganda.

[18] This issue is raised very clearly in Barbara Oomen, "Donor-Driven Justice and Its Discontents"; Martien Schotsmans, "'But We Also Support Monitoring': INGO Monitoring and Donor Support to *Gacaca* Justice in Rwanda," *International Journal of Transitional Justice* 5 (2011): 390–411; and Adam Branch, *Displacing Human Rights: War and Intervention in Northern Uganda* (New York: Oxford University Press, 2011).

CIVIL SOCIETY AND TRANSITIONAL JUSTICE

It is important to note, as all authors writing on civil society do, that there are many different ways to define "civil society." Civil society is always conceived in some relationship to the state – but the nature of that relationship, as well as the specific functions of civil society, may differ from author to author. Roger Duthie gives a good summary of the various approaches, which commonly include an anti-governmental model, in which civil society is defined through its opposition to a state (especially a repressive state); an associational model, in which civil society is comprised of private, voluntary associations located outside of the state and the market; and a public sphere model, in which civil society is defined through its function in providing a space for public deliberation, which is seen to strengthen democracy.[19]

Although there is no consensus in the TJ literature on the definition of "civil society," there is nonetheless a broad agreement on the kinds of roles that civil society actors, specifically, take on in TJ – in both post-authoritarian and post-conflict contexts, as well as in ongoing conflict. These roles combine various aspects of the definitions offered earlier (opposition to a repressive state; private, voluntary associations; space for deliberation). David Crocker and David Backer identified these roles early on.[20] Combining their analyses, these roles include investigation, monitoring and advocacy, facilitation and consultation, service delivery, research and education, and parallel authority.

These practical supporting roles that civil society actors play in TJ efforts are widely recognized, but they represent only one level of understanding civil society's potential contributions to TJ. Many observers make claims for civil society as a set of mediating actors between TJ initiatives and processes of democratization and/or peacebuilding. That is, on the conceptual level, some observers claim that TJ can contribute to democratization and/or peacebuilding through enhancing social capital and civic trust – concepts both linked to civil society.[21] Building on theories of social capital, such observers tap into the body of knowledge built by Robert Putnam, Francis Fukuyama, and others, which discuss how trust and generalized reciprocity are "positive externalities of collective activities undertaken for some

19 Roger Duthie, "Building Trust and Capacity: Civil Society and Transitional Justice from a Development Perspective" (New York: International Center for Transitional Justice, 2009), 5.

20 See Crocker, "Civil Society and Transitional Justice"; and Backer, "Civil Society and Transitional Justice." See also David Crocker, "Civil Society and Transitional Justice and International Civil Society: Toward a Normative Framework," *Constellations* 5, no. 4 (1998): 492–517; and Naomi Roht-Arriaza, "Civil Society in Processes of Accountability," in *Post-Conflict Justice*, ed. Cherif Bassiouni (Ardsley, NY: Transnational, 2002): 97–114.

21 A recent book-length, critical exploration of these connections is Laura K. Graham, *Beyond Social Capital: The Role of Leadership, Trust, and Government Policy in Northern Ireland's Victim Support Groups* (London: Palgrave Macmillan, 2016).

other purpose."[22] By joining associations of any kind (not necessarily related to politics), people build social capital that can then be deployed for other purposes, such as civic engagement.

Indeed, the leading INGO working on TJ, ICTJ, regularly claims that TJ promotes civic trust, and the concept is mentioned in a range of UN documents on TJ.[23] Since the Secretary-General's 2004 report, "The Rule of Law and Transitional Justice in Post-Conflict Societies," the UN has also signaled the importance of civil society engagement with TJ. In general, UN documents have not done much more than to affirm that civil society should be consulted on TJ and to give guidance on how such consultations might take place. Recently, however, this guidance has become more nuanced through the reports of the newly established Special Rapporteur on the promotion of truth, justice, reparation, and guarantees of non-recurrence, an office currently held by Pablo de Greiff. The reports that de Greiff has issued continue the work of affirming the role of civil society in TJ and pointing out the specific ways in which international actors could better support civil society engagement.[24] The reports are also reflective of the theoretical work de Greiff has published over the past ten years. In his August 2013 report to the General Assembly, de Greiff reproduces the explanatory account he gives of the relationship between TJ and the building of civic trust that he has outlined in other places, including in his article on the relationship between TJ and development.[25] We therefore see the issues of social capital, trust, and civil society officially reflected in UN documents.

Cynthia Horne writes, "There is a strong presumption that well designed and implemented transitional justice measures foster trust, which in turn supports

[22] Daniel N. Posner, "Civil Society and the Reconstruction of Failed States," in *When States Fail: Causes and Consequences*, ed. Robert I. Rotberg (Princeton, NJ: Princeton University Press, 2003), 242. Posner suggests that if donors wish to cultivate civil society in failed states, they should be wary of advocacy CSOs engaged in issues related to good governance. Posner believes advocacy organizations are more effective in scenarios where there is already a functioning state. In contexts of failed states, such organizations are too often set up precisely to follow donor agendas and capture donor funds. He counsels giving support instead to CSOs originally set up to promote interests independent of donor agendas. See ibid., 251.

[23] As of late 2016, ICTJ described itself on its web site thus: "We are an international non-profit organization specializing in the field of transitional justice. ICTJ works to help societies in transition address legacies of massive human rights violations and build civic trust in state institutions as protectors of human rights." See "Our Work," ICTJ, accessed December 15, 2016, www.ictj.org/our-work. See also, e.g., the ICTJ briefing paper: Paul Seils, "Towards a Transitional Justice Strategy for Syria" (New York: International Center for Transitional Justice, 2013), 2, ictj.org/sites/default/files/ICTJ-Syria-Analysis-2013.pdf; and UN Security Council, "The Rule of Law and Transitional Justice in Conflict and Post-Conflict Societies: Report of the Secretary-General," S/2011/634* (October 12, 2011), paras. 7 and 17.

[24] See, e.g., UN General Assembly, "Report of the Special Rapporteur on the Promotion of Truth, Justice, Reparation and Guarantees of Non-Recurrence, Pablo de Greiff," A/HRC/24/42 (August 28, 2013), esp. paras. 21, 29, 64, 73–74, 75, 79, 89, 100, 105(c), 105(d).

[25] See UN General Assembly, *Report of the Special Rapporteur on the Promotion of Truth, Justice, Reparation, and Guarantees of Non-Recurrence*, A/68/345 (August 23, 2013), esp. paras. 25–29 and 36–39.

democratization."[26] Indeed, theorists from Alexis de Tocqueville to Putnam have long emphasized the importance of associational life, or civil society, to building the trust needed to support democracy. Notions of social capital and trust have transferred into spheres of international policy, now playing key conceptual roles in policymaking at the World Bank, UN agencies, and other forums. Yet, as Horne notes, there is little empirical research and exploring this presumption with respect to TJ: "The focus of much of the writing on trust and TJ tends to be on how to choose the appropriate transitional justice measure in order to foster trust, with little attention paid to establishing an empirically verifiable relationship between the two."[27] De Greiff, for his part, addresses gaps in empirical grounding in an early article on the link between TJ and trust, writing:

> Whether any of this will in fact obtain, i.e., whether transitional measures will foster the sort of civic trust that I see as the essential part of a "reconciled" society, whether official apologies will actually help citizens grant their trust to trustworthy institutions, etc., are empirical questions which cannot be decided a priori. Indeed, experience suggests that we should have modest expectations at best.[28]

In sum, civil society potentially plays a wide variety of roles in TJ efforts, but some of these roles are clearer and more specific than others. While some donors (like UNDP) are trying to take an approach to civil society actors that moves beyond seeing them merely as project implementers or simple contractors,[29] it is not clear

26 Cynthia M. Horne, "Trust and Transitional Justice," in *Encyclopedia of Transitional Justice*, ed. Lavinia Stan and Nadya Nedelsky (New York: Cambridge University Press, 2011). Pablo de Greiff and Roger Duthie also make this link in various writings.

27 Horne, "Trust and Transitional Justice."

28 Pablo de Greiff, "The Role of Apologies in National Reconciliation Processes: On Making Trustworthy Institutions Trusted," in *The Age of Apology: Facing Up to the Past*, ed. Mark Gibney (Philadelphia: University of Pennsylvania Press, 2008), 121. De Greiff has consistently held the view that we should have modest expectations for the outcomes of TJ measures. Others who draw on his work, however, including organizations advocating for TJ, may not be as modest in their claims for a causal relationship between TJ to trust building. It would be useful, in this regard, to have a clearer picture of the mechanisms by which TJ might actually build trust. There appears to be at least two mechanisms. The first, similar to Putnam and other social capital theorists' conceptualization, might be that TJ can spur people to organize and act collectively around a TJ project. These actions would, on their own, build social capital, which could then be used for other social goods. The second, which is dissimilar to Putnam and others, but which is widespread in the TJ literature, is that TJ uses "signaling" from a state to a citizenry to create trust. That is, undertaking TJ measures signals to victims and others that the state has become more rights respecting, and this would create a shift in perceptions among recipients of the signals, making them more trusting of state institutions. On the face of it, there is more empirical research in related fields to support the first, associational mechanism than there is to support the second, signaling mechanism. There is a literature that examines signaling in international relations, often using game theoretic models, and led by notable political scientists such as James Fearon. It is unclear if or how this literature may or may not support TJ claims on signaling, and we have not seen it referenced anywhere in the TJ literature.

29 UNDP, "UNDP Strategy on Civil Society and Civic Engagement," New York, October 1, 2012, 5; available at www.undp.org/content/dam/undp/documents/partners/civil_society/publications/2012_UNDP_Strategy-on-Civil-Society-and-Civic-Engagement_EN_final.pdf.

whether other donors are taking this approach, or even how consistent the approach is across UNDP activities and country offices. It is also unclear how much this approach is being applied to donor support specifically to TJ.

APPROACH AND METHODOLOGY

The claim that TJ can contribute to strengthening civil society is one that INGOs and the UN promote as an important reason for undertaking TJ; we have little evidence, however, for this claim, as intuitive as it may be. Better understanding the relationship between international assistance and civil society actors (and how international actors do or do not support such civil society strengthening in TJ contexts) marks a step on the road to unpacking these issues. While our research cannot fill all of the gaps, our book's goal is to make significant headway in describing *how* the relationships work between international assistance and civil society actors engaged with TJ, and *what factors influence* their behaviors, in order to start to develop hypotheses on the relationship between international assistance and the impact of TJ measures.

Conceptual Reference Points

Our initial research (prior to undertaking the case studies) identified several bodies of literature as important theoretical points of reference for the project. First is the literature on tensions between local and global approaches to justice – a literature that itself is based on broader conceptualizations of "the local" in processes that are often profoundly shaped by external actors (like donors), such as peacebuilding and development. Within this literature, we focus mainly on the interactions (or "frictions," to use Anna Tsing's terminology) between international agendas/actors and local or national agendas/actors.[30] The literature guides our investigation into civil society perceptions of the motivations, interests, and behaviors of actors providing international assistance, and vice versa. (We are not, in this study, particularly interested in understanding local conceptions of justice, and how these may differ from international normative frameworks, since other scholars have covered this ground.[31])

A second point of reference is literature on networks of local/national CSOs – including their relationships with international networks and actors (including donors). This includes the pioneering work of Risse, Ropp, and Sikkink on transnational advocacy networks, and Paffenholz's investigation of CSOs in peacebuilding

[30] Anna L. Tsing, *Frictions: An Ethnography of Global Connection* (Princeton, NJ: Princeton University Press, 2004).

[31] See, e.g., Rosalind Shaw and Lars Waldorf with Pierre Hazan, eds., *Localizing Transitional Justice: Interventions and Priorities after Mass Violence* (Stanford, CA: Stanford University Press, 2010).

contexts.[32] To what degree are international actors (like donors) doing enough, or doing the right things, to support or cultivate such actors and networks? Donors have latched onto both "civil society" and "networks" as a kind of social good that they should be promoting, but with little guidance or evidence basis (in the TJ field at least) about how to do it or how to know when things are going well.

A third is the literature on international development assistance and foreign policy. We have drawn on the many rich histories of development assistance by Thomas Carothers, Diane de Gramont, Carole Lancaster, and others.[33] Although they do not address TJ directly, these accounts provide the needed context for understanding why donors started to include TJ as part of their development assistance, starting with aid in the mid- to late 1990s to initiatives like the South African Truth and Reconciliation Commission or the Guatemalan Historical Clarification Commission. They also offer frameworks for understanding donor decision-making. Additionally, the work of William Easterly, Jeffrey Sachs, and Ben Ramalingam involved in critiques of aid and of "aid effectiveness" has been a relevant touchstone for our work. Although our own research is exploratory in nature, and the TJ field in general lacks the robust data needed to draw conclusions on effectiveness, this literature contributed to our thinking on donor motivations and decision-making.[34] Finally, we found the work of Judith Goldstein and Robert Keohane on the role of ideas in foreign policy, and the work of David Halloran Lumsdaine on "moral vision" in foreign policy, of use in understanding how and why TJ has figured in donor choices for funding in recent decades.[35] These frameworks were more explicitly developed in Part II of this volume, where we provide two novel conceptual interpretations of the case studies.

Methodological Overview

We relied on a qualitative, case study methodology to answer the questions of *how* the interactions between international donors and civil society actors actually work,

32 See, most recently, Thomas Risse, Stephen C. Ropp, and Kathryn Sikkink, *The Persistent Power of Human Rights: From Commitment to Compliance* (New York: Cambridge University Press, 2013); and Thania Paffenholz, "Civil Society," in *Post-Conflict Peacebuilding: A Lexicon*, ed. Vincent Chetail (Oxford: Oxford University Press, 2009).

33 See, e.g., Thomas Carothers and Diane de Gramont, *Development Aid Confronts Politics: The Almost Revolution* (Washington, DC: Carnegie Endowment for International Peace, 2013); and Carole Lancaster, *Foreign Aid: Diplomacy, Development, Domestic Politics* (Chicago: University of Chicago Press, 2007); and Ben Ramalingam, *Aid on the Edge of Chaos* (New York: Oxford University Press, 2013).

34 See, e.g., William Easterly, ed., *Reinventing Foreign Aid* (Cambridge, MA: MIT Press, 2008); and Ramalingam, *Aid on the Edge of Chaos*.

35 The connection between TJ and the work of Goldstein and Keohane was made in Paige Arthur, "How 'Transitions' Reshaped Human Rights," *Human Rights Quarterly* 31, no. 2 (2009): 321–67. See David Halloran Lumsdaine, *Moral Vision in International Politics: The Foreign Aid Regime, 1949–1989* (Princeton, NJ: Princeton University Press, 1993); and Judith Goldstein and Robert O. Keohane, eds. *Ideas and Foreign Policy: Beliefs, Institutions, and Political Change* (Ithaca, NY: Cornell University Press, 1993).

and *which factors* influence behaviors and outcomes. Thus, the primary unit of analysis is the relationship between these two sets of actors (donors and civil society). Since these interactions take place in highly complex and variable contexts, we believed it was important also to develop thick descriptions of the TJ landscape in the country over time, the international assistance landscape over time, and the civil society landscape over time (in particular, networks of civil society actors). The contextual descriptions are also intended to spur further research on the links between donor approaches and broader TJ impacts, such as the one mentioned earlier on the development of civil society networks, because so little currently exists.

In order to better describe and understand the financial flows from international donors to TJ, primarily bilateral donors, we turned to OECD's online database on ODA.[36] This database gives grant-level information for all bilateral funding from OECD member states, and from some multilaterals (the UN Peacebuilding Fund, for example) going back to the 1970s. It is the main source for statistics on international assistance, but it has been completely untapped in the TJ and human rights fields. Working with a software engineer, we pulled data from 2000 to 2012, and then developed a methodology and a research tool to comb painstakingly through it, using hundreds of keyword searches in four languages to identify TJ-related grants.

Thus, the TJ International Assistance Database was created.[37] As a result of this collection and refinement process, we now have a better (though still incomplete) picture of year-over-year data on international contributions to a range of TJ initiatives. We thus now have some basis for comparing how much money has been spent on different types of initiatives, by which donor, for which type of actor (state/NGO), and in which country. Although research is still ongoing for the database, we have found (so far) more than 2,000 grants totaling more than $500 million (USD). As useful as this data is, however, we emphasize that for this particular project, we used the data mainly to guide and supplement our qualitative case study research, not to run experiments. In fact, the data contains critical gaps and is incomplete: not all assistance to TJ is considered ODA, and many (perhaps most) of the big expenditures on courts, in particular, cannot be found in the ODA data, as they often run through other channels. Moreover, funding to TJ is often granted through basket initiatives of which TJ is just one piece, and it can therefore be difficult to determine how much of the overall grant is actually supporting TJ. We make these gaps explicit when we use the data in our case study analyses.

The case studies involved a mix of desk and field research. We chose a purposive sample since our goal is to explore what is occurring and provide descriptions, rather than to make the kinds of claims more appropriate to a probabilistic sample.

36 To access the OECD's Creditor Reporting System (CRS) database and perform simple keyword searches, see "Query Wizard for International Development Assistance" on the OECD web site, available at stats.oecd.org/qwids/. A very recent resource that also uses OECD data, but in a much more user-friendly way, is Open Aid Data, available at www.openaiddata.org.

37 Paige Arthur, "TJ International Assistance Database, 2002–2012" (unpublished data, 2014).

The sampling strategy was as follows: all countries had to be recipients of foreign assistance for TJ, since our primary unit of analysis is the relationship between donors and civil society. Countries had to have experienced at least two TJ measures, whether national, hybrid, or international in character. This criterion was intended to ensure that both donors and civil society actors have had sufficient opportunity to engage with TJ over time, and it thus excluded countries where TJ is too "young" or insufficient (this included, at the time, Tunisia). Since our goals are mainly descriptive and explanatory, it made sense to include diversity as a criterion for purposive sampling: we thus selected cases from different regions and undergoing different types of transitions (post-authoritarian and post-conflict, acknowledging that the lines between the two may be blurred). Finally, there were practical considerations in our selection that we should acknowledge. One is that a case study had to be feasible within the budget and time frame of our project. For this reason, we chose Guatemala over Colombia in Latin America, as Guatemala is more geographically compact. Another is that the case had to be approved by the US State Department. For this reason, Kenya was excluded as a possibility.[38]

The countries selected were Guatemala, Bosnia and Herzegovina, Morocco, Uganda, and Cambodia. Data for the case studies was drawn from document review, semi-structured interviews with a range of target groups in each of the five case study countries, and grant data from the TJ International Assistance Database. We interviewed more than 100 key informants, who were divided into two groups, each with its own interview guide. The first set of key informants was donors. Here we primarily used purposive sampling, seeking to identify the most important donors in each of the countries, using the TJ International Assistance Database and other sources. We then used a cross-sectional strategy within those donor institutions in order to capture perspectives in different agencies and locations (e.g., embassies, ministries of foreign affairs, and/or development agencies). In some cases, we were able to interview the full population or close to the full population of such donors, as this population was small. We developed an interview guide to capture data on three areas: donor approaches to TJ funding, donor approaches to civil society, and the perceived impact of international assistance on civil society actors and networks.

The second set of key informants was civil society actors. We used purposive sampling to identify actors who are or have engaged with official and/or nonofficial TJ initiatives. We then developed an interview guide to capture data on civil society actors' capacities and social structures for action and on their perspectives on international assistance to TJ. Questions were divided into three areas: the political and social environment in which CSOs work, CSOs' relationships and networks with other civil society actors, and CSO perspectives on donors and international assistance. Both sets of guides are provided as annexes to this book.

38 We were told that TJ was a sensitive issue for the US embassy in Kenya.

Once the interview guides were developed, they were tested in the first country case study, Bosnia and Herzegovina, in April 2014, and then refined for subsequent case studies in May–June 2014. They were translated into relevant languages (Bosnian, Spanish, French, and Khmer). Subsequently, the case studies were updated in countries where TJ issues continued to shift from 2014 to 2017, most notably in Uganda and Guatemala, but also in Cambodia.

After completion of the case studies, we returned to the theoretical reference points that shaped the research questions and the interview guides. Drawing on the case study data, we developed two conceptual pieces. Yakinthou's chapter circles back to the frictions framework to explain the interactions between international and national actors on TJ. Arthur's chapter mines the international development assistance literature for frameworks to help explain the factors in donor decision-making on TJ. Our conclusion refers back to the literature on civil society and networks in order to make some general recommendations for how donors can better support civil society actors working on TJ.

OVERVIEW AND STRUCTURE

This book is structured in two parts. We begin in the first with the case studies themselves.[39] In the second part, readers will find the conceptual pieces that draw on the case studies to explore the relationships between donors and civil society actors. We then conclude with a robust summary and some pointed recommendations for how international assistance to TJ could be improved, with a view toward greater inclusion of civil society.

Part I Understanding the Five Cases

Guatemala

Anita Isaacs and Rachel Schwartz describe how civil society has faced an uphill battle in its struggle to build a broad-based coalition around TJ in the wake of four decades of brutal armed conflict in Guatemala. They argue that international assistance for TJ has witnessed a number of transformations in the two decades since the signing of the peace agreement. Most notably, shifting donor priorities have led to the decline and reorientation of support. Though donor representatives have flexed their political muscle to back civil society activists pursuing truth, repair, and justice for past human rights abuses, the reconceptualization of TJ as part of a broader "rule of law" agenda has moved critical financial support away from traditional victim-centered TJ activities. Over time, the effects of international assistance on civil society have been mixed. On the one hand, international support

39 For those who are interested, we have also appended our interview guides for the case study research in an annex to this book.

has fostered civil society cooperation by building broader networks and facilitating the exchange of information and expertise. More recently, this greater willingness to collaborate has extended to government agencies, building bridges between state and civil society actors. While human rights groups draw a clear link between increased state assistance and their own declining budgets, importantly, international support has opened channels of communication between state and civil society actors, particularly with respect to justice issues.

Yet, on the other hand, shifting donor priorities have fostered unequal access to international financial support, favoring the more well-connected and experienced NGOs, which have been better able to adapt their objectives and activities to international community preferences. Meanwhile, the lack of technical capacity keeps smaller, predominantly indigenous, victims' organizations from receiving much-needed support to attend to local demands and dependent on larger organizations that represent their interests. Further, fierce competition for limited donor resources, alongside long-standing ethnic, class, and ideological divisions, disrupts organizations' capacity to maintain tight connections between leadership and the grassroots and perpetuates a climate of civil society mistrust and fragmentation. The potential for developing much-needed social capital, both bonding and bridging, is accordingly undermined.

Bosnia and Herzegovina

Christalla Yakinthou argues that the shape of international assistance to civil society in Bosnia and Herzegovina was set very early by a combination of factors, but especially by the Dayton Agreement, the early robust exercise of the Bonn Powers, and a heavy investment in criminal prosecutions as a result of commitment to the ICTY. This combination of a constitutional structure that ended the war but embedded the divisions that sparked it, a heavy focus on one aspect of TJ without commensurate consideration for supportive elements, and missed opportunities for building intergroup trust has left multiple marks on the development of a robust and connected civil society. In addition, as the international community in Bosnia and Herzegovina has swung from heavily hands-on to highly hands-off and afraid of rocking the political boat, donors perceive that they have lost a meaningful ability to respond to negative politico-legal challenges that have adversely affected the TJ environment.

Yakinthou's chapter describes how these factors are reflected in civil society and its relationship(s) with the donor community and the broader public: CSOs that meaningfully challenge the political status quo are few and far between, a great deal of civil society work on TJ falls into larger patterns of ethnic division, issues exist around the legitimacy of much work that is done, and vulnerable groups complain of increasing marginalization. While a significant amount of pioneering work in TJ is being and has been done, particularly around criminal prosecutions, the recovery of missing persons, and documentation of human rights violations, there is also a widespread perception that TJ is not addressing core legacies of the conflict, and that this work has had minimal impact on broader Bosnian society. The chapter shows the chasm and the tensions between professionalized and non-professionalized CSOs, picking up on the way NGOs and CSOs have adjusted their work to focus on delivering projects – the broader liberal twenty-first-century theme of "projectitis" – and the impact of this approach on collaboration, independence, and the flourishing of a socially meaningful CSO sector.

The broader social context amplifies these weaknesses. The public views CSOs as making a profession of human rights work, irrelevant, and unable to address pressing social concerns. Coupled with extreme levels of ethnic tension in the country, low social capital and trust, and generally high unemployment (especially youth unemployment), CSOs working on TJ appear as marginal actors in a context of high conflict potential. Though donor support for prosecutions continues, appetite for funding alternative TJ work appears to be flagging, contributing, as in Cambodia and Guatemala, to a highly competitive and mistrustful environment for civil society actors, who also may not be well placed to contribute to understanding how tensions of the past affect the future.

Morocco

Paige Arthur draws some distinctive conclusions in her study of TJ in Morocco, which focuses on the European Union's funding for the much-discussed community reparations program – an innovative attempt to deal with the collective harms of massive human rights violations that operated from 2007 to 2011. The program was run by a state body, the Moroccan National Human Rights Council. Groups from affected regions in Morocco could apply through a competitive process for small-scale funds to support community-level initiatives. Analysis of this unique financing structure led to the finding that when donor funds are channeled largely to official or state institutions – as the funds for the community reparations program were – this act may implicitly legitimize the state's own approach to TJ and delegitimize civil society actors' key roles as interlocutors and counterweights to the state. Indeed, civil society actors were quite critical of the community reparations program; instead, they supported what they saw as more meaningful but more politically sensitive issues like dealing with impunity for past crimes.

Situating the community reparations program in the larger context of TJ in Morocco, Arthur finds that although a vibrant set of civil society actors (including the national victims' organization) had previously been the driving force behind TJ, civil society collaboration on TJ declined after the close of the Moroccan Truth and Equity Commission in 2006, and it remains quite weak today. In general, the Morocco case study suggests that TJ in itself does not enhance cooperation and social capital of organizations, nor has international assistance contributed to such enhancement. In retrospect, therefore, it might have been a positive move for the European Union to complement its support for the state-run community reparations program with specific support for civil society actors either to engage with and monitor the program or to pursue their own TJ-related initiatives, even if these were not linked to the state's (and the National Human Rights Council's) approach to TJ.

Uganda

Tania Bernath shows how the government's lack of commitment, tension between government and the international donor community, and a lack of civil society capacity can have a corrosive effect on the progress of TJ in a country. The case examines donors' long-term interest in supporting the Justice, Law and Order Sector, which includes the state bodies responsible for designing and implementing TJ, as well as trends in donor support to civil society working on TJ. It also looks at the use of a novel funding arrangement – the multilateral basket fund called the Democratic Governance Facility – which aims to promote coordination among donors on a range of issues, including TJ.

Bernath describes how the draft National Transitional Justice Policy, which provides a framework and common language around TJ initiatives, has been in process for several years, but it has stalled due to lack of government prioritization. Similarly, trials at both the national and international levels have been delayed, although as of 2016 they are under way. While a number of CSOs (supported by donors) have emerged as leaders and experts on TJ issues, they continue to work largely independently and have not formed an effective counterweight to government resistance to TJ. This lack of progress has left a number of key donors and UN partners frustrated. Many have lost confidence in the process, with CSOs working on TJ bearing the brunt of this frustration. Now, donors are starting to move on – shifting their priorities from peacebuilding to development, where TJ figures less prominently.

Cambodia

Laura McGrew looks at Cambodia, with its significant Khmer Rouge and civil war legacy. Cambodia is now a post-conflict country with a considerable TJ footprint, primarily in the ongoing work of the Extraordinary Chambers in the Courts of Cambodia (ECCC) and related CSO efforts to document, memorialize, and recover from the legacy of violence. McGrew argues that international assistance to TJ in Cambodia has been hampered by the voluntary structure of contributions to the ECCC, donor personnel's lack of knowledge of TJ principles and processes, the separation of funding streams for the ECCC versus related CSO TJ activities, the dwarfing of funds to CSOs in comparison to the ECCC, a lack of knowledge *within* donor agencies of what different departments are funding and monitoring, and donor fatigue. Nonetheless, international assistance has provided important inputs to TJ mechanisms for civil society, and the ECCC itself would never have happened without donors taking initiative.

McGrew argues that although the ECCC has opened space for CSOs, the court was and remains donors' main focal point for TJ in Cambodia – with the result that donor interest in funding civil society actors working on TJ has ebbed and flowed with the performance of the ECCC. As the ECCC became bogged down in problems of funding, political interference, and corruption allegations, support for CSOs and TJ networks correspondingly declined, and the aid-dependent CSOs found difficulties in mobilizing new sources of funding (except for some new funding streams from the US). As with Guatemala, CSOs have also not maintained previous levels of cooperation between themselves. One bright spot (bucking the trend of donor fickleness) suggested by McGrew's research is an initiative led by the German Civil Peace Service, which has funded a ten-year commitment to build the capacity and coordination of local organizations working on TJ-related issues. Worryingly, however, she concludes that in spite of the extensive international assistance to TJ (and previously to rule of law) in Cambodia, recent government crackdowns on CSOs indicate that donor and CSO goals to link TJ initiatives to ongoing impunity have not been particularly effective in the face of Cambodia's authoritarian government.

Part II Conceptualizing the Connections

Leading off Part II, Christalla Yakinthou examines the case studies using the "frictions" frame Anna Tsing developed in her pioneering anthropological work. Yakinthou argues that in order to better understand how international assistance affects civil society actors, one must more closely observe the tensions, processes, and legacies that often remain unacknowledged, but that shape key decisions over TJ priorities. She argues that while we often scrutinize TJ mechanisms, projects, and outcomes, we infrequently see the interactions across time and between actors that lead to choices ultimately supporting or sidelining particular approaches, harms, and groups over others, as well as how these interactions change and what new processes those changes set off.

Guided by the surrounding (and sparse, but growing) literature on friction and TJ, and the relational literatures on hybridity in peacebuilding and TJ, Yakinthou draws out resonant themes to TJ from Tsing's work. From these, she sets four frames: engaged universals and traveling packages; purification of conceptual and historical spaces; gatekeepers and the illusion of universals; and collaborations, shifts, and (co) imagining the universal ideal. In the second part of the chapter, she applies each of these frames to the data that has emerged from the case studies, to understand how and why goals or institutions were pursued, redirected, and abandoned. The frames direct us toward how hierarchies of power were created and recreated and the consequences of such re/creations.

The data reveals that TJ engagements and priorities are created and recreated across space and time according to several factors, including differing understandings of TJ principles, or "universals," legacies of donor countries such as colonial or foreign policy forays into the grantee or regional context, donors' domestic legacies and motivations, the motivations, and power relationships *between* CSOs (and between donors). These factors affect both the choice of what to focus on and what to ignore, but also affect adherence to goals over time.

The four frames show that while universally understood principles may be attached to TJ, the interaction between the universals as fixed concepts and their interpretation in the five case studies have created gaps, mutations, and innovations that have been sometimes constructive, and sometimes destructive. These interactions change our understanding of the "rules" of TJ, as they also change the routes through which civil society and donor actors try to reach their goals. In Cambodia and the ECCC, we see how friction between international actors shapes accountability agendas and their implementation. In interactions between international actors and victim-survivor groups in Bosnia-Herzegovina and Guatemala, we see how actors can function together ostensibly under the same universal principles, but while pursuing very different goals that may or may not be mutually beneficial. The indicators together show us how these interactions create shifts, fractures, limitations, new gaps, and also, importantly, new opportunities across the spectrum of actors engaged in the pursuit of TJ and the ideas that result. They give us important clues as to how to create more integrated, inclusive, and strategic TJ engagements.

Paige Arthur's contribution in Part II consists of a framework of decision-making specifically related to donor funding for TJ, based on our five case studies as well as a review of the literature on international assistance and the (rather sparse) literature on assistance to TJ. Arthur argues that donor decision-making is marked by the interplay of four key factors – ideas, interests, institutions, and information. She shows how funding decisions are multifaceted and difficult to predict, as they are bound variously by the principled and causal ideas that provide the universe of possibilities for action on TJ; strategic interests, which may or may not conflict with TJ; the context of particular institutional arrangements (which, in the case of TJ, tend to be limited or nonexistent); and the limited amount of practical and theoretical knowledge that donors have of TJ, including knowledge about TJ's effectiveness.

Arthur concludes (unsurprisingly) that we should not expect to see donors supporting TJ when it conflicts with their strategic interests, in particular those relating to security. She notes that ideas, especially causal ideas linking TJ to a variety of democratization, peacebuilding, or rule of law outcomes, have played a critical role in expanding the possible universe of actions for donors. These ideas, however, have not been given sufficient form and content through institutionalization in most donor agencies, whether in the form of specific TJ policies, or in the form of in-house TJ expertise. The result is a donor decision-making process for TJ characterized by fragmentation, incoherence, and possibly ineffectiveness in many (though certainly not all) instances. She finds, additionally, that the clearest idea with the most vocal and powerfully placed constituencies inside and outside of institutions – namely, the idea of the power of trials, advocated by influential lawyers – has garnered the most success among donors so far, measured in terms of funding.

Among the many consequences of these findings, Arthur highlights the fact that when donors do choose to fund TJ, it may not always be supported in the most relevant way. The combination of high-profile, "trendy" ideas and low institutionalization and information can easily lead risk-averse donors to fall into general patterns of donor behavior: preferring to invest in visible, finite "outputs" like commissions, courts, or memorial sites on the one hand, or in countable deliverables like expert trainings, small-scale community workshops, and research reports. They may resist supporting the more politically risky, long-term, and difficult-to-measure civil-society-led social change work that is actually at the core of meaningful TJ initiatives – precisely the kind of work that requires strong civil society actors to succeed. She ends by reflecting on the possibility that the apex of globalized TJ has been reached, and that the potential withdrawal of donor funds may spur creativity and change in the TJ field.

In our conclusion, we home in on civil society. We reflect on what our case studies have told us about the relationship between TJ and civil society, touching on issues of network strengthening that broadly framed our investigation. Unsurprisingly, we found mixed results, including some clear instances where vertical and horizontal networks have been strengthened, or where linking or bridging capital has been built. What was uncertain in the instances was the sustainability of these achievements, where they occurred. We then move into five "missed connections" and corresponding recommendations for making those connections. The recommendations are intended specifically for bilateral and multilateral donors, who all too often lack strategies; have an imbalanced approach to funding different TJ initiatives; struggle with information deficits about TJ practice and theory, TJ impact, and even their own past funding on TJ; are constrained by short-term and project-oriented approaches; and may not be giving enough attention (or the right attention) to a weak and divided civil society sector. Our hope is that donors can use these recommendations as a lever, to help them start to act in a more informed, strategic way – including treating civil society as a partner on a long and winding road (with inevitable setbacks), and encouraging cooperation among a more diverse range of civil society actors.

CLOSING: A SHIFTING CONTEXT FOR TRANSITIONAL JUSTICE

In October 2007, ICTJ and the United Kingdom's Department for International Development hosted a roundtable for donors in London to discuss the future of funding for TJ. Attended by more than sixty representatives from donors, UN agencies, and CSOs, the meeting's aim was "taking stock and moving forward," so donors could engage more effectively with TJ processes, national authorities, and civil society actors. Recognizing the immense role of international donors in TJ in recent years, the conference report observes:

> Yet there is no shared policy framework across international donors and a number of questions still need to be answered. There is a growing demand for evidence and longer-term results. Transitional justice is too often seen in simple terms as a trade-off between peace and human rights. Development agencies committed to eliminating world poverty need to justify funding transitional justice initiatives, some of which can be extremely expensive, with other immediate priorities, such as working towards physical security, health, and education for all.[40]

Fast forward ten years to 2017, and we find that the field has yet to move forward on these questions. Indeed, TJ seems to have stayed remarkably the same, as the world around it has shifted appreciably.

As we write this introduction in early 2017, we note how dramatically the context for TJ (and human rights work in general) has changed – not only since the 2007 roundtable – but even since we began our project three years ago. Refugees from the conflict in Syria have drawn attention (and funds) from donors in Europe; the US-led war on terror has ramped up rather than down, as Al Qaeda and Islamic State of Iraq and Syria (ISIS) forces have grown; and the United States has elected a new president, Donald Trump, whose beliefs stand in stark contrast to those of the human rights community on many issues (torture, Guantánamo, freedom of expression and the press, the value of international norms and institutions, etc.). We note bright spots for TJ: in Colombia, the government and the Revolutionary Armed Forces of Colombia rebels have agreed to a peace settlement in which TJ is an integral part, and in which civil society has played a critical role. But there are also dark spots: in South Sudan, successive peace initiatives, which include TJ, have failed in the face of mounting (and devastating) conflict.

The landscape of TJ is likely to change as a result of these shifts in global dynamics, and TJ may not hold the same place it once did among donor priorities. If this is the case, the relationships between international actors and the civil society initiatives they support (or ignore) may change again. Now more than ever, national civil society actors may need to drive TJ in the face of recalcitrant states and increasingly disengaged donors. Will the donors who are left be doing the right things to support them?

The need for greater coherence (the "how" of international assistance), clarity (the "why"), and coordination (the "with whom") has never been more urgent. In this book we argue that, with a few exceptions, the main bilateral donors providing funding to TJ have, on the whole, lagged behind in their inclusion of civil society

[40] ICTJ and UK Department for International Development, "Donor Strategies for Transitional Justice: Taking Stock and Moving Forward," report of seminar proceedings in London, UK, October 15–16, 2007.

actors as a core component of their TJ strategies (where these exist). Moreover, bilateral donors funding TJ have also lagged behind both the theory and practice of TJ, which has long understood civil society to play a crucial role both as support and counterweight to the state. Whereas theorists and practitioners of TJ argue for (and build strategies around) inclusion of civil society in order to build legitimacy, ownership, trust, and social capital, bilateral donors on the whole have focused their funding on state-led efforts – i.e., disproportionately funding state institutions – with civil society too often left as an afterthought.

This book offers insights into missed connections, from the perspectives of both donors and civil society actors. These insights are important for enhancing donors' and civil society actors' awareness of better ways of using their (collectively) decreasing funding, but they are also important because TJ (or even social change) in the wake of conflict and authoritarianism is unlikely to move forward without a powerful civil society sector acting as a counterweight to divided or backsliding governments and fragmented and mistrustful societies.

PART I

Understanding the Cases

1

From Reconciliation to Rule of Law

The Shifting Landscape of International Transitional Justice Assistance in Guatemala

Anita Isaacs and Rachel A. Schwartz

Between 1960 and 1996, Guatemala suffered a brutal internal armed conflict that pitted the counterinsurgent state against guerrilla forces. By the time the conflict ended with the signing of the 1996 peace accords, the toll of dead and disappeared had reached an estimated 200,000, with an additional 500,000 to 1.5 million people displaced.[1] Records of the atrocities reveal a highly skewed balance of abuses committed by the state. Some 93 percent of acts of violence registered by the United Nations (UN)-sponsored Historical Clarification Commission (CEH) were attributed to state actors, with 91 percent taking place between 1978 and 1984, the peak conflict years. In contrast, violence by guerrilla groups represents 3 percent of all violations registered.[2]

During the early 1980s, violence related to armed conflict assumed an ethnic dimension, as counterinsurgent forces adopted a scorched-earth policy to eliminate the guerrillas' perceived base of support in the indigenous highlands. Truth commission findings document 626 massacres of Mayan communities as well as widespread acts of sexual violence against Mayan women. Patterns of mass killings led international experts to conclude that between 1981 and 1983, the Guatemalan state committed "acts of genocide" against five Mayan ethnolinguistic groups: the Q'anjob'al, Chuj, Ixil, K'iche, and Achi.[3] In the Ixil area alone, findings suggest that between 70 percent and 90 percent of communities were completely wiped out.

Between 1994 and 1996, the UN helped broker a set of comprehensive peace accords between the Guatemalan state and the leftist Guatemalan National Revolutionary Unity (URNG), which brought the armed conflict to a close and set the stage for a number of international assistance efforts in support of transitional justice (TJ) processes. These include not only the decade-long UN Verification Mission in Guatemala (MINUGUA), which monitored progress toward compliance

[1] Comisión de Esclarecimiento Histórico (CEH), *Guatemala: Memoria del Silencio* (Guatemala: United Nations Office for Project Services, 1999), 17, 30.

[2] Ibid., 42. [3] Ibid., 39.

with the peace agreements, but also a number of bilateral and multilateral initiatives to support the pursuit of truth, repair, and criminal justice.

In this chapter, we take stock of these international assistance efforts. We examine how funding levels, mechanisms, and priorities with respect to TJ have evolved. We also analyze the effects of international assistance on Guatemalan civil society itself, exploring how support for TJ has shaped the capacity, knowledge, and objectives of local and national civil society organizations as well as the linkages among them.

Our analysis highlights several core claims. First, we find that international donor interest in TJ assistance in Guatemala has steadily declined, as a result of both donor fatigue and shifting priorities in favor of issues such as security and development. In conjunction with this shift, international donors have come to conceptualize TJ within a much broader rule of law agenda. While this speaks to the core forward-looking TJ objective of "nonrepetition," it also devalues the victim-centered, accountability, conciliatory, and reparative pillars of TJ. To the extent that international donors maintain a more traditional TJ focus, they provide support in three key areas: 1) political, which includes public pronouncements and expressions of solidarity; 2) technical, which includes training and professionalization to bolster civil society capacity; and 3) programmatic, which includes monetary support for TJ activities.

Beyond the changes in assistance itself, we find that, on balance, international donor support has had a number of worrisome effects on Guatemalan civil society. First, dependence on international funding streams has forced civil society organizations to reshape their own institutional objectives to align with donors' new security and rule of law agendas, which focus more on cooperation with government agencies. Civil society is also adversely impacted by the overall decline in international funding. While several international donors make a concerted effort to consult largely indigenous civil society groups whether in the capital or in rural departments, current funding mechanisms and constraints continue to favor the better-organized, more internationally plugged-in, urban-based organizations. Further, international funders are missing an opportunity to strengthen social capital. In fact, competition for limited funds appears to be generating renewed fragmentation and mistrust among human rights, democracy, and justice organizations.

To elaborate on these claims, this chapter proceeds as follows. We first provide some brief notes on the methodology and limitations of our study. Second, we give background information on TJ efforts in Guatemala since the 1996 signing of peace. Third, we examine the evolution of international assistance for TJ during this period, with particular attention to the overall decline and streamlining of funding. In the fourth and fifth sections, we analyze the shifting international funding priorities and the types of international support civil society organizations continue to receive when it comes to TJ issues, before turning to the effects of international assistance on civil society in Guatemala. In the sixth and seventh sections, we discuss how changes in funding preferences have reshaped civil society objectives and activities and increased cooperation with state actors. In the eighth and ninth sections, we assess how funding mechanisms make it difficult for rural victims' groups to access financial and technical support and how limited funds generate a climate of mistrust. We conclude with some broader reflections on how international assistance can most effectively promote TJ and contribute to the strengthening of civil society.

NOTES ON METHODOLOGY AND LIMITATIONS

As a starting point to determine which organizations to interview for this chapter, we used the TJ International Assistance Database, which includes international funding for TJ programs since 2002.[4] While the database identifies which international donors have provided support, in most cases, it does not provide the exact civil society recipients of funds. As a result, we drew on roughly fifteen years of research experience interviewing civil society representatives involved in the struggle for TJ to determine the interview sample.

We conducted interviews with eighteen civil society representatives from fifteen different organizations, ten international community representatives from eight different international donor governments and agencies, and two representatives from a quasi-state human rights institution (Human Rights Ombudsman's Office, PDH). The civil society interviewees represent five types of groups: victims' organizations engaged in the search for disappeared family members and the pursuit of truth and justice (Mutual Support Group [GAM], Guatemalan National Widows' Coordinating Committee [CONAVIGUA], Families of the Detained and Disappeared in Guatemala [FAMDEGUA]); human rights organizations working on a number of issues, among them crimes of the past (Archbishop's Office on Human Rights in Guatemala [ODHAG], Myrna Mack Foundation, Unit for the Protection of Human Rights Defenders of Guatemala [UDEFEGUA], Center for Legal Action on Human Rights [CALDH]); academic/research institutes (Latin American Faculty for Social Sciences [FLACSO Guatemala], International Institute for Learning on Social Reconciliation [IIARS], Institute for the Comparative Study of Legal Sciences [ICCPG]); legal assistance organizations (Legal Firm for Human Rights-Bufete Jurídico); and organizations providing other technical assistance, such as forensic support and archival documentation and analysis (Center for Forensic Analysis and Applied Sciences [CAFCA], Forensic Anthropology Foundation of Guatemala [FAFG], Historical Archive of the National Police [AHPN]).

The international representatives we interviewed came from a mix of donor governments and cooperation missions (US Embassy and USAID, Embassies of

[4] Paige Arthur, "TJ International Assistance Database, 2002–2012" (unpublished data, 2014).

Sweden, Norway, and Spain) and multilateral organizations (UN Development Programme [UNDP], Office of the High Commissioner for Human Rights [OHCHR], UN Special Rapporteur for Freedom of Expression).

Our sampling strategy presented several limitations. First, as a result of staff turnover, it was particularly difficult to find individuals with institutional memory who could discuss changes in strategies, priorities, and the climate for assistance over time. This limitation was most pronounced in the case of international donors. While veteran Guatemalan civil society leaders were able to provide their perspective on funding trends, and we were able to discern changes by analyzing projects funded over time, fewer international donor representatives we spoke with could provide a longer-term view.

Second, due to time and resource constraints within the scope of this project, we were unable to travel to the rural departments most affected by conflict violence to interview local community organizations receiving international TJ funding. Several civil society representatives we spoke with, however, have very strong ties to organizations at the local level and were able to explain their activities and challenges. Additionally, through our own insights, we were able to corroborate their observations with our own field-based knowledge and understanding.

TRANSITIONAL JUSTICE IN GUATEMALA

Despite the election of a civilian president in 1985, Guatemala's internal armed conflict did not come to an end until the signing of comprehensive peace accords eleven years later on December 29, 1996. The agreements stipulated key rights protections, including individual political and civil liberties, indigenous rights, and the right to resettlement for wartime refugees and internally displaced peoples. An agreement reconfiguring the political role of the armed forces aimed to establish civilian democracy on a surer footing. And although the controversial issue of unequal land tenure, a root cause of the armed conflict, was left unaddressed, an agreement on socioeconomic aspects and the agrarian situation acknowledged poverty and inequality as central peace and development concerns.

In a separate agreement, the peace accords also established the terms for the UN-sponsored CEH. Signed on June 23, 1994, the CEH accord established a commission to "clarify with all objectivity, equity, and impartiality the human rights violations and acts of violence ... connected to the conflict," to issue a report with its findings, and to provide recommendations to encourage "peace and national harmony."[5] CEH truth-seeking efforts would build on the work of the Catholic Church to document abuses and disseminate findings through its Recovery of

[5] See "Agreement on the Establishment of the Commission to Clarify Past Human Rights Violations and Acts of Violence that Have Caused the Guatemalan Population to Suffer," MINUGUA (Washington, DC: USIP Library, 1998), www.usip.org/sites/default/files/file/resources/collections/peace_agreements/guat_940623.pdf.

Historical Memory (REMHI) project, which released its report in 1998.[6] The CEH began work in 1997, visiting nearly 2,000 communities to record testimony.[7]

Compiled in its official report, *Memoria del Silencio*, the exhaustive work of the CEH rendered powerful findings about the systematic state abuses perpetrated during the thirty-six-year period of armed conflict. But none had a greater impact than the conclusion that the Guatemalan state had committed "acts of genocide," a charge that vindicated indigenous victims' organizations, but that was swiftly rejected by the country's military, political, and economic elite. On February 25, 1999, the CEH commissioners held an official ceremony to present the report to the state, which President Alvaro Arzú refused to receive.[8] Despite the international backing of truth commission findings and a domestic court decision to convict former dictator Ríos Montt of crimes of genocide, the charge remains deeply contested in Guatemalan society today.

Stemming from CEH recommendations, the state took steps toward complying with another TJ obligation through the creation of the National Reparations Program (PNR) in May 2003. The PNR committed to five types of repair for victims: 1) material restitution, 2) economic compensation, 3) psychosocial care and rehabilitation, 4) symbolic measures to dignify the victims, and 5) cultural reparations.[9] A 2005 reform increased the PNR budget from 300 million to 500 million quetzales (roughly $40 million to $67 million) and extended its mandate from thirteen to thirty-six years.[10]

Since its creation, the PNR has been riddled with political and economic challenges. Due to infighting over control of the program and the nature of reparations provisions – including whether they would be given on the basis of genocide – the PNR did not become operational until 2006. Further, reparations have mostly taken the form of one-time individual checks, rather than the collective, integral measures set out by the program. Critics contend that since the PNR's inception, politicians have used it as a clientelist tool to garner local support. Due to these problems, victims remain disillusioned, and most have yet to receive the reparations they are due. International pressure for the state to comply with its reparations obligations continues to mount, as victims pursue avenues such as the

6 Marcela López Levy, "Recovery: The Uses of Memory and History in the Guatemalan Church's REMHI Project." In *Truth and Memory: The Church and Human Rights in El Salvador and Guatemala*, ed. Michael A. Hayes and David Tombs (Herefordshire: Gracewing, 2001), 103–17.

7 Joanna R. Quinn and Mark Freeman, "Lessons Learned: Practical Lessons Gleaned from inside the Truth Commissions of Guatemala and South Africa," *Human Rights Quarterly*, 25, no. 4 (November 2003): 1117–49.

8 Susan Fitzpatrick-Behrens, "Angels in Guatemala: Confronting a Legacy of Official Terror," North American Congress on Latin America (NACLA) (January 5, 2010), accessed June 29, 2014, nacla.org/news/angels-guatemala-confronting-legacy-official-terror.

9 Gustavo Porras, "Introducción," in *La Vida No Tiene Precio: Acciones y omissiones de resarcimiento en Guatemala* (Guatemala: Programa Nacional de Resarcimiento, 2007), 28.

10 Rodrigo Carrillo, "Programa Nacional de Resarcimiento: Cuatro años haciendo camino al andar," in *La Vida No Tiene Precio*, 58–59.

Inter-American Court on Human Rights to press their demands.[11] The future of the program remains highly uncertain today. In April 2016, the newly elected government of Jimmy Morales shuttered the PNR's regional offices and laid off nearly 200 employees, placing the fate of tens of thousands of requests for reparations in limbo.[12]

In addition to truth seeking and reparations, Guatemala has witnessed several domestic criminal prosecutions related to past abuses. Criminal prosecutions of low-level police and military personnel began in 2009 with cases such as the disappearances of six indigenous peasants by ex-paramilitary member Felipe Cusanero and the disappearance of student leader Fernando García by police officers. Since then a number of other trials have taken place, leading to the convictions of five special forces members for the massacre of Dos Erres and five civil patrollers for the massacre of Plan de Sánchez.[13]

The most prominent trial was brought against Ríos Montt and former director of military intelligence Mauricio Rodríguez Sánchez in April 2013. The trial has its roots in international efforts to prosecute Ríos Montt in Spain's Audiencia Nacional under the doctrine of universal jurisdiction beginning in 1999. After nearly a decade of delays, the Audiencia Nacional issued arrest warrants in 2006 and heard victim testimony in 2008 and 2009; however, Guatemala's Constitutional Court blocked the extradition requests, stalling the international proceedings. But following the 2011 general elections, Ríos Montt stepped down as a member of Congress and was eligible to face justice in Guatemala.

On January 26, 2012, formal charges were announced, relating to crimes that took place in the northwestern Ixil region in the early 1980s. After several procedural delays, the trial began, making Ríos Montt the first president to face prosecution for crimes of genocide in a national court. The nearly two months of hearings included more than ninety testimonies of Ixil victims and a host of expert witnesses such as forensic anthropologists, military specialists, and international researchers. Despite the defense's attempts to invoke an amnesty and stall the proceedings, on May 10 the three-judge panel concluded that Ríos Montt was guilty of crimes of genocide and war crimes, sentencing him to eighty years in prison (Rodríguez Sánchez was acquitted).[14]

[11] See "Case of the Río Negro Massacres v. Guatemala, Judgement of September 4, 2012," Inter-American Court of Human Rights, accessed June 28, 2014, www.corteidh.or.cr/docs/casos/articulos/resumen_250_ing.pdf.

[12] Gabriel Woltke, "Jimmy Morales quiere terminar la tarea de OPM: cerrar la Sepaz," *Nómada*, April 15, 2016, https://nomada.gt/jimmy-morales-quiere-terminar-la-tarea-de-opm-cerrar-la-sepaz/.

[13] See "Guatemala Dos Erres Massacre Soldiers Sentenced," *BBC News*, August 3, 2011, www.bbc.com/news/world-latin-america-14383071; "Ex-paramilitaries Jailed for Guatemala Massacre," *BBC News*, March 21, 2012, available at www.bbc.com/news/world-latin-america-17454434.

[14] See Open Society Justice Initiative, "Judging a Dictator: The Trial of Guatemala's Ríos Montt" (Open Society Foundations, 2013), www.opensocietyfoundations.org/sites/default/files/judging-dicatator-trial-guatemala-rios-montt-11072013.pdf.

The sentence, however, would be short-lived. Ten days later, the Constitutional Court, citing procedural irregularities, annulled the proceedings in a tight three-to-two vote. The overturning of the sentence drew ire from victims' organizations and members of the international community, while prominent members of Guatemala's political and economic elite, including former president Otto Pérez Molina, maintained that the Guatemalan state did not commit genocide.[15] In early 2015, the new trial was delayed due to Ríos Montt's ailing health, and in June 2016, it was definitively suspended following a successful motion filed by the prosecution to separate the cases of Ríos Montt and Rodríguez Sánchez for the retrial. But more recently, a judge ruled that Ríos Montt would be subject to a special trial for the Dos Erres massacre. The new proceedings were slated to begin in October 2017.

Meanwhile, some criminal prosecutions related to conflict-era human rights abuses continue. In July 2014, the first guerrilla perpetrator was convicted for the massacre of twenty-two peasants in El Aguacate, Chimaltenango.[16] In January 2016, the Public Prosecutor's Office (MP) captured eighteen high-ranking former military officials in connection with the discovery of more than 550 bodies at the Zone 21 military base, also known as Creompaz, in Cóban, Alta Verapaz.[17] In February 2016, a military colonel and civilian commissioner were sentenced to 120 and 240 years in prison, respectively, for forced disappearance and crimes against humanity in a case of sexual slavery involving fifteen women held at the Sepur Zarco military base in Izabal.[18] While such trials remain hotly contested within a Guatemalan society that remains highly polarized when it comes to confronting the past, top judicial officials and the human rights community persevere in their commitment to pursuing justice for conflict-era abuses.

THE DECLINE AND STREAMLINING OF INTERNATIONAL ASSISTANCE FOR TRANSITIONAL JUSTICE

Amid the notable advances in TJ, international assistance for such activities in Guatemala has steadily declined in recent years. As a result of high levels of criminal violence, government corruption, and poverty and malnutrition, issues such as public security, justice sector reform, and economic development have received top billing on international donor agendas, relegating TJ to the back burner. This

[15] See "Presidente de Guatemala afirma que 'no hubo genocidio' durante dictadura de Ríos Montt," *EFE*, January 6, 2015, www.nacion.com/mundo/centroamerica/Presidente-Guatemala-genocidio-Rios-Montt_0_1461853885.html.

[16] Henry Morales, " La Justicia guatemalteca condena a un jefe guerillero por masacre durante la guerra civil," *El Faro*, July 5, 2014, www.elfaro.net/es/201407/internacionales/15646/La-Justicia-guatemalteca-condena-a-un-jefe-guerrillero-por-masacre-durante-la-guerra-civil.htm.

[17] Saul Elbein, "Bringing up the Bodies in Guatemala," *Al Jazeera America*, February 23, 2016, http://america.aljazeera.com/multimedia/2016/2/the-bodies-under-the-base.html.

[18] Maya Thomas-Davis, "Guatemala: Justice for Sepur Zarco Sex Slavery Victims," *Al Jazeera*, March 3, 2016, www.aljazeera.com/indepth/features/2016/03/guatemala-justice-sepur-zarco-sex-slavery-victims-160303072107762.html.

shift is striking in light of the long and storied history of international support for peacebuilding and TJ in Guatemala since the peace negotiations.

As peace talks in Guatemala got under way in 1994, the UN deployed a humanitarian mission known as the UN Verification Mission in Guatemala (MINUGUA) to accompany negotiations between the government and guerrilla representatives. During its initial phase, MINUGUA served as a peacekeeping mission, whose objectives were to put an end to the violence and oversee the implementation of the Comprehensive Agreement on Human Rights. By 1997, MINUGUA had deployed 188 uniformed personnel to Guatemala and had spent just over $4.5 million.[19] Following this initial phase from 1994 to 1997, MINUGUA set its sights on the longer-term objectives of encouraging the Guatemalan government to reform state institutions and enshrine the promises of the peace accords into law. MINUGUA's mandate expanded to cover a range of issues, including "indigenous affairs, macroeconomic and fiscal policy, labor issues, land rights and agrarian policy, military and public security reform, and gender issues, among others."[20]

In these years, MINUGUA provided technical assistance to state institutions and national civil society organizations through a trust fund supported by nine member states: Belgium, Canada, Denmark, Germany, the Netherlands, Norway, Sweden, the United Kingdom, and the United States. During the decade MINUGUA was in operation, trust fund donations totaled $19.8 million, with 45 percent used for projects to strengthen the justice sector and defense of human rights, 21 percent to strengthen the National Civilian Police, 13 percent to promote legislative reforms to guarantee peace accord provisions, and 10 percent to support the publication and dissemination of MINUGUA's work. At its peak in 2000, MINUGUA included 532 national and international staff.[21]

On November 15, 2004, at the beginning of the administration of President Óscar Berger, the Mission's mandate officially came to an end. MINUGUA's final report declared that "with the end of international verification, the Guatemalan peace process [had] matured into a new and important phase in which national actors are assuming fuller responsibility for monitoring and promoting the goals of the Peace Accords." There was thus a perception within the international community that, ten years since the beginning of peace negotiations, Guatemala had made significant strides in guaranteeing democratic rule and fulfilling the central tenets of the agreements. Given this impression, the international community determined it could pull back a little and allow national actors to take the reins.

19 See "United Nations Verification Mission in Guatemala," United Nations Peacekeeping Operations, accessed June 28, 2014, www.un.org/Depts/DPKO/Missions/minugua.htm.

20 UN General Assembly, "The Situation in Central America: Progress in Fashioning a Region of Peace, Freedom, Democracy, and Development, Report of the Secretary-General," A/59/746 (March 18, 2005).

21 Ibid.

While the withdrawal of MINUGUA did not signal a complete UN departure, it did coincide with a broader programmatic turn away from a traditional TJ focus to a more general human rights and rule of law orientation on the part of international actors. Shortly after MINUGUA's closure, the Guatemalan government and the UN agreed to create a stand-alone Office of the High Commissioner for Human Rights (OHCHR), which began operations at the beginning of 2006. OHCHR priorities include "widening democratic space, the protection of human rights in development and in the economic sphere, countering discrimination, [and] combating impunity."[22] In addition to offering technical assistance, OHCHR monitors the human rights situation, publishing reports and investigations that make specific recommendations to state authorities. The Guatemalan government solicited OHCHR accompaniment for an additional three-year period beginning in 2015 – the third mandate extension since the office was created.

In addition to UN human rights activities through MINUGUA and OHCHR, international support through bilateral funding from donor governments also enjoys a long history in Guatemala. USAID began supporting peace process goals through two projects in 2001. Its three-year Human Rights and Reconciliation Program bolstered human rights groups, supported advocacy on behalf of disappeared children, and carried out activities designed to preserve the historical memory of conflict violence. From 2001 to 2008, USAID's Support for Demobilization, Incorporation, and National Reconciliation Program allowed forensic anthropologists at the FAFG to enhance their analysis equipment and provided support to groups offering psychosocial attention to victims. According to USAID project documents, USAID provided roughly $19.3 million in all for victim-centered TJ activities between 2001 and 2011.

In large part, funding from European governments in the early 2000s demonstrates similar trends. According to projects recorded by the TJ International Assistance Database, bilateral aid from European donors focused heavily on truth seeking, the search for the dead and disappeared, and psychosocial support for victims. For example, up until 2008, the mission of Austria provided support to forensic anthropologists' efforts to exhume victims, while the Dutch government supported similar efforts through 2010. Through 2010, the Spanish government funded historical memory projects as well as other activities to dignify and commemorate victims.[23]

Two significant transformations with respect to international assistance took place around 2010. First, donor governments began dedicating a larger share of funds to justice sector reform, in large part through the UN International Commission against Impunity in Guatemala (CICIG), a hybrid investigative and prosecutorial body created to reform the judicial system and accompany the MP in trying

[22] "OHCHR in Guatemala 2013–2014," Office of the High Commissioner for Human Rights, accessed June 28, 2014, www.ohchr.org/EN/Countries/LACRegion/Pages/GTSummary1314.aspx.

[23] Arthur, "TJ International Assistance Database."

emblematic cases. This reorientation of funds was due not only to the CICIG's growing caseload, which came to include cases against ex-president Alfonso Portillo and numerous military officers for embezzlement,[24] but also to the deteriorating security situation in the country, where the homicide rate reached a peak of 42 per 100,000 people.[25]

The shift in funding levels and priorities can be seen most clearly in the case of the United States, which has contributed nearly $5 million per year to the CICIG, roughly the same amount it contributed to TJ programming through UNDP during the four years between 2010 and 2014 combined.[26] Another example is the Spanish national government, which had strongly supported exhumations and grassroots victim organizations through the late 2000s, but ceased all TJ funding in 2013 to direct assistance to combatting malnutrition and gender violence, according to an embassy official. Even worse, some countries, which had maintained strong human rights support in Guatemala since the peace process, have closed their embassies, among them the Netherlands, Switzerland, and Norway.[27]

The streamlining of international funding for TJ initiatives through the creation of PAJUST (TJ Accompaniment Program), administered by UNDP, represents a second major shift. PAJUST was built on the work of two previous UNDP programs carried out in the mid-2000s: the "Dignification and Psychosocial Attention to Armed Conflict Survivors" Program (DIGAP) and the "Alliances with Civil Society" Program (PASOC).[28] PAJUST serves to coordinate donor efforts by pooling resources and holding group meetings to define funding priorities. Rather than maintain bilateral TJ programs, donor governments contribute to the PAJUST budget, which is allocated according to a set of defined goals and criteria.

Through financing provided by USAID, Sweden, Canada, Denmark, the Netherlands, the Basque government, the Catalan government, and the UN Peacebuilding Fund totaling nearly $35.9 million for the initial five-year period

24 See CICIG, *Caso Alfonso Portillo (Causa No. 7102–2001)*, accessed April 24, 2016, at www.cicig.org /index.php?page=7102–2001.

25 UNODC, "Transnational Organized Crime in Central America and the Caribbean: A Threat Assessment" (Vienna: United Nations Office on Drugs and Crime, 2012), 12.

26 On funding to the CICIG, see Joshua Partlow, "How a Peaceful Political Uprising Happened in War-Scarred Guatemala," *Washington Post*, September 5, 2015, www.washingtonpost.com/world/the_americas/how-a-peaceful-political-uprising-happened-in-war-scarred-guatemala/2015/09/05/88664b34-5195-11e5-b225-90edbd49f362_story.html; on funding for PAJUST, see PAJUST's internal Program Document: Programa de Acompañamiento a la Justicia de Transición (PAJUST), "Documento de programa," UNDP (June 2010), accessed June 28, 2014, www.gt.undp.org/content/dam/guatemala/docs/prodocs/undp_gt_pajust.pdf.

27 Civil society and international donor representatives discussed the recent closures of the Swiss and Dutch embassies, while closure of the Norwegian embassy was announced following research for this chapter. The Norwegian embassy's announcement is "Embassy in Guatemala to Be Closed," Government of Norway, November 4, 2015, accessed April 16, 2016, www.regjeringen.no/en/aktuelt/embassy-guatemala/id2460226/.

28 PAJUST, "Documento de programa."

(2010 to 2014),[29] PAJUST works to support state institutions as they comply with their obligations to armed conflict victims under international law and to bolster civil society organizations that advocate on victims' behalf.[30] PAJUST programming is oriented around the four pillars of TJ: truth, reparations, criminal justice, and nonrepetition. A fifth area, "articulation," refers to efforts to promote greater cooperation between state and civil society actors. Two projects have garnered the vast share of PAJUST support: 1) the AHPN, which works to catalogue, analyze, and put to legal use millions of National Police documents discovered in 2005; and 2) the FAFG, which leads efforts to exhume the remains of conflict victims and return them to family members.

Representatives of donor governments explained the emergence of PAJUST to channel TJ funding as the result of three main factors. First, decreases in funding for international missions and the contraction of in-country staff in the late 2000s meant that embassies no longer had the human resources to administer their own aid programs. By working through UNDP, donor governments have been able to alleviate the burden on in-country personnel. Second, international mission officials realized that, in some cases, they were duplicating efforts because of a lack of communication. PAJUST has provided a platform for international donors to coordinate funding and avoid this overlap. Finally, channeling funds through PAJUST has allowed donor governments to create some distance between themselves and TJ efforts, which have become more politically charged over the past several years. Several embassy officials explained that separating their bilateral agenda and interests from the issue of TJ funding allowed for a better relationship with the Guatemalan government. As one cooperation mission official noted, "Funds go through UNDP because they are more independent from governmental interests than [our mission]."

While PAJUST has constituted a welcome attempt to streamline international support, it also signals a decline in international donor interest and broader changes in donor priorities, which have placed a premium on issues like violence, impunity, and poverty rather than addressing past abuses. The creation of PAJUST also reflects increasing political sensitivities and a concern that international assistance for TJ might disrupt bilateral diplomatic relations with the Guatemalan government.

TRANSITIONAL JUSTICE AS A "RULE OF LAW" ISSUE

Alongside changes in funding levels and priorities, international donors have undertaken a strategic shift, reconceptualizing TJ as a "rule of law" issue. Rather than focus

[29] See "Programa de Acompañamiento a la Justicia de Transición – PAJUST," accessed May 24, 2017, available at www.gt.undp.org/content/guatemala/es/home/operations/projects/democratic_governance/Pajust.html. We were not able to get updated information for Phase II of PAJUST, which began in 2015.

[30] "Programa de Acompañamiento a la Justicia de Transición (PAJUST)," UNDP, accessed June 28, 2014, www.gt.undp.org/content/guatemala/es/home/operations/projects/crisis_prevention_and_recovery/Pajust/.

on truth seeking, reparations, and justice as means of coming to terms with the past, the international community has pursued a much more future-oriented approach, emphasizing the importance of reforming institutions to ensure that conflict-era abuses are not repeated. An important effect of this shift in framing has been increasing assistance for and cooperation with Guatemalan government agencies, now seen as crucial to bolstering the rule of law and human development. As we discuss in greater depth later in this chapter, this shift has largely been understood as burying the unfinished work of addressing past human rights abuses in order to pursue a much more politically palatable security and justice agenda.

As noted earlier, outside of PAJUST, increasingly fewer internationally funded programs deal specifically with traditional TJ issues. The CICIG has become the major international donor initiative over the past eight years, garnering considerable financial support from the governments of Canada, Finland, Germany, the Netherlands, Norway, Sweden, Spain, the United Kingdom, the United States, and the European Union.

While the CICIG does not explicitly take on cases related to conflict-era human rights abuses, it does fulfill the objectives of TJ in the sense that it promotes critical institutional reforms to ensure nonrepetition. While recognizing that conflict-era violence is not the CICIG's primary focus, international donor representatives described its work and that of other judicial sector programs as coinciding with the goal of pursuing justice for the past. As one donor government representative stated, "[Our programs] seek to provide space for the system to work. And so, we merge TJ and the rule of law." As another foreign diplomat stated, "I'm not sure where TJ ends and justice begins." Thus, as the peace process becomes more distant and the Guatemalan judicial sector remains weak, international donors have begun to conceive of TJ within a broader focus on the rule of law and institutional strengthening. International government representatives cited these reasons for the perceived decline in explicit TJ funding.

But the move away from supporting TJ initiatives per se, toward their merger into a rule of law agenda, has also precipitated a turn from funding national civil society to providing greater financial assistance for state institutions. Outside of MINUGUA, funding in the early 2000s was largely directed at victim-centered civil society groups working to exhume the remains of those killed and disappeared and to provide psychosocial care. But by the late 2000s, donor assistance, on the whole, increasingly supported state institutions such as the MP, the Judicial Body (OJ), and the National Institute of Forensic Science (INACIF), among others.

PAJUST is an exception to this general trend. Per project documents, the PAJUST budget favors assistance for civil society organizations over state institutions, with the former receiving roughly twice as much funding as the latter ($16.3 million to $8.2 million). This disparity is, in large part, due to the substantial support – some $10.3 million – the FAFG has received for exhumations and forensic analysis.

Yet even while allocating a significant share of funds to civil society, PAJUST works with eight different state agencies to strengthen the government's stake in TJ efforts. As one diplomatic representative commented, "PAJUST is ensuring that there is state ownership as well." Further, civil society cooperation with the state is one of the key criteria according to which PAJUST funding decisions are made. According to one UNDP official, a central pillar of PAJUST's work is articulation, which includes, among other dimensions, "promoting more cooperation between civil society organizations and the state."

Overall, strengthening state–nongovernmental organization (NGO) relations has become a central emphasis within international donor agendas, a significant contrast to the immediate postwar years when the international community felt a more pressing need to revive Guatemala's heavily battered civil society and focus on victim-centered activities to promote healing and reconciliation. There has been a growing recognition that despite a reinvigorated civil society sector, the broader objectives of strengthening the rule of law cannot be achieved without more robust state institutions that can deliver security, justice, and also basic services to the population.

POLITICAL, TECHNICAL, AND PROGRAMMATIC SUPPORT FOR TRANSITIONAL JUSTICE

To the extent that the international community continues to back TJ activities, international and civil society organizations cite three main types of support, which go beyond monetary contributions: 1) political support; 2) technical assistance; and 3) programmatic funding.

Political support refers to the pronouncements of backing, accompaniment, leadership, and mediation with the Guatemalan government that international actors offer to national civil society groups. One example of political support as it relates to TJ is the presence of diplomatic officials, particularly ambassadors, at emblematic trials for conflict-era abuses. In 2010, US ambassador Stephen McFarland attended the trial of two former members of the National Police eventually convicted in the disappearance of activist Fernando García. His successor, Ambassador Arnold Chacon, attended the Ríos Montt genocide trial in 2013, along with several other ambassadors and high-level international officials such as then-CICIG commissioner Francisco Dall'anese. Chacon's successor, Ambassador Todd Robinson, has continued this practice, attending the Sepur Zarco sexual slavery trial.[31] Their attendance, along with behind-the-scenes political pressure exercised by other international government officials has been designed

[31] See Lauren Carasik, "Justice Postponed in Guatemala," *Boston Review*, May 28, 2013, www.bostonreview.net/world/justice-postponed-guatemala.

to send the message to the Guatemalan government that the rule of law ought to be respected.

Diplomatic and other donor representatives contend that this political support is just as important as the financial backing they provide, as it bolsters the demands and amplifies the voices of civil society groups while showing that the international community is watching. "Just being there and being photographed with human rights defenders matters," stated one diplomatic official, in reference to the international presence at judicial proceedings and civil society forums.

While donor governments have been active in offering political support for TJ efforts, diplomatic officials reported certain constraints. There are often difficult tensions between making political statements and respecting Guatemalan national sovereignty and institutional affairs. As one official expressed, "Guatemala is a country that is protective of its processes, like any country. We have to be careful and proceed with the utmost respect." In light of the negative reactions of the Guatemalan government and ex-military groups to international accompaniment, another official even argued that the Ríos Montt trial illustrated how international support can sometimes hurt the process. But embassy officials have responded to national criticisms by focusing, above all, on the precedence of the rule of law. "Why attend the trials?" asked one diplomatic official. "To show that the process is important ... When we get criticized, we focus on the process." Another tactic donor governments have used is sending lower-level officials to observe human rights trials – they maintain a lower profile while also demonstrating support to the human rights defenders with whom they have ties.

The second type of support, technical assistance, refers to the external human resource inputs that enhance the training of personnel and the strengthening of capacities and internal procedures of an organization. Though civil society representatives and international officials both indicated that this type of assistance is critical, they had a hard time naming instances of technical support related to TJ specifically. Beyond the CICIG, virtually the only instance cited was Swiss support to bring internationally renowned archivist Trudy Peterson to train personnel at the AHPN on the handling and analysis of archival materials. While not specific to TJ, some international actors, including USAID, the Swedish embassy, and UNDP, cited micro-grant programs they administer to improve the technical capacities of smaller, younger local organizations – for instance, USAID's USA Forward.

The third type of support, programmatic support, refers to the direct financial support international donors provide for TJ initiatives. None of the international actors, other than UNDP through PAJUST, described having explicit TJ funding mechanisms. As noted earlier, to the extent that international actors focus on TJ, they have increasingly come to frame it within the broader scheme of justice and the rule of law – objectives that while anchored to the TJ pillar of nonrepetition, nonetheless depart from the victim-centered activities of the past.

Donor decision-making processes for programmatic support take into consideration a host of factors. In the case of PAJUST, UNDP evaluates eight criteria in determining which proposals to fund: 1) whether the project responds to program objectives; 2) whether the organization has worked with UNDP in the past; 3) whether the organization has the capacity to manage funds; 4) whether the organization is part of existing networks with other groups; 5) the extent to which the organization coordinates with state institutions; 6) whether the project includes a gender focus; 7) whether the project involves a focus on indigenous communities; and 8) the amount requested for the project. Governments that provide bilateral assistance reported using similar standards to make funding decisions.

PAJUST funding decisions are made during donor roundtables in which contributing governments make recommendations to UNDP and search for consensus on funding priorities. The donor governments that contribute to PAJUST reported having less control over the monitoring of projects, but consider this a natural and necessary sacrifice given the reduction in their personnel. Despite this challenge, international representatives did report undertaking an extensive consultation process with civil society and state actors under the auspices of UNDP to determine the PAJUST agenda.

While PAJUST serves as the main mechanism for synchronizing donor efforts, in general, international donors – both foreign governments and multilateral institutions – enjoy close collaboration and extensive communication with one another as a result of a number of coordinating platforms. The primary organizational body is the Group of 13 (G13), a group of eight countries (Canada, Italy, Germany, Switzerland, Norway, Spain, Sweden, and the United States) and six multilateral organizations (the Inter-American Development Bank, International Monetary Fund, Organization of American States, European Union, World Bank, and UNDP) to coordinate support.[32] Originally created by six countries in 1999 following the devastation of Hurricane Mitch, the group has expanded and seeks to support Guatemala "to achieve an equitable society, sustainable economic growth, and the rule of law."[33]

The G13 operates at three levels. At the top is the "Dialogue Group" comprised of ambassadors (or the highest in-country diplomatic official) and directors of participating multilateral institutions. The Dialogue Group holds political and strategic discussions on pressing issues, which have, at times, concerned TJ issues such as the Ríos Montt trial. At the second level is the "Cooperation Coordination Group," which is made up of political counselors, heads of mission, and officials in charge of multilateral assistance. This group discusses international funding efforts broadly and makes proposals to the Dialogue Group. Finally, the third level consists of thematic roundtables made up of mission and embassy staff. These groups discuss in

32 See "Acerca del G13," Grupo de Donantes G13, accessed June 28, 2014, www.g13.org.gt/content/acerca-del-g13.

33 Ibid.

greater detail projects and funding efforts related to five key areas: 1) security and justice; 2) health; 3) education; 4) water and environment; and 5) food security. Discussion and coordination of TJ support takes place under the auspices of the security and justice roundtable.

In addition to the G13, the European Union embassies along with those of Norway and Switzerland have created the "Grupo Filtro," a platform for dialogue between European diplomatic officials and Guatemalan human rights defenders. Through monthly meetings on thematic issues or important cases, European government representatives and civil society actors can share information and coordinate strategies.

Thus, even while overall financial assistance is on the decline, the international community exhibits a high degree of coordination and diplomatic officials understand their role not only in financial, but political terms. While bound by the constraints of shifting country priorities, both embassy and multilateral officials have been willing to use their visibility and standing to press human rights and TJ demands even as funds dry up.

RESHAPING CIVIL SOCIETY OBJECTIVES AND ACTIVITIES

The perceived decline in international assistance for TJ and the shift in donor priorities have been acutely felt by the civil society organizations that emerged during the latter years of the armed conflict and peace process. Reduced funding levels and an increasing international focus on security, institutional reform, and economic development have forced groups emerging from victims' demands for truth, repair, and justice to reorient their objectives and activities away from their core TJ claims.

This stands in stark contrast to the years surrounding the peace process, when international assistance was instrumental in reviving Guatemalan civil society on the basis of peacebuilding and TJ. During the peace negotiations, the UN-sponsored framework peace agreement mandated the establishment of the Assembly for Civil Society (ASC) to prepare nonbinding, consensus position papers for the negotiating parties' consideration. While these excluded proposals on operational aspects of the peace process, the ASC was expected to submit proposals on each of the five substantive themes that comprised the peace agenda – human rights, resettlement of refugees, indigenous rights, socioeconomic development, and democratization.

Participation in the peace process through the ASC was a formative experience. Emerging out of an armed conflict in which civil society had been turned inward and against each other, the consultative and collaborative process imposed upon the ASC forced its members to begin to listen to one another, to recognize each other's expertise, and to learn how to seek compromise. In the opinion of several participants, the ASC engendered a semblance of solidarity and trust that, though hard to sustain, continues to inspire them, reminding them of the possibility and value of collective action.[34]

Significantly, participation in the peace process also cultivated the seeds for civil society activism in postwar TJ processes. Accompanied by the international community, human rights and victim rights associations emerged from the peace process battle-tested, politically savvy, and intent on pursuing a full accounting for past abuses. Shortly after the passage of the Accord for Historical Clarification, the Guatemalan Archdiocese and its affiliate human rights organization, the ODHAG, announced the creation of its own historical memory project, known as the Project for the Recovery of Historical Memory, or by its Spanish acronym, REMHI. Victim rights organizations mobilized, compiling databases for use by both the REMHI and the subsequent UN-led CEH investigating teams, which also included local professionals as staff members. As important, victims' organizations representing widows and orphans like CONAVIGUA or relatives of the disappeared like GAM and FAMDEGUA organized their grassroots bases. They persuaded victims of the need to testify, reassured them of the safety of doing so, and accompanied and even translated for them as they appeared before the CEH.

These same groups, joined by human rights advocates, also participated actively in crafting the contours of a reparations program and subsequently in staffing its ranks. Further, they refused to discard the possibility of one day convicting perpetrators of crimes against humanity. Civil society organizations set about collecting forensic evidence, parsing through a trove of records discovered in the AHPN, and building survivor willingness to serve as witnesses in eventual human rights trials.

Since these initial postwar years, international donor assistance for TJ in Guatemala has created novel spaces for civil society coordination and dialogue, particularly in the case of PAJUST. As mentioned earlier, UNDP convenes regular meetings with its civil society partners, which have allowed for the general sharing of information and experiences as well as the coordination of activities. Through PAJUST, UNDP has also created thematic roundtables that bring together organizations working on the same issue, but may have different capacities. For example, there is a thematic roundtable on the search for the disappeared, which brings together groups that specialize in forensic science like the FAFG, organizations advocating for families of the disappeared like the GAM and FAMDEGUA, and groups concerned with TJ but that specialize in lobbying the state, such as the Myrna Mack Foundation. By combining their distinct expertise, the roundtable has worked to create a manual on the search for the disappeared, which will be published by UNDP. Another example is a past workshop on psychosocial care, which allowed for the sharing of methodologies across organizations.

34 Roman Krzanic, "Civil and Uncivil Actors in the Guatemalan Peace Process," *Bulletin of Latin American Research* 18, no. 1 (1999): 1–16 and Tania Palencia Prado, "Peace in the Making: Civil Groups in Guatemala" (London: Catholic Institute for International Relations, 1997).

Brought together under the auspices of donor consultations and programs, participants in these networks stressed the advantages of sharing information, brainstorming together, and engaging in collective action. As one interviewee put it, "we receive more respect by making statements together, rather than if any one organization were to go it alone." By making civil society cooperation a central concern, programs like PAJUST have encouraged Guatemalan civil society organizations to come together and draw on their diverse yet complementary expertise to mount a unified front.

Yet, despite roughly two decades of strengthening civil society networks with the help of the international community, members of Guatemalan civil society mark a clear separation between past and present, perceiving a dramatically changing panorama, particularly with respect to the tone and approach of international support.

On the one hand, donors who were once key allies have withdrawn significant funds and, in the case of the Dutch, Swiss and Norwegians, closed their embassies altogether. On the other hand, the restructuring of donor priorities has forced civil society organizations (CSOs) to rearticulate their organizational missions and activities in new and unfamiliar terms to adjust to the new funding landscape and survive. While many organizations and networks had already framed their work as part of a broader human rights and justice agenda, changes in donor goals and strategies have had a significant effect on those groups that have historically worked closest with armed conflict survivors, which have been forced to reorient their programming most dramatically. GAM, for instance, has procured USAID funding for a project on crime prevention; CAFCA has nearly abandoned its work on exhumations to develop expertise in criminal investigation techniques; the FAFG is seeking support for a project on disappeared migrants; and CONAVIGUA has been forced to set aside much of its work with widows and orphans of the armed conflict to focus on topical issues such as domestic violence because, in the words of one leader, "no one wants to fund projects that deal with the past anymore."

While CSO representatives understand the increasing donor focus on violence-related issues, they also express exasperation at the growing security emphasis of international assistance today. Lamenting the excessive focus on violence perpetrated by Guatemala's gangs, or *maras*, one civil society leader noted, "if you don't work on *maras* and tattoos, it's like they don't want to listen to you. Everything is about *maras* and tattoos."

The increasingly reductive donor approach has frustrated veterans of Guatemalan civil society, who hoped that the combination of civil society strengthening and stymied progress on TJ goals would generate greater support. For example, some thought the Ríos Montt verdict and the outcry following its overturning would stimulate international assistance. "We thought that this moment would bring an avalanche in funds," one CSO representative said. But instead donors appear to have falsely concluded either that TJ had been rendered in Guatemala, or that

Guatemala had reached the limits of TJ. Others suggest that donor fatigue and frustration are to blame for the retrenchment. Donors are fed up, as one CSO put it, "with working in a context in which there are no results." Yet, at the same time, donor fatigue may also reflect diplomatic concerns with taking an overtly political stand amid the deeply polarized national context.

Whether a product of donor frustration or increasing reticence due to political interests, civil society representatives see this attitude as shortsighted. One human rights activist challenged the view that TJ efforts have been exhausted, contending that, "it's not that we didn't take advantage of the time. It's that we never had power." Further, human rights lawyers point out that cases related to past abuses "take years to see through," at times more than a decade. Given the long list of trials pending and the limited capacity of the justice system to process them in a timely manner, the belief that TJ goals could be accomplished with restricted funding and without more substantial civil society oversight is misguided. Many international community representatives agree. As one diplomatic official contended, "Survivor groups tell us this all the time. It is not sustainable to have an eighteen-month project when judicial trials take years."

Overall, the shift in funding priorities away from traditional TJ activities as well as the overall decline in international financial support has left civil society organizations with a sense of abandonment mid-struggle. While shifting donor objectives have proven fruitful for those groups able to articulate their activities in terms of the rule of law or security, organizations that maintain a more victim-centered approach have struggled to cope amid the changing landscape.

INCREASING CIVIL SOCIETY–GOVERNMENT COOPERATION

Another important, and perhaps more positive, effect of international support for TJ has been the strengthening of state–civil society cooperation, an increasing emphasis of donors as they seek to shore up state capacity. To be sure, civil society actors have always been key players in making demands on the state. The establishment of the CEH, the PNR, and the CICIG are illustrative of their tangible successes.

Yet it is only in more recent years that CSOs have worked on a more sustained basis with state agencies to promote justice and human rights. For example, the Guatemalan Human Rights Defenders Unit (UDEFEGUA), which monitors and reports threats and attacks on civil society activists, coordinates its actions with the quasi-governmental Human Rights Ombudsman's Office (PDH). Whenever possible it also reaches out to engage the government, including the Presidential Commission on Human Rights (COPREDEH), the Interior Ministry (MINGOB), the Ministry of Defense, and the MP, seeking to build relationships of exchange and confidence between communities and the public officials charged with protecting their security. This coordination is not only crucial to the protection of human rights workers but, as one UDEFEGUA representative put it, is necessary "so that people begin to lose their mistrust."

The professionalization of the MP undertaken during the early years of the CICIG permitted effective and sustained collaboration between civil society and the state during the tenure of attorney general Claudia Paz y Paz (2010–2014) and continued under her successor, Thelma Aldana (2014–2018). The major human rights law firm, the Bufete Jurídico, joined forces with public prosecutors in trying perpetrators of human rights violations, including during the Ríos Montt trial. Further, AHPN documents have supported investigations of wartime crimes, and several organizations have provided technical assistance to the MP. For example, MP personnel have attended human rights courses at the Guatemala City-based academic institute FLACSO. CAFCA has lent its newly acquired expertise in criminological methodologies designed to assist in the investigation of cases where there is no crime scene to cases of forced disappearances. Overall, the skills, techniques, and expertise developed by many civil society organizations in the postwar years have served to strengthen and professionalize state agencies undergoing critical processes of institutional reform.

International community representatives have lauded the greater willingness of state and civil society leaders to work together as a key achievement of their support. As one PAJUST representative remarked, among civil society, "there is a greater level of maturity in terms of sitting down and working with state institutions."

But civil society leaders, while noting advances in cooperation with the state, also draw attention to the deteriorating climate for TJ as a result of two successive governments with tight military links. Under former president and ex-general Otto Pérez Molina (2012–2015), who was ousted from office following a massive corruption scandal, the government slashed funding for TJ activities carried out by the Secretariat of Peace (SEPAZ), and even closed the Peace Archives housing stores of documents related to state abuses during the armed conflict.[35] Similar trends have continued under President Jimmy Morales (2016–present), whose party, the National Convergence Front (FCN), was founded by hardline ex-military officers implicated in past human rights violations. The budget for the PNR was cut in half, leading to the temporary closure of the national office in Guatemala City and regional offices in fourteen different departments.[36]

Thus, while CSOs have managed to forge closer links with some state agencies, such as the increasingly independent MP, other state organs under tighter executive control have attempted to roll back recent progress, leaving TJ efforts stuck in limbo. "There is nothing to transition to or from," one CSO interviewee noted. Another

35 See Éder Juárez, "Víctimas de la guerra protestan por cierre de Archivo de la Paz," *La Hora*, June 5, 2012, http://lahora.gt/hemeroteca-lh/victimas-de-la-guerra-protestan-por-cierre-de-archivo-de-la-paz/.

36 See Gabriel Woltke, "Jimmy Morales quiere terminar la tarea de OPM: cerrar la SEPAZ," *Nómada*, April 15, 2016, https://nomada.gt/jimmy-morales-quiere-terminar-la-tarea-de-opm-cerrar-la-sepaz/.

likened the pursuit of justice and accountability in Guatemala to "a crab. It walks backwards."

DIFFERENTIAL CIVIL SOCIETY ACCESS TO INTERNATIONAL ASSISTANCE

Though international support for TJ has brought a number of benefits, they have tended to accrue to the more well-connected, experienced human rights organizations rather than smaller, indigenous victims' groups. The gains of international assistance have thus been uneven, fostering capacity among more professionalized civil society groups while making it difficult for newer organizations outside of existing networks to access programmatic and technical support.

Indigenous and nonindigenous civil society activists agree that Mayan Guatemalans constitute the most politically, economically, socially, and culturally marginalized sector of Guatemalan society. There is an equally widespread consensus that the same heavily indigenous communities that bore the brunt of the violence during the armed conflict are now suffering the effects of rising social conflict and escalating repression.

Yet a number of technical and logistical barriers stand in the way of providing greater funding to those groups most in need. While UNDP explained having a rather extensive consultation process with its existing civil society and state partners through PAJUST, its funding standards and practices tend to exclude less experienced organizations that are seeking support. As one international official explained, "Unfortunately, local indigenous organizations that don't meet the criteria probably don't have a chance. There needs to be a capacity to administer the funds."

Though channeling funds through PAJUST has weakened the direct links between donor governments and civil society partners, diplomatic officials make periodic field visits and rely on information from other international organizations to monitor project progress and receive feedback. For example, while Swedish embassy officials reported making field visits twice per year, they also communicate extensively with Diakonia, a faith-based Swedish development organization that provides TJ funding and has tighter links with organizations at the local level. Donor missions such as those of the United States and Sweden also employ foreign service nationals, Guatemalan experts that serve as the link between the diplomatic community and local organizations. These local experts often bring with them experience working within civil society and existing relationships with other civil society leaders, facilitating greater trust, communication, and collaboration. Yet donor government officials concede that they do not make it to the interior of the country as often as they would like to or should, and that there is a significant imbalance between their engagement with Guatemala City-based human rights organizations and rural indigenous victims' groups.

While limitations exist for civil society groups seeking funding for the first time, some international officials explained using targeted efforts to identify new partners. For example, the Norwegian mission and UN organizations hold forums at the beginning of each funding cycle to get to know new potential participants in its grassroots-oriented Maya Program. The success of these efforts, however, depends on young organizations having knowledge about these opportunities and the ability to make contact with international funders. As one diplomatic official stated, "We have tended to give money and renew grants for the same organizations. But what about those who do not know how to write proposals and may be doing better work?"

Despite the imbalance in direct funds to urban versus rural organizations, several of the national-level human rights CSOs describe extensive, ongoing contact with indigenous communities and organizations – in other words, the indirect channeling of international assistance to the grassroots level. For example, organizations like the FAFG, the Bufete Jurídico, the human rights defenders group, UDEFEGUA, and a leading human rights organization, CALDH, whose work is centered in rural indigenous communities, have established effective partnerships with both local- and national-level, predominantly Mayan organizations. The same is true of the Church-based ODHAG, which has developed close ties with indigenous communities through local parishes, and the ICCPG, through its training workshops with rural women and indigenous communities. Each of these organizations stresses the important work they are doing in concert with and on behalf of marginalized rural communities, whether in excavating mass graves and returning remains, protecting human rights in areas of heightened social conflict, bringing perpetrators of wartime violence to trial, fostering local-level efforts to preserve historical memory and facilitate social reconciliation, or providing workshops and training intended to inform communities about their legal rights.

These successes notwithstanding, they should be juxtaposed with the crisis currently confronting victims' associations, like CONAVIGUA, FAMDEGUA, and GAM, which have enjoyed the longest standing and closest contacts with severely affected communities in the Mayan highlands. Those relationships are under severe strain today, a function of the serious budget crunch making it particularly hard for these organizations to stay afloat. Representatives of each of these groups described how budgetary constraints had forced them to cut both personnel and travel funds. A representative from one explained, "We are one third the size that we used to be, so we just can't keep in touch with our base like we used to." Another echoed those sentiments, confessing that lack of funds means that "our relationship with communities now is not as close as it used to be."

Discussions with civil society leaders about their organizational history of international assistance highlight a generalized perception of unevenness in the distribution of support for TJ. Representatives of well-funded organizations emphasized the advantages of knowing where and how to apply for funding. It is a matter of "knowing which doors to knock on," one interviewee observed. It is also a matter of having a requisite skill set that includes language skills, cultural affinities, contacts, and a capacity to draft winning proposals. One interviewee described himself as an adept "seller of dreams," and the director of ODHAG conceded to having well-established contacts and affinities with faith-based international NGOs. Although a significant number of Guatemalan CSOs possess these skills, others do not. Representatives of indigenous NGOs, local organizations, and even nationally based indigenous victim organizations that work directly on TJ issues are at a distinct disadvantage in soliciting funds.

CIVIL SOCIETY FRAGMENTATION, MISTRUST, AND DEPENDENCE

Competition for scarce international assistance in combination with the social fissures lingering from the armed conflict has bred fragmentation and mistrust within civil society that continues today. For all their collaboration, activists are also open about these challenges, and international donors also recognize deep divisions as serious obstacles to civil society coordination.

Civil society representatives are not just skeptical of the government, but mistrustful of each other, which one CSO leader described as reflecting "institutional jealousies." Echoing views expressed by many of her colleagues, one human rights activist described the challenges as indicative of profound "class and racial divisions" in addition to ideological differences and resentments. These are, as she explained, carryovers from internal struggles among wartime guerrilla armies that continue to divide the Guatemalan left today.

Those divisions, class-based, ideological, and racial, become intensely personal. There is a prevailing sense, as one representative of a predominantly indigenous organization put it, that, "in Guatemala there are ladinos and Mayas, and they don't want to involve us." Those feelings were echoed in conversations with nonindigenous activists, who attributed the difficulties to "the lack of agreement amongst us." In one pointed instance, a ladino representative turned the tables around to blame indigenous Guatemalans for the tension. "They see us as ladino, and don't want anything to do with us," he remarked.

Such deep-seated divisions have had serious material effects on TJ efforts. They paralyzed the reparations program in the mid-2000s following spats over which civil society factions would have political control.[37] Further, they hinder the work of civil society networks, with activists describing their withdrawal from organizations because of fights and arguments that become personal and prevent concerted action. The representative of one organization dismissed one prominent coalition of human rights organizations, explaining that she left because there "was a lot of discussion without action."

[37] Interviews with authors, March 7–13, 2009; See also Porras, "Introducción," 34.

Though progress has been made in building greater civil society cooperation, donors coincide with CSO leaders in noting that divisions remain very deep and enduring. Donors explained the need, at times, to be strict and demand cooperation and consensus-building as a condition of support, both political and financial. But they also acknowledge that overcoming these long-standing divisions will remain a tremendous challenge, particularly in a country where thirty-six years of armed conflict shredded the social fabric. As one official contended, "Because we are dealing with a fragmented society, we see a fragmented civil society. We need dialogue across the board ... There is a lot of room to join forces and present a stronger voice." Rifts are largely seen as a result of desires for "prestige and prominence" among organizational leadership. But diplomatic officials also admit that the cutthroat funding environment and competition for scarce resources are certainly causes as well. "We can play a role in strengthening civil society, but we may also play a role in causing fragmentation," recognized one official.

CONCLUSION

In sum, international assistance for TJ has witnessed a number of transformations in the two decades since the signing of the peace agreement. Most notably, shifting donor priorities have led to the reorientation of financial support. Though donor representatives have flexed their political muscle to back civil society activists pursuing truth, repair, and justice for past human rights abuses, the reconceptualization of TJ as part of a broader rule of law agenda has moved critical financial support away from traditional victim-centered TJ activities.

Over time, the effects of international assistance on civil society have been mixed. On the one hand, international support has fostered civil society cooperation by building broader networks and facilitating the exchange of information and expertise. More recently, this greater willingness to collaborate has extended to government agencies, building bridges between state and civil society actors. While human rights groups draw a clear link between increased state assistance and their own declining budgets, importantly, international support has opened channels of communication between state and civil society actors, particularly with respect to justice issues.

Yet, on the other hand, shifting donor priorities have fostered unequal access to international financial support, favoring the more well-connected and experienced NGOs, which have been better able to adapt their objectives and activities to international community preferences. Meanwhile, the lack of technical capacity keeps smaller, predominantly indigenous, victims' organizations from receiving much-needed support to attend to local demands and dependent on larger organizations that represent their interests. Further, fierce competition for limited donor resources, alongside long-standing ethnic, class, and ideological divisions, disrupts the capacity of organizations to maintain tight connections between leadership and the grassroots and perpetuates a climate of civil society mistrust and fragmentation. The potential for developing much-needed social capital, both bonding and bridging, is accordingly undermined.

Though the current fiscal climate and prevailing priorities of the international community do not bode well for the future of TJ support, donors in Guatemala can continue to use their political clout and visibility to back civil society demands for accountability and to provide a platform for civil society cooperation with increasingly independent and capable state agencies like the MP. In addition, even with diminished funds, they can be more attentive to and seek to correct for the inherent inequalities in access to international support, which currently work against those most in need: the rural Mayan communities that suffered the brunt of conflict violence and continue to face the social and economic effects. While the political and financial constraints on international TJ support are unlikely to ease any time soon, bilateral and multilateral assistance remain important antidotes to rising concerns about democratic backsliding in Guatemala two decades after the signing of peace.

2

Fighting Windmills, Ignoring Dragons

International Assistance to Civil Society in Post-Conflict Bosnia and Herzegovina

Christalla Yakinthou

Bosnia and Herzegovina (BiH) is a multi-ethnic, post-communist, and post-conflict country whose war was triggered by a nexus of events including the Soviet Union's decline, Yugoslavia's breakup, and rising nationalism in the western Balkans. The (both) domestic and regional war spanned 1992–95 and was marked by the longest siege of a capital city in modern warfare, and by the perpetration of some of the worst war crimes and crimes against humanity on European soil since World War II. Twenty-two years after the war's end – by North Atlantic Treaty Organization (NATO) intervention – and the implementation of the corresponding Dayton Peace Agreement, BiH citizens bear a pockmarked legacy of two decades of transitional justice (TJ) and peacebuilding. Civil society organisations (CSOs) working on TJ are viewed by the public as disengaged from people's needs, and supporting donor organisations do not fare much better. The perception of CSOs as "doing well from the conflict" rubs up against countrywide resentment (though each community has very different reasons) of a criminal prosecutions process spanning two decades, synonymous with the term "transitional justice" in BiH. All this sits upon a scaffolding of rising domestic levels of unemployment (particularly youth unemployment), among the lowest wages in Europe, stagnant investment, deeply divided and divisive education systems, and rising and dangerously high levels of tension between communities.[1]

This chapter argues that there is a lot to learn from the way TJ has been "done" in BiH; sadly, most lessons are warnings about intervention models that embed ethno-nationalist divisions, things that go wrong when civil society becomes dependent on international aid, and the atomisation of ground-up initiatives reckoning with the past, largely because of systematic stonewalling by an unrepentant and unaccountable political system. This chapter is organised into three main sections.

I thank Paige Arthur and Louis Monroy-Santander for their invaluable comments and reflections on this chapter. In addition, I thank Louis Monroy-Santander for his editorial assistance and the ICMP for its support over and in advance of the fieldwork period.

[1] Dorte Hvidemose, "The Missing Peace: The Need for a Long Term Strategy in Bosnia and Herzegovina" (Sarajevo and London: Nansen Dialogue Center and Saferworld, 2010).

The first provides a background of the conflict and TJ initiatives, and this chapter's methodology. The second focuses on findings related to international assistance, particularly the culture of dependency cultivated in CSOs. It looks specifically at the funding landscape, decision-making and the delivery of assistance, the roles of international actors and their efforts to balance types and degrees of intervention, and internal and external challenges to cultivating more effective practices. The final section looks from the perspectives of civil society, outlining civil society reflections on TJ funding, goals and decision-making, the relationship between "projectitis" and donor disengagement, and finally at the creation of and competition around networks and the resultant fracturing of and between organisations, and the possibilities of collaboration with political stakeholders.

BACKGROUND

By late 1991, two of BiH's three national communities – the Bosnian-Serb and Croat communities – had claimed separate territories within the country's borders, a consequence of tensions, mass expulsions, and recreation of boundaries within neighbouring Croatia and Serbia.[2] An independence referendum was held in February 1992, where a 65 per cent turnout of the population, predominantly Bosnian Muslims (or Bosniaks) and Bosnian Croats, voted overwhelmingly for separation from Yugoslavia, while most Bosnian Serbs refused to vote. The subsequent independence declaration sparked attacks by Serb paramilitary organisations on Croat and Bosniak areas. International recognition of BiH's independence in early April prompted the siege of Sarajevo, marking the beginning of war. The siege was brutal and long – with as many as 3,500 shells falling on the city every day over the course of four years, snipers shooting civilians, and mortars targeting public buildings.[3] The conflict killed 11,541 people were killed in the siege, and another approximately 50,000 were injured. While the conflict was ongoing, an inquiry triggered by British journalists exposed various concentration camps in Bosnian Serb-held territories in the country. This led to the formal establishment of the International Tribunal for the Former Yugoslavia (ICTY) to prosecute war crimes, genocide, and crimes against humanity.[4] The ICTY's establishment did not serve the desired deterrent effect; war ended only in late September 1995, after a three-week NATO bombing of Serbian strongholds. This forced the Serbian side to the

[2] Milan Sitarski and Ivan Kujova, "Bosnia and Herzegovina: Federalism, Equality and Sustainability. A Study of BiH Redesign to Secure Institutional Equality of Constituent Peoples" (Mostar, Bosnia-Herzegovina: Institute for Social and Political Research, 2016).

[3] See the Markale market massacres in February 1994 and August 1995, the latter triggering the NATO airstrikes that ended the war. For information, see Denis Dzidic, "Sarajevo Massacre Remembered," Balkan Transitional Justice, August 28, 2012, www.balkaninsight.com/en/article/markale-massacre-commemorated.

[4] The ICTY was established in 1993 by UNSC Resolution 827.

negotiating table; the presidents of Bosnia, Serbia, and Croatia consequently signed the Dayton Peace Agreement in December that year.

The 1992–95 war led to approximately 104,732 deaths,[5] 31,500 disappearances,[6] more than two million refugees, and up to 50,000 victims of sexual violence.[7] The war was characterised by extensive human rights violations, war crimes, and crimes against humanity. Documented crimes include widespread ethnic cleansing, forced displacement, the burning of homes and towns, detention and concentration camps, torture, enforced disappearance, systematic rape as a war crime, purposeful attacks on civilian populations, and other atrocities. Most notorious were the Omarska, Prijedor, and Trnopolje concentration camps, where torture, starvation, summary executions, and rape were commonplace.[8] A number of officials overseeing the camps have since been indicted and prosecuted for war crimes, genocide, and crimes against humanity at the ICTY.[9] Srebrenica, so long a mixed town, in July 1995 became the site of genocide when nearly 8,000 Bosniak men and boys were murdered at the end of a three-year siege. The genocide unfolded in front of Dutch United Nations (UN) peacekeepers sent to defend the area – declared a UN-protected safe zone – and with some likely level of awareness of its possibility in advance from several international diplomats.[10] While all three communities committed terrible crimes, these camps and the genocide, as well as various systematic massacres, were part of a broader strategy of ethnic cleansing of Bosniaks and Croats in the northern and eastern parts of the country. These actions allowed territorial separations that shaped Republika Srpska after the war. Tremendous violence therefore lies at the heart of the reformation of BiH's internal borders, and as Refik Hodzic argues, ongoing denial of this violence has

5 Figures from Jan Zwierzchowski and Ewa Tabeau, "The 1992–1995 War in Bosnia and Herzegovina: Census-Based Multiple System Estimation of Casualties Undercount" (paper presented at the International Research Workshop on "The Global Costs of Conflict" organised by the Households in Conflict Network (HiCN) and The German Institute for Economic Research, Berlin February 1–2, 2010), www.icty.org/x/file/About/OTP/War_Demographics/en/bih_casualty_undercount_conf_paper_100201.pdf.

6 Jeremy Sarkin, Lara Nettlefield, Max Matthews, and Renee Kosalka, "Missing Persons from the Armed Conflicts of the 1990s: A Stocktaking" (Sarajevo: International Commission on Missing Persons, 2014), www.icmp.int/news/icmp-report-presents-all-aspects-of-missing-persons-issue-in-bih/, 11.

7 Graeme Simpson, Edin Hodžić, and Louis Bickford, "Looking Back, Looking Forward: Promoting Dialogue through Truth-Seeking in Bosnia and Herzegovina" (New York: United Nations Development Programme), 66.

8 Omarska was the first camp exposed to international attention, giving an initial but confused glimpse into the war's horrors. See Ed Vulliamy, "Shame of Camp Omarska," *Guardian*, August 7, 2016, www.theguardian.com/world/1992/aug/07/warcrimes.edvulliamy.

9 Martina Fischer, "Dealing with the Past from the Top Down and Bottom Up: Challenges for State and Non-State Actors," in *Transitional Justice and Reconciliation: Lessons from the Balkans*, ed. Martina Fischer and Olivera Simic (London: Routledge, 2016).

10 Florence Hartman and Ed Vulliamy, "How Britain and the US Decided to Abandon Srebrenica to Its Fate," *Observer*, July 4, 2015, www.theguardian.com/world/2015/jul/04/how-britain-and-us-abandoned-srebrenica-massacre-1995.

a continuing destabilising effect on victim communities' perception of the present and the future as stable and safe.[11]

Dayton formally ended the conflict, institutionalising ethnic divisions. Governance is exercised by a formal consociational structure, though the state became an international protectorate. A rotating Council of Ministers composed of representatives of the three major identity groups forms the head of government. BiH is composed of two post-war entities: the Federation of Bosnia and Herzegovina (Federation), composed primarily of Bosniaks and Bosnian Croats; and Republika Srpska (RS), composed primarily of Bosnian Serbs and a minority of non-Serb refugees, internally displaced persons, and returnees. Each entity has significant legislative and political autonomy. Bosniaks resent the creation of the RS, carved out of ethnic cleansing, and fear the entity's separatist tendencies. Bosnian Serbs in the RS, for their part, resent being harnessed to the Bosnian state, and feel that crimes committed against them during war have not received adequate attention.[12] There is minimal interaction between communities except in the capital of Sarajevo, which remains mixed, though increasingly less so. A third area, the Brčko District, is jointly governed by the two entities.

The international oversight body, the Office of the High Representative (OHR), oversees Dayton's implementation and the effective functioning of state institutions. Formally, the OHR can remove elected officials and overrule the parliament – though its impact is now minimal. As Bosnia is a European Union (EU) pre-accession country, the role of the High Representative is now exercised by the EU Special Representative.[13] The OHR settled quickly and definitively in BiH, taking a highly hands-on approach.[14] Monroy-Santander has pointed out that "(a)s the OHR began imposing decisions on state symbols, identity, banking and constitutional arrangements it crippled local ownership and made political leaders develop strategies of ethnic mistrust between the three constitutive peoples."[15] The external ownership of BiH's peacebuilding and state-building arguably triggered domestic alienation. Subsequent international critiques of CSOs as

[11] Refik Hodzic, "Post-Karadzic Bosnia and Herzegovina: The End of the Criminal Justice Era," International Center for Transitional Justice, April 11, 2016, www.ictj.org/news/karadzic-bosnia-herzegovina-criminal-justice. Also, Refik Hodzic, "Flowers in the Square," International Center for Transitional Justice, April 11, 2015, www.ictj.org/flowers-square-prijedor.

[12] Martina Fischer and Olivera Simic, eds., *Transitional Justice and Reconciliation: Lessons from the Balkans* (London: Routledge, 2016).

[13] Agon Demjaha and Luzlim Peci, *Interethnic Relations in the Western Balkans: Implications for Kosovo* (Pristina: KIPRED, 2014).

[14] For more on this, see Michael Ignatieff, *Empire Lite: Nation-Building in Bosnia, Kosovo and Afghanistan* (New York: Vintage Books 2013); Outi Keränen, "Acts of Contention: Local Practices and Dynamics of Negotiated Statebuilding in Bosnia-Herzegovina 1995–2010" (PhD diss., London School of Economics, 2013); and Roland Kostic, "Reconciling the Past and the Present: Evaluating the Dayton Peace Accords 1995" (Uppsala: Uppsala University Press, 2009).

[15] Louis Monroy-Santander, "Mapping Reconciliation: Looking at Bosnia's Peacebuilding," *New Birmingham Review* 1, no. 2 (2013): 283.

disengaged from broader societal needs, corrupt, and weak should be viewed within the difficult context that has called for, shaped, and funded them.

"Truth" about the conflict and its resolution is divided into three "ethnic" perceptions. Each community has its own heavily politicised, mono-perspective media. Politicians are generally inflammatory towards other communities. Mono-ethnic political parties instrumentalise victims and war narratives to defeat their opponents. One civil society interviewee went so far as to say that parties were "feeding nationalism to camouflage their own incompetence and their inability to solve large social problems."

The education system is also a dividing factor; practices like the "two schools under one roof" policy mean that, even in mixed areas, students from different communities do not interact in school. It is not surprising that recent studies show high – and rising – levels of distrust between young people of the ethnic communities. This tension is likely exacerbated by ethno-nationalist education systems, a lack of coherent teaching about the past, inflammatory media, and the second highest level of youth unemployment in the world, currently sitting at 57.5 per cent.[16]

Transitional Justice Efforts in Bosnia-Herzegovina

TJ has a difficult legacy in BiH, due to widespread perceptions (however unfair) of a prosecutions process with a budget inverse to its impact, and to a civil society sector viewed by the broader public as self-interested and fund-chasing. There is, thus, a prevailing perception that TJ is something that the international community brought to BiH neatly packaged, doing little for intercommunity reconciliation.[17]

Criminal Justice and Institutional Reform

The ICTY is the largest TJ initiative in BiH, tarring surrounding efforts with its brush. It indicted 161 people across four types of crimes, and from all Balkans countries involved in the regional wars: genocide, crimes against humanity, violations of the laws of war, and grave breaches of the Geneva Convention. Proceedings are ongoing for twelve accused, and have been concluded for 149 individuals. Eighteen have been acquitted, eighty sentenced, thirteen referred to relevant national jurisdictions, and thirty-six have had their indictments withdrawn or died

[16] World Bank, "Improving Opportunities for Young People in Bosnia and Herzegovina," World Bank, February 14, 2013, accessed April 20, 2016, www.worldbank.org/en/news/feature/2013/02/14/improving-opportunities-young-people-Bosnia-Herzegovina. Also see World Bank/ILO compiled data year-by-year: "Unemployment, Youth Total (% of Total Labor Force Ages 15–24 (Modeled ILO Estimate)," World Bank, http://data.worldbank.org/indicator/SL.UEM.1524.ZS. Most recent available data is for 2014.

[17] Claire Garbett, "Introduction," in *My Neighbour, My Enemy: Justice and Community in the Aftermath of Mass Atrocity*, ed. Harvey M. Weinstein and Eric Stover (New York: Cambridge University Press, 2010).

before sentencing.[18] The tribunal has been the object of criticism: it has given minimal voice to victims,[19] sentences have been consistently too mild, and at an estimated cost of just under USD 2.3 billion as of 2014,[20] it is top-heavy and expensive per prosecution. It made little attempt at outreach to conflict-affected communities, especially early on. At the same time, it prosecuted intellectual authors of war crimes, leaving a jurisprudential legacy particularly around gender-related crimes and rape as a war crime, the creation of hybrid tribunals, and the development of local judiciaries. It generated millions of pages of testimony documenting what happened and how – a tremendous feat. But Hodzic has warned that one of the tribunal's unintended and dangerous effects has been the complex interweaving of collective zero-sum ideologies of victimhood and perpetration that have "paralyzed any meaningful conversation on reconciliation and anathemised notions of acknowledgement and forgiveness."[21] Moving conversations beyond this has not proven easy.

As the ICTY contemplated winding down, a specially created War Crimes Chamber of the Federal Court of BiH and cantonal courts in the two entities were proposed by the OHR, established to prosecute mid- and lower-level war crimes cases for crimes relevant to BiH. In 2005, they began processing the remaining 10,000 cases. Progress has been slower than hoped, and major legal mistakes led to decision reversals in genocide cases.[22] Such events have damaged the court's reputation. Additional difficulties include limited accessibility of records and evidence gathered by the ICTY, limited availability of ICTY trial records in the national languages, and significant witness protection issues.

In preparation for the ICTY's closure and since the early 2000s, donors have largely focused on the capacity building of local jurisdictions. This has been a significant task for domestic and international actors, including building prisons, courts, and administrative structures, creating infrastructure and technical capacity, developing Bosnian judges and court officials, and vetting the judiciary.

18 "Key Figures of the Cases," International Criminal Tribunal for the Former Yugoslavia (no date), accessed April 15, 2016, www.icty.org/en/cases/key-figures-cases.

19 Claire Garbett, "Justice and 'National Ownership': An Assessment of the Institutional Development of the War Crimes Chamber of Bosnia and Herzegovina," *Human Rights Review* 13, no. 1 (2012): 65–84. See also Maria Eastmond, "Reconciliation, Reconstruction and Everyday Life in War Torn Societies," *Focaal: Journal of Global and Historical Anthropology* 57 (2010): 3–16; David Hoogenbom and Stephanie Vieille, "Rebuilding Social Fabric in Failed States: Examining Transitional Justice in Bosnia," *Human Rights Review* 11, no. 2 (2010): 183–98; and Chandra Lekha Sriram, "Beyond Conflicts and Pursuing Accountability: Beyond Justice versus Peace," in *Palgrave Advances in Peacebuilding: Critical Developments and Approaches*, ed. Oliver Richmond (London: Palgrave Macmillan, 2010).

20 Daniel McLaughlin, "International Criminal Tribunals: A Visual Overview" (New York: Leitner Center for International Law and Justice, 2013), www.leitnercenter.org/files/News/International%20Criminal%20Tribunals.pdf.

21 Hodzic, "Post-Karadzic Bosnia and Herzegovina."

22 AFP, "Hundreds of Bosnian War Criminals to Be Released and Retried," *Journal*, December 7, 2013, www.thejournal.ie/bosnia-war-criminals-released-1209704-Dec2013.

Two justice sector reforms stand out: the 1999–2002 police vetting, and the 2002–2004 judiciary vetting. In 1999, the UN Mission in Bosnia-Herzegovina implemented a three-year comprehensive review of the police service to deal with paramilitary police units, the lack of entity police cooperation, and post-Dayton serving officers who had committed significant human rights violations. The three-step process vetted some 24,000 officers, and while questions remain around fair treatment of decommissioned officers, it increased numbers of women and minorities and reduced the generally inflated police force numbers.[23] Judicial reform began some seven years after Dayton. The process began with a push from the international body, the Independent Judicial Commission, and was subsequently driven by the OHR. This process took some twenty-one months and was considerably resource-intensive. A reappointment process sought to fill approximately 1,000 posts and to introduce a gender and ethnic balance in the judiciary.[24] Significant progress was made to restore public trust and to increase judicial efficiency, however broader judicial reform remains challenging in BiH, and is a focus of its EU accession process.[25]

Reparations

Efforts to hold parties responsible for wartime reparations have been both international and domestic. At the interstate level in 2007, BiH brought a civil case to the International Court of Justice (ICJ) against Serbia. The ICJ ruled in a binding decision that while Serbia "could and should" have prevented the genocide, it was not guilty and was not required to pay interstate reparations.[26] A group of Srebrenica survivors has separately pursued various civil cases against the UN and the Dutch government between 2007 and 2014, ending in Dutch courts finding limited liability on the part of Dutch peacekeepers, ruling in favour of reparations.

Domestically, a recent landmark ruling by BiH's war crimes court ordered two Bosnian Serb soldiers to pay reparations to their victim for wartime rape, opening the way for further prosecutions.[27] Entity-led reparation efforts include social security and veteran protection systems set up to improve living standards across the communities, though these are neither cross-communal nor traditional reparations efforts, but instead intra-entity. In addition, state-level legislation has included property restitution under Dayton and a 2004 law on missing persons (though the reparative element of this law remains dormant). Beyond this, reparations have been

[23] Alexander Mayer-Rieckh, "Vetting to Prevent Future Abuses: Reforming the Police, Courts, and Prosecutor's Offices in Bosnia and Herzegovina," in *Justice as Prevention: Vetting Public Employees in Transitional Societies*, ed. Alexander Mayer-Rieckh and Pablo de Greiff (New York: SSRC, 2007).

[24] Ibid., 211.

[25] Gary Robbins, "Bosnia and Herzegovina's Unfinished Judicial Reform," *New Europe*, April 25, 2010.

[26] Marlise Simons, "Court Declares Bosnia Killings Were Genocide," *New York Times*, February 27, 2010, www.nytimes.com/2007/02/27/world/europe/27hague.html.

[27] Julian Borger, "Bosnia Rape Victims May Claim Compensation for First Time," *Guardian*, June 30, 2015, www.theguardian.com/world/2015/jun/30/bosnia-victims-compensation-landmark-ruling.

legislated independently at the entity and cantonal levels.[28] There has been significant criticism of the way reparation payments are calculated, estimating value according to tiers of harm suffered. There is also a preference for war veterans and veteran groups over victims' associations, which disadvantages victims across all economic, political, and social levels, imposing difficulties for mobilising and developing supportive power structures.

Truth-Seeking, Memory Work, and Documentation

Recovery, identification, and return of the missing and disappeared during war has been a cornerstone of truth-seeking work over the past two decades. As part of this work, the International Commission on Missing Persons (ICMP) became a key TJ actor in BiH and the region. Over the past twenty years it has exhumed and identified almost 23,000 persons.[29] The ICMP has supported families of the missing and disappeared, helping them form organisations, lobbying domestically and internationally, and supporting calls for medical, legal, and psychosocial support from the state and the international community. It is a hybrid institution, functioning also as a grant-awarding body for smaller (usually victim-focused) initiatives. In its transition out of BiH, the ICMP helped set up the Missing Persons Institute (MPI), a domestic and multi-ethnic body that ensures the protection, cataloguing, and excavation of mass grave sites, the inclusion of families of the missing in the searching process, and the establishment of a central record of the missing. Established as a result of the Law on Missing Persons in 2005, the MPI is a state-level institution.

Two efforts were made to create domestic truth commissions, failing for largely political reasons and lack of local legitimacy. Several local-level inquiries have been held.[30] A public acknowledgement of sorts and recognition of the Srebrenica genocide occurred in 2005 when the then-president of the RS, Dragan Čavić, apologised publicly after the release of the Srebrenica Commission's findings. However, more than a decade on, RS political elites view that apology as anathema, replaced by frequent denial.[31]

28 For an overview of various efforts in the region, see Peter Van der Auweraert, *Reparations for Wartime Victims in the Former Yugoslavia: In Search of a Way Forward* (Geneva: International Organization for Migration, 2013), www.iom.int/files/live/sites/iom/files/What-We-Do/docs/Reparations-for-Wartime-Victimes-in-the-Former-Yugoslavia-In-Search-of-the-Way-Forward.pdf.

29 Sarkin, Nettlefield, Matthews, and Kosalka, "Missing Persons from the Armed Conflicts of the 1990s," 11.

30 Including the Commission Investigating the Events in and around Srebrenica between July 10 and 19, 1995 (Srebrenica Commission), which was forced on the RS by then-High Representative Lord Paddy Ashdown, the State Commission for Finding the Truth on the Suffering of Serbs, Croats, Bosniaks, Jews, and others in the Period 1992–95 (Sarajevo Commission), the Commission for the Avdo Palić Case, and the Truth and Reconciliation Commission of the Bijeljina Municipality (Bijeljina Commission).

31 Hodzic, "Post-Karadzic Bosnia and Herzegovina."

Over the past eight years, a Balkans-wide effort at a regional truth commission, called RECOM, has garnered the support of some 1,000 CSOs, artists, media organisations, individuals, and victims', veterans', and survivors' associations. RECOM was designed to support a complex and interwoven regional narrative about the Balkans conflicts, promoting multi-perspectivity and avoiding the simplistic ethnic narratives prevalent in every country of "us" victim and "they" aggressor. However, it is a dormant initiative for the time being.[32] In 2007, the United Nations Development Programme (UNDP) began a process called Supporting National Capacities in Transitional Justice for BiH, which resulted in a draft Transitional Justice Strategy for BiH: a comprehensive document addressing fact-finding, truth-telling, reparations, and memorials. This process took two years, involving a fifteen-member expert working group of institutional representatives at the entity and state levels and civil society actors. The strategy also fell victim to political division and remains unimplemented.

There are also various civil society-led documentation and memorialisation efforts, including documentary film, oral history, short-term visual art memorials, and archives. Of note are initiatives including the Sarajevo Roses,[33] the Red Chair Memorial,[34] the Bosnian Book of the Dead,[35] and the repeated (blocked) efforts and micro-memorials of families of children murdered during house raids in Prijedor in 1992 to create a permanent site of memory.[36] A number of memorial ceremonies happen annually around the ICMP's return of remains, the most organised of which is the 11 July Srebrenica burials, during which men and boys murdered in the genocide who have been identified over the previous year are interred in the Potocari Cemetery, where the genocide began.

NOTES ON METHODOLOGY AND LIMITATIONS

Primary data was collected through nineteen semi-structured interviews with thirty-eight individuals from CSOs and three donor organisations (National Endowment for Democracy [NED], the UK government, and UNDP). In addition, a roundtable

[32] Fischer, "Dealing with the Past from the Top Down and Bottom Up," 25.

[33] To learn about this project, see "Sarajevo Roses," Urban Association, accessed April 15, 2016, http://udruzenjeurban.ba/english/sarajevo-roses/.

[34] For more, see Elvira Jukic, "Sarajevo Remembers Siege with Sea of Red," *Balkan Insight*, April 6, 2012, accessed April 20, 2016, www.balkaninsight.com/en/article/sarajevo-marks-siege-after-20-years.

[35] For more, see Dzenana Halimovic, "Bosnian Researcher Counts War Dead, and Faces Threats for His Methods," Radio Free Europe, November 21, 2008, accessed April 20, 2016, www.rferl.org/content/Bosnian_Researcher_Counts_The_Dead_And_Faces_Threats_For_His_Objectivity/1350799.html.

[36] For more on this, see Amer Jahic, "Prijedor Authorities Silent on Memorial for Child Victims," *Balkan Insight*, May 29, 2015, accessed April 15, 2016, www.justice-report.com/en/articles/prijedor-authorities-silent-on-memorial-for-child-victims; Refik Hodzic, "Flowers in the Square"; and Haris Subasic, "The Culture of Denial in Prijedor," Transconflict, January 29, 2013, accessed April 15, 2016, www.transconflict.com/2013/01/the-culture-of-denial-in-prijedor-291/.

discussion was held with seven individuals representing three bilateral donors (the Swiss, Swedish, and Dutch governments) and two multilateral donors (the EU and UNDP). Interviews were conducted between April and May 2014, based on standard interview guides for this project. Because this was the first case study in this book's set, the interview guide was treated as a pilot, and questions were adapted as interviews progressed. Approximately one-third of interviews required an interpreter, as the lead researcher does not speak Bosnian. Secondary data was collected in the literature review outlined in the bibliography.

Interviewees were selected through secondary research and numerous consultations with regional and country experts, including former and current International Center for Transitional Justice (ICTJ) and ICTY staff members working on TJ in BiH, academics writing on the topic, and other practitioners. The researcher sought a representative sample of CSOs that were local, national, and international, and that were both professionalised and grassroots/volunteer. This case study profited from the assistance of the ICMP. The case study author had a number of pre-visit conversations with ICMP staff members regarding the substantive and logistical aspects of fieldwork. When an initial list was made to reflect this spectrum, in collaboration with ICMP advice, it was validated by aforementioned experts. Interviews with donors were selected through an analysis of the TJ International Assistance Database, and key actors were verified by the ICMP and UNDP.[37] A nine-day agenda was developed for the research team with ICMP assistance, which also provided almost all of the research team's transport while on mission. This collaboration facilitated a highly productive and efficient trip, but also introduced a risk of bias, from various perspectives. In some cases, ICMP staff were present in interview rooms; in others (such as in the RS) interviews were conducted before or after (usually unrelated) discussions between ICMP staff members and interviewees. In two cases, the preceding/succeeding discussions were about a strained network, and in another about a project the interviewees had asked the ICMP to fund. The researchers struggled to balance this element, but the extent to which it affected the content of data collection is difficult to measure.

A number of gaps exist within the research, including the fact that it was difficult in a very restricted time to interview a deep cross-section of CSOs across the country and ethnic bases, and an absence of interviews with ICTY representatives or individuals who worked on its outreach. Interviews were conducted in Sarajevo, Srebrenica, Tuzla, Bijeljina, Banja Luka, and Prijedor. Time restrictions meant that we were not able to include potential interviews in Mostar and Zenica. However, the author feels that a representative sample of actors and perceptions was obtained within those constraints. Similarly, logistical and time difficulties meant that some key donors could not be interviewed, and time with the interviewed donors was limited. Follow-up interviews were conducted over Skype and telephone with

37 Paige Arthur, "TJ International Assistance Database, 2002–2012" (unpublished data, 2014).

British Foreign and Commonwealth Office and NED representatives, but we did not interview the Norwegian government, a key donor in the country. There is, however, secondary material containing research on the work of the Norwegian government and embassy in BiH.

Finally, some CSO interviews, and the donor roundtable, were attended by a US State Department representative for reasons outlined in this book's introduction. In general, it appeared that branding the project as a "State Department" initiative helped ensure interviewee interest in the research and secure interviews with senior personnel. Likewise, the presence of the Bureau of Democracy, Human Rights, and Labor Affairs representative encouraged interviewees to be more frank in their assessment of donors, because, as they told us, it was their first opportunity to relay critical information about funding approaches back to a donor – an interesting and unintended side effect. Any skewing of the data as a result of this presence is difficult to measure, but is acknowledged.

THE IDENTITY CRISIS OF INTERNATIONAL INTERVENTION

Context: Encouraging Civil Society Dependency and Lacking Transitional Justice Strategies

To understand the connections (missed or otherwise) between international assistance and civil society in a TJ framework, it is important to observe how those relationships evolved into what they are now. A first point is to be made on the impact of power-sharing peace agreements – not only on TJ provisions but also on shaping relationships down the line. Dayton speaks to this over two periods: the immediate and the long term.[38] The segregation embedded by Dayton and the deep inter-group divide both impacts and is reflected in civil society and its relationships with donors in many ways.[39] Dayton affected the way donors see their roles supporting peacebuilding in the country, and how they orient around the political context. In interviews, donors said the political constraints of Dayton set engagement parameters for TJ early on. One interviewee commented, "From a political point of view, it was always going to be close to impossible to have the perfect set-up for a reconciliation process and some of the other elements ... This led us towards a focus on a [criminal] justice agenda."

Another highlighted additional challenges around domestic leadership, adding to the previous interviewee's comment: "We focused on the judiciary, rather than

38 For more on the relationship between TJ and power-sharing in post-conflict contexts, see Christalla Yakinthou and Sky Croeser, "Transforming Tunisia: Transitional Justice and Internet Governance in a Post-Revolutionary Society," *International Journal of Transitional Justice* 10, no. 2 (2016): 230–49.

39 Florian Bieber, "After Dayton, Dayton? The Evolution of an Unpopular Peace," *Ethnopolitics* 5, no. 1 (2005): 15–31.

broader society . . . In Bosnia, you need to find three separate Nelson Mandelas to push the state forward, and then another five at the regional level." In this statement, one is struck by the early orientation towards one form of TJ at the expense of others, and one also sees the seeds of separation between civil society and the broader societies from which it has arisen. Speaking of the recent environment, one donor strongly argued that the broken political context shaped their (lack of) focus on particular approaches: "I would say that maybe for some areas, we gave up simply because there is a [political] deadlock and we don't really see the solution in the short term. I speak of the truth commissions. We can invest, but the question is whether there is added value in continuing to invest in this process." But there have been further costs to this approach: grantees and a donor representative emphasised that donor agendas and fear of "rocking the boat" in the early post-Dayton period were responsible for the emergence of a civil society unwilling to tackle tough political issues: "A political civil society was muted by the international community, which was cautious about funding projects that would exacerbate political polarisation or politically charged work."[40]

Funding Landscape: Who Funds What

In the immediate post-war context, funding was overwhelmingly channelled into humanitarian assistance and relief via international NGOs, and general funding in BiH moved from humanitarian to reconstruction, to institution building, to reform. Because of the donor community's relatively small size, and its long-term engagement in the country, there are very high levels of openness between the major group of bilateral and multilateral donors. The extent to which their funding priorities are coordinated is unclear, but it seems that they are aware of one another's priorities.[41]

In terms of total amount of funding to TJ in BiH, our data points to three priority areas: recovering remains of missing persons, domestic war crimes trials, and memorialisation activities.[42] According to an ICMP official, the ICMP's work on missing persons has cost approximately USD $134.2 million between 1996 and 2013.[43] The donor community spent $61,150,200 specifically for domestic war crimes

[40] It is important to note the collapse between the terms "civil society" and "NGO" in BiH, as civil society is understood as the NGO community. While I try to use the terms "CSO" and "NGO" as consistently as possible, where they are already blurred by interviewees I follow their usage.

[41] Hvidemose, "The Missing Peace."

[42] Please note that we exclude funds for the ICTY, on the grounds that it is not a BiH institution and that its work is not exclusive to BiH. For funding of the ICTY, see Marieke Wierda and Anthony Triolo, "Resources," in *International Prosecutors*, ed. Luc Reydams, Jan Wouters, and Cedric Ryngaert (Oxford: Oxford University Press, 2012), 113–70.

[43] Government funders are listed by the ICMP as: Canada, Chile, the Czech Republic, Denmark, Finland, France, Germany, Greece, the City of the Hague, the Holy See, Iceland, Ireland, Italy, the Netherlands, Norway, Poland, Spain, Sweden, Switzerland, Thailand, Turkey, the United Kingdom, the United States, and the EU. (ICMP Fact Sheet, May 29, 2017.)

trials from 2004 to 2012, according to annual reports of the registry of the Court of Bosnia and Herzegovina, with the largest donors (in rank order) being the United States, the United Kingdom, the EU, the Netherlands, Germany, Sweden, and Norway.[44] The third major focus of TJ funding has been memorialisation, specifically of the Srebrenica genocide and the building of the Potocari education centre alongside the cemetery/memorial. The memorial site cost roughly $5 million to build, including funds from the United States and the Netherlands; and it has subsequently received supporting funds for its operation.[45] Documentation projects like the Balkans Investigative Reporting Network (BIRN) have received consistent levels of support from small groups of donors. Overall, we found roughly $6 million in support to civil society actors such as BIRN, the TRIAL Advocacy Center, the Association of Women from Prijedor (IZVOR), etc., in the TJ International Assistance Database.

The Organisation for Economic Co-operation and Development (OECD) data and primary interview data has shown key TJ donors in BiH to include the following parties. In terms of bilateral funding, the United States provided substantial support to the War Crimes Chamber ($16.38 million through 2012). Also, primarily through the State Department, the United States provided the ICMP with seed funding and sustained support for the work of BIRN. It contributed to the Srebrenica memorial, the development of documentary film programmes, projects to strengthen political institutions, the Youth Initiative for Human Rights (YIHR) and civic education programmes, and the Post-Conflict Research Center. The United Kingdom, primarily through the Foreign and Commonwealth Office, supported the Srebrenica memorial and related education programmes, war crimes prosecutions and justice sector reform more broadly, the ICMP, and the MPI's communications strategy. Its contributions to the War Crimes Chamber totalled $8.4 million through 2012.

The Netherlands' Ministry of Foreign Affairs focused on support for the ICMP, the War Crimes Chamber ($6.8 million through 2012), the Srebrenica memorial, and the restoration of human rights mechanisms. Norway focused early on the Srebrenica memorial, while giving sustained attention to the ICMP, the ICTY War Crimes Chamber, judicial capacity building and the justice sector, administrative and infrastructural support for first instance and war crimes courts, and outreach on war crimes trials by BIRN. Norway's Ministry of Foreign Affairs has provided support for reconciliation projects undertaken by the Research and Documentation Center, human rights monitoring, education and advocacy

44 The Registry of the Court of Bosnia and Herzegovina, "Annual Report, 2012" (Sarajevo: Registry of the Court of Bosnia and Herzegovina, 2012), www.sudbih.gov.ba/stranica/43/pregled.

45 News stories estimate the cost at between $5 million and $5.7 million. See "Clinton to Unveil Bosnia Memorial," *BBC News*, August 4, 2003, http://news.bbc.co.uk/2/hi/europe/3123485.stm; and "Clinton Unveils Bosnia Memorial," *BBC News*, September 20, 2003, http://news.bbc.co.uk/2/hi/europe/3124642.stm.

(including projects introducing TJ into tertiary education curricula), and multimedia documentation efforts.

Sweden has been engaged predominantly via the Swedish International Development Cooperation Agency (Sida). It has supported the ICMP, as well as basket funds for the transfer of responsibilities for war crimes prosecution to domestic courts, and the development of domestic capacities. It has supported war crimes prosecutions both financially ($4.39 million through 2012) and through secondments to war crimes chambers, as well as supporting the development of state prisons holding war crimes perpetrators, for the Research and Documentation Center, and early engagement with truth commission projects.

Switzerland, via the Federal Department of Foreign Affairs, has long engaged with post-conflict peacebuilding via funding to the UN and judicial development. It has supported NGO projects on the free flow of information and media, strengthening civil society, democratic participation, the UNDP-led TJ strategy, the Research and Documentation Center, and the Center for Victims of Torture. It contributed just over $1 million to the War Crimes Chamber through 2012.

Other bilateral funders include Germany, which focused mainly on the War Crimes Chamber ($4.79 million through 2012) and the ICMP (at least $640,000 through 2012); and Austria, Spain, and Italy, all of which contributed more than $1 million to the War Crimes Chamber.

In terms of multilateral funding, EU institutions supported the war crimes court, the ICMP, and the "Together against Torture" network, as well as capacity building for victims' organisations. From 2002 to 2012, the main recipients of EU funds have been the War Crimes Chamber ($8.4 million) and the ICMP (at least $3.6 million).[46] From interviews we learned that the EU has focused on building domestic infrastructure to clear the backlog of war crimes cases. It will provide some €15 million ($17 million) to war crimes processing over the next five years.[47] UNDP has been in BiH since 1996, supporting the War Crimes Chamber, sustaining support for the TJ strategy, providing witness support during trials, and enhancing civil society effectiveness. We have only found roughly $500,000 in UNDP support in our research so far, much of it related to its activities around the TJ strategy.

In sum, we found donors provided roughly $195 million to formal TJ entities (the ICMP and the War Crimes Chamber) during the time period under consideration. By contrast, based on information gleaned from the TJ International Assistance

[46] Registry of the Court of Bosnia-Herzegovina, "Annual Report, 2012." The ICMP data is from Arthur, "TJ International Assistance Database, 2002–2012."

[47] An EU representative first mentioned this in an author-led roundtable discussion with donor representatives, April 25, 2014. Subsequent news stories confirm the EU contribution. See Denis Dzidic, "Reform Justice Sector or Lose Funds, EU Tells Bosnia," Justice Report, April 21, 2015, accessed on April 15, 2016, www.justice-report.com/en/articles/reform-justice-sector-or-lose-funds-eu-tells-bosnia; and Denis Dzidic, "EU Finally Approves Bosnia Funds for War Crimes," Balkan Transitional Justice, December 22, 2015, accessed on April 15, 2016, www.balkaninsight.com/en/article/eu-finally-approves-bosnia-funds-for-war-crimes-12-22-2015.

database, civil society-related work has received far less support. Beyond the Srebrenica-Potocari memorial site (roughly $5 million), we have found less than $7 million for civil society-related projects during the same period, to organisations like BIRN, TRIAL, YIHR, and IZVOR, as well as support for torture rehabilitation work and UNDP engagement with civil society. Although this figure is likely not comprehensive, we have no reason to believe that it is missing large sums that will make a huge difference in the comparison, since the average grant disbursement per year for civil society actors in our database is $44,000. It is important to keep in mind, however, that this sum does not include funding from private foundations – but rather only bilateral and multilateral donors.

Decision-Making and Delivery of Assistance

The EU's work with civil society development and TJ in BiH is funded through two channels. Its Instrument for Stability (IfS) package assists victims participating in court proceedings via the NGOs that support them. The European Instrument for Democracy and Human Rights (EIDHR) has a section that prioritises civil society development. The EU's civil society annual budget is €5 million ($6.7 million). One EU representative interviewed mentioned that after 2018 it would be likely EU support would turn to the development of civil or commercial law because "at some stage you will move on as a donor and hope that the country does as well"; an offhand comment, but one that may actually hold an accurate mirror to its perspective on priorities in long-term funding.

Of bilateral donors, the Netherlands, Switzerland, the United Kingdom, and Sweden all have significant embassy/local-level decision-making capacity and flexibility. The Netherlands kept the same key funding themes for several years, and has a strongly delegated system. Development cooperation in BiH ended in 2011, and the only part that remained open was funding on Srebrenica, reduced from €5 million to €2 million ($6.7 million to $2.7 million) by late 2016.[48] Previously, the focus was on larger programmes, with a four-year strategy. These strategies were drafted by embassies and sent to the relevant ministry to ensure support for local priorities. At the same time, the Netherlands has been drawing from basket funding to support transitioning societies, and while the budget is set in The Hague (at the time of interview, it was €350,000 [$470,000] per year and was reduced in 2015), it is used exclusively to support CSOs. This funding is distributed according to specific calls for proposals. For these grants, quality and innovation are prioritised. Limited funding has not been an issue for the embassy, whose representative considered that they had been able to "accommodate what we have wanted while focusing on a limited number of themes."

48 Though the embassy does not exclude the possibility of financing activities related to war crimes prosecutions for Srebrenica.

Sweden's country strategy is set from Stockholm via specific global civil society policy. Swedish work has a strong development focus, as Sida manages its global development budget. This is not the case with other bilateral funders, whose development funding is represented through ministries or local embassies. This means that there is not always a unified vision or approach to development goals, or to the Paris Agenda.

The Swedish have historically provided a larger amount of support for a smaller number of organisations, responding to emerging global best practice. There is a clear move towards providing long-term core support where possible, broad goals that allow much country-level discretion, and working directly with Bosnian NGOs rather than through Swedish intermediaries. It is unclear to what extent this transition has taken place on the ground.

The British approach appears exceptional in grounding itself in local priorities, as set by CSOs, Bosnian policymakers, and UK government representatives. Its strategy combines conflict analysis, renewed every five years, and annual consultations with other donors, CSOs, youth groups, media, and government actors. Its representative said: "We spend a lot of time checking and rechecking our assumptions and where we can best spend our money. The UK is a small donor. We need to be precise as to where we put our money. That allows us to make more targeted interventions." The workshops are cross-border, and begin with these groups posing challenges to existing UK funding patterns. After this, people are broken into smaller groups to identify "various areas [where] we need to put more focus and tension." This information is distilled down and compared against existing priorities. Those priorities are modified accordingly, and a call for proposals is subsequently sent out. "We try to give as much feedback as we can, we ask applicants to go back and think through whether the project is likely with these tools to provide the change sought. There is a great deal of discussion to shape each project."

The US-based National Endowment for Democracy (NED) policy is included here as a comparator, set to a greater degree by the needs of its grantees. NED, partly as a result of the flexibility provided by its unique status (it is a non-governmental funding body whose funding comes primarily from the US Congress), positions itself as a grantee-driven endowment. "We don't design programs and then have calls for proposals. We develop relationships with organisations that fit the profile of NED partners. They come to us with ideas and approaches. We then assess that against what other donors are doing, where the gaps are, how much money we have, etc." NED strictly maintains that topics and focuses are chosen by grantees.

Role(s) of International Actors: Balancing Types and Degrees of Intervention, and Lessons in Unintended Impacts

International actors have a specific legacy in BiH, directly impacting international funding and support roles both at the initial post-war stage and over time. Running through our interviews was a tension linked to this history, between an understanding that heavy-handed interventionism was damaging to (especially but not exclusively) BiH's civil society sector, and a realisation that standing back when things go badly has not helped. How to get this balance right was a recurring theme among donors and civil society actors interviewed, and one with which our donor interviewees genuinely struggled, in both their discussions and interventions. To that end, several types of roles became apparent through the course of our interviews: heavily hands-on, neutral arbiters, hands-off, and collaborative – though collaborative appeared more as an ideal type rather than an example of a real role.

One of the most important roles identified by interviewees from both civil society and donor communities was a need for international actors to function as neutral arbiters. This was important at two levels: as key network actors, bringing CSOs together that may otherwise not collaborate, and as connectors across ethno-political lines. This has been particularly important in BiH as a result of the widespread suspicion and mistrust between communities; something that is also reflected in civil society. Both the ICMP and UNDP have played this role over time, and while the OHR is most closely associated with the role of arbiter, its struggle to find the balance has been well documented.

While the OHR has played the role of forceful arbiter over the past twenty years,[49] it is now phasing out. Paddy Ashdown's retirement in 2006 marked a high water point, and a recognition that the OHR's approach might have been *both* profoundly productive (especially regarding justice sector reform) and unproductive, that the seeds of its far-reaching reforms sprouted deformed domestic ownership across a number of levels. Thus, a shift towards encouraging this elusive domestic ownership occurred, but with it came frustrations associated with self-imposed silence.

Some international actors expressed frustration with the debilitating status quo as regret around the OHR's reduced influence, given the current stalemate on any political issue that needs agreement of both the Federation and RS. One donor reflected:

> No one would disagree that we would like to see ownership as the leading principle, but that approach makes it very difficult for us to respond when we see things go wrong, because ... it becomes hard to push and apply conditionality and financial leverage, other than on issues that you directly fund. But in a more general sense there has been a very standoffish attitude.

This swing by donors between engagement and disengagement was a source of discussion for many interviewees across the spectrum.

In the period leading up to accession, the EU is the most significant international actor in BiH, and has taken over the OHR. It is characterisable as (so far) playing

[49] Edward Meyer and William Nash, "Balkans 2010: Report of an Independent Task Force" (New York: Council on Foreign Relations Center for Preventive Action, 2010).

a highly hands-off role in terms of political engagement, but one whose impact extends far beyond its engagement. While no date has been given for accession, the EU deploys considerable resources in BiH. It has significant potential to become an important connector between CSOs and government and political actors, both as a result of its enlargement funding and the conditions for accession. We see this has begun happening in some areas, and its long-term democratisation agenda was cited as impacting government–civil society relations, at least on a small scale. That is, its size and incentives offer CSOs space for at least a cursory dialogue with political elites, where the latter are forced to engage at some level with the former. However, it is characterised here as hands-off because the EU veers towards a general unwillingness to confront sensitive political topics. An interviewee described this approach as follows:

> [EU] institutions have agreed on a certain level of silence about the past [in BiH] because it's so sensitive ... it demonstrates a total lack of knowledge of how to approach things in this country. And the EU is the major player, it dwarves everyone else. But it has no idea, it is like an elephant crashing through.

Unintended Impacts

The hands-on approach of the OHR has not produced significant social change, though it has transformed institutional structures and capacity. This, together with the slow and clumsy course of the ICTY's work and subsequent domestic prosecutions, has affected how international actors are perceived within the country and by their grantees. The international community's emphasis on criminal justice after a lack of intervention during the war created considerable cynicism, as has the time it has taken the ICTY to produce results. This has been amplified by recent key ICTY reversals of war crimes sentences on appeal, and by reductions in perpetrators' sentences.[50]

This spills beyond ICTY boundaries: in July 2013, a European Court of Human Rights decision reversed various war crimes convictions made by the Bosnian War Crimes Chamber, due to a misapplication of law, resulting in the release of fourteen war criminals and affecting other cases.[51] The impact of this decision was given by a number of donors participating in the roundtable discussion as an example of how the international community is hamstrung by its own legacy, and how uncertainty around dealing with this legacy limits its ability to engage meaningfully and quickly to major events:

50 Eastmond, "Reconciliation, Reconstruction and Everyday Life in War Torn Societies."

51 Denis Dzidic, "Bosnia: Court Controversies and Freed War Criminals," Balkan Transitional Justice, December 26, 2013, accessed April 20, 2016, www.balkaninsight.com/en/article/bosnia-court-controversies-and-freed-war-criminals.

> Everything that happened in the lead-up to that judgment has led to a very real, fundamental reversal of the results achieved . . . This judgment has been applied to many cases, including genocide cases, and it shouldn't have been applied, in our view. But there was no real discussion of it, at all within the international community! . . . You would expect it to be a far higher-level issue, considering how much support the international community has given to the war crimes prosecutions.
>
> Something extremely fundamental happens and here we are . . . [shrugs] because it's an independent system, and we can't dictate to the constitutional court, etc. . . . that is now the attitude. This ownership idea has become very central. And I find that as the international community we do not have the tools, apparently, or the means to respond to issues that are crucial, also for TJ.

In this case, a clear link was made between the lack of meaningful international response and the direct degradation of public trust in international justice and TJ, including civil society work.

Internal Challenges for Donors: Time-Poor and Lacking Communication

All donors interviewed recognised that social change is long term, and that BiH NGOs address a wide array of issues with limited funding in an oppressive political climate. The most significant challenges donor interviewees identified were a lack of internal communication with relevant departments, and a lack of time to think about the relationship between programming and impact.

Structural impediments to effective international assistance were a significant theme of our interviews. Internal communication and coordination between different governmental departments or policy priorities seems to be consistently challenging for donors, particularly between departments of foreign affairs and development agencies. The Swiss representative, who has access to more directly useful resources for TJ assistance, highlighted the value of a regional strategy and an awareness of relevant approaches: "The fact of having a regional dealing with the past advisor, not really because he knows the context here but because he can suggest some mechanisms or approaches, facilitates the work of diplomats working on this portfolio." In an extremely time-pressed context where embassy staff numbers are being reduced and people have multiple portfolios, there is little time and few resources for rethinking how programming can better develop civil society's capacity to create and deepen sustainable networks for change. The Swiss use of a regional TJ advisor may be one small bridge to increased effectiveness.

Embassy-level actors dealing with civil society and TJ issues uniformly said they struggle to find clear and relevant guiding documentation. Institutional memory depends on handover notes and tracing key individuals who have knowledge of previous programming. One donor reflected:

> I would have found it very helpful if there had been some kind of guidance document on our framework when I came to the country ... one would expect ... when you become a diplomat in a country like this ... that there is a strong body of guidance information regarding what you are supposed to do. But the reality is that Bosnia is not treated any differently to any other country we go to.

More than one donor highlighted this as a serious constraint on good programming, and indeed it can only impede programmatic and country coherence. Related to the lack of time to think about programming and impact, the Swiss are unique in that their foreign ministry has had a targeted "Dealing with the Past" programme since 2003. This is part of a significant Swiss global foreign policy priority, allowing the local embassy to work within stable parameters. But with this exception, most key donors do not have a TJ strategy at either the country or the global level.

The need for international donors to provide support for communication between civil society and political elites was uniformly identified as important by donors and grantees, and we will see it echoed strongly in the civil society section later in this chapter. One important method identified by all was better policy advocacy by donors. However, this was identified as a strength of development-oriented assistance, rather than actors that fund at the embassy level. The following comment by a donor interviewee highlights such challenges: "Most embassy staff just don't have time. It's one of the things that comes on top of your regular job. You don't have time, you don't have the proper skills of how to do [policy advocacy]." The interviewee talked about the gap between foreign office and development approaches: "It's not the funds. It is a combination [of funding and advocacy]. The fact you have funds means you can use it as leverage." The goal of pairing funding to NGOs with donor advocacy at the governmental level was also repeatedly emphasised as valuable by our civil society interviewees, and something that needs sustained improvement on the part of (particularly bilateral) international actors.

External Challenges for Donors: Disconnected CSOs and Obstructive Political Actors

There was general consensus among interviewees that several factors would/have help/ed CSOs strengthen their independence and ability to operate as political actors. Many interviewees focused on the value of providing core funding rather than project-focused funding, and the importance of finding strategies to overcome intransigent political elites. In our interviews with grantees, there was general and strong agreement of these factors as key to empowering CSOs within such challenging contexts.

In February 2014, a series of public protests in Tuzla by former private sector employees against recent company closures and non-payment of compensation and health care protection quickly turned into nationwide protests against rising unemployment and political corruption.[52] In this light, a number of donor interviewees reflected on the absence of "their" CSOs in the 2014 protests. This was considered symptomatic of the disconnect between CSOs working on TJ and the rest of the country, and the perception of TJ CSO inability to lead social change:

> This year's public outcry was really interesting because it was not driven by the NGOs we work with. They weren't there. That does not imply that the NGOs we work with are bad, at all. But it does imply that they work in very specific areas, and they are as effective as they can be in this context. They make their point. They do stuff, but these people were not the ones I had seen, they are not the popular leaders who will lead . . . they are not people everyone knows, they do not have the status in society that they are going to bring change. They work in very specific areas. But that doesn't make them leaders of big changes in society. So it seems like two different worlds.

However, donors at the time of interview appeared unaware that NGOs had been actively barred from meetings to organise the protests,[53] highlighting how deep public distrust is of TJ NGOs. Because they are perceived by the public as in the pocket of the international community, TJ NGOs will continue to struggle to connect to more organic social change movements. At the same time, without the freedom to pursue goals that they determine, they are unlikely to be able to improve their standing in society.

While recognising the historical relationship between international intervention in BiH and civil society ineffectiveness, the provision of core funding was considered one way of counteracting civil society dependence on international funding for programmatic direction. While this would not solve the problem of donor dependency, it would enable CSOs to respond quickly to emerging issues, to join their resources to social movements, and ultimately to reconnect with issues that are too political for donors to fund directly. Donors were acutely aware of this difficulty:

> Because if you give them core funding, then it gives them the flexibility to pursue the issues that are important to them, rather than having to deliver project results related to our agendas. But is a challenge . . . We, both as part of our new strategy and as part of our approach to CS, we are trying to rethink our approach a little bit, to see if we can do things differently but it is not easy.

One interviewee used the example of government efforts in 2013 to conduct the first post-war census to illustrate the value of CSO flexibility. As part of census information, the inclusion of ethnic identification data was planned. A group of

52 Briony Jones, "Educating Citizens in Bosnia-Herzegovina: Experiences and Contradictions in Postwar Education Reform," in *Transitional Justice and Reconciliation: Lessons from the Balkans*, ed. Martina Fischer and Olivera Simic (London: Routledge, 2015), 193.

53 Randall Puljek-Shank and Willemijn Verkoren, "Civil Society in a Divided Society: Linking Legitimacy and Ethnicness of Civil Society Organisations in Bosnia-Herzegovina," *Cooperation and Conflict* 52, no. 2 (2016): 184–202.

organisations "quickly formed around these issues and [was] able to [successfully] advocate for changes." A similar example was given by another donor around a network that formed against attempted government restrictions to limit access to information laws. On the other hand, there was also general recognition of misalignment of donor and CSO strategies, and lack of inclusion of CSOs in setting donor agendas in post-conflict regions. This was considered by one donor relational to weak CS, and the cycle of donor dependency: "We [as donors] have these issues and agendas that we think are important, but then how do you work with civil society in a way that sort of creates them as a strong independent force, but without this dependency? It is really hard." However, while it was an important theme for CSO interviewees, few donors commented on whether it would be useful to involve civil society in donors' own strategy setting. Of our interviewees, only NED and the British do so already.

Finally, civil society effectiveness is hamstrung by obstructive political elites, and the issue of political deadlock ran through many conversations. The dilemma of how and when to include political actors in CSO policy-oriented work was of regular focus. One donor illustrated with a project on sexual violence against women, which drew vertical and horizontal societal stakeholders, but did not create policy-level change: "It's just that whatever you do, the impact remains limited because at the top level, everything is completely stuck. And so ... we simply lack the vision or creativity to know what else can be done, and at the same time our own capacity is very limited." This points to the idea that donors are both empowered, in relation to their grantees, and disempowered, in relation to BiH politicians and their ability to block progress.

Some donors, in cooperation with grantees, are changing their collective approach. The UNDP representative reflected that while NGO project ideas and proposals may be very good, "When it comes to high level politicians, everything is blocked ... We need to figure out a new way to approach this." In recognition, UNDP incorporates government officials and NGOs in their project planning to overcome this. The key question is how one thinks about supporting CSOs within a broader context of a shifting donor landscape, a deeply locked political environment, and a climate where the CSOs most likely to survive are those that have been most professionalised.

CIVIL SOCIETY AT A CROSSROADS: STUCK BETWEEN "THE NGO MAFIA" AND MARGINALISATION

Context

In order to understand the impact of international assistance on CSOs working on TJ in BiH, it is useful to have a better understanding of the civil society landscape in the post-conflict era. On paper, BiH has an extremely active civil society sector, with approximately 12,000 CSOs registered. About half, some 6,600, are operative. Only approximately 7 per cent of active NGOs deal with democracy-specific issues.[54] Of those, Simpson, Hodžić, and Bickford estimate that approximately 312 NGOs deal with TJ.[55] The sector is institutionally weak, increasingly underfunded, and largely dependent on international support. There is significant competition for resources, and the overwhelming majority of NGOs working on TJ are based in the Federation, usually in Sarajevo, carrying with them associated imbalances.[56]

Dayton's complex governmental, political, and legislative structure directly influences the context in which civil society operates. There is a correspondingly high level of ethnic homogenisation within NGO structures, and ethno-nationalist agendas often filter into NGO structures and programming. Very few NGOs have offices in both entities, and most employ staff from only one community. In addition, there is vastly different legislation in each entity governing the formation and operation of NGOs, differences in entity-level funding structures and opportunities for NGOs, and different levels of government in each entity. NGOs in the RS are more centralised in their internal dynamic and decision-making structures, while NGOs in the Federation tend towards the opposite. Sarajevo-based organisations generally receive the lion's share of funding from, and exposure to, donors, creating a capital–periphery divide within civil society. Global hierarchies are transferred to hierarchies within the NGO world. At the same time, those hierarchies are not flat spaces – groups access various levels of social capital to communicate messages and to alter or access decisions of the powerful; we see how later in this chapter.

Both RS- and Federation-based CSOs rely on government funding for survival, and with funding allocation comes the distribution of largesse, though this impacts each entity's CSOs differently as each has a different approach to funding. In the RS, some CSOs receive considerable core and project support, while others receive nothing, whereas the general approach in the Federation appears to spread smaller amounts more evenly across more organisations.

Two interviewees argued that civil society in BiH is at a crossroads; between the need to transition out of its (predominantly) post-conflict service-provision role and the need to move towards higher levels of professionalisation and specialisation, encountering many tensions. While there was a call from both donors and other civil society actors for NGOs to "professionalise," many actors also talked about the disease of "projectitis" or "projectomania," that is, an industry sustained and driven by project-focused work without its own vision. This is a symptom of high levels of

54 Ivana Howard, "Building Civil Society in BiH: Challenges and Mistakes," in *State or Nation: The Challenges of Political Transition in Bosnia and Herzegovina*, ed. Eldar Sarajilic and Davor Marko (Sarajevo: Center for Interdisciplinary Postgraduate Studies, University of Sarajevo, 2011).

55 Simpson, Hodžić, and Bickford, "Looking Back, Looking Forward."

56 Fischer, "Dealing with the Past from the Top Down and Bottom Up," 25.

dependency on and orientation towards, the donor community, and an absence of CSOs' own agenda, separate from the dictates of donors and project activities.

"Projectitis" presents a problem: while many NGOs are underfunded and overburdened, there is a hive of activity around issues whose local relevance is questionable, and whose methods are tired and unable to reach broader communities. This drives donor frustration and public cynicism. But as donor funding shifts thematically it consequently shifts project proposals. This need to retool to fit cyclical donor priorities has arguably not helped CSO legitimacy in the eyes of the broader public/s, destabilising the field. In addition, large NGOs are heavily professionalised, making them more efficient, but also putting them out of local communities' reach for a number of reasons including but not restricted to "fundable" project design requiring forms of interaction that are alien and intimidating to small, non-urban communities.[57]

A CSO actor linked the 2014 protests to these issues: frustrated and desperate citizens disconnected from civil society, manipulated by political elites, and importantly, without an active citizen culture. This resonates with the work of Obradović-Wochnik, who argues: "Low levels of social capital and trust have led to generally low participation in civil society across post-Socialist Eastern Europe."[58] These perspectives on the protests, which mirror donor responses, highlight the notion that this seemingly disconnected story does not have a single, easily waved-away cause, but is a complex moment that points towards a series of actions, interactions, and reactions between international and domestic actors during and after the conflict, regional historical circumstances, and domestic factors – which loop back to global economic power structures, investments, and incentives.

Reading the Runes? Civil Society Reflections on TJ Funding, Goals, and Decision-Making

The overwhelming perception among CSOs regarding donor goals for TJ falls into two camps: the first is that donors have no discernible TJ funding strategy, and the second is that if there is a strategy, it is aligned with donor countries' national priorities and demands, as well as global funding trends, rather than on regional or local needs. The sentiment that "if there are goals, they don't communicate them clearly to us" was regularly shared. We were frequently told that very little was ever shared from donors about fund allocation and how decisions are made. Generally, foundations like Mott Foundation, Open Society Foundation (OSF), Sida, and NED were considered to have approaches to working with grantees that interviewees found most useful, responsive, collaborative, engaged, and trustful. By contrast, the

57 Jelena Obradović-Wochnik, "The 'Silent Dilemma' of Transitional Justice: Silencing and Coming to Terms with the Past in Serbia," *International Journal of Transitional Justice* 7, no. 2 (2013), 328–47.

58 Ibid., 346.

EU was frequently accused of not respecting or placing emphasis on building relationships with grantees.

Some CSO interviewees expressed the feeling that significant donor funds go to the same limited pool of NGOs (known locally as the "NGO mafia"). The perception was that the donor community at worst played favourites, and at best stuck to the organisations with which they already had relationships (and particularly favoured international NGOs over local, though no examples were given) at the expense of victim and survivor organisations. More generally, transparency about grant application results was on the whole considered poor, and CSOs frequently stated that more feedback on the process would be of great benefit to them. In addition, a number of CSOs criticised donors for following "sexy issues," forcing NGOs to adapt projects to restrictive and locally irrelevant themes. This criticism, particularly levelled at the EU, is the flipside of donor frustration with irrelevant programming.

The Faustian Pact of Projectitis and Donor Disengagement

Most interviewees argued that there was a structural problem with the TJ funding context. Some pointed us to a misalignment of donor and civil society priorities and a problem with an international community with a "short attention span." A number of grantees perceived that donors orient towards projects framed in terms of clear deliverables with short(er) turnarounds. They believe there is less patience for long-term projects whose markers of success may be less clear, but whose work towards social change may be just as important. There was a general perception that "donors want attractive things, physical things like the Srebrenica memorial."

Orienting towards projects in the absence of TJ strategies has not aided collaboration between CSOs, and has exacerbated competition. For example, funding particular victim or survivor groups and not others has created its own consequences. Within the broader legacy of the war, Srebrenica holds a unique place for the international community in BiH because of its collective inaction during the genocide. Because of this, Srebrenica victims have more visibility than victims and associations from other areas. While this is not to say that Srebrenica associations have received significant (or even adequate or sufficient) levels of financial support for related projects, the more coherent and more sustained international attention to Srebrenica leaves victims from other atrocities (for example, the collective centres and camps in Tuzla and Prijedor) feeling forgotten. The clear unevenness of international attention on stories of displaced people, victims of massacres, and camp survivors across the country makes it difficult for victims from other areas such as those mentioned earlier to get support for work they may want to do, as well as for the emergence of a coherent narrative. This contributes to tensions and corrosive divisions within victim groups, creating perceptions of hierarchies of victimhood.

The general tension around donor fatigue is captured by a grantee working on education and TJ: "In situations like ours, it's the second generation that opens these doors [to address the trauma of conflict], not the first. So now we are all stuck. Donors are frustrated with our lack of progress, and we are frustrated with their lack of support." This idea was reiterated by a number of actors, but perhaps most representatively by the following:

> The donors invested a huge amount of money after the war on reconciliation. For them this chapter is finished. Now they are more looking at reforms, restricting of government, corruption, transparency, connecting education with the labor market, and the social sector. This is especially the EU focus; all of new IPA [Instrument for Pre-Accession Assistance] has this frame. Yes, they are mentioning nationalistic rhetoric, but there is no funding focus there at all. I think the problem is they spent a lot of money on this in the past, and they don't want to re-spend, especially for projects specifically focused on reconciliation. But I am afraid that none of the above issues will be solved if we don't look at the interethnic tension.

Indeed, interviewed service-provision NGOs painted a bleak future, in a context of ongoing victim needs not being met by the state, and untenable levels of resource-stretching. Multiple grantees said the move away from supporting service-delivery NGOs would harm both the TJ landscape and Bosnian society. Psychosocial and legal support NGOs also appear disproportionately affected by funding reductions, and repeatedly told us they are barely able to provide basic services to people seeking help. One NGO staff member told us: "In some cases the capacities of these organisations are not meeting the [need] . . . You are not selling strawberries, you are dealing with issues that are very, very sensitive." Another NGO representative, not based in Sarajevo, said:

> Some organizations are near extinction. This deprives us from having future support. We are unable to further expand our own activities because we are busy filling gaps left by other orgs that cannot exist . . . The available capacities just do not exist anymore . . . In the area of the missing we have assisted with 100 appeals to our constitutional court, which adopted numerous decisions on these grounds. But this is insufficient to fully meet the needs of people here. None of us are legal experts and there isn't a lawyer we can connect to within 300 km.

Interviewees outside Sarajevo explained that small grassroots NGOs providing support to survivors and returnees were doing important work but fell between grant cracks. These NGOs have little access to power, and few resources to apply for relevant grants that would give them core or project support. Grantees both inside and outside of Sarajevo believed that the changed funding landscape would hit small grassroots organisations hardest, particularly associations of families of missing persons and NGOs and CSOs with an annual budget in the range of 2,000 to 10,000 KM ($1,350 to $6,800).

This is particularly acute because there is no government support for victim trauma-healing work. It appears that reductions in funding these organisations by key donors is related to their perception that it is an area where support should come from the EU or the Bosnian state, but neither appears to be filling the gap, and the government's free legal aid system is fragmented and underdeveloped.[59]

Networks

In the context of such deep ethno-political divisions and limited financial support, networks that build linking and bridging social capital become increasingly important. However, grantees interviewed pointed to impediments and strain caused to their relationships with other organisations by competition for project funding. According to one person, "We are all competing, in a way. We have networks, but struggle in making those networks effective. It is hard to get organizations to collaborate on advocacy projects in particular. It's hard to get timely cooperation."

Pulling the Plug on Outreach

Few lessons were learned from the ICTY's outreach mistakes. When the BiH State Court and local courts were established, a Public Information and Outreach Section (PIOS) was established in 2005. The innovative work being planned was significantly and quickly pared back by massive structural changes to PIOS, which shifted its work from robust engagement to mere responses to information requests.[60] The Prosecutor's Office also has an independently run public relations department. The main purpose of these two offices has been to "display that the new BiH judicial institutions are transparent, independent, and effective" – a difficult task in the face of an overwhelming lack of public trust in the domestic judiciary to try war crimes fairly.[61] One observer described in detail the early development of the Court Support

59 In 2009, the UNDP's "Access to Justice" programme developed a free legal aid network working through and with local NGOs. More information about the programme can be found at UNDP's web site, "Access to Justice: Supporting the Rule of Law and Transitional Justice," United Nations Development Programme, accessed June 2, 2017, www.ba.undp.org/content/bosnia_and_herzegovina/en/home/operations/projects/crisis_prevention_and_recovery/access_to_justice/.

60 Refik Hodzic, "Living the Legacy of Mass Atrocities," *Journal of International Criminal Justice* 8, no. 1 (2010): 128.

61 Stephanie Barbour, "Making Justice Visible: Bosnia and Herzegovina's Domestic War Crimes Trials Outreach," in *Transitional Justice, Culture, and Society: Beyond Outreach*, ed. Clara Ramirez-Barat (New York: SSRC, 2014), 103; see also OSCE mission to Bosnia and Herzegovina, "Delivering Justice in Bosnia and Herzegovina: An Overview of War Crimes Processing from 2005 to 2010" (Sarajevo: Organisation for Security and Co-operation in Europe, 2011).

Network, a PIOS initiative with great potential but that was cancelled in its first year. The network relied on NGOs to share information about cases, and to make use of their access to outlying communities. Most importantly for this study, "the differing mandates and modus operandi of the NGOs did not bode well for their ability to unite in a common endeavor unless they were given continued tangible support while cementing their connections."[62] In both of these examples, networks needed time, trust, and resources to develop into self-sustaining partnerships. Incoherent donor strategies were as much to blame for the weaknesses of these initiatives as fractured NGOs and dismissive publics.

Activating Linking and Bridging Social Capital

The Balkans Investigative Reporting Network (BIRN) is a network that spans the Balkans, made up of journalists, editors, and media reporters. BIRN staff members talked about the benefits of having deeply engaged donors. In March 2012, the BiH State Court adopted a procedure stating that the initials of people convicted of war crimes, as well as the location in which the crime was committed, would be anonymised and only the first ten minutes of the trial would be made public. This made trial reporting very hard. The interpersonal trust BIRN developed with court staff and lawyers allowed it to get around censorship by gaining access to anonymised information. At the same time, its staff considered that a good relationship with its donors helped pressure the state to reverse a part of its decision (the anonymisation of names): BIRN's donors were part of the EU's biannual Structured Dialogue meetings with the judiciary in BiH, and presented the issue both times to BiH representatives. BIRN simultaneously launched a petition and social media campaign called "Stop Censorship about War Crimes." These factors may have led to the partial reversal of the State Court's approach to anonymisation.

The Advantages of Hybridised Worlds: NGOs Living in Multiple Spaces

Two hybrid organisations highlight the relationship between place, the self-conscious construction of and simultaneous lack of control over identity, and public legitimacy. Track Impunity Always (TRIAL) is both a national and an international NGO, headquartered in Geneva, holding consultative status at the UN Economic and Social Council. Its hybrid status means that it is uniquely situated vis-à-vis its relationships to power players domestically and internationally. This affects how it is perceived. On one hand, it has a largely positive and constructive relationship with state actors, which could be (in part) attributed to the fact that "maybe they realize we are reporting on them in Geneva." This allows them to feed into government decision-making conversations. On the other hand, its status as an (also)

[62] Barbour, "Making Justice Visible," 106.

international NGO has been uncomfortable for its (national) staff members, especially during field engagement, where they are perceived as "having it good" in comparison with "local-local" (non-hybridised) NGOs. What gives them legitimacy to engage state actors is also what delegitimises them in other circles.

The ICMP's non-forensic division is headquartered in Sarajevo, while its forensic work is headquartered and based in Tuzla and Banja Luka, both in the RS. It purposefully juggles its identity as an international and fully national body for the key strategic reason that if it did not, its ability to dig across borders would be significantly harmed. It has worked closely with the ICTY (and subsequently with the BiH State Court) to ensure that remains are processed in a way that would enable criminal prosecutions and to show the full scope of crimes committed. In its own evolution, it has drawn on its global networks, including the International Committee of the Red Cross and the Argentinian Forensic Anthropology Team, especially in its shift from humanitarian to law-based processes for ICTY prosecutions. It has supported networks that provide medical and psychosocial support to families of the missing and war crimes witnesses, as well as working closely with media (and media education) and across documentation efforts.

Disconnected, Unconnected, and Fragile: Victims' and Survivors' Groups

Victims' and survivors' organisations are among the most deeply politicised subset of the NGO sector, with very few cross-cutting relationships and networks with victims' organisations from other identity groups. All of these organisations remain exclusively mono-identity, and it is difficult for them to build alliances across ethnic identities.

The Regional Coordination of Family Associations of Missing Persons from the Former Yugoslavia exemplifies the value of continued (sometimes quiet) support by its donor organisation, and the fragile work involved in building lasting networks between victim groups across distrustful communities. It is a fledgling network, established out of an ICMP initiative in the late 1990s for collaboration between family associations. It emphasises that the missing persons issue needed to be worked across multiple governments, and that responsible parties across the divide need to be held accountable to achieve progress. Its representatives believe that the Regional Coordination has led to cooperation within state-led institutions working on the issue. The organisation formed in 2005 but registered only in 2010, underlining the amount of time trust-building initiatives take to formalise. By 2011, it officially represented twenty-six family associations from BiH, Serbia, and Croatia. All three Bosnian ethnic groups are represented, as well as other regional groups. While it can be a significant moral actor on the issue of missing persons, its potential remains underexploited. Key challenges are political sensitivity, the group's vulnerability to ethnic point-scoring, and general lack of funding, which limits both support and activities, impeding its ability to conduct its business and attract younger members.

The decrease in CSO funding in the region affects organisations such as this one. This is important to the organisation's basic functioning: as those leading the coordination body are generally not comfortable, conversant, or trusting of conference calling and other remote meeting tools, they rely on face-to-face meetings. Without funding, such meetings are difficult and so the organisation remains stuck. The group's fragility is deeply linked to the broader regional political context, which makes relationships among actors vulnerable to derailing over the smallest perceived slight.

Across communities, the capacity of victim organisations varies considerably. The Organization of Families, formed in 1997, is one of the most internally sophisticated victims' organisations in BiH. A network in and of itself, it is closely related to the RS entity, with little need for broader family networks. It has utilised its significant access to funding and entity-level political power to co-opt victim agendas within its group, and to be dominated by the RS battle for political legitimacy, and especially to amplify the genuine victim narratives within its group. This organisation is part of a small group of RS NGOs classified as "Special Public Interest." At the other end, representing victims of the same ethnicity, is the Serb Union of Family Associations of Missing Persons. This organisation, existing in the same state, receives no public funding and very little bilateral or multilateral donor support. Founded in 2004 by twenty-four groups, the Union works on searching for missing persons, appealing court decisions, and speaking on behalf of families to receive housing and other rights. It relies on ICMP assistance and small grants, running on a constant state of fragility.

The Mothers of Srebrenica and Zepa Enclaves is an organisation that, as a result of the savvy and determined leadership of Munira Subasic, sidestepped its limited financial resources, becoming a significant force for Srebrenica accountability, giving victims back their identity, and naming perpetrators of atrocities. It is composed of some 8,116 women genocide survivors, who established the group (it was then a network) in the immediate post-war period with strong ICMP assistance.

The organisation has leveraged international power networks, local heads of embassies, and member voices to achieve its goals. It has used both legal and popular avenues, filing civil actions in the district court of The Hague against the Dutch government and the UN for failure to prevent genocide.[63] When the government formally decided to place the Srebrenica memorial in the Tuzla-Doboj canton, far from the massacre site, the Mothers of Srebrenica surveyed its members, showing overwhelming support for the memorial to be built in Srebrenica at the site where the UN peacekeeping force had headquartered, and where the vast number of killings began. It harnessed the international community, including embassies and key public figures like then-US President Clinton, to lobby for the memorial's

[63] For details, see *Mothers of Srebrenica et al.* v. *State of The Netherlands and the United Nations*, International Crimes Database, accessed April 30, 2016, www.internationalcrimesdatabase.org/Case/758/Mothers-of-Srebrenica-v-the-Netherlands-and-the-UN/.

location and raise its profile once unveiled. This tactic was effective, despite internal political opposition, and the memorial now stands on the main site of the massacre.

At the same time, like many victims' and survivors' organisations, the Mothers of Srebrenica complained that NGOs often profit from false associations with the group, claiming to have cooperation with it to gain project support from donors. Another Srebrenica survivor supported this, saying that "so many NGOs are working here, but they are not local, and we don't know what they do. What do they do?" He also stated that he did not feel victims' and survivors' groups were perceived as part of a solution for a peaceful Bosnia, but rather that: "We, the victims, are told we are stuck in the past. We are seen as part of the problem, not part of the solution."

New Ways of Working? Negotiating Collaborations with Political Stakeholders

The RS-based Helsinki Committee for Human Rights works on new education materials for secondary schools, focusing on a traveling school, teaching history and the conflict in BiH. Both the development process and the product itself are a collaboration between RS activists, educators, survivors of atrocities, and the project's staff. The effort is a useful example of incorporating institutions from early on, and using the EU democratisation process as a lever for change:

> Our position is helped because major donors like the EU are now requesting CSOs to have partnerships with institutions . . . so now we explain [to state actors] why this is important and how it's connected to EU integration and the democratization process of the country. They see that link immediately. "Now," we say, "you have a chance to be part of it. If you are not part of it, it is going to happen anyway. The history teaching will have to change . . ." And slowly they come on board.

Ownership was transferred to an implementation team of representatives of the pedagogical agency of the RS, and a director of a Prijedor secondary school. This strategy speaks directly to suggestions UNDP and grantees made regarding the value of leveraging global power actors for increasing the chances of success for sensitive projects.

CONCLUSIONS

Surrendering to the Shadows of Its Legacy: The International Community in BiH, from Intervention to Assistance

The ongoing need for constitutional reform sits like a dark cloud over political and civil society development in BiH. Dayton's legacy, and its role as a major impediment to progress in the country, was identified as a continuing problem across almost all interviews, both donor and CSO. One donor sketched the need for constitutional reform as "this huge hulking thing hanging over, blocking everything." The same donor argued that one effect of the political corruption enabled by the constitution included pushing away potential civil society leaders who "very actively choose to avoid politics, and I can't blame them."

The OHR set the tone for an interventionist international leadership, and donors responded. When the OHR realised the unintended consequences of its leadership style, it pared back its influence. The donor community was part of this push-forward/pull-back, and donors see it as a tension between local ownership and international assistance to create effective progress on TJ. One donor reflected on the relationship between the current quagmire and the international community's handling of various crises: "I think we see in the last one or two years some rethinking, an awareness that things have gone so badly in this country." At the same time, they expressed a feeling of being stuck: "There isn't a solution. There is an awareness that things have gone badly and need a solution. There are thoughts, but there is no suggestion for reform."

This general reluctance to intervene was an issue raised by both donors and grantees, affecting the kinds of TJ projects funded, the kinds of organisations that receive support, and the kind of support given. But donor relationships with grantees and with civil society more generally are not set only by those constraints: donors in-country respond to headquarter priorities, which cycle regularly according to global and domestic policy priorities. In addition, donors with particular legacies in the conflict, like the Dutch, have a very specific TJ funding profile – centred directly on Srebrenica and truth-telling. However, this engagement is not just top-down and driven by donor guilt or headquarter priorities; the Dutch response to its legacy in Srebrenica resulted from (sometimes uncomfortable) interactions with and responses to pressure from victims' associations pushing for acknowledgment. It is not simply a one-way interaction of the powerful providing and the disempowered receiving.

The donor landscape has realigned over the past few years, and while donor numbers are decreasing, the engagement of those left is steady. Donor interviewees mentioned that TJ funding is undergoing consolidation and reduction of the number of funders. The major negative impact of this realignment has been on the range of small grants to civil society actors, which are now much more limited. This affects organisations that work on ground-up initiatives to support victims and survivors, on memory, and on documentation. A number of grantees and a multilateral donor told us that this change was closing grassroots NGOs "out of the competition," because the grants left require a more professionalised and sophisticated engagement, infrastructure, and capacity of CSOs. This has been amplified by the EU presence, whose IPA, EIDHR, and IfS funding far outstrips all other major donors and has changed the funding landscape significantly. Because some funders have framed their project calls and their available funds around their own general global trends (LGBTQ, domestic violence, and other thematic priorities), many groups working on TJ in BiH have harnessed (or fallen victim to) these shifting donor priorities that may not necessarily be linked to post-conflict contexts and needs, adding to the contextual dislocation and the growing disconnection of TJ CSOs from core issues around social change.

The Shadow Cast on Civil Society

This chapter has argued that particular institutional and historical factors go a way towards explaining the often-dysfunctional engagement between donors and CSOs in BiH. The Dayton Peace Agreement ended the war, but an unintended consequence of Dayton's consociational architecture has been the empowering of ethno-nationalist elites in both the Federation and the RS to further their own agendas, while definitively blocking fragile efforts towards both political and popular reconciliation at the legislative levels. At the same time, the international community's enactment of the Bonn Powers created both an external ownership of BiH's peace- and state-building processes, and a dislocation of domestic capacity. This watered the seed of domestic alienation, and increased public cynicism towards both an international community that stood by during the massacres but took over afterwards, and towards the CSOs that are perceived as having little to do with making citizens' lives better. With important exceptions, civil society actors working on TJ in BiH have limited capacity and influence, are heavily reliant on donor support, and viewed with suspicion by the broader communit(ies).

This chapter has shown that global power hierarchies have also been echoed in hierarchies within civil society (such as between Sarajevo-based and NGOs not based in the capital, or between victim-survivor groups), but that power is also reciprocal and wielded and reinterpreted by local-level actors to move towards their own goals. However, things are neither clear nor linear. The creation of a professionalised civil society has made organisations more efficient, but has also isolated those actors from the communities they are supposed to represent. Some have adapted themselves to changes in donor frameworks and continued their work, but in other cases the allocation of project-tied funding has blurred organisations' identities, as they shifted their work focus. Some have taken clear advantage of the presence of international funds to create "career NGOs." Together, all of this has increased cynicism among the broader public(s) who have a nickname for such civil society actors: the "NGO mafia," and has led to a field characterised by the twenty-first-century liberal-peacebuilding disease of "projectitis."

The TJ landscape has itself been shaped by the early and disproportionate focus from the international community on criminal justice (including the War Crimes Chamber and the ICTY), without commensurate attention to how such processes must be supported by a strong and well-thought-out combination of state- and civil society-led initiatives in order to succeed – including and especially victim-centred initiatives, which, with the exception of the support of the ICMP, have been almost entirely neglected. In this regard, the ICMP's work is important as a balancing factor because of the consistent and high levels of donor support over time, and because of its contribution to truth-telling aspects of the prosecution process.

The accumulation of these issues leaves us with a broader problem to confront going forward. While each community has different reasons, resentment of TJ is countrywide. At best, international assistance has supported two decades of TJ with some important, but lopsided results, and at worst, it has helped cultivate a civil society that struggles to both survive and be taken seriously in a broader context of rising inter-group mistrust, record youth unemployment, and embedded political corruption. Without broader political change in BiH or a radical rethinking of the format, focus, and goals of international assistance to TJ in the country, and a more honest and horizontal connection with as well as between organisations that seek social change, international assistance to TJ will continue to face profound obstacles and civil society actors will remain removed from real social change initiatives.

3

Sending the Wrong Signal

International Assistance and the Decline of Civil Society Action on Transitional Justice in Morocco

Paige Arthur

Morocco has had a unique experience with transitional justice (TJ) over the past fifteen years. In this chapter, I argue that although international assistance to TJ has been limited in Morocco (in comparison to other recipient countries), it still has had a marked effect: namely, it has resulted in a tacit legitimation of the Moroccan state's approach to TJ, to the detriment of civil society (and victim) approaches, which typically oppose the state. A key difference in approach between the state and civil society concerns dealing with the issue of impunity for past human rights violations (as well as ongoing human rights violations): impunity remains central to the goal of TJ for civil society actors, while it is downplayed or ignored by state actors.

One factor in this result is the fact that the main TJ donor in Morocco is the European Union (EU), and the main recipient is a Moroccan state body, the National Human Rights Council (Conseil National des Droits de l'Homme, CNDH). While some of the money that the EU has granted to CNDH has subsequently passed through to civil society organizations, there has not been a corresponding donor focus on supporting the main civil society and victim organizations active on TJ, which have been critical of CNDH's approach. As a result, civil society efforts to act as a counterweight to the state on TJ have suffered. Indeed, I argue that there has been a general decline in civil society action and collaboration on TJ since the close of the Moroccan Equity and Reconciliation Commission (Instance d'Équité et Réconciliation, IER) in 2006. After this point, responsibility for TJ shifted from civil society to the state, and donor money followed this trajectory, mainly from the EU. While international assistance did not cause this shift, it has contributed to it.

This chapter is organized as follows. First, I offer a brief overview of TJ in Morocco. Second, I introduce the methodology and its limitations in relation to

I am grateful to IREX for its generous support for the research in this chapter. I would also like to thank Fadoua Loudiy, Naomi Roht-Arriaza, and Christalla Yakinthou for offering helpful comments and insights on earlier drafts. A special recognition of indebtedness goes to Fatna El Bouih in Casablanca and Mohamed El Khamlichi in Al Hoceima for their expertise and guidance while doing research in those cities.

this case study. Third, I describe the landscape of international assistance, give an overview of the key programs being funded, and discuss donor and beneficiary perspectives on international assistance. Fourth, I analyze the impact of this assistance in light of some of the intended goals of enhancing trust, collaboration, and gender equality, as well as some unintended consequences for beneficiaries, in particular, the difficulties and exclusions created by EU grant regulations, and the implicit EU confirmation of CNDH (and thus the state) as the key TJ actor in Morocco.

BACKGROUND

In the late 1990s, King Hassan II authorized some limited initiatives to investigate and deal with the systematic violation of human rights that had taken place since Moroccan independence from France and Spain in 1956. Hassan II became king upon the passing of his father, Mohammed V, in 1961. Most of his reign is known as the "Years of Lead," a dark term that refers to his rule through repression. The king and other power holders in society – known in Moroccan Arabic as the *makhzen*, a term that refers collectively to the security forces, economic oligarchs, and elites tied to the king – used enforced disappearance, arbitrary arrest, torture, mass trials, and inhumane conditions of detention in secret prisons as a means to control or destroy the regime's opponents through the end of the Cold War. Those opponents included leftist organizations that sought revolution; military leaders and soldiers who staged coups; and, more recently, Islamist groups. They also included members of a long-standing self-determination movement for Sahrawi people in the Western Sahara, the Polisario Front. Although most of the violations occurred under the rule of Hassan II, there was also significant repression in the Rif right after independence, resulting in a severe crackdown in 1958 and 1959 and a decades-long isolation of the region.[1]

Since the end of the Cold War, Morocco has come under increasing international pressure to respect human rights, curb corruption, and institute democratic reforms. In 1990, Hassan II created a national human rights institution called the Consultative Council of Human Rights (Conseil Consultatif des Droits de l'Homme, CCDH), whose mandate centered on advising the king on the promotion and protection of human rights. The creation of the Ministry of Human Rights followed in 1993. In 1997, opposition leaders formed a government for the first time in Moroccan political history. And in 1998, Hassan II requested the CCDH to investigate and resolve all cases of disappearance within six months.

[1] Before his ascension to the throne, Hassan II was commander in chief of the army, and therefore repression in the Rif was under his direct command. For a thorough overview of the abuses, see Instance d'Equité et Réconciliation, *Synthèse du Rapport Final* (Rabat, 2005), www.ccdh.org.ma/fr/rubriques/documentation/publications/rapport-de-linstance-equite-et-reconciliation/rapport-final-de-lier. The full report is available in Arabic and French.

In a subsequent press release, the CCDH established a list of 112 people who had been disappeared by the state, with fifty-six declared dead and others whose circumstances were unknown. The figure represented only a small proportion of the real number of disappeared; however, since the CCDH is a state body, the press release marked for the first time the state's recognition that enforced disappearance had taken place. The state also announced an unconditional amnesty for all parties.[2]

In spite of these political openings, the "deep state" in Morocco (represented by the *makhzen*) remained largely unchanged. With Hassan II's death in 1999, his son Mohammed VI took power, inaugurating a more meaningful liberalization process that, fifteen years later, has given rise to conflicting interpretations about how committed the king is to reform – or how much reform he can enact given the countervailing forces in Moroccan society.

The TJ process – initiated under Hassan II's reign but deepened under Mohammed VI's – has been equally marked by this ambivalence. In interviews for this project, it was clear that some view TJ, and the state's human rights institutions in general, as a means of coopting human rights activists and movements without adopting significant change; others see it as a reasonably good-faith initiative to negotiate with and respond to the proposals from human rights actors in civil society.

Civil society actors have played a crucial role in TJ from the very beginning. National-level organizations such as the Moroccan Human Rights Association (Association Marocaine des Droits Humains, AMDH), the Moroccan Forum for Truth and Justice (Forum Marocain de Vérité et Justice, FMVJ), and the Moroccan Human Rights Organization (Organisation Marocaine des Droits de l'Homme, OMDH) are long-standing groups that represent different perspectives and political sensibilities (and political parties). AMDH was established in 1979 and many of its founding and current members are ex-detainees.[3] It was and continues to be on the far left of the political spectrum, and it continues to call for radical political change. FMVJ is a national umbrella structure of victims and victims' groups created in 1999, whose founding president, Driss Benzekri, would later head the IER and the CCDH. Founded in 1988, OMDH is a national human rights organization that has seen a rapprochement with the state over the years, according to some observers. Of these three, AMDH appears to have the strongest public presence currently, as it is a well-organized, broad-based membership association that mobilizes its chapters consistently and was a key player in Morocco's Arab Spring.

While there are many other human rights organizations in Morocco, these three are mentioned because they formed the core of the push for TJ in the late 1990s and early

[2] See Susan Slyomovics, *The Performance of Human Rights in Morocco* (Philadelphia: University of Pennsylvania Press, 2005), 21–22; Fadoua Loudiy, *Transitional Justice and Human Rights in Morocco: Negotiating the Years of Lead* (New York: Routledge, 2014), 5; and Mediateur Pour la Démocratie et les Droits de l'Homme, *Evaluation du Rapport de 'L'Instance Equité et Réconciliation': Un Bilan Pour l'Avenir* (Rabat, 2009), 10–11 (hard copy on file with author).

[3] For more on AMDH, see its website at www.amdh.org.ma/en/about-amdh.

2000s. After its investigations in 1998, and in response to continued domestic and international pressure, the CCDH advised the king to create a reparations program in 1999 for victims of systematic human rights abuse. While many victims participated, the program generated serious debate and heavy criticism from all human rights organizations: for example, the program was not linked to a truth-telling exercise; it was not accompanied by accountability for those responsible; and there were a number of operational limitations, such as an overly tight deadline for applications (which resulted in excluding some 6,000 applications from consideration); a poorly constructed compensation scheme; and the fact that some human rights violations were not covered.[4] Additionally, the scheme did not take into consideration the specific needs and experiences of women victims or family members.[5]

In November 2001, the three organizations (AMDH, FMVJ, OMDH) joined forces to create a broad-based symposium that is often mentioned as the origin of the IER. The proposal for the IER emerged from the symposium, and it was adopted by Mohammed VI. The commission began its work in 2004, and it delivered its final report at the end of 2005. The commission was headed by the charismatic Driss Benzekri – the founding president of FMVJ – and the sixteen commissioners mainly consisted of CCDH members, including victims (such as Benzekri himself).

The IER issued a set of recommendations that included a new reparations program for individuals (to address the gaps of the previous program), a community reparations program for regions that were particularly hard hit (or "punished") during the Years of Lead, and a slate of reforms for the constitution, the security sector, the judiciary, etc. The CCDH, with Benzekri at its head, was given the task of implementing the recommendations. It pushed ahead with individual and community reparations, as well as with initiatives to modernize the archives, produce scholarly histories of the Years of Lead, and develop sites of memory. As of June 2014, the government had made reparations to 26,063 victims and their rights holders, costing 1.8 billion Dirham (roughly $210 million).[6] The community reparations program, funded largely by a grant from the EU with additional support from the Ministry of the Interior, supported 148 small projects in thirteen regions. While it is officially over, some of the projects are still in the process of finishing up.

4 Mark Freeman and Veerle Opgenhaffen, *Transitional Justice in Morocco: A Progress Report* (New York: International Center for Transitional Justice, 2005), 11–12.

5 This issue was not discussed at the time, but was later noted during the operation of the IER. See Julie Guillerot, *Morocco: Gender and the Transitional Justice Process* (New York: International Center for Transitional Justice, 2011).

6 CNDH, "Résumé du rapport présenté par de M. Driss El Yazami, president du Conseil National des Droits de l'Homme devant le Parlement," June 16, 2014; on file with the author. Conversion rates to US dollars here and henceforth in this report are based on exchange rates accessed on xe.com on August 1, 2014.

The reforms that the IER recommended, however, were largely stalled until 2011, during the Arab Spring when activists galvanized the public to push for change. Harnessing the energy of the Egyptian and Tunisian uprisings, protesters called for mass rallies in all major cities in Morocco on February 20, 2011. Immediately after the marches, Mohammed VI announced that he would make major changes to the constitution, including many of those called for in the IER recommendations (although the IER recommendations were not necessarily a specific frame of reference for the protesters). This included a reform of the CCDH to enhance its mandate and its independence from the state. Now called the National Human Rights Council (Conseil National des Droits de l'Homme, CNDH), it also saw a change in leadership, and a new mandate both to harmonize Moroccan law with international conventions and to work with state actors to implement human rights reforms, including of the security sector.[7]

While there was some evidence of cooperation among civil society groups, many interviewees stressed that civil society generally maps onto divisive political party affiliations. Political life in Morocco is highly fractured, with more than thirty political parties and an apparently high distrust in parties in general. These divisions have consequences for civil society, and each national human rights organization is seen as close to one party or another; even FMVJ, which by definition was an umbrella group that included everyone from radical leftists to Islamists, was perceived by some as dominated by a particular political party, especially after its most recent congress in 2013.

As of 2014, the focus of human rights actors was no longer on the IER directly, but on ensuring the implementation of the proposed reforms, which remained promises on paper. In terms of the context for undertaking TJ-related initiatives, it should be emphasized that "TJ" as such was not high on the agenda for any particular organization, except perhaps for FMVJ, which continued to represent victims' needs, and which specifically saw TJ as integral to the project of transitioning to a democracy. In general, the political receptivity for civil society action on TJ was very similar to action on other HR-related issues – with one crucial difference being the continuing political sensitivity of TJ issues related to criminal accountability and state acknowledgment of wrongdoing. While there are certainly sensitivities around other human rights issues (for example, migration, lesbian, gay, bisexual, and transgender rights, religious freedom), they may not touch at the core of the state – and the "deep state" – in the same way as TJ does.

Interviews revealed two competing perspectives on the TJ process as it stood in 2014: the first viewed the TJ process as having produced a useful framework for pushing the state to deal with the past; the second viewed it as a process that the state

[7] I will refer to both CCDH and CNDH in this chapter, similar to my interviewees in Morocco. CCDH refers to the pre-2011 institution, and CNDH to the institution in 2011 and after. This unfortunately gets confusing, as some programs span the change from CCDH to CNDH.

had used to coopt human rights activists and to avoid dealing with the hard issues of impunity and genuine reform. To a certain degree, this conflict was rooted in differing perceptions of CNDH as a mediating body between state and civil society. For some, CNDH was an opportunity for civil society to propose solutions and negotiate with the state, while for others, it was a means for the state to coopt and neutralize civil society's role as a counterweight to state power.[8] AMDH, for example, did not allow its members also to be members of CNDH, in order to protect its independence from the state. Indeed, the CNDH's paid staff were drawn from civil society organizations (including one senior leader who was formerly the head of FMVJ and a member of AMDH), suggesting a kind of revolving door between state and civil society.

It is impossible to tell which of these two interpretations is more reflective of reality, but it should be noted that the president of CNDH in 2014, Driss El Yazami, was a well-known and highly respected human rights activist who lived in exile in France for more than thirty years, where he was secretary-general of the International Federation for Human Rights (FIDH). Moreover, CNDH did use its power sometimes to publicly criticize the state's human rights record, and it also investigated cases of detention and torture in good faith. As one interviewee said, "The police are afraid of CNDH; there's a direct link between CNDH and the king."

But there may be a long way to go. The state continues to violate freedoms essential to the full flowering of civil society, including freedoms of the press, of expression, and of association. State officials have dragged their feet in registering organizations whose views they disagree with. And, especially in the wake of the February 20 movement, there were reports of trumped-up charges against those associated with the protests, including bloggers, artists, and organizers. As one interviewee put it, "Repression has evolved." Even so, the old tactics apparently have not completely died out. A 2013 report by the UN Special Rapporteur on the Prevention of Torture, Juan Méndez, highlighted continuing arbitrary detention, forced confessions, and torture, especially of those deemed a threat to the state, such as members of Sahrawi political organizations and Islamist groups.[9] This tighter security approach was also related to the 2003 Casablanca bombings and fear of further attacks.

In this context, it can be no surprise that a general pessimism reigns among many victims and human rights actors – not just in relation to a more comprehensive approach to TJ that includes addressing impunity alongside other initiatives, but also in relation to the human rights situation in Morocco writ large.

8 The secretary-general of CNDH, Mohammad Sebbar, addressed these critiques in an interview in Morocco's *Tel Quel*. See Omar Radi, "Le Maroc va mieux, merci," *Tel Quel*, February 14, 2012, telquel.ma/2012/02/14/le-maroc-va-mieux-merci_1093.

9 See UN Human Rights Council, "Report of the Special Rapporteur on Torture and Other Cruel, Inhuman or Degrading Treatment or Punishment, Juan E. Méndez," A/HRC/22/53/Add.2 (April 30, 2013).

NOTES ON METHODOLOGY AND LIMITATIONS

This case study followed the overall methodology for this research project, including use of the standardized interview guides. Data was collected through two means: semi-structured interviews based on the questionnaires developed for this project and review of a range of documents. The documents included the final report of the IER; the websites of civil society organization (CSOs) and donors; reports by international nongovernmental organizations (INGOs) like the International Center for Transitional Justice (ICTJ), Human Rights Watch, and Amnesty International; news stories; academic literature; official documents from the EU and the State Department; materials developed by participants in the community reparations program; and three evaluations of the community reparations program; among other things.

I conducted twenty-seven interviews with more than forty people, mainly in person (two by phone) in June 2014. Sampling was purposive. A large proportion of interviewees consisted of CNDH staff or members, as CNDH was the implementer of the individual reparations program (funded by the state) and the EU-funded programs for community reparations and to support initiatives on archives, history, and memory. Since very little (if anything) had been written about any of these programs at the time this research was conducted, it was important to gather information on how they were structured.

To develop the interview list outside of CNDH, also based on a purposive sampling strategy, I consulted the TJ International Assistance Database and conducted preliminary interviews with experts on Morocco to determine which organizations would be critical to data collection.[10] Based on these investigations, I attempted to interview the three national human rights organizations involved in the IER process; I was only successful in getting interviews with AMDH and FMVJ, as OMDH was not available during the limited research period. Other national organizations interviewed were Association ADALA and the Medical Association for the Rehabilitation of Torture Victims (Association Médicale de Réhabilitation des Victimes de Torture, AMRVT).

Given the fact that the most recent TJ initiatives have focused on the EU-funded community reparations and archives, history, and memory, I decided to concentrate my time on interviewing civil society actors who could shed light on their involvement with those initiatives in two out of the thirteen regions covered by the community reparations program. These included three organizations working in the Hay Mohammadi neighborhood in Casablanca and two organizations in Al Hoceima (in the Rif region), all of whom benefited from the community reparations program. Only two regions were visited based on the limited time and resources; information on other regions was gathered through interviews with Rabat-based CNDH staff members and through a review of two

10 Paige Arthur, "TJ International Assistance Database, 2002–2012" (unpublished data, 2014).

evaluations of the reparations program commissioned by the EU. I also conducted interviews with two people who were knowledgeable about current efforts on archives, history, and memory.

Finally, I conducted interviews to gain information on the context. This included a range of people: victims who had participated in the reparations/IER processes, academic observers, a former IER commissioner, international observers, local staff members of INGOs working in Morocco, and a group of thirteen members of a local youth council in Al Hoceima.

There were a number of limitations, however. The most significant of these was that the sample size for interviews related to the community reparations program was small – two local coordinators with a general perspective on the program, as well as five organizations/grantees, in two of the thirteen regions that benefited from the program. The size of the country and the difficulty in getting around quickly was a key factor in this gap. As mentioned, I compensated partly for the gap through review of two comprehensive evaluations and interviews with Rabat-based people with knowledge of the program in the other regions.

Additionally, I conducted most of the interviews in French, a language in which many elites in Morocco are fluent. This said, some interviewees either did not speak French or preferred to speak in Arabic. It is therefore possible – in either case – that interviewees were not able to express themselves in the exact manner that they intended, or were not interpreted in a precise way.

Finally, in terms of interviews related to marginalized groups, efforts were made to capture perspectives of women and Amazigh (Berber) groups. However, due to lack of time and contacts, I was not able to capture sufficiently the Sahrawi perspective on TJ, as there was only one relatively brief interview that directly touched on the Western Sahara – in spite of it being a critical issue for TJ.

On a positive note, the fact that the number of donors we found for TJ in Morocco was quite small (four) meant that I could interview most of them: the EU, the Netherlands Embassy, and the National Endowment for Democracy (NED). I made repeated attempts to interview a UNIFEM (now UN Women) representative, without success.

INTERNATIONAL ASSISTANCE AND TRANSITIONAL JUSTICE

Types of International Support

TJ in Morocco has been driven primarily by local actors, including civil society actors. Until the involvement of the EU starting in 2007, all early TJ-related funding came from the state. For example, both the individual reparations programs and the IER were entirely funded by the state. This said, international actors have played several roles in Morocco's evolving TJ process.

First, international actors, primarily NGOs, have provided technical assistance and solidarity. Interviews suggest that international NGO actors like the International Center for Transitional Justice (ICTJ), FIDH, and Amnesty International played a useful supporting role to national NGOs. Prior to the IER process, national human rights organizations had contacts with international human rights networks. For example, Amnesty International had long played a role in generating international interest on Morocco's HR record through its reports. And FIDH was a natural contact, as it was located in Paris and its secretary-general was Moroccan (Driss El Yazami, who subsequently became the head of CNDH). ICTJ in particular was consistently singled out for its positive contributions to the IER process, including the development of the individual reparations program and working with civil society organizations on follow-up activities to the IER.[11] UNIFEM also played a role in providing technical assistance on including gender as a crosscutting issue in the community reparations program.

A second (albeit less significant) role of international actors has been political support and action. In fact, the role of donors in TJ processes has been ambiguous. A number of interviewees stressed the role of donors' policies rather than funds ("The real level is the level of policy") and lamented the fact that major donors, especially the EU, were not pressuring the Moroccan state to act. Although the EU has been by far the biggest donor, its approach to TJ was seen by some as technical rather than political. A review of documents related to the IER grants (for example, the EU action plans for Morocco) supported this view – in the sense that the political context (and obstacles) for proposed reforms and actions was not mentioned. Moreover, the action plans steered clear of the political issues related to impunity and institutional accountability for past HR abuse. In fact, the word "impunity" only appeared twice in the 103-page document. In general, while the donors who have engaged on TJ obviously did support it, there was no evidence that they were using policy to push for TJ in Morocco.

The third role concerns international donors' financial support for TJ. The major TJ donor in Morocco has been the EU. As part of its 2005 action plan for Morocco, it committed €3 million over a four-year period to a community reparations program, known as IER1 (using the acronym of the Truth and Equity Commission, on whose recommendations it was based). In the 2009 action plan, it committed a further €8 million over four years for work related to archives, history, and memory, known as IER2.

The EU's funding of €11 million dwarfed all other financial support to TJ in Morocco combined, which barely amounted to $0.5 million, according to interviews and to data we could find in the TJ International Assistance Database. There were only two other significant donors. First was the Netherlands Embassy,

[11] Many interviewees were aware that I was a former ICTJ staff member, so there is a possibility for positive bias on that basis.

which supported ICTJ's activities promoting security system reform with funds totaling roughly $107,000 from 2009 to 2011. (It is unknown whether ICTJ had earmarked funds from a particular donor for its Morocco work prior to 2009, and there is no record of such funds in the TJ International Assistance Database.) Second was the NED, which supported FMVJ's follow-up work to the IER from 2007 to 2012 with roughly $300,000, and it continues to support FMVJ as of this writing. NED also gave $26,000 to another civil society organization, the Association Mouvement Rihanate Citoyennes, to do outreach around the community reparations process in 2010. Very small sums were also given by the Swiss and Belgian Embassies to support follow-up activities of the IER – for example, the Swiss contributed $2,000 to cover publication costs for a report about women's experiences of human rights violations that had originally been commissioned by the IER.[12]

The evolution of this assistance changed over time. Technical assistance and solidarity was more intense prior to and during the IER and the early years of the community reparations program. This activity was signaled by the numerous international conferences and workshops sponsored by ICTJ and others during this time, up through 2011. Financial assistance has been most intense during the post-IER period, with EU funding starting only after the close of the IER. While one might expect that the most intense period of international assistance would coincide with a flourishing of civil society action on TJ, this was clearly not the case in Morocco – one reason being that EU money was directed to the CCDH/CNDH, a state body.

International Funding: Following the IER's Lead

Before discussing donor and beneficiary perspectives on international assistance, it is important in the Moroccan case to understand the key programs and entities benefiting from international assistance, namely, the EU-funded programs known as IER1 and IER2.

Toward the end of the IER's work in 2005, members of the IER's committee on community reparations – led by Yazami, the former secretary-general of FIDH and the future head of CNDH – were looking for potential funders for the program. The origins of the community reparations program (IER1) stemmed from consultations during the time of the IER with civil society organizations, including victim organizations, primarily in the south.[13] Recommendations for community reparations for eleven affected regions (later expanded to thirteen) were included in the

12 Data is from Arthur, "TJ International Assistance Database"; the NED's Morocco webpage at www.ned.org/where-we-work/middle-east-and-northern-africa/morocco (accessed June 12, 2014); and various EU and CNDH documents.

13 This claim is from interviews, but also corroborated by the introductory booklet accompanying IER1's "box set" of materials. See CNDH, "Programme de réparation communautaire au Maroc: Contributions à la justice transitionnelle" (Rabat: CNDH, 2012), 1 (on file with author). Unfortunately, none of these materials is presently available online.

IER's final report. Two criteria were used to identify the regions: 1) they had detention centers and suffered socioeconomic marginalization; or 2) they had experienced a violent repression. A committee headed by Yazami took forward the recommendations. Because it seemed unlikely that the state would fund such a program, Yazami spearheaded fundraising efforts.

Although interviews are not conclusive about why the state did not choose to fund the community reparations program on its own, one story is that competition with the Moroccan state's recently launched National Initiative for Human Development (l'Initiative Nationale pour le Developpement Humain; INDH) was a factor (the INDH, which was launched in 2005, will be discussed further later in this chapter). The EU was approached, as it has close relations with Morocco under its European Neighborhood Policy and, indeed, as of this writing, Morocco was the largest recipient of EU funds under the Neighborhood Policy.[14] The EU commissioned a report on the merits of the community reparations program from two experts (one Tunisian, one Italian); the report recommended supporting the program and also made proposals on its structural design.[15] As a result, financial support for what became IER1/2 was included in the 2005 action plan for EU-Morocco – the action plan being a four-year-long framework for agreed activities – and it was continued in the 2009 action plan. The most recent action plan (2013) no longer includes specific activities related to IER recommendations, although it does briefly mention the IER as a general reference framework.[16]

The roughly €5 million program (€3 million from the EU, the rest from the Ministry of the Interior) ran from 2007 through 2011, although a number of projects continued through 2014.[17] A total of 148 projects was funded through a rigorous call for proposals process, in which civil society organizations could propose projects relating to four themes: preservation of memory, capacity building, revenue-generating activities, and integration of women. In order to implement the program, a number of novel structures were created: first, the money was directed through a government-owned savings and investment fund, the Fondation Caisse de Dépôt et Gestion (FCDG), rather than the CCDH, as the FCDG was better placed to

14 See the EuropeAid webpage for Morocco at ec.europa.eu/neighbourhood-enlargement/neighbourhood/countries/morocco_en.

15 Unfortunately, the report does not seem to be publicly available, in spite of its obvious relevance to the design of other community reparations programs.

16 EU Council, "Relations avec le Maroc: projet de plan d'action Maroc pour le mise en oeuvre du statut avancé (2013–2017)" (December 9, 2013), 13; available at eeas.europa.eu/delegations/morocco/documents/eu_morocco/plandactions_fr.pdf.

17 The €5 million figure was given by interviewees directly concerned with managing the funds, who said that the Moroccan state paid a little less than half of the total program costs. However, the figure for the contribution from the Moroccan state is at odds with the one given in the official brochure that accompanied a "box set" of IER1 materials. According to that brochure, the total budget was 159,853,207 Dirham ($19 million), with 95,853,207 Dirham ($11.5 million) from the state; 39,865,000 Dirham ($4.8 million) from the EU/UNIFEM; and the rest from other sources. See CNDH, "Programme de réparation communautaire au Maroc,".

manage and disburse funds on the scale needed for the program. Further, in each region, a tripartite oversight structure called the "local coordinating committee" was created to bring together the CCDH, civil society, and local state representatives. While these appeared to function differently in each region, the animating idea was to bring civil society actors into contact with state actors in ways that would build trust and lasting relationships. The coordination bodies helped with outreach and communication, and in some cases to troubleshoot blockages as they arose, particularly when these blockages were caused by the state. From the very beginning, gender was integrated into the IER1 program. UNIFEM ran some pilot initiatives before the program got under way in order to test gender inclusion, and it was a member of the overarching Steering Committee (alongside the CCDH, the FCDG, and the EU). There was always at least one organization on each local coordinating committee representing local women's groups.

Toward the end of the community reparations program, the EU agreed to provide €8 million from 2010 to 2014 for a second program on archives, history, and memory – known as IER2. Activities were devoted to developing Morocco's archives, promoting professional and scientific history of the Years of Lead, and encouraging memory initiatives, such as the transformation of Morocco's former detention centers into sites of conscience or other spaces for the community. While much of the funding for IER2 was devoted to developing the archives and commissioning studies for potential museums, it also included a request for proposals (RFP) process for small history/memory projects. IER2 ended up funding seven of these projects (out of sixteen applications).

By all accounts, IER2 had significant difficulties in achieving its objectives for a number of reasons, including delays in starting the program, burdensome EU regulations, and a disorienting change in strategic direction associated with the creation of CNDH in 2011. Local/national civil society actors were included mainly in museumification studies undertaken in Al Hoceima, Ouarzazate, and Casablanca. However, all of these possible museum projects were stalled due to lack of funding or lack of an appropriate building, and there was no evidence of ongoing civil society engagement. Indeed, most of the funds allocated for IER2 went unspent.

The View from Donors

IER1 and IER2 were inspired directly by the IER's recommendations and were implemented by the CCDH/CNDH. Yet they, and particularly the community reparations program, were problematic to civil society actors for a number of reasons. In general, civil society actors saw these programs as a way for the government to avoid the more difficult political issue of democratic reform, but still claim that it was advancing a TJ agenda. Victim participation was notably absent. Several interviewees dismissed the program, and one interviewee heaped scorn on it.

The question therefore arises: why, among everything the EU could have supported, did it support these programs in particular? Why did other donors not step in to support other types of initiatives, perhaps in addition to these?

Various actors involved held different perspectives on this issue. Beginning with donors, it is important to understand that while each donor had a sophisticated analysis of the context, and each highlighted different aspects of TJ's role in that context, TJ was nonetheless just part of a "basket" of activities that might be funded under broader thematic headings. That is to say, none of the TJ donors had a particular strategy to support TJ; instead, support for TJ was folded into longer-term strategies to promote democracy and human rights.

The EU, for example, saw TJ as part of a larger policy of promoting democratic transition. On the symbolic level, it was suggested that EU member states saw parallels between TJ in Morocco and TJ in European countries like Germany, Spain, and the United Kingdom (Northern Ireland). For them, learning from their own history had been important on the road to peace, and so they may have gravitated toward activities in the cultural domain such as archives, history, and memory projects as an important means of assisting a country to take ownership of its own past. Thus, for the EU, the choice to support IER1/2 was a natural one, as the IER recommendations fit easily into the EU's interest in promoting good governance as well as with its values and its own historical experiences. In addition, for some donors such as the Dutch Embassy, support for TJ was part of a general commitment to human rights issues, and also motivated by the fact of a large Moroccan diaspora in the Netherlands. However, what this amounted to was a series of piecemeal approaches in which donors could be seen to be doing something, even if what they were doing was not particularly strategic.

The reasons behind the lack of strategy were different, however, for different donors. In the case of the EU, for example, support for TJ was part of a bureaucratic decision-making process that involved large-scale, multiyear planning (the action plans). Once the action plans were set, they were highly inflexible. For a donor like the Dutch Embassy, however, the lack of strategy was a result of the fact that decisions were ad hoc and tied to individuals within the Embassy. The Dutch funding for ICTJ's work on security system reform is an indicative example. Support for ICTJ was ad hoc, rather than part of a larger strategy for promoting TJ; evidenced by the stopping of funding once ICTJ withdrew from Morocco in 2011. If such a strategy had been in place, then ICTJ's decision would have merely prompted the Embassy to try and find another NGO to take the work forward; both FMVJ and OMDH, for example, had been ICTJ's collaborators on the project and may well have had the capacity to fill the gap.

Related to the lack of a strategic approach is the issue of the small scale of international support to civil society-led projects on TJ. The Dutch support for ICTJ mentioned earlier is one instance of this. More broadly, while there was a communication mechanism for the EU and the bilateral governments, hosted by the EU (as Morocco's largest donor), TJ was reported not to have been a high priority in these meetings, which were described as information-sharing sessions and an opportunity for donors to exchange ideas and prevent duplication of projects across the spectrum of their funding focuses; a good start, but hardly a comprehensive approach to funding TJ or democratic development. It is therefore fair to characterize both the behavior of individual donors and donors' collective approach to TJ in Morocco as piecemeal, small-scale, and lacking a strategy to bring together various elements.

Political interests naturally played a role in TJ funding as well: decisions of *whether* and *what* to fund. TJ remained a politically sensitive issue in Morocco, particularly concerning the issue of criminal accountability and state responsibility for past human rights violations. As a result, some donors, including the United States, trod softly around these issues, especially as Morocco was an ally in the war on terrorism and it was more stable and liberal than most other regimes in its neighborhood. Support for TJ incurred risk in maintaining good relationships with the Moroccan state. It was perhaps no surprise, in this sense, that the EU's approach has been to support TJ, but to fund elements that courted little political risk.

Finally, donor fatigue was setting in. As one donor said, "Five years ago, funding the IER's recommendation was sexy; now it's not. There is a feeling now that [this] is over." The focus had shifted to the constitutional reforms of 2011. This shift is also evidenced by the fact that TJ was not included in the most recent (2013) EU action plan for Morocco. After IER2, there would be no further funding specifically related to the implementation of the IER recommendations.

The View from Beneficiaries

In general, beneficiaries of funding for TJ in Morocco were knowledgeable about the constraints on donors. They had very different perspectives, however, on the wisdom and relevance of specific donor actions.

While there was some diversity of views within CNDH, interviewees noted that TJ was something that matched the EU's interests, since many EU member states had undergone TJ-like initiatives. They felt that both the EU and UNIFEM (as of 2011, incorporated into UN Women) had clear goals that were well communicated. Moreover, they felt that they were directly involved in setting those goals – this is obviously true, in the sense that the EU was supporting the implementation of recommendations developed by the IER, rather than its own initiatives. The EU Delegation's physical presence in Rabat meant that they "understand our dynamic."

The national-level human rights organizations also had a general understanding of TJ funding, and were certainly aware of the EU's support for IER1/2. They had, however, a somewhat different perception of donor goals and decision-making processes on TJ. With respect to the EU, they saw the EU funds as a matter between the EU and the Moroccan state; civil society actors were not really involved. This perception was confirmed by a CSO-led evaluation in 2007 of the EU-Morocco action plan that included support for IER1/2, among many other things, which stated, "The Action Plan concluded between the EU and Morocco was elaborated and negotiated without consultation with nor even information from CSOs. This is contrary to all the engagements that express support for civil society participation in democratization processes."[18]

In general, interviews with civil society actors suggested that it was not a particularly common practice for donors to consult them – except in the general way in which donors like the Dutch Embassy are in constant consultation mode, as they look for organizations and projects to fund. Some civil society interviewees, rightly or wrongly, interpreted this activity as a kind of ad hoc project seeking that sometimes benefits those who already have connections, rather than a means of sustainable investment in civil society actors.[19]

National-level organizations evinced little support for IER1 or IER2, as mentioned earlier. But interviewees generally were not critical of the EU's choices – and nearly all of them had either received or applied for EU funds at one time or another. Instead, interviewees seemed sanguine about the EU's potential as well as its structural limitations: for example, some explained that the EU tends to award funds of a (large) size that would be difficult for a small organization to absorb, and they therefore thought it was logical for the EU to give money to CNDH, a state institution.

Local grantees of IER1/2 did not have much perspective on funding for TJ. They obviously did know that the EU supported TJ, as they received money from the EU. However, the vast majority of grantees were not TJ or even human rights organizations, and thus they are not seeking money from other donors on these issues. For most, it was also their first time working with EU funds. Interviews suggested that, at this level, organizations did feel that the EU had clear goals, at least as they were expressed through the community reparations program. They did not, however, feel that they had much contact with the EU or any input on decision-making or structures. For most, the EU was an abstract entity that required a lot of reporting, rather than a partner. Interviewees also had some questions about how well the program met local needs – a subject that will be addressed in the next section.

[18] The report explicitly took the action plan to task for ignoring most of the IER's recommendations on institutional reforms, and it is based on workshops that included representatives of AMDH and OMDH, among others. Moroccan Euromediterranean NGO Network, "Évaluation du Plan d'Action Maroc/U.E. Dans le Cadre de la PEV" (report of a conference held in Rabat, October 25–26, 2007), 24; available at www.fes.org.ma/common/pdf/publications_pdf/PEV/PEV.pdf.

[19] Indeed, we came across one specific case where a TJ-related project did receive funding through having a personal connection with the donor. Many civil society actors expressed strong opinions about the way that embassies decide on funding. There is a perception among some that embassy staff members "don't do their jobs" and "wait until the end of the year" when they then have to find projects to fund. The opinions themselves may or may not be valid, but it is important to acknowledge that this kind of negative perception exists. (By contrast, we did not hear strong positive opinions of the ways that embassies decide on funding from our interviewees.)

Good Intentions Gone Awry?

Three themes surfaced repeatedly with respect to the issue of the relevance of international assistance to TJ in Morocco. First, and as noted earlier, many national actors, including victim groups, simply did not see IER1/2 as the most relevant TJ need; they focused instead on institutional reforms as a priority. Given the fact that institutional reforms were effectively blocked before 2011, however, it is unclear what kinds of TJ projects these national actors would have preferred to see getting donor support.[20] Small projects were funded at this time related to reforming the security institutions (including the grant to ICTJ from the Dutch Embassy), but the work did not get very far for political reasons.

Second, a consistent issue raised with respect to the community reparations program was whether development or income-generating projects were relevant to reparations for past human rights abuse. This issue was raised consistently among all three groups interviewed: CNDH, national organizations, and local grantees. As background, it is important to recall that the RFP for IER1 asked for proposals for four types of projects: 1) preservation of memory; 2) capacity building; 3) income generation; 4) inclusion of women. Of these, the largest proportion (roughly 40 percent) of grants under IER1 went to income-generating projects, most of which apparently failed, in the sense that they did not produce sustainable income.[21] Examples of projects included a women's carpet-making cooperative; numerous agricultural initiatives, such as flower cultivation; and a cooperative for disabled women to produce beauty products. In the cases of Hay Mohammadi and Al Hoceima, it appears that all of these initiatives failed – even though in Al Hoceima there are attempts to keep two of them going in spite of the fact that they are not generating income.[22]

The perceived relevance of these projects hinged on a couple of things: on the one hand, whether the small scale of the projects made them appropriately "reparative" in communities that have immense developmental needs; and, on the other, whether there was a sufficient symbolic component to call these projects "reparations" rather than "development." With respect to the first issue, it was said

[20] One civil society actor said that they believed the EU's support for IER1/2 had legitimated the state's lack of action on impunity and reform.

[21] The rough proportion given by the FCDG was: 1) preservation of memory: 20 percent; 2) capacity building: 30 percent; 3) income generating: 40 percent; and 4) inclusion of women: 10 percent. The proportion of grants given directly followed the proportion of applications received, according to the interviewee. The weakness of these projects is discussed in the unpublished evaluations of the IER1 program (on file with the author), but was also discussed with people in Hay Mohammadi and Al Hoceima.

[22] As another example of confusion, one of the projects that IER1 supported in Al Hoceima promoted turkey farming among women. However, turkey farming is exactly the kind of small development project that women in the region fundraise for anyway – reparations or no. I picked up a brochure about turkey-farming projects by women's cooperatives in the office of a local development NGO (brochure on file with author); these projects had nothing to do with reparations.

repeatedly that regions like Al Hoceima need more hospitals, a university, and a highway connecting it to the rest of the country (i.e., to Taza) – not isolated projects for fifteen to twenty to fifty people at a time (projects that then unfortunately failed to produce sustainable results for communities). On the second issue, everyone agreed that there was significant confusion between the IER1 program and the INDH, the much larger national development program that the state launched nearly simultaneously (in 2005). In spite of communication efforts, interviewees said that local communities had trouble understanding what IER1 was and how it was different from the INDH, especially early on; this confusion was complicated by the fact that the INDH then helped with co-funding many of the IER1 projects.

By contrast, supporters of the community reparations program stressed its symbolic function and its role in reconstructing relationships between the community and the state. They also mentioned that income-generating projects had been included in the first place in response to victim communities expressing this preference during the initial consultation process. Some supporters felt that the symbolic function would have been strengthened if communities better understood the difference between reparations and development and, additionally, if the projects selected had had a clear benefit to everyone. A number of interviewees – on both the donor and grantee sides – said that they felt that local organizations did not always propose projects that aligned with the "spirit" of the program. In this sense, it is perhaps unfortunate that the RFP did not result in more proposals for projects related to the preservation of memory, which some felt was more closely aligned with a symbolic effort that benefits communities as a whole.

The third point of controversy that was frequently mentioned concerned the transformation of some of the former detention centers into sites of conscience or community centers, in particular, the former Derb Moulay Chérif prison in Hay Mohammadi and some of the sites in the south around Tazmamart and Agdz. The IER made specific recommendations around creating these sites of memory, and indeed suggested that the transformation of some sites was already under way.[23] Yet, as of this writing, there has been little progress on any of these sites. Instead, the focus within CNDH has shifted toward creating more general museums completely unrelated to the detention centers, which will represent the entire history and patrimony of a particular region, with no specific focus on past human rights violations. Plans for such museums are central to the IER2 program, which has proposed these more general museums in Al Hoceima, Casablanca, and Ouarzazate. These museums will not, therefore, be sites of memory or sites of conscience.

Interviewees held a variety of perspectives on this situation – some voicing extreme disappointment at the fact that the former detention sites had not been

[23] In 2005, the IER wrote: "The IER specifically recommends the conversion of former illegal detention centers (Tazmamart, Agdz, Derb Moulay Chérif in Casablanca, etc.). Steps in this direction are already being taken." IER, *Synthèse du Rapport Final*, 45 (my translation).

transformed, and others supporting a more general approach to "memory" that would celebrate a region's entire heritage and perhaps contribute to tourism. It should be noted that much of this general support for heritage spaces came from interviewees in the Rif, which did not have a secret detention site during the Years of Lead; therefore, there is no choice to make between a "Museum of the Rif" and a detention center, as there is in Casablanca and Ouarzazate.

The reasons for this shift in focus away from transforming the detention sites are a bit murky, but it is clear that it is actually not related to decisions made by donors like the EU; instead, the decisions have been made by Moroccans. One factor is that there are logistical problems in undertaking the proposed transformations; these problems, which include (for example) evicting people who are still living on the premises of Derb Moulay Chérif, provide the state with an excuse for not moving forward – and it is unclear whether there is political will to move forward. Another factor is that the change in leadership with the creation of CNDH in 2011 (a year after the IER2 program was launched) also led to a change in priorities with respect to CNDH's approach to memory and history. Many interviewees both inside and outside of CNDH noted that Yazami wanted to take a more scientific approach to the past, which can be summed up in the phrase "passing from memory to history," and which has deprioritized memory-related projects. In this sense, the EU has allowed CNDH leadership to set the priorities for what it believes to be most relevant with respect to memory and history work for IER2 – resulting in these general museum projects rather than projects more specifically related to the Years of Lead.

Finally, a striking feature of the community reparations program – given the fact that its intention was to benefit victims – is how little it appeared to work directly with victim organizations. In Al Hoceima, this is because victim organizations simply declined to participate, because of their fundamental disagreements with the program. In Hay Mohammadi, individual victims were integrated into various projects, but not organized groups as such. This lack of participation of victims' organizations was not lost on interviewees, some of whom thought that the program would have funded more relevant projects had it worked directly with victims' organizations. One project in Hay Mohammadi that was designed directly to address victims' needs was the creation of a center to treat torture victims. However, the center had to close after a year because of lack of funding, as EU funds alone were not enough to sustain it, and state actors did not step in to fill the gap.

In sum, these various points of contention show how the good intentions of both the major donor and Moroccan authorities (that is, establishing a community reparations program) got sidetracked in the program's implementation. Most of these points relate to insufficient engagement with victims' groups about the fundamental value and direction of the program. Of course, persuading victim groups of this value would have been difficult, given the fact that the state did not commit itself to other reforms the groups themselves prioritized. The small scale of the program in relation to the state's development program (the INDH) did not help matters.

THE IMPACT OF INTERNATIONAL ASSISTANCE

Trust and Collaboration

A crucial finding of this case study concerns a marked decrease in collaboration among civil society actors working on TJ after the close of the IER in 2005. Through a seemingly vicious circle, this decline was both a consequence of and a contributor to the rise of the CCDH/CNDH as the most important TJ actor in Morocco. While international assistance did not cause this decline, it did contribute to it through several means. Moreover, there is little evidence that the projects chosen for support by donors have had any positive effects on civil society trust or collaboration, or its ability to act as a counterweight to the state on TJ.

Some background on the evolution of civil society engagement on TJ is useful here. All interviewees highlighted the cooperation of the three key civil society actors on TJ – FMVJ, AMDH, and OMDH – in the early 2000s as they reacted to the state's inadequate proposal for reparations for victims ("They completely rejected it," as one interviewee put it) and developed counterproposals that included the creation of the IER. While they may have had to "add water to their own wine," as one interviewee said, in order to work with one another, it does seem that they did so up to the time of the IER itself. The key area of disagreement, as mentioned, was how to address impunity; AMDH felt it could not be sacrificed, whereas OMDH thought it useful to table the issue for practical reasons. Activities at the time included nonofficial negotiations with the state (there were no official contacts) and sensitization and outreach to media and politicians, as well as outreach to international actors such as FIDH and ICTJ. Through this means, the organizations were reinforcing their relationships both locally and internationally in order to push forward a TJ agenda.

With the creation of the IER in 2004, AMDH decided against cooperating with the commission, due to its limited mandate (for example, not including HR violations up to 1999), as well as the decision that individual perpetrators would neither be named nor held accountable. At the same time, the head of FMVJ, Driss Benzekri, stepped down in order to become the IER's leader, perhaps signifying a clear split in approaches between the two organizations, even as they had an overlapping membership. AMDH would later organize a set of public hearings of victim testimonies that – contrary to the IER's – would allow victims to name their torturers. Nonetheless, AMDH did participate in a civil society monitoring committee of the IER, which was comprised of the three key organizations plus many of the civil society associations that had participated in the original 2001 symposium.

When the IER concluded its work, all three key organizations welcomed the final recommendations, which more than one interviewee called "very correct." This included AMDH – even though it had disagreed with the process used to arrive at the recommendations. This agreement, however, did not seem to result in renewed collaboration and strategy setting among the three organizations, in order to continue pushing forward the TJ agenda. There may be several reasons for this. First, the CCDH, now with Benzekri at its head, was tasked with implementing the recommendations, initiating a new dynamic in the TJ process. The role of civil society organizations may therefore not have been as clear as it had been before, as the state was now taking the lead. Second, some of the most important recommendations relating to institutional reforms very dear to civil society organizations were, as one interviewee put it, "put in the Frigidaire until 2011" – the Arab Spring. There was little political opportunity to advance, in spite of a variety of programmatic initiatives on security sector reform, etc., which included joint efforts among a number of organizations, including the project referred to earlier between ICTJ, OMDH, and FMVJ.[24]

It is relevant to note here the important role of the personal level in relationships among organizations, especially in the national-level human rights organizations. Many of these groups are populated by former victims, including in the leadership, many (if not most) of whom were (or continue to be) left-wing activists. (Examples: the head of Medical Association for the Rehabilitation of Torture Victims and FMVJ are brothers; the secretary-general of CNDH formerly worked at both FMVJ and AMDH; the director of programs at ADALA also was formerly with AMDH.) It was my impression that people often know one another personally, have long histories, and sometimes have strong opinions on human rights tactics, especially on the question of whether to work with the state on democratic reforms, or instead to push the state into crisis through activism. This said, it is clear that prominent former victims have greatly enhanced social capital, as they occupy leadership positions in a variety of key organizations.

Liberalization of the state – however insufficient – was clearly an important factor in emboldening civil society organizations to work together on TJ. Moreover, cooperation among national human rights organizations strengthened in reaction to the state's flawed proposal for reparations in the late 1990s; organizations came together to make counterproposals (in particular, for the IER) that were more in line with civil society expectations for TJ. Even during the IER, when some organizations, such as AMDH, criticized the IER and held alternative public

[24] ICTJ led a two-year project on security sector reform in 2009–10, working with a range of local human rights NGOs, including FMVJ and OMDH. One output of the program was a joint ICTJ–OMDH study: Abdallah Ounnir, "Réflexion pour l'adoption d'une stratégie nationale de lutte contre l'impunité" (no date, hard copy on file with the author).

hearings, the national human rights organizations were all contributing toward a truth-telling process, albeit in different ways.

Yet this cooperation and shared purpose lessened substantially after the close of the IER. Organizations did not establish a new, shared agenda on TJ, even if there was ad hoc collaboration on particular issues (i.e., the death penalty). Collaboration was also tested over the issue of how much to work with the state rather than to act as a counterweight to it – for example, how much to work with the CCDH/CNDH or not after the close of the IER.

Moreover, the relative roles of civil society actors within this collaborating structure changed over time. FMVJ, clearly a national leader on TJ prior to the IER, no longer possesses the same prominence it once did. Some attributed this change to the loss of its charismatic leader, Driss Benzekri; others to the IER process itself, which some see to have disrupted FMVJ's previous role as a strong moral counterweight to the state.

What has the role of donors been in this process? First, donors themselves made observations on this lack of collaboration, so they were clearly aware of it. In a general sense, both donors and civil society actors mentioned that civil society actors were reluctant to enter into real partnership, which would entail co-fundraising and sharing of both resources and decision-making. Donors perceived, for example, that peer organizations often competed with one another rather than collaborated, and AMDH/OMDH was an example given of organizations that did not collaborate with one another. A number of donors and civil society actors also mentioned that organizations of different types may be less likely to collaborate. "Types" meant many things in this instance – established organizations not wanting to work with an organization that was only two years old, older leaders not wanting to ally with younger leaders, service organizations not having good links to advocacy organizations, etc. This point, however, would seem to suggest that organizations of similar types were more likely to collaborate. As we have seen with the national human rights organizations, this was not always the case.

While donors have supported a handful of collaborative projects (such as the NED's multiyear support of FMVJ and the Dutch Embassy's support for ICTJ's work on security sector reform), more generally, the structure of international assistance clearly contributed to a competitive, individual, project-driven approach rather than a collaborative, strategy-driven approach. This is simply the nature of competing for RFPs in a marketplace where civil society actors must distinguish themselves from competitors in order to receive funding. In terms of decision-making processes, both NED and the Dutch Embassy used competitive RFP processes, and (as discussed), the EU-funded IER1/2 also relied on competitive RFPs.[25]

[25] The embassy, for example, does a yearly competition in which it both looks for interesting projects and receives concept notes from NGOs; it has a human rights fund of roughly €500,000 per year that is specifically for CSOs.

An issue like TJ, however, is one that really does often require collaborative action to be successful. And long-term, core support would be important to encouraging organizations taking a "strategy" rather than a "project" approach. Perhaps there was more scope for donors to consider insisting on joint proposals from civil society actors on TJ – as challenging as these are from many angles.[26] One donor lamented, "Donors are part of the problem" – meaning that it was easier to work with individual CSOs than with groups or networks, and easier to work with existing partners than to find new ones.

Mixed Outcomes of IER1/2

This weak impact of donor-funded projects on trust and collaboration can be seen more directly through the lens of IER1: the community reparations program whose stated objectives included the strengthening of civic trust. My research examined the operation of the program in two regions: Hay Mohammadi, a poor neighborhood in Casablanca and also the location of one of Morocco's most notorious detention centers, Derb Moulay Chérif prison; and Al Hoceima, a town in the Rif region, which experienced severe repression in the late 1950s and the 1980s, as well as decades of economic marginalization. Analysis of these two sites offers different perspectives on the relationship between community reparations and civil society.

In terms of networks among civil society actors, there is little evidence that IER1 contributed in either case to building relationships either among civil society actors or between civil society and state actors. In both cases, projects were carried out generally independently of one another, although civil society actors did meet in some cases for trainings or as part of the local coordinating committee. There was only one reported instance of civil society actors continuing a relationship after the end of the IER1 program (between Casamémoire and Association Initiative Urbaine in Hay Mohammadi). Additionally, the one capacity-building project considered as part of this case study – which brought together seventeen community organizations from the Hay Mohammadi neighborhood – was considered by its own project manager to have resulted in no durable outcomes. The primary reason for this failure was that the organizations that participated in the program lacked both money and access to funders, and therefore could not develop any projects after the conclusion of the capacity-building project. There was, however, evidence that civil society actors leveraged preexisting relationships to aid them in their projects. For example, in Al Hoceima, leaders of an income-generating project that taught rural women in the Rif

[26] For example, even in instances where donors have tried to encourage partnership, it has run up against the fact that organizations prefer not to collaborate. One donor discussed it in the context of a new program funded by UN Women: "UN Women has been encouraging collaboration. It has a €1.4 million project with seven different NGOs working on human rights, awareness raising, and lobbying. UN Women is coordinating them to capitalize on their union. But each organization sees their project as separate. Each wants to manage the funds. [In general] many women's groups come together for ad hoc actions but not for long-term projects."

how to cultivate roses (and bring them to market) have leveraged their relationships with a local development network to continue training, even as the project faces difficulties in actually generating income, and thus continuing.

Moreover, the local coordinating committees – which were, in theory, the key vehicles for generating social trust between state and civil society actors – in these two instances suggested mixed results in terms of establishing durable relationships between civil society and state actors. It should be noted that the committees in the two cases were structured somewhat differently: in Hay Mohammadi, all of the grantees were included in the committee, whereas in Al Hoceima, none of them were. In Al Hoceima, interviewees' consensus was that the committee was not useful because the state representatives ultimately were not particularly interested in or supportive of their projects. As one person noted, "The elites here are representative of their parties in Rabat. If the parties are in the opposition, then they will be against things emanating from the state." After initial meetings with the committee, grantees primarily worked with the CCDH representative, and interviewees suggested that promises made by the elected representatives were not often upheld in a satisfactory or timely way. In Hay Mohammadi, the role of the coordinating committee was positive in some instances – for example, facilitating access to national archives. However, not all interviewees saw the committee as useful, and one in particular stopped going to meetings.

A further finding in terms of relationship building in Al Hoceima was that IER1 elicited a negative reaction from a range of key actors. A number of human rights and victim organizations declined to participate in the program. In particular, the local chapter of FMVJ was invited to be on the coordinating committee, but refused. Other organizations, such as AMDH, publicly criticized it, as they considered it trivial and irrelevant to larger needs for social and political justice.[27] Local political elites also were sometimes opposed, since they may or may not be invested in state-level initiatives, depending on their political party affiliations.

On a positive note, however, such blockages could sometimes be constructive. In Al Hoceima, civil society relationships with CNDH itself appear to have been strengthened through the program, and in particular through the efforts of the local representative and the subsequent establishment of a regional office (after 2011). Grantees said that when they faced obstacles, especially with local political elites, they approached CCDH/CNDH, which helped them with specific issues (for example, finding co-funding for a theater project, securing a point of sale for roses). This said, it was not clear that this strengthening lasted past the end of the program.

[27] It should be noted that the fact that these programs generated public criticism may also be interpreted in a positive light. Two of the evaluations of the IER1 program emphasized that the program had opened up public debate and reinforced the notion that public discussion of the Years of Lead was permissible. See the unpublished evaluation of IER1's pilot projects on gender (2010, p. 91) and the unpublished final evaluation (2013); both on file with the author.

EU Grant Regulations: A Special Challenge for Beneficiaries

A unanimous point of view – one that everyone was quite emphatic about – was that administering EU funds was "difficult" and "heavy," with rules that one interviewee described as "frankly stupid." That EU funds are difficult to administer is a well-known fact – including to those who work at the EU. So this may seem like an obvious statement and, perhaps, pointless to expand upon. It is useful, however, to isolate some of the challenges raised as they pertain to TJ funding in this particular context.

First, although one of the key objectives of the community reparations process was to recognize and empower victims and victims' groups as civic actors, there are many ways in which the cumbersome EU procedures may have in fact contributed to their exclusion. Each of the following were means by which interviewees noted exclusion to operate:

- The grants issued through IER1 and IER2 were administered through a competitive RFP process, which naturally favored organizations that could put together a professional proposal.
- Proposals were required to be submitted in French.
- Organizations were required to co-fund a certain percentage of their project's costs.

Many interviewees noted that it was difficult, if not impossible, for the most marginalized communities to participate in the process, as they were impoverished, had high rates of illiteracy, did not speak French, and, in some cases, had Amazigh rather than Arabic as a first language. While the CCDH did make sincere efforts to assist groups through an "accompaniment" process, most CNDH and civil society actors thought that these were a good idea, but ultimately insufficient.

Second, the fact that the EU required the use of its logo on anything produced using EU funds (including business cards for CNDH staff members) meant that the community reparations program was publicly branded as an EU program. According to interviews, this did lead to some discussions in communities about whether the state was appropriately assuming its responsibilities for repairing past human rights abuse.

Third, there was concern with the IER2 program in particular that EU requirements to purchase goods and services from EU providers, as well as to partner with EU educational institutions, were preventing the projects from moving forward. These requirements meant that it was difficult sometimes for Moroccan institutions to take ownership of the projects. As an example of this dynamic, we can cite the fact that of the seven grants for history and memory projects given through the IER2 program, two were given to a French institution, the Centre Jacques Berque, and one to a Spanish citizen who is of Rifain origin. It is not known whether nearly half the grants were given to these institutions/individuals *because* they were Europeans, and it should be noted that there were very few applications (sixteen). Interviews suggest that there is a perception that this was the case, even if that perception is false.

A Bright Spot for International Assistance: Gender Inclusion

One issue on which there was positive evidence of international influence on TJ relates to the inclusion of a gender perspective across a range of TJ initiatives: the IER, individual reparations, and community reparations. The history here provides helpful context to understand the contribution of international actors, including donors. Interviewees emphasized that women's groups were not particularly interested in TJ in the early days (1999 to 2001), and they did not see TJ as an important issue for women. Although women's groups were invited to participate in the 2001 symposium that led to the creation of the IER, as well as the civil society monitoring committee that accompanied the IER, this did not translate in a practical way into a gendered approach to the IER's work. As one interviewee put it, "Even women's organizations did not have a gendered lens on TJ." This gap existed in spite of the fact that the IER was comprised of representatives of human rights organizations, which were already supportive of women's rights. The impetus for integrating gender into the work of the commission came not from networks with women's groups, therefore, but rather from the work of women staff members of the IER, such as IER commissioner and former political prisoner Latifa Jbabdi (the only woman commissioner), as well as from international actors such as the ICTJ.

With respect to the community reparations process, gender was integrated on the conceptual level from the beginning. To operationalize this commitment, UNIFEM was a member of the overarching Steering Committee (alongside the CCDH, the FCDG, and the EU), and there was always at least one organization on each local coordinating committee representing local women's groups. (In the case of the two regions visited in this case study, there was more than one women's group on each coordinating committee.) This said, there did not appear to be any new or durable relationships established as a result of working on the community reparations process, as mentioned in the preceding section – whether among women's groups or among women's groups and other kinds of civil society actors. Additionally, the incorporation of UNIFEM and women's organizations into the institutional structures did not immediately or unproblematically lead to the adoption of a gendered approach to the work. Indeed, a mid-term evaluation of the program found that a gender approach was almost completely absent from the early projects funded. Interviewees suggested that it might have been better to offer training on gender to all project managers, so that gender truly could have been integrated in a crosscutting way. They also agreed (as did a final evaluation of the program) that gender was better incorporated in the later projects funded through the second RFP process.[28]

Many interviewees emphasized the positive role of the ICTJ with the IER and the individual reparations program, and of UNIFEM with respect to its participation in IER1. Moreover, the EU's requirements for gender as a crosscutting theme added an extra push to these efforts. Without these actors, it seems clear that the distinctive gender dimensions to political violence in Morocco would not have been part of either discourse or plans.

Even with these clear contributions, there were some complications. Interviews suggested that the most marginalized women beneficiaries of the community reparations program often required elite intermediaries to navigate the difficult EU proposal process. To take the example of the cooperative for rose cultivation, this was a group of largely illiterate Amazigh women (according to interviewees). It would have been impossible for them to develop a professional proposal – in French, no less – and to manage the project according to the EU's requirements without such help. Therefore, it would be interesting to know more about the degree to which the program facilitated these kind of connections, or whether they were preexisting – and then, ultimately, to know whether these kinds of intermediary relationships are fruitful and durable. In the case of the rose cooperative, the project leader was from the community herself, but obviously had moved away and acquired an education.

An Unintended Consequence: CNDH Consolidates Its Role

Among the set of Moroccan actors that have engaged on TJ, the position of the state has changed significantly over the past fifteen years. A key turning point came, as mentioned, with the accession of the charismatic Benzekri to the leadership of the CCDH, and the CCDH being charged with implementation of the IER's recommendations. Subsequently, it received significant funding from the EU in order to assist in that (selective) implementation. While we might normally expect civil society to act as a watchdog, ensuring that the CCDH/CNDH made progress, we have instead seen a withering of civil society action and interest on TJ, for reasons explained earlier.

The EU's long-term support to IER1 and IER2 (via the CCDH/CNDH) implicitly legitimated the state's approach to TJ and delegitimized civil society actors' key roles as both interlocutors and counterweights to the state. In retrospect, it might have been a positive move for the EU to complement its support for IER1 and IER2 with specific support for civil society actors to engage with and monitor these programs.

[28] Unpublished evaluations (2010 and 2013) are on file with the author; the 2010 evaluation is also included in IER1's "box set" of documents, films, and other media, which are not yet available online.

Therefore, although TJ remains nationally owned and driven, the Moroccan state is effectively shaping the priorities. This fact begs the question of who the national/local owners are, since clearly there are deep rifts within Moroccan society on these issues – rifts that are not necessarily reflected in the composition of CNDH, which naturally is comprised of those civil society actors who believe the time really has come to move from opposition to proposition. Interaction with donors, such as it is, has served to reinforce this dynamic, although donors did not cause it.

This enhanced legitimacy has resulted in an unforeseen consequence: CNDH itself seems to have become an international actor on TJ due to the notoriety of the Moroccan experience with TJ. CNDH interviewees mentioned that they receive international delegations asking for information on the IER and community reparations from places like South Sudan, Mali, and elsewhere on a nearly constant basis.[29] CNDH members also figure as technical advisors to the TJ process under way in Tunisia. In a recent speech to Parliament, CNDH President Yazami noted that Morocco's "pioneering example continues to inspire many other countries in the region that have opted for the same path."[30]

CONCLUSION

In spite of the fact that Morocco would not be considered a major recipient of international assistance on TJ (relative to many other countries), there is much to be learned from its experience. In the wake of the IER in 2005, and with the implementation of its innovative community reparations program, Morocco was considered a powerful positive example of TJ and a source of TJ expertise for the region and beyond. As of 2014, however, after progress mainly in the realm of reparations for victims and limited truth telling, TJ in Morocco had been blocked: CNDH continued to implement certain pieces of the IER's recommendations, but avoided the most politically sensitive issues.

This chapter identified a number of factors shaping this outcome, which I argue was not caused by donors, although donors contributed to it. Taking their lead from CNDH, donors took a piecemeal approach to the implementation of the IER's recommendations: they focused on the least politically challenging issues, like community reparations and memory projects, and played down the interests of civil society organizations to tackle the hard question of impunity for grievous human rights abuse – abuse that continues. Although the community reparations program, which was supported by the EU, was partly intended to foster trust between civil society and the state, as well as among civil society actors, those goals were hard to achieve given the challenges with the program's design (which was shaped by cumbersome EU rules) and the fact that it lacked

[29] One person suggested that the demand to share lessons was overwhelming and interfering with normal work.

[30] CNDH, "Résumé du rapport présenté par de M. Driss El Yazami," 1.

substantial engagement with and support from victim organizations. On a positive note, TJ in Morocco showed improved sensitivity to the gendered nature of human rights abuse as a result of international engagement, including that of donors.

Ultimately, however, with CNDH now consolidated as the most important actor on TJ in Morocco, donors have stopped engaging on TJ entirely. Ten years after the cautious optimism that followed the IER, a deep pessimism in regard to state commitment to and civil society engagement on TJ is the order of the day. This is a particularly tragic outcome in a country where TJ was conceived and driven primarily by committed human rights and victim organizations.

4

Off the Agenda as Uganda Moves toward Development

Uganda's Transitional Justice Process

Tania Bernath

Since independence, Uganda has yet to experience a peaceful transfer of power. After transitioning from British colonial rule to self-government in 1962, communities in Uganda have witnessed military coups, dictatorships, and armed rebellions. The most well known of these conflicts emerged from the Lord's Resistance Army (LRA) insurgency and ongoing violence in northern Uganda that began in 1986 and diffused into other countries after incomplete peace talks in 2006.

The conflict in northern Uganda saw between 1.8 million and 2 million people internally displaced. Of this number, approximately 1.2 million internally displaced persons (IDPs) originated from the Gulu, Kitgum, and Pader regions in the north, with the remaining coming from Teso and Lango. More than 200 camps and "protective villages" were established to accommodate IDPs, with 50 percent of their populations comprised of children. These camps grew and became densely populated; locations housed some 60,000 people.

IDP camps, however, provided women and children limited protection from rape, torture, and killings committed by both the LRA and the government army, the United People's Democratic Front (UPDF). Violence perpetrated by these groups, and resulting diseases from poor camp conditions, contributed to hundreds of thousands of deaths. Further, it has been estimated that more than 25,000 children were forcibly conscripted during the war, many from within IDP compounds. Night commuting, when children walked from IDP camps to larger cities to avoid LRA abduction, impacted up to 45,000 children.[1]

I am incredibly grateful to Paige Arthur for her support, assistance, and unending patience. This chapter would not have been written without her help. I would also like to acknowledge Victor Ochen for his insights and feedback, which have been critical to my understanding of Uganda and to the research. I would also like to acknowledge everyone I interviewed and talked to in Uganda for this research for his or her time, candidness, and honesty.

[1] Civil Society Organizations for Peace in Northern Uganda (CSOPNU), "Counting the Cost: Twenty Years of War in Northern Uganda" (March 2004), 8, www.oxfam.org/sites/www.oxfam.org/files/uganda.pdf.

In this chapter, I argue that as the government's commitment to implement transitional justice (TJ) has waned, and as Uganda has moved from a postwar to a development phase, TJ has lost momentum among donors. Donor strategies related to TJ have long focused on strengthening the state's Justice, Law, and Order Sector (JLOS), and they have also provided support to some civil society actors. But TJ is rarely referred to in donors' most recent strategies, and interest has shifted away from dealing with the past to focusing on the present. Although donors have supported civil society organizations (CSOs) working on TJ on an individual basis, such groups have not benefited from a broad-based and coordinated approach to capacity building. Without a strong civil society acting as a counterweight to ongoing state inertia, it is difficult to see how TJ will move forward appreciably.

The most concrete outcomes to date are the national and International Criminal Court (ICC) trials in 2016, marking the first time that anyone responsible for crimes committed in the Ugandan conflict may be brought to justice. Even without a capacity-building strategy, a core group of TJ CSOs has developed and become national leaders on the various aspects of the complicated TJ agenda. While their work has largely been complementary, and CSOs do work together, this has more often been opportunistic rather than strategic – whether in relation to their actions, advocacy, or dealings with government. Additionally, although the relationship between government and civil society started out strong, it has since deteriorated, further adding to fragmentation and breakdown of the TJ process. Still today, the draft National Transitional Justice Policy (NTJP), which has been years in the making, has not been adopted into law. Thus, no reparations have been provided, the truth has not been told, and no government actor has been held to account for their actions or for negligence in protecting the population.

This chapter starts with an overview of TJ in Uganda, followed by a note on the methodology and limitations of the study. It then describes international assistance to TJ in Uganda, in sections on aid to state actors and aid to civil society actors. This chapter subsequently turns to the ways that international assistance has imprinted both the TJ process and CSOs working on TJ. It concludes with an overview of the political, financial, foreign policy, and administrative factors that have driven donor decision-making.

TRANSITIONAL JUSTICE IN UGANDA

Starting in the 1990s, conflict-affected communities in the north began to make demands for an amnesty to bring an end to the conflict with the LRA and other armed groups. In 2000, the Amnesty Act was enacted, and the Amnesty Commission (AC) was established by an Act of Parliament: among its duties was to demobilize, grant amnesty, resettle, and reintegrate former fighters on the one hand, and to promote dialogue and reconciliation between government and warring factions on the other.[2] Since it started its work, the AC has demobilized 27,000 people, who have denounced rebellion and been integrated into their community as part of the process.[3] In 2012, the Amnesty Act lapsed. After pressure from the northern communities, however, it was reinstated.

While the war was still raging in northern Uganda in December 2003, the government referred the situation with the LRA to the ICC.[4] In 2005, the Court unsealed the warrants of five suspected perpetrators – all members of the LRA – of serious crimes in the conflict.[5] Since then, three of the five have died. Finally, in 2016, one of the two remaining members of the LRA, Dominic Ongwen, turned himself over to the ICC, leaving only Joseph Kony at large. The fact that Dominic Ongwen started in the LRA as a child soldier has raised significant legal questions on the role of children in the conflict and their accountability for abuses.[6]

The peace talks held in Juba between 2006 and 2008 marked a negotiated end to the conflict. The talks between the Ugandan government and representatives of the LRA were hosted and mediated by the government of South Sudan and supported by both international and local CSOs. The process initially involved a few CSOs and subsequently evolved to include Joaquim Chissano, the Special Envoy of the United Nations (UN) Secretary-General, as well as official observers from the African Union (AU), Kenya, Tanzania, the Democratic Republic of the Congo, Mozambique, the United States, and the European Union (EU).

Although the Juba Peace Agreement was never signed in full, in 2007, the Agreement on Accountability and Reconciliation (or "agenda item 3" of the peace talks) was signed.[7] It addressed "serious crimes, human rights violations and adverse

[2] For an overview, see Joanna R. Quinn, "The Supposed Accountability/Peacebuilding Dilemma in Uganda," in *Transitional Justice and Peacebuilding on the Ground: Victims and Ex-combatants*, ed. Chandra Lekha Sriram (New York: Routledge, 2013), 206.

[3] This figure is accurate as of July 2016. See Parliament of the Republic of Uganda, "The Amnesty Commission Decries Inadequate Funding" (no date), accessed December 12, 2016, www.parliament.go.ug/new/index.php/about-parliament/parliamentary-news/889-amnesty-commission-decries-inadequate-funding.

[4] For a helpful overview of the political and security context of the amnesty, see Sverker Finnström, "Reconciliation Grown Bitter? War, Retribution, and Ritual Action in Northern Uganda," in *Localizing Transitional Justice: Interventions and Priorities after Mass Violence*, ed. Rosalind Shaw and Lars Waldorf with Pierre Hazan (Stanford, CA: Stanford University Press, 2013), 137–40. On the ICC referral, see the "Uganda" page on the ICC website, accessed December 12, 2016, www.icc-cpi.int/uganda. Note that the letter of referral was sent in December 2003, but the referral was announced in January 2004.

[5] On the reasoning behind not including crimes committed by government forces, see Kurt Mills, *International Responses to Mass Atrocities in Africa: Responsibility to Protect, Prosecute, and Palliate* (Philadelphia: University of Pennsylvania Press, 2015), 129–74.

[6] See Adam Branch, "Dominic Ongwen on Trial: The ICC's African Dilemmas," *International Journal of Transitional Justice* 11, no. 1 (2017): 30–49; Mark A. Drumbl, "Victims Who Victimize," *London Review of International Law* 4, no. 2 (2016): 217–46; and Human Rights Watch, "ICC: First Major Hearing on LRA Crimes," January 21, 2016, www.hrw.org/news/2016/01/21/icc-first-major-hearing-lra-crimes.

[7] See "Agreement on Accountability and Reconciliation between the Government of the Republic of Uganda and the LRA/M" (June 29, 2007), http://peacemaker.un.org/uganda-accountability-reconciliation2007.

socio-economic and political impacts" from the conflict and obligated the government to establish a TJ framework that would include the development of a truth-telling mechanism, reparations for victims, and the formation of a special division of Uganda's High Court to prosecute perpetrators of serious crimes.[8]

Drawing from its commitments on accountability and reconciliation in the Juba Agreement, the government established a TJ Working Group (TJWG) under the auspices of JLOS, which is the overarching configuration of government institutions working in the administration of justice (established in 1999 with its first strategic investment plan starting in 2001).[9] The TJWG is under the leadership of the Honorable Principal Judge, and it includes core agencies whose mandates are directly linked to promoting accountability and reconciliation.[10] As a hybrid entity, the TJWG includes civil society actors like the International Center for Transitional Justice (ICTJ) and the Refugee Law Project (RLP), as well as key members of JLOS, donors, and UN agencies.

The TJWG was tasked with "developing and managing an effective TJ system for Uganda" and was divided into five thematic subcommittees: 1) war crimes prosecutions; 2) truth and reconciliation; 3) traditional justice; 4) finance; and 5) integrated systems. No subcommittee has specifically focused on remedy and reparations, as these issues were seen to cut across all the aforementioned areas, has been to "develop and manage an effective TJ system for Uganda." One major task has been to put together the NTJP, which considers all the TJ elements. The draft NTJP, considered the first of its kind in Africa, has been ready for consideration since 2014.[11]

In 2008, the government also established the War Crimes Division of the High Court, later renamed the International Crimes Division (ICD). The ICC Act of 2010

8 See Michael Otim and Marieke Wierda, "Uganda: The Impact of the Rome Statute and the International Criminal Court" (New York: International Center for Transitional Justice, June 2010), 3, www.ictj.org/sites/default/files/ICTJ-Uganda-Impact-ICC-2010-English.pdf.

9 For more information, see the JLOS webpage, "Our History," accessed December 12, 2016, www.jlos.go.ug/index.php/about-jlos/our-history. The sector is comprised of: the Ministry of Justice and Constitutional Affairs; the Ministry of Internal Affairs; the Judiciary; the Uganda Police Force; the Uganda Prison Service; the Directorate of Public Prosecutions; the Judicial Service Commission; the Ministry of Local Government (Local Council Courts); the Ministry of Gender, Labor and Social Development (Probation and Juvenile Justice); the Uganda Law Reform Commission; the Uganda Human Rights Commission; the Law Development Centre; the Tax Appeals Tribunal; the Uganda Law Society; the Centre for Arbitration and Dispute Resolution; and the Uganda Registration Services Bureau.

10 These include the judiciary: the Ministry of Justice and Constitutional Affairs; the Ministry of Internal Affairs; the Ministry of Finance, Planning and Economic Development; the Directorate of Public Prosecutions; the Uganda Police Force; the Uganda Prisons Service; the Uganda Law Reform Commission; the Uganda Human Rights Commission; the Amnesty Commission; and the Uganda Law Society.

11 For more information on the NTJP, see Michael Otim and Kasande Sarah Kihika, "On the Path to Vindicate Victims' Rights in Uganda: Reflections on the Transitional Justice Process Since Juba" (New York: International Center for Transitional Justice, June 2015), 5–6, www.ictj.org/publication/uganda-reflections-transitional-justice-since-Juba.

domesticated provisions of the ICC's Rome Statute, following the Geneva Conventions Act, which had defined violations of the Geneva Conventions as national offenses back in 1964. The ICD is authorized to investigate and prosecute individuals suspected of war crimes, crimes against humanity, and genocide, as well as terrorism, trafficking, and piracy offenses. A primary intention behind setting up the ICD was to complement the work of the ICC by making a significant contribution to securing justice for victims of Uganda's two-decade conflict in the north between the LRA and the Ugandan army. The ICD's jurisdiction is not limited to LRA members or members of the Ugandan army; however, the existence of the Amnesty Act has proven to be a complicating factor in taking LRA cases forward.[12]

The first and only case to date relating to the conflict in northern Uganda concerns a former LRA commander, Thomas Kwoyelo, who was charged with multiple counts of war crimes under the Geneva Conventions Act. Although Kwoyelo was charged and brought to court in 2009, the case has suffered multiple delays due to legal obstacles related to the applicability of Uganda's amnesty law. The trial was finally due to resume following a decision by the Supreme Court in April 2015 that ruled that the amnesty law was not applicable to the case because the crimes that Kwoyelo committed were not done in the furtherance or cause of the war. The court's ruling was a major achievement, making clear that there is not a blanket amnesty for all crimes committed by the LRA. Unfortunately, further roadblocks are anticipated due to a lack of funding for outreach, witness protection, and (victim) support schemes.[13]

NOTES ON METHODOLOGY AND LIMITATIONS

Document review and qualitative research methods were used in this research, which was conducted in 2014 with some follow-up done in 2016 over Skype and telephone. Methods included semi-structured individual interviews with key stakeholders with donors including the United States, Ireland, the Netherlands, and the multi-donor Democratic Governance Facility (DGF); staff of UN agencies, including the Office of the High Commissioner for Human Rights (OHCHR), UN Women, and the UN Development Program (UNDP); staff of government agencies (JLOS); and staff of the main TJ CSOs in Uganda. Interviews were conducted with foundations such as the Uganda Fund, the MacArthur Foundation, Trust Africa, and Diakonia. Additionally, on a subsequent assignment in 2016, the researcher met with donors from Norway and Sweden, giving the researcher insight into their current priorities.

12 Otim and Wierda, "Uganda," 3–4.

13 See the decision, "Uganda v Kwoyelo (Constitutional Appeal No. 01 of 2012)," April 8, 2015, www.ulii.org/node/15751; and Sharon Nakandha, "The Kwoyelo Case at the ICD: The Realities of Complementarity in Practice," *International Justice Monitor*, May 5, 2016, www.ijmonitor.org/2016/05/the-kwoyelo-case-at-the-icd-the-realities-of-complementarity-in-practice/.

The researcher also organized a half-day meeting in Gulu, northern Uganda, which brought together fifteen CSO representatives from the north (mostly from Gulu), including traditional leaders. Group discussions at the meeting centered on impressions of TJ in Uganda, views and perceptions of donors, and perceptions of what types of interventions would be needed in the future.

One limitation of the research is the lack of focus on the religious community that has historically played and still plays a critical role in TJ activities in Uganda, especially around issues of reconciliation. Another is that TJ CSOs did not always distinguish between their TJ projects and other tasks when describing their perceptions about donors, since they carry out many additional projects not necessarily linked with TJ. It was not always clear that CSOs' perceptions of donors were strictly related to TJ initiatives.

OVERVIEW OF INTERNATIONAL ASSISTANCE FOR TRANSITIONAL JUSTICE IN UGANDA

In this section I provide an overview of international assistance for TJ in Uganda, first for state actors and then for civil society. Since much of the funding related to TJ in Uganda runs through larger entities and basket funds, it is important to highlight that budgets are not always fine-grained enough to determine how much of the allocations are spent on TJ, rather than other things.

Assistance to Government Actors on Transitional Justice

Donor support of state actors working on TJ has focused on the work of the AC, the peace negotiations, and JLOS (which includes the ICD, the TJWG, and the Uganda Human Rights Commission [UHRC]).

To support the work of the AC, an $8.2 million trust fund was set up in 2000 by the World Bank, with financing from Denmark, the Netherlands, Norway, Sweden, and the United Kingdom. The project targeted 28,800 ex-rebels with social and economic reintegration including financial and educational support, and by July 2011 had resulted in the demobilization of 3,342 reporters, the reinsertion of 3,438 reporters and the reintegration of and other assistance provided to 6,030 reporters.[14]

Donors also supported the peace negotiations from 2006 to 2008. Just prior to the start of the peace process, the UN Office for the Coordination of Humanitarian Affairs

[14] See the World Bank, "Demobilization and Integration in Uganda: Laying the Foundation for Post Conflict Recovery by Building Regional Peace" (Washington, DC: World Bank, 2013), www.worldbank.org/en/results/2013/03/20/demobilization-and-integration-in-uganda-laying-the-foundation-for-post-conflict-recovery-by-building-regional-peace.

established the Juba Initiative Fund with $4.8 million in funding from Canada, the United Kingdom, the Netherlands, Norway, and Sweden (among others).[15]

JLOS, described earlier, is comprised of institutions with closely linked mandates of administering justice, maintaining law and order, and protecting human rights. Many of the donors that had contributed to supporting the AC and the peace negotiations, including the Netherlands, Ireland, Sweden, Austria, and Norway, were also committed to supporting this type of coordination of government agencies. Donor support has become an ever-smaller proportion of the overall JLOS budget over the years, which is in the low hundreds of millions of dollars (as of 2015/16, JLOS's budget was $280 million).[16] At their height (2008–12), these contributions reached $19 million to $28 million per year, up until the beginning of donor withdrawal around 2011–12, owing to corruption scandals and disagreement with the Anti-Homosexuality Bill (which will be discussed in what follows).[17]

Of this funding for JLOS, it is difficult to discern how much has been allocated to TJ-related work. Indeed, TJ only starts to figure in JLOS's five-year Strategic Investment Plans starting with the third plan, covering the years 2012–17, where it appears in several of the key outcomes.[18] In general, the main entities with activities linked to TJ – namely, the ICD, the TJWG, and the UHRC – have been supported through the regular JLOS budget. Additional support has also been provided to specific TJ initiatives; for example, in 2008, support was provided directly to the ICD from Canada, Ireland, and Denmark.[19] It should be noted, however, that the vast majority of the JLOS budget has little or nothing to do with TJ, as it includes the Ugandan Police

[15] See International Crisis Group, "Northern Uganda: Seizing the Opportunity for Peace," Africa Report no. 124 (April 26, 2007), 3, https://d2071andvipowj.cloudfront.net/124-northern-uganda-seizing-the-opportunity-for-peace.pdf. The governments of Uganda and South Sudan provided additional funds to this initiative to support the talks. The Juba Initiative Fund and the Amnesty Commission in charge of disarmament, demobilization, and reintegration in Uganda are referenced here, although their work is not considered part of TJ in Uganda.

[16] In 2015/16, JLOS's budget was $280 million (1.05 trillion Schillings), with the largest share going to the Ugandan Police Force (roughly 50 percent). By contrast, the unit containing the ICD – the Directorate of Public Prosecutions – had a budget of $8 million. "The Justice, Law and Order Sector: Annual Performance Report, 2015/16" (Kampala: Justice, Law, and Order Sector, no date), 141, www.jlos.go.ug/index.php/news-media-events/newsroom/latest-news/item/571-jlos-performance-2015–16-key-facts-and-figures.

[17] According to grant-level data in the TJ International Assistance database, donors provided $116.85 million to JLOS between 2002 and 2012. The largest contributions came from the Netherlands ($38 million), Ireland ($34 million), Sweden ($15.8 million), Austria ($14.9 million), and Norway ($9.1 million). Note that although the data matches well with JLOS financial reports, it is likely incomplete, especially for the earlier years. Paige Arthur, "TJ International Assistance Database, 2002–2012" (unpublished data, 2014). The most current data for JLOS can be viewed by donor country on Open Aid Data; see Open Aid Data, "Government & Civil Society: Uganda," accessed February 26, 2017, www.openaiddata.org/purpose/285/151/7/.

[18] See Justice, Law, and Order Sector, "The Third JLOS Strategic Investment Plan, 2012/13–2016/17" (Government of Uganda, no date), 19–31. In the previous plan, dated August 2006 and therefore pre-Juba, there is only one passing mention of TJ.

[19] Presumably, this additional support was needed since a special criminal division to deal with international crimes was not foreseen in the operative (pre-Juba) Strategic Investment Plan.

Force, the prison system, and so on. The section that houses the ICD, for example, which is the Directorate of Public Prosecutions, has a relatively small budget (in 2015/16, it was only 2.3 percent of the $280 million JLOS budget).[20] We should expect that only a fraction of the donor funds allocated to JLOS have directly supported TJ.

State actors have also received support on TJ from the UN Peacebuilding Fund. From 2011 to 2012, the UN Peacebuilding Fund provided $14 million in support to UN agencies in cooperation with state and civil society partners to carry out projects in northern Uganda, especially Acholi regions. Of the three projects funded, the largest one, called "Peacebuilding through Justice for All and Human Rights," dealt directly with TJ issues. Funded at $5.9 million from 2011 to 2012, the project involved collaboration between UN (UNDP, OHCHR, UNICEF, UNFPA) and national authorities (JLOS, UHRC, and Acholi regional authorities) in relation to trainings and practical support to state actors, as well as community-level dialogues and consultations. Thematic issues included sexual and gender-based violence (SGBV) and children.[21]

Other support related to TJ has come through the Peace Recovery Development Plan (PRDP), a government-led framework to consolidate peace and security in the northern regions that was significantly funded by donors. As a separate development plan for Uganda's conflict-affected regions, it was conceived in alignment with the country's overall National Development Plan (NDP), providing a framework not just for the government but for donor strategies on conflict-sensitive development.[22] Peacebuilding and reconciliation is one of the four primary objectives of the PRDP; however, in the first phase, only 2.7 percent of the total budget was allocated toward the peacebuilding and reconciliation pillar, with most of this going to the amnesty and demobilization program.[23] Many observers considered

20 "The Justice, Law and Order Sector: Annual Performance Report, 2015/16," 142.

21 Iris Wielders and Lorna Juliet Amutjojo, "Final Evaluation Report of UN Peacebuilding Fund Programmes in Acholiland, Northern Uganda" (New York: UN Peacebuilding Fund, January 26, 2012), 33–40, www.unpbf.org/wp-content/uploads/Uganda-2012.pdf.

22 One estimate puts donor funding at 70 percent of the total expenditure for the PRDP. See Delta Partnership in Association with REEV Consult for the National Planning Authority, "Development Partnerships Thematic Report: Mid-term Review of the Uganda National Development Plan" (Kampala: National Planning Authority, October 2013), 30, npa.ug/wp-content/uploads/NDPI-MTR-Development-Partnerships-Report.pdf. For a helpful overview of the PRDP, see Elliot Bertasi, "Post-conflict Reconstruction and Development: The PRDP for Northern Uganda" (Knoxville, TN: Baker Scholar Projects, 2013), 26–28, http://trace.tennessee.edu/cgi/viewcontent.cgi?article=1022&context=utk_bakerschol.

23 The first phase of PRDP (2009 to 2012) had a budget of $606 million over three years; in the second phase, it decreased to $455 million – although actual expenditures for both periods were much less for a variety of reasons, including the 2012 corruption scandal discussed in this chapter. For PRDP budgets, see Government of Uganda, "Peace, Recovery and Development Plan for Northern Uganda," September 2007, 113–16; and Alex Otto, Oroma Gladys, and Cho Woo Willy, "Concerns over Northern Uganda Development Plans," Institute for War and Peace Reporting, accessed December 14, 2016, https://iwpr.net/global-voices/concerns-over-north-uganda-development-plans. See also Jonathan Marino, "Is the PRDP Politics as Usual? Update on the Implementation of Uganda's Peace, Recovery and Development Plan," Briefing Note no. 2 (Kampala: Refugee Law Project, December 2008), 8, http://refugeelawproject.org/files/briefing_papers/RLP.BP0802.pdf.

the investment in this pillar to have been insufficient, as it "was mainly focused on infrastructural development – neglecting the crucial peacebuilding and reconciliation strategic objective."[24] Addressing people's confusion about whether or not building infrastructure in the north (schools, police stations, etc.) should be considered "reparations" from the government, ICTJ noted that these are public goods that ought to be provided to citizens whether they are victims or not, and therefore they are not reparations.[25]

Financial support to state actors has also been supplemented with technical support – sometimes delivered by experts from donor governments (e.g., Canada), by UN actors like OHCHR, and by international CSOs, such as ICTJ, Avocats Sans Frontières (ASF), and the Public International Law and Policy Group (PILPG).[26] Technical assistance has consisted of trainings, workshops, and/or study tours for state bodies such as the ICD, the TJWG, and the UHRC. Assistance has also included feedback on key technical documents, such as the ICC Act, the ICD's Rules and Procedures, and the NTJP.[27]

[24] Robert Senath Esuruku, "Horizons of Peace and Development in Northern Uganda," ACCORD, August 19, 2011, www.accord.org.za/ajcr-issues/horizons-of-peace-and-development-in-northern-uganda/. The Advisory Consortium of Conflict Sensitivity (ACCS), a partnership that brings together the International Alert, Safer World, and Refugee Law Project, also noted: "Although an assessment of PRDP I found that more efforts needed to be focused on the strategic objectives of building peace and reconciling communities in the North, the total budgetary contributions for the PRDP II allocated to this objective were reduced from $17.5m to $12.5m. Out of the four objectives, the one that includes peacebuilding and reconciliation activities only received 3 percent of the total budget, while the other 97 percent went to the other three objectives." ACCS, "Northern Uganda Conflict Analysis" (Kampala: Advisory Consortium of Conflict Sensitivity, September 2013), 32–34, http://refugeelawproject.org/files/briefing_papers/ACCS_Northern_Uganda_Conflict_Analysis_Report.pdf. (The assessment cited by ACCS in the document is: Office of the Prime Minister, "Peace, Recovery, and Development Plan for Northern Uganda (PRDP) Phase II. July 2012–June 2015" [November 2011].)

[25] ICTJ, "Reparations for Northern Uganda: Addressing the Needs of Victims and Affected Communities," Briefing Paper (2012), 5–6, www.ictj.org/sites/default/files/ICTJ-Briefing-Paper-Reparations-Uganda-2012-English.pdf. Carrington and Naughton underscore this point in Graham Carrington and Elena Naughton, "Uganda: Unredressed Legacy: Possible Policy Options and Approaches to Fulfilling Reparations in Uganda" (New York: International Center for Transitional Justice, 2012), 15, www.ictj.org/publication/unredressed-legacy-possible-policy-options-and-approaches-fulfilling-reparations-uganda.

[26] For example, USAID funded PILPG to provide technical assistance on the ICC Act. See Casals & Associates, Inc., "Final Report: Northern Uganda Transition Initiative (NUTI), May 2008 to May 2011" (Washington, DC: USAID, no date), 11, http://pdf.usaid.gov/pdf_docs/pdacw909.pdf.

[27] As just one example, according to grant-level data in the TJ International Assistance database, Canada sent experts on international criminal law, restorative justice, and conduct of investigations early in the life of the ICD (2009), for a project entitled "Technical Support to the Government of Uganda in the Implementation of the Agreement on Accountability and Reconciliation." For one summary of various international study tours as well as technical assistance, see "The Justice, Law and Order Sector: Annual Performance Report, 2013/14" (Kampala: Justice, Law, and Order Sector, no date), 28–30, http://askyourgov.ug/request/133/response/89/attach/2/JLOS%20ANNUAL%20PERFORMANCE%202014.compressed.pdf.

Assistance to Transitional Justice Civil Society Organizations

Funding for TJ CSOs came from many of the same bilateral donors that provided support to JLOS. Norway, Sweden, and Austria have provided a wide array of funding program support to the largest number of TJ CSOs, according to grant-level data found in the TJ International Assistance Database. The United Kingdom, the United States, and Canada have also provided some project funding. In total, we have found $7 million to $8 million in bilateral funding provided to CSOs for TJ-related activities between 2006 and 2011, with almost half of it from Norway.[28]

In addition to bilateral funding, starting in 2011, Austria, Denmark, Ireland, the Netherlands, Norway, Sweden, the United Kingdom, and the EU established the Democratic Governance Facility (DGF). The DGF is a multimillion-euro basket fund (€27 million to €30 million per year[29]) whose goal is to "strengthen democratization, protect human rights, improve access to justice, and enhance accountability."[30] It works with a wide array of partners: state institutions and constitutional bodies, professional associations, academic and research institutions, inter-political party platforms, the media, and a diversity of CSOs including nongovernmental, community, and faith-based organizations.[31]

Rights, Justice, and Peace is one of DGF's priorities and the pillar under which TJ work falls. The annual budget for this pillar has varied, ranging from 30 percent to 40 percent of the total budget. However, as with other broad institutions, it is hard to discern how much of this money is spent on TJ-related activities. Within the "rights, justice, and peace" component, the subcomponent that is most directly related to TJ, "Promoting peace and reconciliation in areas affected by conflict," receives only 4 percent of the total DGF budget, or approximately €1 million to €1.2 million per year. TJ also appears in a larger subcomponent on access to justice, although most of these funds appear to be directed to legal aid and other non-TJ-related services. RLP, ICTJ, and the African Youth Initiative Network (AYINET), as well as TJ-related networks (discussed later) have received funding from DGF for TJ projects.

The ICC Trust Fund for Victims has allocated more than €3 million since 2007, working through partners to provide support to victims suffering conflict-related injuries with material and psychological support. AYINET, the Center for Victims of Torture, and many other groups have benefited from this fund.[32]

28 Arthur, "TJ International Assistance Database."

29 See DGF Annual Reports for 2011/12 to 2015/16, available on the DGF web site at www.dgf.ug/annual-reports.

30 See "What Is the DGF?" DGF, accessed December 12, 2016, www.dgf.ug/what-dgf.

31 See DGF, "Annual Report 2015/2016," 13, www.dgf.ug/publication-resources/dgf-annual-report-2015–16.

32 The Trust Fund for Victims, "Annual Report Summary, 2016" (ICC Annex II: List of Projects in Northern Uganda), accessed December 12, 2016, www.trustfundforvictims.org/sites/default/files/imce/summary_EN_ONLINE.pdf. For a list of the fund's implementing partners, see the website of the ICC Trust Fund for Victims, www.trustfundforvictims.org/partners.

The UN Peacebuilding Fund mentioned earlier also provided some support to civil society. The "Peacebuilding through Justice for All" project, which mainly benefited state actors like JLOS, also had RLP as a partner.

Finally, other major donors to TJ CSOs have been foundations such as MacArthur, Open Society, the Uganda Fund, and Trust Africa. The Uganda Fund, which was created by the MacArthur Foundation, provides support both to national organizations and to community-based organizations in northern Uganda, with a focus on war-affected children and youth. One of the four strategic priorities of the Uganda Fund has been TJ and reconciliation. The total budget for the Uganda Fund is $7 million – although it is unclear how much of this is allocated to the TJ-related priority area. MacArthur and Open Society have also provided funding to TJ CSOs, community-level reconciliation, and peacebuilding initiatives. However, allocations for these various activities is not clear. Another foundation based in Senegal, Trust Africa, also provided modest funding to work with victims.

DONOR STRATEGIES AND APPROACHES ON TRANSITIONAL JUSTICE

I turn now to a discussion of donor strategies. In general, donors have engaged in several coordinated strategies in Uganda. As mentioned, the PRDP provides an overarching framework for strategy and decision-making around funding in the north to which donors have aligned their development strategies. Previous sections have also outlined the use of the DGF basket fund, funding country-wide work. Additionally, there is the JLOS Development Partners Group, which is comprised of agencies that support JLOS through various mechanisms, including sector budget and project support. The group has a membership of Austria, Denmark, Germany, Ireland, the Netherlands, Norway, Sweden, UNDP, OHCHR, UNICEF, ICRC, UN Women, UNFPA, and USAID. The United Kingdom and the EU Delegation participate as non-contributing members.

As these descriptions suggest, there has been real donor engagement on TJ, especially in relation to criminal justice. However, donors have not developed a discrete strategy on TJ, as they have waited for the government to provide that strategy through the NTJP. Given the lack of movement by the NTJP, donors do not appear to have developed a "Plan B," and instead appear to be moving on to other issues.

Donor Focus on Criminal Justice

Strengthening JLOS has been a major preoccupation of donors since its establishment in 2001. In 2008, when the ICD's forerunner was created, it received direct funding from donors and was also supported within the JLOS budget. The wide support from donors signaled to TJ CSOs that the ICD (and by extension international justice) was a donor priority. Donor prioritization of strengthening JLOS is also reflected in the level of coordination and engagement that they have had with the body through the JLOS Development Partners Group.[33]

Impressions of donors' TJ priorities in the immediate post-Juba period were reflected in an article written by one prominent CSO leader: "Many funders chose to prioritize particular aspects of the peace agreements, with many opting to fund prosecutorial initiatives. From the beginning, the success of the talks and the highly wrought contents of the agreements attracted pro-ICC funders to pour money into Uganda, seeing a potential case study for positive complementarity between the ICC and domestic peace processes."[34] This notion that donors primarily emphasize criminal justice over other TJ activities was articulated clearly by another donor interviewee, who highlighted support for bringing cases to the ICD: "Of the $700 million in aid given to Uganda each year, very little is allocated to TJ. TJ is an outlier for us, and it is largely due to the lack of concreteness of [the sector]." Focus is placed instead on bolstering the ICD and the amnesty law: "We really want to push ICD to bring a case," the donor indicated. "There have been few LRA that have taken the amnesty. It is mostly the Allied Democratic Forces (ADF), so we feel there is some scope there."

More recently, as mentioned, TJ has been highlighted as a priority in the JLOS third Strategic Investment Plan; however, it is difficult to understand how this commitment is manifested given the lack of details within the strategy itself and without clarity on budget allocations. The lack of action by the government on the NTJP also puts this prioritization into question. Some donors appear to have hitched their strategies to an expectation that the Ugandan government will push forward a TJ agenda (through prosecutions or through the NTJP).[35] Now that the first ICD trial is finally moving forward after many years of delay, it remains to be seen how this might affect the process overall.[36]

33 "JLOS Development Partners," JLOS, accessed December 12, 2016, www.jlos.go.ug:442/index.php/about-jlos/development-partners.

34 Stephen Oola, "The Coalition for Reconciliation in Uganda (CORU): Important Lessons for Proactive Civil Society Engagement in Catalyzing Transitional Justice Discourse," paper presented at the African Transitional Justice Research Network workshop "Advocating Justice: Civil Society and Transitional Justice in Africa," August 30–31, 2010, Johannesburg, South Africa, 9. See also Oola's more recent work: Stephen Oola, "In the Shadow of Kwoyelo's First Trial: The ICC and Complementarity in Uganda," in *Contested Justice: The Politics and Practice of International Criminal Court Interventions*, ed. Christian De Vos, Sarah Kendall, and Carsten Stahn (New York: Cambridge University Press, 2015).

35 A review of how TJ is represented in both JLOS's and DGF's operative strategy documents shows that the NTJP is assumed to be moving along: it is listed as an "assumption" for DGF's TJ-related objectives and goals, and it is listed as an "output" for JLOS, rather than an objective. This suggests that donors did not believe that adoption of the NTJP was something that might require special effort or strategy. See DGF, "DGF Programme Logframe" (Kampala, November 2013), 14–15; and JLOS, "The Third JLOS Strategic Plan, 2012/13–2016/17" (Kampala: Justice, Law, and Order Sector, 2012), 63, 67, 68.

36 The ACCS observed, "The designing of the transitional justice framework has largely been centralised within the Justice Law and Order Sector (JLOS), with limited contributions from other stakeholders including critical line ministries (such as Health, Gender and Education), civil society, and local communities. The result has been a prioritization of formal punitive justice processes – which to date have had limited impact on promoting peace and reconciliation amongst communities in the North." ACCS, "Northern Uganda Conflict Analysis," 32.

Donors' Consistent Support for Women's Issues

Attention to women's rights, gender equality, and repairing SGBV harms have been a consistent focus within donor strategies – both for individual country strategies and for those coordinated through multi-donor trust funds such as the UN Peacebuilding Fund and the UN Joint Programme on Gender Equality.[37] However, it is not always clear if all funds for these programs are considered "TJ," especially if they are not explicitly linked to the recognition of past human rights violations.[38]

Relevant work includes repairing the wounds of war-related sexual violence through medical and psychological rehabilitation, which has been critical since there is no reparations program for victims. AYINET's focus has been on completing surgeries for victims of sexual violence in conflict (e.g., fistula surgeries) and for other surgeries (e.g., to extract bullets, treat keloids, heal burns and contractions, and rehabilitate mutilations and other physical cases). RLP has also engaged in this work as part of its Beyond Juba project with funding from DGF.[39] The Uganda Fund and the MacArthur Foundation launched a specific TJ and reconciliation initiative, partnering with community-based organizations to provide redress to women and girl SGBV victims.[40]

Donor Strategic Engagement with Civil Society

Donors have rarely publicly communicated their goals about TJ in any formal way – apart from their multiyear strategy documents, such as some of the ones mentioned earlier, which are not particularly fine-grained. TJ CSOs are not consulted as a group to feed into donors' strategy development or decision-making on TJ. Instead, TJ CSOs hear about funding opportunities in general formal sessions set up by donors, through bilateral meetings, or through hearing about funding opportunities

[37] A five-year program (2010–14) with the participation of twelve UN organizations and a budget of $16 million with funding from the UK Department for International Development (DfID) through the Multi-Partner Trust Fund.

[38] Some of the projects focus on providing support to present-day SGBV, which is a major and growing problem in Uganda. However, these projects don't necessarily consider the consequences of war-related violence, which is a separate, but related issue. Additionally, it is not uncommon for donor strategies to reference Security Council Resolution 1325. See, e.g., Swedish Ministry for Foreign Affairs (MFA), "Strategy for Development Cooperation with Uganda March 2009–December 2013" (Stockholm: Ministry for Foreign Affairs, 2009), www.government.se/49b749/contentassets/06c3e920079f4d158709369664d9447d/cooperation-strategy-for-development-cooperation-with-uganda-2009-2013; and DfID, "Annual Review 5, Post Conflict Development Plan (PCDP), 2009–2016" (London: Department for International Development, June 2016), 13, https://devtracker.dfid.gov.uk/projects/GB-1-200250/documents.

[39] DfID, "Annual Review 5, PCDP 2009–2016": 13.

[40] For more information on the organizations and types of projects that have benefited from the Uganda Fund, see "Current Grants," Uganda Fund, accessed December 12, 2016, http://ugandafund.org/grants/current-grants.

from donors and then being encouraged to apply. When donor civil society forums have taken place, they have been done on an ad hoc basis and have largely been one-way conversations, often taking place after donor priorities have been set. When the DGF first started in 2012, it held a networking forum where it shared its goals and then invited potential partners to apply for funds. At that time, some of the TJ CSOs that had previously obtained funding from one of the DGF contributing countries were urged to apply to the DGF.

The lack of any structured forum or way to communicate has led CSOs to go on "fishing trips" from embassy to embassy, where they network for project funding. These trips were a source of frustration and confusion for some CSOs. One interviewee said: "At the end of these trips, I don't feel like I know anything more about the donor's priorities. I feel that they can tell me one thing one day and they say that it is not a priority, and then I can go back again and ask for that thing again another day and I may get it." CSOs do not pick up on these statements as a matter of diplomacy, seeing them instead as indicators of scattered interests. "I don't think many donors have priorities or a strategy about TJ," the person concluded.

Specifically in relation to DGF funding, according to its "Partnership Approach" paper, DGF recognizes the potential for networks as drivers of positive change, linking policymakers and advocacy groups with grassroots actors, facilitating two-way information flows, creating opportunities for coalition building, and delivering tangible impact to widespread target groups.[41] TJ CSO observations, however, suggested that partners received less individualized attention to projects and engagement than with other donors. Attention appeared to be on ensuring organizations met their administrative requirements rather than getting feedback on the technical aspects of their projects.[42]

TJ CSOs reported that the most consistently supportive donors were foundations such as the Macarthur and the Uganda Fund, and bilateral donors such as Norway, Sweden, and Austria. These donors have provided core funding, been most involved in the projects, and have proven the most flexible and least onerous

41 DGF, "The Partnership Approach" (Kampala: Democratic Governance Facility, August 2012), 5, dgf.ug/images/docs/DGF%20Partnership%20Approach%20paper%20FINAL%20-%20August%2012.pdf.

42 A study conducted by INTRAC (and funded by the Danish government) on the impact of multi-donor funds, including the DGF, on civil society had some relevant findings: "The literature review and field research indicated that increased multi-donor support to civil society may have unintended, negative consequences in relation to an independent, diverse, civil society. Donor investment in joint civil society funds should consider both the benefits and possible costs in relation to their broader civil society policies. For example, there is some evidence of civil society concern that the convergence of donor priorities in a limited number of joint funds may reduce the sources of funding for many, particularly smaller, CSOs. It may encourage others to divert from their primary mission to obtain funding since there are fewer alternative sources of funding; reduce CSO access to individual donors; and undermine the mediating role donors have played between civil society and governments." INTRAC, "Study on Support to Civil Society through Multi-donor Funds: Final Report" (Oxford: INTRAC/Danida, January 2014), 5, www.globaltfokus.dk/images/Pulje/Arkiv/Fagligt_Fokus/Study_on_Support_to_Civil_Society_through_Multi-Donor_Funds.pdf.

in terms of reporting. Another positive instance of donor–grantee relationships concerns Diakonia, a faith-based organization that receives funds from the Swedish government and works worldwide, partners with fourteen human rights CSOs based in various regions throughout Uganda, and has a well-thought-out, long-term strategy to build the capacity of each of the organizations it funds.[43] Other donors, such as the United Kingdom, the United States, the UN, and the ICC Trust Fund have provided project support; interviewees report, however, that they are more bureaucratic and may have short timelines and more onerous reporting.

Reframing Transitional Justice for New Donor Priorities

In recent years, donors have started to shift attention to new priority areas, for a variety of reasons. One is that with the TJ process stalled at the state level, they have not seen civil society advocating for TJ among donors in a way that appeals effectively to their interests and agendas. The dilemmas that donors face funding TJ CSOs projects was reflected clearly at RLP's Fourth Institute for African Transitional Justice in 2014.[44] During a donor roundtable on "the changing impact of development assistance to post-conflict recovery programmes and transitional justice initiatives in Africa," a DGF representative emphasized that donor groups want to act in the "current context." He is quoted as saying, "Looking at what happened fifteen years ago, and trying to rectify the damage done is not trendy," and urging "TJ practitioners to emphasize the future implications of their work wherever possible." Additionally, the report says that, in his view, "Ugandan survivor and victim groups are significantly less organized and less effective in lobbying for support than similar groups in Nepal and Mozambique, where he previously worked." He cited this as another possible reason that donors had not prioritized TJ in Uganda.[45] The USAID representative

43 For more about Diakonia's approach in Uganda, see "Uganda," Diakonia, May 10, 2017, www.diakonia.se/en/Where-we-work/Africa/Uganda/. TJ is included in its current strategic plan (2015–19) as one (of many) strategic priorities; see "Diakonia Uganda Intervention Areas and Strategic Priorities 2015–2018," www.diakonia.se/globalassets/documents/diakonia/news-and-media/diakonia-uganda-intervention-areas-results-framework-2015–2019.pdf. Another relevant model for supporting civil society is the Independent Development Fund (IDF), established in 2008, which is an indigenous grant-making organization incorporated in Uganda by leading CSO networks and development partners. The initial partners were the Royal Danish Embassy, DFiD, the Swedish Embassy, and the Royal Netherlands Embassy, and it currently receives funding from DGF. The IDF is engaged in the delivery of a range of support services to the country's CSOs as a strategy to strengthen their individual capacities to better contribute to the national human rights, good governance, and poverty reduction efforts. For more about IDF, see its website at www.idf.co.ug.

44 The annual meeting, which convenes TJ actors from across the region, was funded by DGF and DfID. See Refugee Law Project, "The Fourth Institute for African Transitional Justice (IATJ) Summary Report" (Kampala: Refugee Law Project, June 2014), www.refugeelawproject.org/files/briefing_papers/14_08_05_IATJ_Summary_Report.pdf.

45 Ibid., 8–9.

expressed a similar frustration, saying: "As development partners we don't know who is taking leadership on the future of transitional justice in Uganda. Is it CSOs that are taking leadership, or is it the state? Unless [this issue] is resolved, it becomes difficult [for donors] to help. We want to help but we need practical direction and clarity."[46]

Another reason is that some of the donors that supported TJ projects in the immediate post-conflict period have shifted to development in their most recent strategies. The Ugandan government signaled this shift in its Vision 2040 document, which makes no reference to TJ or indeed the unaddressed legacies of the conflict.[47] Taking their lead from the Ugandan government, donors are now aligning their own strategies to this forward-looking, ahistorical "vision." For example, the most recent UN Development Assistance Framework (UNDAF) for 2016–20 does not mention TJ or the conflict, in contrast with the previous one (2010–14), where it appeared several times. Additionally, the PRDP, which had "peace and reconciliation" as one of its pillars, is now in its third phase, and is linked directly to the National Development Plan of the government's Vision 2040.[48] Bilaterally, some donors' newest strategies mark a distinctive departure from their previous strategies in that they deemphasize the legacies of the conflict. Sweden's newest (2014–18) strategy is a case in point, as it makes little reference to the past.[49] Likewise, the EU's strategy for Uganda – which between 2014 and 2020 will allocate upward of €578 million total, with 29 percent (€100 million to €168 million) for good governance and €25 million for civil society strengthening – makes no reference to the past.[50]

In its third Strategic Investment Plan, JLOS makes mention of TJ; however, it is unclear how much of a priority it is for the government considering that it does not

46 Ibid., 9.

47 Government of Uganda, "Uganda Vision 2040" (National Planning Authority, 2013), http://npa.ug/wp-content/themes/npatheme/documents/vision2040.pdf. See ICTJ's gloss on Vision 2040 in Virginie Ladisch, "From Rejection to Redress: Overcoming Legacies of Conflict-Related Sexual Violence in Northern Uganda" (New York: International Center for Transitional Justice, 2015), 2, www.ictj.org/sites/default/files/ICTJ-Report-Uganda-Children-2015.pdf.

48 In PRDP 3, reintegration, reconciliation, and TJ are mentioned as part of strategic objective 1 (out of three strategic objectives). The document recognizes that "the failure to implement a comprehensive justice and reconciliation process has resulted in a lack of closure to the conflict for many" (7). TJ is seen as a key component of reintegration as "many new conflicts are rooted in the unfinished issues from the war" (22). However, there is no budget attached to understand how much funding is allocated to each strategic objective. "The Peace Recovery Development Plan for Northern Uganda (PRDP3) July 2015–June 2020" (Kampala: Government of Uganda, August 2015).

49 In the Swedish MFA's 2014–18 strategy, the conflict is mentioned only once in passing, whereas it had been a more central feature of the 2009–13 strategy. See Swedish MFA, "Strategy for Development Cooperation with Uganda March 2009–December 2013," 5, and "Results Strategy for Sweden's International Development Cooperation with Uganda, 2014–18" (Stockholm: Ministry for Foreign Affairs, 2014), 3, www.regeringen.se/contentassets/eb64cf708f5841e196fe04c01414b3f0/results-strategy-for-swedens-international-development-cooperation-with-uganda-20142018.

50 See "Uganda 11th European Development Fund (EDF) National Indicative Programme" (Kampala: Government of Uganda/European Commission, December 2014), 12–14 and 25, https://eeas.europa.eu/sites/eeas/files/11th_edf_for_uganda_en.pdf.

necessarily feature in other publications regarding JLOS priorities.[51] Instead, JLOS emphasizes other aspects of its work: prison reform, community policing, juvenile justice, etc. Access to justice and human rights are also foregrounded as priorities – but for current abuses, not for those committed in the past. Perhaps more tellingly, Sarah M. H. Nouwen has documented government resistance to including TJ in JLOS's Third Strategic Investment Plan (2012–17). "Even with persisting donor interest, transitional justice has already lost some of its appeal to officials," she writes, citing numerous interviews. "JLOS, the GoU's leading actor on transitional justice, in 2011 omitted transitional justice from its first draft of its strategic investment plan for the next decade [*sic*]. At donors' insistence, transitional justice in the end received one page in the report, even though, according to the relevant JLOS actors, transitional justice is 'only transitional, and will thus not even be years,' and therefore need not be incorporated into any long-term plans."[52]

THE INTERNATIONAL IMPRINT ON TRANSITIONAL JUSTICE

Early discussions of TJ in Uganda are directly related to the response to the referral of Uganda to the ICC and the debates that ensued. The aim of this section is to explain the evolution of international assistance provided to TJ and its impact over time.

Beginnings and Key Actors

Both the desire to find a peaceful end to Uganda's conflict and the invitation of the ICC to Uganda were the key events that catalyzed the focus on TJ in Uganda. The "peace versus justice" debate that ensued following the referral of Uganda to the ICC caught the attention of international TJ observers,[53] and in 2005 OHCHR and ICTJ entered Uganda. Several TJ CSOs and coalitions were calling for a peaceful end to the conflict and for a comprehensive TJ agenda – one that not only included

[51] For example, in a recent brochure (paid for by the Austrian government) by JLOS about its work, TJ is completely absent: not only is TJ not mentioned, but there is no discussion of the ICD or even of the conflict. The terms "war," "conflict," "ICD," "ICC," and "LRA" do not appear anywhere. See JLOS, "Uganda's Justice Law and Order Sector – JLOS – Innovations Changing the Lives of Ordinary Ugandans" (Kampala: Justice, Law, and Order Sector, 2015), www.entwicklung.at/fileadmin/user_upload/Dokumente/Publikationen/Downloads_Laender_DivBerichte/Uganda/JLOS_Spreads__2_.pdf.

[52] Sarah M. H. Nouwen, *Complementarity in the Line of Fire: The Catalyzing Effect of the International Criminal Court in Uganda and Sudan* (New York: Cambridge University Press, 2013), 167–68. An evaluation of Austria's conflict resolution work between 2010 and 2015 also mentions Austria's role in ensuring that TJ was included in JLOS Third Strategic Investment plan. See Austria Development Cooperation, "Evaluation: Review of the Uganda Country Strategy 2010–2015" (Vienna: Austrian Development Agency, 2015), 29, www.oecd.org/derec/austria/Review-Evaluation-Uganda-2010–2015.pdf.

[53] See, e.g., Adam Branch, "Uganda's Civil War and the Politics of ICC Intervention," *Ethics & International Affairs* 21, no. 2 (2007): 179–98.

international justice, which was already on the agenda because of the ICC, but also truth-telling, reconciliation, and reparations.

TJ was a new concept in Uganda in 2005 when a handful of international and national TJ CSOs emerged on the scene. Over the past ten or so years, they have developed a high level of understanding of the relatively complicated TJ landscape in Uganda, played different but complementary roles, and become conversant with the TJ field on both the national and international levels.

With initial funding from the Austrian government and more recently from the DGF, ICTJ is one of the two main international CSOs that has been active in Uganda since 2005. It has played a strong capacity-building role, especially in the early stages of the post-Juba period. Since then, it has been instrumental in keeping TJ on the national agenda. ASF, the other main international CSO, was established in late 2007 in Uganda and partnered with the Ugandan Law Society. ASF has not only played a strong capacity-building role but provided crucial technical support to JLOS and the ICD. ASF has received funding from Australia Aid, Belgian Ministry of Cooperation and Development, UK's Department for International Development (DfID), the EU, and the MacArthur Foundation.

In terms of key national CSOs, RLP, based in Kampala, was one of the first CSOs to become involved in TJ. With funding from Norway and Sweden for its signature Beyond Juba project, it has established itself as a key player and has been instrumental in laying the groundwork for different aspects of TJ. The Justice and Reconciliation Project (JRP), based in Gulu, has benefited from consistent project and core funding from Norway; it has been involved in traditional justice, reparations, and community truth-telling. Another leader in the TJ movement, AYINET, based in Lira, has had consistent funding for its TJ work from the ICC Trust Fund, Trust Africa, and DGF, and it has been involved since 2005 in supporting victims with urgent medical and psychological needs and helping to build victims' capacity to support themselves.

Networks of CSOs have developed since 2002 and have been organized around different aspects of the TJ agenda. Some have developed under the leadership of an organization or individual, while others have come together as a coalition of actors recognizing that they might make a deeper impact as a group. There are coalitions that only exist on paper, and others that have been developed for opportunistic reasons, without proper buy-in or a broader constituency.

One of the first networks was the Civil Society Organizations for Peace in Northern Uganda (CSOPNU), a coalition that advocated for the end of the war and brought together eighty-six CSOs from northern Ugandan in 2002. Given the change in context, many of the humanitarian agencies that were part of the coalition left; although CSOPNU received funding from DGF as recently as 2011–12, the coalition lost momentum and is no longer active.[54] The Coalition for Reconciliation in Uganda (CORU) came together, initially under RLP's leadership. The coalition was a critical player in ensuring that – along with formal justice and accountability – reconciliation and truth-telling were central to the discussion at the Juba Peace talks. In 2006, the Uganda Victims Foundation (UVF), the only group that represents victims nationally, was established. With initial funding from REDRESS, UVF emerged following an international meeting of the Victims' Rights Working Group in London and a second in Kampala attended by participants and representatives of several NGOs, including AYINET, which was the host of the network at the time.

By 2009, the Northern Uganda Transitional Justice Working Group (NUTJWG), a network of between eighty and 130 human rights and CSOs from Teso, Lango, West Nile, and Acholi regions, was established. NUTJWG received funding from the Uganda Fund, the MacArthur Foundation, and DGF through a partnership with JLOS. Since its establishment, however, this coalition, although still functioning, has weakened, as there were allegations that funds were misused, and it has suffered from deficits in leadership. The latest edition is Human Rights Network Uganda (HURINET), a coalition of human rights organizations in Uganda, which received funding from MacArthur with the aim to build a similar coalition of TJ actors.

Acting as donor, partner, and interlocutor to the government, UN agencies including OHCHR, UN Women, and UNDP have played an active role on TJ. They have partnered with TJ CSOs, especially ICTJ, on several projects. They have also provided technical advice to the government and TJ CSOs, and set up forums for interaction. They also sit on the JLOS Development Partners Group alongside the donors.

Once the government committed itself to establishing a TJ framework, the TJWG was created within JLOS to facilitate the process. The TJWG is a hybrid body comprised of donors, select members of JLOS, UN agencies, and CSOs. The main task of the TJWG has been to develop the NTJP. With significant feedback and consultation with TJ CSOs both formally and informally (especially in the beginning phases of the process), a draft policy has been developed, which has been instrumental in providing a framework and common language around TJ in Uganda. The policy is comprehensive in nature and treats a wide range of TJ issues. These include: international justice, traditional justice, truth-telling, reconciliation, reparations, and amnesty. Subjects such as victim participation, special emphasis on the gender dimensions of the conflict, witness protection, and complementarity of all these approaches are also addressed. Donors have been involved in the draft NTJP, as well as other international actors such as ICTJ, ASF, OHCHR, and UN Women. These international actors have given feedback and

54 On DGF funding to CSOPNU, see DGF, "Annual Report 2011–12," 16.

been part of workshops where the policy has been discussed, bringing international expertise to the process.[55] They have also publicly expressed concerns as the NTJP has languished without government action.[56]

The sections that follow summarize some of the key points of debate that have engaged national and international actors – often, although not always, on different sides of the issues discussed.

Justice for International Crimes

Debate around the issue of justice for international crimes in Uganda was originally centered around the work of the ICC. On the one hand, it is the area of TJ most widely supported by the government and donors and, conversely, the least supported by the northern Ugandan communities when the situation was first referred in 2003. The TJ CSOs were caught in the middle: fearful of any threat to making peace, members of the Acholi religious community in northern Uganda advocated unsuccessfully for the indictments to be overturned, arguing that traditional justice was sufficient for those who had a role in the conflict. At the time, CSOs were divided on what role the ICC could play in shaping Uganda's TJ process. On the one hand, the ICC was seen as a threat to the fragile peace process. Also, because it was requested by President Museveni and omitted crimes committed by government forces, it lacked neutrality and credibility. On the other hand, its presence was a key factor in pushing the TJ process along in Uganda. It was a factor in the setting up of the ICD, and it has played a role in educating victims about their role in the formal justice process in Uganda through outreach activities. The ICD is based in Uganda and has even held pretrial hearings in Gulu; therefore, unlike the ICC, it is accessible to the people living there.

Not only has international interest and funding supported the work of the ICD, international actors have also provided significant technical assistance. ASF's TJ work has focused on providing technical assistance to the ICD, including assisting in the drafting of its Rules of Procedure and Evidence and providing legal analysis on major issues such as the Amnesty Act. Additionally, as mentioned earlier, donor prioritization of the ICD has meant that other elements of TJ have at times taken a backseat in the process.

55 As one example, development partners such as Ireland demonstrated interest in the NTJP through their participation in the stakeholder consensus-building workshop on the draft NTJP in 2013. See "Opening Remarks by Hon Eng Hillary Onek, Minister for Internal Affairs," at Stakeholder Consensus Building Workshop on the Draft National Transitional Justice Policy, May 21, 2013, Kampala, Uganda.

56 See references to the policy in: Austria Development Cooperation, "Evaluation: Review of the Uganda Country Strategy 2010–2015," 23; and "Speech by His Excellency Dónal Cronin, Ambassador of Ireland & Chair of the JLOS DPG," at the Twentieth Annual JLOS Government of Uganda/Development Partners Review, October 15, 2015, Kampala, www.judiciary.go.ug/files/downloads/JLOS%20speech%20October%202015%20-%20Final.pdf.

Amnesty

These different perspectives of the government, international actors, and the northern communities on the situation in northern Uganda has impacted the debate on amnesty. Some argue that the amnesty has contributed to peace, as it was the reason for the return and demobilization of approximately 26,000 former combatants. Others insist that the amnesty and the work of the AC has not taken victims' needs into account and caters only to perpetrators. Until recently, as mentioned, the amnesty hindered the ICD's ability to prosecute serious crimes.

These competing perspectives also impacted the eventual reinstatement of the amnesty. In anticipation of the expiration and possible renewal of the Amnesty Act in 2012, the JLOS TJWG launched a review that suggested four possible options as a way forward.[57] There was strong consensus that the act could not continue in its current form, because it undermined accountability mechanisms for international crimes, impacted ongoing criminal justice processes, and condoned impunity for sexual and gender-based crimes. Many saw it as imperative to harmonize the act with national and international law. In the end, however, amnesty was reinstated in 2013 after religious leaders from northern Uganda petitioned Parliament in favor of its continuation. This reinstatement was further recognized and supported by northern TJ CSOs.[58] This profound division has fostered mistrust all around. It has impacted relations between TJ CSOs, as well as between TJ CSOs and state actors.

Traditional Justice

Traditional justice refers to localized approaches to justice and reconciliation in communities. It has been recognized in the draft NTJP as playing a role in conflict and dispute resolution, as well as in providing redress to victims especially at the local level. Attention to traditional justice is widely supported at the local level in communities, and it is seen by many as having the potential to play a pivotal role in local-level disputes, especially for those who do not have access to the formal court system.[59] Although not seen as relevant for international crimes within the framework of the NTJP, it does have an important complementary role with the formal justice system. JRP and RLP been active players in seeking to clarify the role of traditional justice mechanisms in TJ in Uganda through research, reports, and consultations.

57 TJWG, "The Amnesty Law (2000) Issues Paper: Review by the Transitional Justice Working Group" (Kampala: Justice, Law, and Order Sector, April 2012), www.judiciary.go.ug/files/downloads/JLOS-Amnest%20Issues%20Paper.pdf.

58 See a press release from NUTJWG highlighting its support for reinstatement of part of the Amnesty Act, and urging the development of a more coherent and legitimate NTJP: NUTJWG, "The Reinstatement of Uganda's Amnesty Act 2000: A Renewed Promise for Peace & Justice in Northern Uganda" (June 2013), www.ugandafund.org/images/FR_1306.pdf.

59 Otim and Kihika, "On the Path to Vindicate Victims' Rights in Uganda," 3.

Traditional justice in Uganda (and elsewhere) has generated wide-ranging debates, and it has faced scrutiny in relation to its effectiveness and lack of conformity to international norms.[60] As such, it is difficult to make general statements about the role of international actors. Some donors supported traditional groups and projects even prior to the end of the conflict. Initially, Denmark and Norway provided support to Acholi religious groups in northern Uganda to explore ways of using local conflict resolution strategies to end the conflict. Funding for Acholi traditional groups ceased soon after the signing of the Juba Peace Accords as donors found that funds provided to the groups were not always well managed, and more capacity building was needed to handle funds.[61] More recently, both UNDP and DGF have been providing support to Acholi groups aimed at building their capacity; programs include training cultural leaders in conflict mediation and dispute resolution. In 2014, DGF took a decision to cease this support when it could not fully account for the funding that was provided.[62]

Truth-Telling and Reconciliation

Truth-telling and reconciliation have been major issues of concern of TJ CSOs and those affected by the conflict; however, these areas have gotten the least attention from donors and the government. Early on, TJ CSOs tried to ensure that truth-telling and reconciliation were incorporated in the peace process. Advancing the truth and reconciliation agenda, however, has been seen as complicated by the role that state actors, such as the UPDF and local government officials, played in the conflict and the potential consequences of bringing this information to light in a formalized way.

RLP's signature TJ project, Beyond Juba, which started in 2007 (initially funded by Norway and Sweden, and later by the DGF), has contributed to many aspects of the TJ agenda, including truth-telling. For example, RLP's countywide mapping exercise, called the National Reconciliation and TJ Audit, documents all major current and past conflicts and their legacies.[63] It has also created the National Memory and Peace Documentation Centre, with support from USAID, the Northern Uganda Transitional Initiative, and DGF. RLP describes the center as "a memorial to the victims and survivors of Uganda's

60 For a critical analysis of traditional justice in the Ugandan context, see Adam Branch, "The Violence of Peace: Ethnojustice in Northern Uganda," *Development and Change* 45, no. 3 (April 2014): 608–30; and Mills, *International Responses to Mass Atrocities in Africa*, 150–59.

61 Based on information provided in an interview in June 2014.

62 See DfID, "Annual Review 5, PCDP 2009–2016," 12.

63 The audit was conducted in twenty districts throughout Uganda and documented more than 125 conflicts – the vast majority of which involved armed violence and went beyond the LRA conflict largely discussed in this chapter. Refugee Law Project, "Compendium of Conflicts in Uganda: Findings of the National Reconciliation and Transitional Justice Audit" (Kampala: Refugee Law Project, 2014), www.refugeelawproject.org/resources/briefing-notes-and-special-reports/345-compendium-of-conflicts-in-uganda-findings-of-the-national-reconciliation-and-transitional-justice-audit.

civil conflicts" and "a space for engaging the community around themes of peace, justice, cultural pride, history and remembrance."[64] JRP has also contributed substantially through research on massacres and mass killings in the conflict. Although unclear at what stage the project stands, the UHRC is undertaking a documentation project, with financial support from DGF and technical support from OHCHR.

Attempts at promoting reconciliation have also not been well addressed. Although in the wake of Juba, civil society pushed for a National Reconciliation Bill that included provisions for a Truth and Reconciliation Commission, observers report that the National Reconciliation Bill "was scuttled when donor governments made it clear that they wanted the ICC Bill fast-tracked."[65]

Reparations

Development actors have been largely silent on the issue of reparations. The majority of funding related to reparations has been to address some of the most urgent medical and psychological needs of war victims, for workshops and consultations largely designed to feed into and influence the NTJP, and for memorialization as a form of reparation. No steps have been taken so far to create a national reparations program. Given the numerous victims, any such program will likely be complicated to design and costly to implement.[66]

Regarding medical and psychological needs, TJ CSOs, with support from DGF, the ICC Trust Fund for Victims, and the UN Peacebuilding Fund, among others, have stepped in to provide these services. Research and consultations, mostly aimed at influencing government policy, have sought to understand the needs and the victims' attitudes around reparations.[67] Some studies have enabled organizations to obtain funding to address victims' problems.

64 For more information, see "The National Memory and Peace Documentation Centre (NMPDC)," Refugee Law Project, accessed December 12, 2016, http://refugeelawproject.org/nmpdc. The DfID claims that the center is "now playing a catalytic role in promoting dialogue on peace and justice in Northern Uganda." See DfID, "Annual Review 5, PCDP 2009–2016," 13.

65 Christian De Vos, "All Roads Lead to Rome: Implementation and Domestic Politics in Kenya and Uganda," in *Contested Justice*, 393. For an overview of the process that led to the National Reconciliation Bill and that corroborates the claim that donors prioritized criminal justice over truth-seeking, see Oola, "The Coalition for Reconciliation in Uganda (CORU)," 9.

66 See Otim and Kihika, "On the Path to Vindicate Victims' Rights in Uganda," 6.

67 On the issue of reparations alone, along with Dyan Mazurana, Teddy Atim, and Helen Kezie-Nwoha, "Making Gender-Just Remedy and Reparations Possible: Upholding the Rights of Women and Girls in the Greater North of Uganda" (Kampala and Cambridge: Isis Women's International Cross-Cultural Exchange and Tufts–Feinstein International Center, 2013), there has been an OHCHR study, "The Dust Has Not Yet Settled: Victims Views on Remedy and Reparation in the Greater North, Uganda" (Kampala: Office of the High Commissioner for Human Rights, 2012), and ICTJ's "Unredressed Legacy: Possible Policy Options and Approaches to Fulfilling Reparations in Uganda" (New York: International Center for Transitional Justice, 2013) – all substantive reports. There have also been reports by AYINET and RLP.

Funding from the Uganda Fund supported the Women's Advocacy Network, a self-organized group of LRA first wives, and JRP (also with assistance from ICTJ) to put a petition together requesting reparations for female victims of sexual violence from Acholi land that Parliament unanimously adopted in 2014.[68] This achievement remains largely symbolic, as to date the government has provided no reparations.

THE IMPRINT OF INTERNATIONAL ACTORS ON CIVIL SOCIETY

Donors and international actors have played roles – with varying degrees of success – in financing civil society work, providing technical assistance and capacity building, and strengthening the social capital of civil society actors in relation to the state and in relation to one another.

Skill Building and Education

Workshops, training, research/studies, outreach, technical support, and consultations are the main methods used in Uganda to educate and build capacity on TJ. Workshops and training have been effective in creating opportunities for dialogue, to share ideas and information, and to seek feedback from government officials, members of the community, TJ actors, and victims. Efforts to bring groups together for trainings and workshops have had the positive effect of encouraging some TJ CSOs to work together and have enhanced TJ CSOs' ability to collaborate around TJ. Training has also been used frequently as a capacity-building exercise. It has been an important strategy for ICD staff – especially judges.

At times, donors have questioned the efficiency and effectiveness of workshops: for example, whether the numerous Kampala-based conferences and workshops on TJ-related issues are the most efficient use of donor funding given their frequency, the fact that they often involve the same people, and the cost. Normally workshops last from one to three days, take place in the conference facility of a hotel, and provide some form of transportation or sitting fee for participants and lunch. In some instances, there have been three or even four workshops in one week. The outcome of these workshops or conferences is not always clear, and their purposes can overlap.[69]

[68] See UN Women, "As Reparations Are Considered in Northern Uganda, Ways Are Sought to Equally Include Female Survivors," March 17, 2012, www.unwomen.org/en/news/stories/2012/3/as-reparations-are-considered-in-northern-uganda-ways-are-sought-to-equally-include-female-survivors.

[69] For example, during my first ten-day visit, there was a National Victims' Conference that lasted for three days, a one-day workshop aimed at CSOs providing feedback on the government's TJ policy, and a TJ workshop on youth and children. The documents provided at the one-day government feedback workshop, while useful, were based on research carried out a year earlier. In addition, the workshop seemed to duplicate earlier JLOS efforts seeking feedback on the draft TJ policy finalized in July 2013. Moreover, the event was poorly attended, while most of the people present had been at the National Victims' Conference a few days beforehand and planned to attend the TJ workshop on youth and children the next day.

Research including population-based studies and consultations have been instrumental to both national and international actors in understanding needs, influencing policy, building local capacity for research, and feeding into the numerous critical debates in Uganda. Interviews surfaced concerns, however, about the proliferation of research and population-based studies conducted in northern Uganda aimed at understanding victims' perceptions. Some of the studies have added new information, while others seem to duplicate information already collected, and at times the findings contradict one another. It is difficult to understand what new information they offer now as most studies have been aimed at influencing government policy, which has now largely been set.

Strengthening Civil Society Organization–Government Relations

CSO and government relations have featured consistently in the approaches of both donors and other international actors, such as OHCHR, ICTJ, and UN Women. In the early stages, JLOS made significant efforts to invite TJ CSOs to participate in TJWG's meetings and to deliberate on the draft NTJP. The TJWG also partnered with CSOs and networks formally and informally (as mentioned, RLP and ICTJ sit formally on the TJWG as the civil society representatives). With support from DGF, JLOS entered into an agreement with NUTJWG to do outreach and consultations to communities on the draft NTJP. ASF, JRP, AYINET, and RLP have also received funding from the ICC to do extensive outreach and consultation with victims and communities. TJ CSOs, including ICTJ, have and continue to invite JLOS representatives to participate in their workshops.[70] RLP and AYINET have also brought TJ CSOs together for coordination purposes on several occasions through their various projects. AYINET has also made efforts to involve the Ministry of Health with the aim of partnering on medical rehabilitation projects. RLP's Beyond Juba project has engaged various government entities including line ministries and parliamentarians on TJ. In March 2017, a forum between RLP and parliamentarians was held.[71]

It is hard to say whether engagement on TJ has resulted in strengthened networks between state and civil society actors. The reinstatement of the amnesty in 2013 has been a major source of discontent for JLOS. After JLOS carried out a review in 2012 and came up with what seemed like a workable compromise on the amnesty, there was a push from the traditional leadership and several TJ CSOs for its reinstatement. For JLOS and other TJ CSOs, this felt like a real step back and has impacted the relationships between JLOS and the TJ CSOs, especially those that called for the amnesty's reinstatement.

70 An evaluation of Austria's overall support to Uganda also highlighted ICTJ's capacity-building work with government and other CSOs. See Austria Development Cooperation, "Evaluation: Review of the Uganda Country Strategy 2010–2015," 26.

71 Refugee Law Project, "Brief on Orientation of MPs on Transitional Justice" (Kampala: Refugee Law Project, 2017), www.refugeelawproject.org/files/others/Orientation_of_MPs_on_TJ.pdf.

Cohesion among Transitional Justice Civil Society Organizations

As mentioned earlier, a handful of TJ CSOs are playing a critical role on TJ in Uganda. In Uganda, the number of TJ CSOs is small, they are largely concentrated in Gulu, Lira, and Kampala, and funding options are few. The TJ work of the major TJ actors is varied and with little duplication. These groups have interacted in trainings and workshops, which has had the positive effect of encouraging some CSOs to work together and has enhanced CSOs' ability to collaborate around TJ. A few of them regularly come together and have partnered on projects. Some of these groupings include JRP, RLP, NUTJWG, and ICTJ. Others include UVF and REDRESS, and JRP and ASF or AYINET and ASF. HURINET, a coalition of human rights organizations in Uganda that was instrumental in organizing the Uganda Coalition for the International Criminal Court, engaged in coordinating activities, with assistance from the MacArthur Foundation.[72]

The limited funding available places CSOs in competition for support, which may compromise their efficacy. This competition prevents CSO actors more generally from sharing information – including information about funding opportunities. In some cases, this has incentivized some CSOs to develop projects anew and to seek out funding for activities they may not have been best positioned to carry out. In one example, in 2014, the Foundation for Human Rights Initiative received funding from the EU to carry out a workshop on TJ. However, given that this organization is usually involved in legal aid and human rights issues, it is unclear why it was best placed to host a TJ workshop.

Outreach and Links with Victim Communities

International support to victims' groups and networks has been instrumental in building awareness of victims' rights. Beginning in 2006, UVF created an independent national victims' association; supported victims to attend conferences, trainings, and workshops; enabled participation in research; contributed to policy development; and built victims' capacity to represent and speak for themselves.

In 2010, UVF received funding from OHCHR, the MacArthur Foundation, and UNDP, which enabled it to grow, reach more groups, and carry out surveys and research. UVF's work has been focused on conducting advocacy based on its research, training victims in TJ concepts, and equipping victims with the skills to advocate for themselves on TJ issues.[73] Since its move from being hosted by AYINET to becoming more independent, and following the initial funding that it

72 For a more in-depth look at HURINET's activities with the coalition, see "Ugandan Coalition for the International Criminal Court (UCICC)," Victims' Rights Working Group, accessed December 12, 2016, www.vrwg.org/about-vrwg/ucicc.

73 More available on the UVF at "Uganda Victims' Foundation (UVF)," Victims' Rights Working Group, accessed December 12, 2016, www.vrwg.org/about-vrwg/uvf.

received, UVF has had little success obtaining consistent and sustainable levels of funding.

Regional and national victims' conferences provided victims with firsthand information about the TJ policy and have enabled them to engage with government actors directly on relevant issues. AYINET, with funding from Trust Africa, for example, convened regional conferences on victim issues in eastern, central, northern, and western Uganda throughout 2014 that culminated in the National Victims' Conference that took place in Kampala at the end of May 2014. These efforts have, to an extent, enhanced victims' social capital by strengthening their voice and connections.

It is important to note, in this regard, the initially successful work of the Women's Advocacy Network and JRP in raising the profile of reparations for women victims of the conflict with the Ugandan Parliament. While the Parliament has not acted on its promise of reparations, the fact of women victims standing collectively as citizens in Parliament – demanding recognition and receiving it – was a striking symbol of strengthened voice.

FACTORS AFFECTING DONOR STRATEGIES AND DONOR DECISION-MAKING

An important factor affecting donor decision-making, which has already been discussed, is donors' linkage of their strategies to the Ugandan government's Vision 2040 agenda. Several other factors are also in play. First and foremost is the importance of maintaining stability and security in a volatile region. Others are financial concerns related to corruption, and foreign policy concerns related to the government's stance on homosexuality. Finally, donors have been coordinating their funding into multi-donor trust funds and basket funds like the DGF; donors providing funds through multi-donor trust and basket funds must make decisions by consensus, which has impacted donor decision-making. These factors have all directly or indirectly impacted funding for TJ.

First, in both the Great Lakes Region and the Horn of Africa, Uganda plays a stabilizing force in an unstable region. According to the UN High Commissioner for Refugees, Uganda is also host to 650,000 people of concern, refugees and asylum seekers from South Sudan, the Democratic Republic of Congo, and Somalia. There are also refugees from Rwanda and Burundi, many of whom are urban refugees who are vulnerable to human rights and security concerns, especially in Kampala. Also, groups listed as terrorist organizations are active in the region. Uganda has a clear strategic importance, in particular to the United States and the EU, but also to others. The Netherlands' most recent strategy for future support to Uganda highlights the country's importance in the region economically and in other leadership roles, but also the need for the continued strengthening of the UHRC and JLOS, its human rights record, particularly around repressive laws and actions, and the establishment of stronger institutions of governance.

Second, a concern over corruption, notably the mismanagement of PRDP funds, has significantly impacted donor decision-making. In 2012, a corruption scandal emerged when individuals in the Office of the Prime Minister (OPM) stole funds allocated for the development of northern Uganda. This discovery led to the first real deterioration in relations between the Government of Uganda and its development partners. According to a Human Rights Watch report, the embezzlement of more than €12 million in donor funds from Uganda's OPM "hit the headlines in many donor capitals in late 2012, prompting serious questions about Uganda's commitment to fighting corruption."[74] The stolen donor funds were earmarked as crucial support for the PRDP and the rebuilding of northern Uganda, ravaged by a twenty-year war, and Karamoja, Uganda's poorest region. The EU, the United Kingdom, Germany, Denmark, Ireland, Sweden, and Norway suspended aid.[75] Ireland and the Netherlands suspended their aid to JLOS.[76] The impact on JLOS was immediate. The leadership gap among development partners was immediately filled by Austria, which did not suspend funding to JLOS.[77] The aid suspension not only disrupted JLOS programming – and by extension TJ-related JLOS activities – but it highlighted how dependent JLOS is on donor funding, calling into question its sustainability.

Third, the passage of the Anti-Homosexuality Bill in 2014 created another rift, when donors – including the Netherlands, the United States, and Sweden – followed through on their threats to pull funding from Uganda. The World Bank also cancelled a loan that it had been planning to provide to the Ugandan government. This action further compounded funding streams both to JLOS and to TJ CSOs that had already been suspended due to the corruption scandal. Given the strong anti-homosexuality sentiment within Ugandan society, CSOs did not understand why donors would take such a firm stand on this issue, as it did not appear to them that the international community had much power to exercise influence. One donor said, "There was no way [to] continue funding a government that legislates against homosexuality." As the donor explained, "This is an important issue at home and we have to pay attention to our own constituents." TJ CSOs were impacted both by the potential loss of funding due to donor protests and by the generally antagonistic environment created between the donor community and the Ugandan government. In the end, however, the bill was overturned and donors' relationships with government ultimately improved.

74 Allard K. Lowenstein, "'Letting the Big Fish Swim?': Failures to Prosecute High-Level Corruption in Uganda" (New York: Human Rights Watch, 2014), 1, www.hrw.org/sites/default/files/reports/uganda1013_ForUpload_0.pdf.

75 Ibid., 1. 76 "The Justice, Law and Order Sector: Annual Performance Report, 2013/14," 137.

77 Austria Development Cooperation (OECD) "Evaluation: Review of the Uganda Country Strategy 2010–2015," 26. The suspension also immediately affected the PRDP: see Deniva, "Impact of Donor Aid Cuts on the Implementation of the PRDP, 2012/13" (no date), accessed December 12, 2016, www.deniva.or.ug/resource-centre/other-key-reports/194-impact-of-donor-aid-cuts-on-the-implementation-of-the-prdp.html.

Finally, the move from bilateral funding to a basket funding model by DGF in 2011 had a dramatic effect on many CSOs working on TJ, which previously had links on a bilateral basis with some DGF donors. Initially, in the move to create DGF's basket fund, the consolidation resulted in less bilateral funding to CSOs. For instance, of the DGF donors, only Norway maintained bilateral links to partners and provided core funding, while others, such as Austria and Sweden, continued to provide some ad hoc funding to CSOs. However, for the most part, TJ CSOs were told to apply to DGF because its participating donors would no longer provide bilateral support.

Consolidation in the DGF basket fund shifted decision-making from individual countries toward more of a consensus-building approach. In this shift, TJ has remained on the agenda, but other priorities have emerged. In general, there is significant interest among many donors to strengthen civil society actors' advocacy, skills, and knowledge about human rights, land, oil governance, and other sensitive issues that are viewed as threatening to undermine the regime's political and financial interests. Evidence-based research and advocacy on transparency in the oil sector, compensation and reparations for land acquisitions and sales, political and legal reform, and protection of human rights, including the rights of the lesbian and gay community – are the issues that the government is most sensitive about.[78]

CONCLUSION

More than ten years ago, the government promised an ambitious TJ agenda that was backed by development partners and the international community. Time has passed with little achievement, despite the commitments made in Juba. Many donors appear to have genuinely supported TJ – and pushed for TJ with the government. In the 2015/16 annual performance review of JLOS, for example, the Development Partners Group lamented the "lengthy, excessive delay in submission of TJ policy to Cabinet" and asked if this was evidence of a "lack of commitment to victims of war?"[79] Without a concerted strategy for getting TJ on the government's agenda, however, donors may be moving on as the government has successfully resisted and avoided TJ. The shift toward development is reflected in recent donor strategies, aligned to Uganda's Vision 2040, that focus on "current realities" (rather than the past) and an ahistorical view on the present situation.

With support and engagement from donors and other international allies (and despite the lack of focus and clear strategy from donors in terms of capacity building), several CSOs have developed and become national leaders on the various

78 Human Rights Watch, "Curtailing Criticism: Intimidation and Obstruction of Civil Society in Uganda" (New York: Human Rights Watch, 2012), www.hrw.org/report/2012/08/21/curtailing-criticism/intimidation-and-obstruction-civil-society-uganda.

79 JLOS DPG, "The 21st Annual Performance Review (2015/16): Joint Assessment" (Kampala: Justice, Law, and Order Sector, 2016), 4, 7, www.jlos.go.ug/index.php/document-centre/annual-review-conferences/21st-annual-jlos-review/393-development-partners-assessment-of-the-jlos-annual-performance-201516/file.

aspects of the complicated TJ agenda. While their work has largely been complementary, it has not been coordinated. They have also not always been united in their actions, in their advocacy, or in their dealings with government. The state–civil society relationship started out strong, but has deteriorated, further adding to fragmentation and breakdown of the process.

Civil society actors are caught in a difficult position in Uganda. The state has not prioritized the NTJP. Moreover, it has actively closed down the space for civil society engagement and expression, which has affected actors advocating for TJ.[80] Meanwhile, although many urgent political issues, such as fights over land, have a historical basis stemming from conflict-era concerns, TJ CSOs have not convincingly made these links in their advocacy with donors. In fact, in general, TJ CSOs' advocacy continues to show weakness, perhaps not sufficiently taking on board donor feedback from RLP's 2014 June workshop, which highlighted not only getting advocating to donors but also reframing their arguments to show the relevance and importance of TJ in Uganda today. As the DGF representative at the meeting noted, "In the end, donors can only do what they are requested to do. The DGF cannot go out on its own and start a major transitional justice program. We can only help if we are effectively requested by civil society and the government to intervene. But today no one is requesting real assistance and as a result transitional justice remains a largely academic field."[81] Further, TJ CSO advocacy also does not seem to reflect new strategies, such as trying to link TJ efforts to government development plans or developing new alliances or campaigns to get the issue of passing the NTJP more squarely on the government agenda. This said, it may be difficult for CSOs to make progress as the state continues to consolidate its power – including with donors' money.

The findings in this chapter demonstrate the frustrating complexity of the still evolving TJ process in Uganda. It is one that has been neither "donor driven" nor "nationally owned," to use the overly simple development assistance jargon. Although donors' focus on criminal justice has certainly shaped the TJ process, that focus has also followed the lead of the Ugandan government. Indeed, the main factors that have influenced donor decision-making – such as the shift from a post-conflict to a development context, the desire for a stable and secure Uganda, issues related to corruption, the government's stance on homosexuality, and the increasing coordination of funding – have little to do with TJ or its goals, even as they have affected, sometimes dramatically so, the chances for TJ or the shape of TJ in Uganda. Currently, real movement on TJ is hitched to the NTJP, which is with the government. Yet donors and civil society actors appear unable to influence or engage the government to move the discussion or process forward. Given this deadlock, unless there is a major change in the Ugandan political context or a shift in donor priorities, it is unlikely that TJ will advance significantly.

80 Human Rights Watch, among other groups, has been documenting this closing of public space. See, e.g., Human Rights Watch, "Curtailing Criticism."

81 Refugee Law Project, "The Fourth IATJ Summary Report," 15.

5

Hybrid Court, Hybrid Peacebuilding in Cambodia

Laura McGrew

This chapter reviews the background of international assistance in Cambodia to transitional justice (TJ) measures. It examines the Extraordinary Chambers in the Courts of Cambodia (ECCC), a joint venture between the Royal Cambodian Government and the United Nations (UN), its origins, and the resultant space created for civil society organizations (CSOs) out of this endeavor. It shows the hybrid nature of TJ in Cambodia, and the frictions and innovations that result from the local versus the international, such as the innovative civil party participation scheme created under the ECCC. This chapter highlights how neither the international nor the local vantage points are monolithic entities.

While the ECCC *has* opened space for CSOs, international assistance has focused primarily on the ECCC, while other TJ measures and support for CSOs were sidelined. In the context of this neglect, the current chapter highlights the importance for donors both to provide capacity building and to improve their (internal and external) coordination. In spite of the extensive international assistance to TJ (and previously to rule of law) in Cambodia, recent government crackdowns on CSOs indicate that donor and CSO goals to link TJ initiatives to ongoing impunity have not been particularly effective in the face of Cambodia's authoritarian government. The impact of international assistance has nonetheless been substantial, and now that the ECCC's presence has opened Pandora's Box, talking about the past is no longer seen as taboo in Cambodia.

BACKGROUND

Between April 17, 1975, and January 7, 1979 (also known as the "Three Years, Eight Months, and Twenty Days"), the regime of Democratic Kampuchea (DK) (also known as the Khmer Rouge [KR]), was responsible for the deaths of approximately 1.7 million people (mainly Cambodians), who died due to extermination, starvation, overwork, and lack of health care. After neighboring Vietnam overthrew the DK government in January 1979, more than a million refugees rushed from Cambodia, mainly to the Thai border. Here, and inside Cambodia, a proxy civil war continued between Eastern Bloc powers (the Cambodian People's Republic of Kampuchea [PRK] led by former KR cadres, with assistance from Vietnam, Russia, and others) and Western Bloc powers (the Cambodian non-communist resistance, including former KR forces, backed by Thailand, the United States, the United Kingdom, and others.) Included in the PRK government were Prime Minister Hun Sen, as well as other key senior members, notably Chea Sim and Heng Samrin. Former King Sihanouk was also linked with the KR in the past. After a decade of civil war, a peace agreement was finally reached in 1991, and in 1992 the United Nations Transitional Authority in Cambodia (UNTAC) brought a massive UN peacekeeping mission to return refugees, uphold human rights, and conduct democratic elections.

Between 1979 and the UNTAC period, the Cambodian government conducted a variety of TJ initiatives, including a show trial against what it called the "Ieng Sary–Pol Pot Genocidal Clique," for which a large number of testimonies in the countryside was collected; the creation of memorial sites in every province, including the Tuol Sleng Museum and Choeung Ek Killing Fields; and the implementation of widespread education programs berating the KR regime and praising the PRK (and Vietnamese) for saving the country. Most of these TJ initiatives were discounted by the West as politicized and biased.

Cambodia is ranked 160th out of 175 on Transparency International's Corruption Perceptions Index.[1] The human rights situation had improved since the 1992–93 UNTAC period, but serious human rights violations continued, and have peaked in the past few years in particular as the opposition party seemed to threaten the primacy of the Cambodian government (many members of which had roots in the PRK and with the former KR). These human rights violations include lack of freedom of expression, assembly, and association; lack of an independent judiciary and parliament; major problems with land and labor rights, including interventions by security forces resulting in deaths; arbitrary detention of human rights activists and others; and rampant impunity.[2] A number of versions of a draft nongovernmental organization (NGO) law were introduced several years ago, and in spite of active resistance by CSOs (and the international community) to some of its more unclear and possibly restrictive provisions, a final version of the Law on Associations and NGOs was promulgated in August 2015. Since then, the government has used the law to break up CSO meetings and trainings. CSOs also fear a cybercrime law that the government has been discussing.

[1] Cambodia is ranked 160th along with Eritrea and Venezuela. See Transparency International, *Corruption Perceptions Index* (Berlin: Transparency International, 2013), http:cpi.transparency.org/cpi2013/results.

[2] United Nations General Assembly, "Report of the Special Rapporteur on the Situation of Human Rights in Cambodia, Surya P. Subedi," A/HRC/24/36 (August 5, 2013); Human Rights Watch, *World Report 2014: Cambodia* (New York: Human Rights Watch, 2014), www.hrw.org/world-report/2014/country-chapters/cambodia.

Gender issues have only recently been discussed in Cambodia. There is a general lack of awareness of gender equity and gender rights, and a high prevalence of sexual and gender-based violence (SGBV). Women are generally marginalized across society, CSOs, and the ECCC. After research and advocacy by a few international gender experts, SGBV under the KR has received more attention, and aspects have now been addressed in one of the ECCC cases (forced marriage and rape within marriage, in Case 002). Several large-scale meetings on SGBV – organized in the shadow of the ECCC hearings – have also served to heighten awareness of gender-related crimes.

There is very little tolerance for different political views in Cambodia. In Cambodia's hierarchical patron-client-dominated society, any criticism of the state is often equated with enemy status. Decisions are still made in a top-down manner: for example, judges still take instructions from the leaders in the executive,[3] and hierarchical relationships are also seen in many other contexts.[4] Some thirty years after the KR period, there is still little trust and social capital in Cambodian society.[5] Systems of hierarchy and patronage further complicate social capital and trust, as political parties polarize populations and especially the ruling Cambodian People's Party requires complete dedication and a mentality of "If you are not with us, you are against us." While kinship relationships in Cambodia are strong, outside of the family there is little historical evidence of other types of associations.[6] In addition, civic trust (trust in institutions) was seen by all interviewees in this study as very low, especially in the judiciary.

THE EXTRAORDINARY CHAMBERS IN THE COURTS OF CAMBODIA

In 1996, nearly twenty years after the KR regime's end, the two co-prime ministers (Prime Minister Hun Sen and Prince Ranaridh) wrote a letter to then–UN

3 International Bar Association, "The ECCC – A Failure of Credibility" (London: International Bar Association, 2012), www.jurist.org/paperchase/Cambodia-1.pdf.

4 Moira O'Leary and Nee Meas, *Learning for Transformation: A Study of the Relationship between Culture, Values, Experience and Development Practice in Cambodia* (Phnom Penh: Krom Akphiwat Phum, 2001), 64. See also Judy Ledgerwood, "Understanding Cambodia: Social Hierarchy, Patron–Client Relationships and Power," Northern Illinois University (n.d.), www.seasite.niu.edu/khmer/ledgerwood/patrons.htm.

5 The most recent available data (2008) from the Asian Barometer concerning interpersonal trust shows that Cambodians are among the most distrustful people in the world (only 7.7 percent say that "most people can be trusted"). See the data on UNESCO's website, "Cambodia – Social Participation Indicator – Interpersonal Trust," UNESCO, accessed July 23, 2016, http://en.unesco.org/creativity/cambodia-social-participation-indicator-interpersonal-trust. Vicheth Sen has found that among a group of 400 respondents, levels of trust between people outside the basic family unit were low, existed somewhat among neighbors in rural areas, but were restricted only to family members in urban areas, Vicheth Sen, "Social Capital in an Urban and a Rural Community in Cambodia," *Cambodia Development Review* 16, no. 2 (2012): 7.

6 Ebihara May, "Svay, a Khmer Village in Cambodia" (PhD diss., Columbia University, 1968), 181; and Sen, "Social Capital in an Urban and a Rural Community in Cambodia," 6.

Secretary-General Kofi Annan asking for assistance with an international tribunal.[7] After years of negotiations between the Royal Government of Cambodia (RGC), the UN (Special Rapporteur Thomas Hammarberg and the UN Office of Legal Affairs), and various donors (especially the United States), in 2005/6 a mixed or hybrid tribunal (the ECCC) was finally agreed upon. Its mandate was to try "senior leaders most responsible."[8] As a hybrid tribunal, it includes international and national co-judges and co-prosecutors, as well as a mix of international and national lawyers and court staff members. Most of the national staff members are closely linked to the government. Although none of the senior political actors in the RGC had been foreseen as possible targets of prosecution as "senior leaders most responsible" for the KR regime, there was widespread sensitivity around the topic of accountability for crimes during the KR period – especially since there has been controversy over defense lawyers at the ECCC calling these actors to testify at the court and their refusal to do so.

The first defendant's trial began in 2009. Called Case 001, it concerned Kang Kech Eav (known as Duch), the former head of Tuol Sleng prison, where more than 12,000 prisoners were tortured and sent for extermination at Choeung Ek Killing Fields. He was found guilty of war crimes and crimes against humanity in 2010, and after an appeal was finally sentenced to life imprisonment. In 2011, Case 002 began against four defendants: Nuon Chea, Ieng Sary, Ieng Thirith, and Khieu Samphan. The case was split into two parts: Case 002/01 focused mainly on forced evacuation of the cities that began immediately after the KR takeover, and established the background for the structure of the DK regime. Its hearings ended in October 2013. Though only two of the defendants remained (Ieng Thirith has been declared mentally unfit for trial, and Ieng Sary passed away in March 2013), a guilty verdict was presented on August 7, 2014 against both defendants, and they were sentenced to life in prison. Case 002/02, of the same defendants, including war crimes, crimes against humanity, forced marriage and rape, and genocide, began in October 2014. Hearings have been completed and closing statements were concluded in June 2017: deliberations may last an additional year. The investigation of Meas Muth, named in Case 003, has been completed. Three persons were originally charged in Case 004: the investigating judge dropped charges against defendant Im Chaem (Case 004/01) in February 2017 while the investigations have been completed of defendant Ao An (Case 004/02) and of defendant Yim Tith (Case 004/02). Due to lack of political will (and funding), many observers doubt the cases will ever be tried; especially considering

7 In 1998, the CSO Cambodian Human Rights and Development Association (ADHOC) gathered 85,000 signatures/thumbprints on a petition calling for a tribunal after Prime Minister Hun Sen reversed his position, calling to forget the past.

8 Royal Government of Cambodia. *Law on the Establishment of Extraordinary Chambers in the Courts of Cambodia for the Prosecution of Crimes Committed during the Period of Democratic Kampuchea* (2004), www.eccc.gov.kh/en/documents/legal/law-establishment-extraordinary-chambers-amended.

a statement from the co-investigating judges in June 2017 calling for a stay of proceedings due to funding shortfalls.[9]

Between 2013 and 2014, the ECCC seemed stalled due to several factors: difficulty obtaining funding for the ECCC, especially for the national side; perceptions that the RGC was at a minimum not interested, and perhaps even blocking forward movement on the court; interference by the RGC in legal matters; and corruption at the court. However, by early 2014, the ECCC had finally lurched from the long-stalled period of inactivity into the aforementioned faltering but consistent series of investigations and trials. Although the RGC had requested the trials in 1997, the years of fraught negotiations reduced the appetites of both the UN Office of Legal Affairs and the RGC, and neither has ever been fully committed to the process. This is especially true of the RGC, particularly because several senior government officials were once former members of the KR regime and did not cooperate with calls to testify or broaden the scope of prosecutions. Nor has the RGC been committed to legal and judicial reform in general. Finally, the initial cooperation may have been related to common rent-seeking practices to profit from relatively highly paid government appointees to the ECCC – once it became clear that skimming would be hampered due to donors' emphasis on applying international financial standards, government support seems to have waned.

The 2014 reactivation seemed to be partly due to several factors: new activity on the prosecution side actively pushing to move cases forward; some developments in the organizational structure of the trial chamber allowing for a more clear and concise timeline; and the UN General Assembly's release of a $15.5 million subvention for a reserve fund. It was too late, however, for several donors who had already realigned their funding with other initiatives and ECCC-related legacy projects, rather than on continued support for outreach and civil parties. Surveying the landscape, it is safe to say that, overall, the ECCC has lost steam. Now that Case 002/02 has been completed except for judicial decisions and expected appeals, and the future of Cases 003/004 is highly uncertain, the ECCC is clearly winding down, with personnel already being laid off and others beginning to search for new employment.

In any case, attention to outreach has been erratic over the ECCC's life. At the beginning, the ECCC had only minimal funding for outreach, little for public

[9] ECCC. Press Release: "Co-investigating Judges Issue Decision on the Impact of the Funding Situation on Cases 003, 004, and 004/2" (August 11, 2017) (Phnom Penh: ECCC, 2017), www.eccc.gov.kh/sites/default/files/media/Press%20Release%20Co-Investinagting%20Judges%20Issue%20Decision%20On%20The%20Impact%20Of%20The%20Funding%20Situation%20ENG.pdf; See also Open Society Justice Initiative "The Future of Cases 003 and 004 at the Extraordinary Chambers in the Courts of Cambodia" (Phnom Penh: Open Society Foundation, 2012), www.opensocietyfoundations.org/publications/future-cases-003-and-004-extraordinary-chambers-courts-cambodia; and Open Society Justice Initiative, "New Report Notes Lack of UN Response to Political Interference at Khmer Rouge Tribunal" (Phnom Penh: Open Society Foundation, 2015), www.ijmonitor.org/2015/10/new-report-notes-lack-of-un-response-to-political-interference-at-khmer-rouge-tribunal/.

information, and none at all for victim participation, though this changed over time. The ECCC's Public Affairs Section (PAS) is responsible for information provided to the Cambodian public, the media, and the international community in support of the work of the court organs (judicial chambers, prosecution, and defense). The Victims Support Section (VSS; previously called the Victim Support Unit) was created only after the internal rules of the court were amended to include civil parties, which later has become a unique hallmark of the ECCC and is often described as one of its major and few successes.[10]

Cambodian victims can participate in the ECCC proceedings in two ways: either by submitting complaints to the co-prosecutors, or by applying to be civil parties. The VSS conducts outreach to civil parties and also manages the civil party process, including the complaints and requests for reparations: there are approximately 3,870 civil parties in Case 002, while ninety participated in Case 001. While 647 people have registered as civil parties in Case 003, only nine have been accepted to date; in Case 004, 1,995 have registered, and thirty were accepted. More than 200 of the mostly elderly civil parties have passed away. The Lead Co-Lawyer's Section heads the legal services for the civil parties. Once the court recognizes them, civil parties are eligible to seek collective and moral reparations and the VSS coordinates the requests and proposals for reparations.

Unfortunately, this "model" hybrid ECCC has been plagued with problems – in particular due to the lack of cooperation by the government side of the court, and the government's flouting of international standards. On the other hand, the gradually increasing recognition of the importance of the bottom-up "local" approach has been reflected in the field of TJ in Cambodia. An almost complete lack of concern in international assistance with the "local" of civil society (and indeed the victims) during the creation of the ECCC and its beginnings, sits in contrast with its more recent prioritization through extensive civil party (victim) participation. As we will see, while international actors held most of the power in the initial creation phase of international TJ initiatives, there has been a limited power shift toward engaged civil society actors.

NOTES ON METHODOLOGY AND LIMITATIONS

The interviewees for this research were selected based upon a review of the TJ International Assistance Database, which highlighted donors and civil society actors involved in TJ activities;[11] the researcher's extensive experience with the ECCC and

10 While the agreement to create the ECCC was signed in 2003, the agreement entered into force in April 2005, the first staff members started in February 2006, the judges were sworn in in July 2006, and the first hearing for Case 001 occurred in February 2007: see the webpage: "Key Events," ECCC, accessed July 23, 2016, www.eccc.gov.kh/en/keyevents. It was only in 2008 that the VSS became fully functional when funding was obtained from the German government.

11 Paige Arthur, "TJ International Assistance Database, 2002–2012" (unpublished data, 2014).

civil society in Cambodia; discussions with the book's editors about the prioritization of the large number of potential interviewees; assistance from a US State Department Foreign Service Officer in making appointments with the US Embassy in Phnom Penh; website review of potential interviewees (including the list of ECCC partners on the ECCC website); and queries made to key informants. In May and June 2014, a total of thirty-seven interviews was conducted with forty-seven persons (seven by telephone): sixteen interviews with donors, six with staff from the ECCC and the Office of the High Commissioner for Human Rights (OHCHR), and fifteen with civil society actors.[12]

The most significant gap was due to research time restrictions in contrast to the large number of potential interviewees, and the difficulty prioritizing. The time limitation also did not allow interviews of other CSOs *not* receiving TJ funding, for purposes of comparison. The second significant gap was the long period of time passed since the initiation of the ECCC (and related CSO activities), and the situation at the time of interviews of a decrease in funding to the ECCC and TJ, and to Cambodia in general with a downsizing of several embassies and of CSO activities (thus it was difficult to find knowledgeable donor interviewees). Third, the high turnover in embassy staff resulted in a large number of the donor interviewees being relatively ill informed about the history of the funding to the ECCC and especially to civil society activities. In addition, as the ECCC was usually funded out of the political/foreign affairs wings of governments, while civil society activities were funded from a variety of sources including development offices, it was difficult to identify interviewees who knew about both the ECCC and CSOs. While most interviewees were happy to be interviewed, some of the embassies were reluctant to meet (perhaps due to the politically sensitive topic and/or their lack of information). Finally, while the researcher was in Bangkok, a coup happened the day before scheduled interviews. These had to be cancelled and rescheduled primarily over the phone.

INTERNATIONAL ASSISTANCE: PRIMACY OF THE EXTRAORDINARY CHAMBERS IN THE COURTS OF CAMBODIA, WITH LITTLE TRICKLE-DOWN EFFECT

Cambodia exemplifies a unique case of a lengthy, convoluted TJ process, yet with substantial international assistance. This international assistance has been characterized, however, by a preponderant focus on the ECCC and a comparative neglect of civil society, at least partly due to key international actors' own historical relationships with Cambodia. While the ECCC winds down, it remains the main focus of most donors (as it has been since its creation in 2006). Meaningful assistance to

[12] Of the thirty-seven interviews, fifteen were conducted in the presence of the US State Department Program Officer from the Bureau of Democracy, Human Rights and Labor.

CSOs was slower in coming. This late support started ebbing by 2014 as international priorities changed; yet, by then, civil society actors had gained footholds in TJ processes and become more influential. Civil society demonstrations around elections and freedom of speech between 2013 and the present have resulted in increasing government crackdowns against civil society, and while donors had turned away from TJ, they are also hard-pressed to come up with innovative measures to deal with the rampant impunity. It has become increasingly clear that the years of international assistance to rule of law and indeed to the ECCC have not had the effect many donors and NGOs desired – that is, reduced impunity.

Historical Legacies and Donor Influence on the Extraordinary Chambers in the Courts of Cambodia and the Transitional Justice Agenda: Frictions and New Creations

TJ strategies for international interventions are related to political interests. In Cambodia, donor countries' cooperation with the ECCC and the TJ agenda has been influenced by their past histories, resulting in an emphasis on the ECCC's retributive justice model (over the goals of truth and reconciliation); various levels of funding for the court or related organizations and services; provision of diplomats influencing the negotiations; assistance (or meddling) in the rules and procedures; and appointment of international staff and officials. These past histories include France's colonial history in Cambodia, Japan's role as a regional power, Germany's historical experience with the Holocaust, and the United States' history in the war in Vietnam. Each of these actors, we see, has had its own role in the court. In addition, because of the imprisonment, torture, and killing of nationals (notably of the United States, the United Kingdom, Australia, New Zealand, and France) by the KR during the KR period, as well as some attacks during the 1990s, these key international players were particularly insistent on prosecutions in an international court.

Initial (and ongoing) funding decisions have been dominated by the "political, retributive, and symbolic" model of TJ – a dominant view promulgated by the United States (and others), focusing on the ECCC and not on other CSO TJ activities (outreach, dialogue, memory work, trauma healing, etc.).[13] After the years of war between Eastern and Western Bloc proxies, both sides were eager to be finished with Cambodia, as the Western-style criminal prosecutions through the ECCC were originally envisioned to finish in three years. As a result, donors' (and the RGC's) desire to close the chapter of the KR past dominated assistance decisions focusing on the large, flashy, and unique ECCC, with little concern for the needs of the Cambodian population.

France, the former colonial power and a civil law country, had the largest influence on Cambodia's legal system and it continues to provide legal assistance

[13] See Annie Bird, "Introduction," in *U.S. Foreign Policy on Transitional Justice* (New York: Oxford University Press, 2015).

to several institutions. In contrast to common law, the civil law system uses investigating judges, and incorporates civil parties in criminal cases. Thus, the ECCC was developed using primary elements of the French-influenced Cambodian civil law system. French diaspora groups and experts such as legal analyst David Boyle provided significant inputs into the set-up of the court, the rules and procedures, and the civil party system. Another major French impact on the court was the inclusion of three languages (Khmer, English, and French). While most experts felt that two languages would have been sufficient (Khmer and English), the acquiescence to France's insistence (as well as pressures from the defense) to include French as an official language required countless delays due to the translation of the tens of thousands of pages of documents, and simultaneous translation during court proceedings.

The United States has also had a significant role in the ECCC, both directly and indirectly. The US Congress was pressured by the Cambodian diaspora, as well as a strong anticommunist voice against both the PRK and Vietnam, to establish the court. The United States played a significant role in the creation of the ECCC directly through Ambassador David Scheffer, the US Ambassador-at-Large for War Crimes Issues, and later Senior Advisor to the UN Secretary-General, as well as in the initial and ongoing collection of evidence against the KR, through its financial and technical support of the Documentation Center of Cambodia (DCCam).

Japan, the largest donor to the ECCC, also had a significant colonial presence in Cambodia during World War II, and a continued interest in maintaining its soft power in the region in spite of – or especially because of – its fluctuating economic situation. In the past two decades, Japan has provided substantial assistance in the rule of law sector, in particular, to the civil code and civil procedure code and related capacity building in the judicial sector.

The court's rules are a mishmash of colonial and donor interests and legacies. As mentioned earlier, the choice of legal system for the ECCC was based upon Cambodia's colonial past (especially France's civil law system), but also its later alignment with the United States and development assistance from other countries. The initial emphasis on the French-based civil law system at the ECCC was adapted to include many unique aspects that marked its hybrid nature – such as panels of judges with a majority of Cambodian and minority of foreign judges, with complicated rules necessitating agreement of at least one foreign judge in all decisions.

Technical assistance from the UN, the United States, Australia, and others in the Cambodian legal system, as well as substantial donor support for human rights, has influenced the ECCC today to include international legal norms, as well as some elements closer to common law countries. The many foreign advisors, judges, and other legal personnel working at the ECCC have also influenced the court's legal culture. These personnel come from a variety of legal backgrounds, and many have had experience in the other international criminal tribunals (the International Criminal Court [ICC], the International Criminal Tribunal for the former

Yugoslavia and the International Tribunal for Rwanda), which have had strong common law influence. The largest donors (Japan, France, Australia, and the United States) have had at least one judge or prosecutor among the ECCC personnel. They, and the United Kingdom, Canada, New Zealand, and Germany have all had significant inputs into the court, including staff appointments.

Most of the framing of the crimes at the ECCC has been done by common law experts, including historian Steven Heder, who was funded early on by the Open Society Justice Initiative (OSJI) to write "Seven Candidates for Prosecution" (Heder also later worked as an investigator at the ECCC).[14] In addition, David Scheffer, then US Ambassador-at-Large for War Crimes Issues, was the main architect of many of the compromises of the ECCC, allowing the UN and the Cambodian government to move forward with the court, though neither side was ever fully satisfied with the results.[15] All of these compromises, however, have created their own challenges, and it has thus taken time for many advisors to understand and work with and within Cambodia's legal system. Furthermore, the culture of impunity and corruption in the country has had strong influence in the legal sector and indeed within the ECCC itself, again requiring cultural understanding from advisors. However, this international influence also has positive impacts: as mentioned elsewhere, if not for the international aid from Germany to the ECCC Victims Unit and to a large group of CSOs, many of the nonjudicial TJ measures would probably have been entirely neglected.

The Development of Civil Society and Other Transitional Justice Initiatives

During UNTAC, CSO presence mushroomed, including many key human rights organizations, most of which continue to exist today. In contrast to the oppression by the socialist system throughout the 1980s, human rights organizations created in the early 1990s in the political space opened up by UNTAC were ideologically aligned with the Western democracies, particularly France, the United States, and the United Kingdom. While the human rights CSOs focused on government impunity for current human rights violations, they were also concerned about the violations of the past, because many former KR remained in the post-UNTAC government. Thus, seeds of distrust between government and civil society were planted from the very beginning of the human rights CSOs' existence.

The most prominent CSO working on TJ in Cambodia is the Documentation Center of Cambodia (DCCam), of which there was frequent mention in the interviews for this case study. DCCam's origins go back to the mid-1990s. In April 1994, the "Cambodian Genocide Justice Act" was passed by the US Congress, which

14 Stephen Heder and Brian Tittemore, *Seven Candidates for Prosecution: Accountability for the Crimes of the Khmer Rouge* (2nd edn.) (Phnom Penh: Documentation Center of Cambodia, 2004), www.wcl.american.edu/warcrimes/khmerrouge.html.

15 See David Scheffer, *All the Missing Souls: A Personal History of the War Crimes Tribunals* (Princeton, NJ: Princeton University Press, 2012).

created the Office of Cambodian Genocide Investigation in the US State Department's Bureau of East Asian and Pacific Affairs. In 1995, a grant was awarded to Yale University to conduct research, training, and documentation on the KR regime, and the DCCam office in Cambodia was set up as an independent research institute. DCCam initially maintained its own special niche of documentation, but soon expanded to many other activities including legal education, outreach, civil party support, victim–perpetrator dialogue and reconciliation, genocide education, etc. DCCam's archive houses thousands of pages of documents, photographs, and films, and it has served as the major source of documentation for the ECCC. An extensive genocide education program has produced a KR history curriculum for Cambodian high schools, as well as a teacher training manual and program. DCCam is in the process of raising funds to create the Sleuk Rith Institute, a permanent documentation center for memory, justice, and reconciliation.

In addition to DCCam, several other CSOs have started TJ programming, including monitoring, outreach, coordination, memory projects, historical dialogue, films, psychosocial services, and projects related to SGBV, gender rights, and gender sensitivity. These CSOs are divided into two groups: those that came from the field of human rights, and those that focused mainly on TJ activities. The key local CSOs involved in TJ that initially came from the human rights world include the Cambodian Human Rights and Development Association (ADHOC), the Cambodian Defenders Project (CDP), and the Cambodian Human Rights Action Committee (CHRAC). Those with TJ-related activities include the Bophana Center, which has worked on documentation and memory work; the Transcultural Psychosocial Organization (TPO), which offers psychosocial services and research, including work on gender; Kdei Karuna (KdK), which works on grassroots historical dialogue; and Youth for Peace (YFP), which does outreach, youth and elder dialogue, and memorialization. Many other organizations have also been involved in TJ work and have received international assistance, and they will be discussed in the course of this chapter.

Evolution of Transitional Justice Funding: The Key Donors

The engagement of both donors and CSOs has been a long process leading from the following key events: 1) the end of the KR regime in 1978; 2) the end of the PRK period in 1991, which had produced several TJ measures supported by Eastern Bloc countries but were then therefore unacceptable to the West; 3) the 1992–93 UNTAC intervention resulting in elections and a coalition government; 4) the 1996 letter written by the two co-prime ministers requesting assistance from the UN to conduct an international trial; 5) the start of the final negotiations between the government, the UN, and bilateral donors in 2003 to create the ECCC; and 6) the 2006 signing of the agreement to create the ECCC, which started its first trial in 2009.

Several of the larger human rights organizations (ADHOC and the Cambodian League for the Promotion and Defense of Human Rights) and bilateral donors (the

United States, France, Japan, Sweden, Netherlands, and the United Kingdom) had been involved with TJ since the second phase in 1991. These CSOs and some donors had been involved in long-term lobbying on human rights and in backdoor negotiations, and donors eventually provided funding. Their ostensible goal was to promote the end of impunity and to promote human rights in Cambodia, though the superpowers were also vying for influence in the region.

Funding for TJ in Cambodia has been entirely dominated by funding to the ECCC: most funding to CSOs has been seen as ancillary – except for funding to DCCam and to various CSOs by Germany's Agency for International Cooperation (Gesellschaft für Internationale Zusammenarbeit, GIZ). Even activities such as outreach and public information were not fully funded at the beginning, as this donor observed:

> We didn't properly fund outreach – we left it for civil society groups to fund piecemeal and hand to mouth ... but by not even giving a budget line for donors to contribute even if subcontracted to civil society, which would have been the right thing to do, made it harder and resulted in less rigorous coverage of information around the country ... We found it very difficult to mobilize funds at that level, even $10,000, which would have made a huge difference to an NGO.

The focus of funding to the ECCC was initially short term, as the ECCC was to finish within three years with an initial budget of approximately $50 million. Through 2016, it has taken at least ten years and received approximately $236 million. Japan has been its primary funder (more than 30 percent), with other major funders including the United States, Australia, Germany, the European Union (EU), and the United Kingdom – among many others.[16] There are separate funding streams to the Cambodian government and UN "sides" of the court. Data from the TJ International Assistance Database and from GIZ suggests that CSOs have received a fraction of this sum: roughly $16 million from 2000 to 2012 for TJ-related activities, with a third of this amount going to DCCam.[17] If we compare contributions to the ECCC through 2012 to those to

16 This sum reflects the total contributions to the court minus the contributions from the Cambodian government. See "ECCC Financial Outlook: March 2016," ECCC, accessed February 18, 2017, www.eccc.gov.kh/sites/default/files/Financial%20Outlook%2031%20March%202016-final_0.pdf.

17 Figures calculated from Arthur, "TJ International Assistance Database." We have found grants totaling $9.71 million, of which $5.88 million was for DCCam, mainly from the United States and Sweden (Sweden discontinued funding for DCCam after 2010). It is important to acknowledge that this data is incomplete and should be seen as indicative rather than exact and exhaustive. We do not, however, have reason to believe that there would be large changes to these figures, even if we were to find additional grants to CSOs in the data, since CSOs typically receive small amounts of money. Adding to the Database figures, GIZ has supported a ten-year project (which will be described in detail later in this chapter) to encourage civil society participation in the ECCC, with a projected budget of roughly €9 million ($10 million) from 2008 to 2017, about half of which (€4,674,000/$5.3 million) was expended between 2008 and 2012. We were not able to identify this funding in the TJ International Assistance Database, and we are therefore grateful for information from Marcos Smith, e-mail message to Paige Arthur, May 25, 2015. On Swedish funding to DCCam, see Anthony Finn, Patricia Curran, and Carol Strickler, "Forward Looking Evaluation of Sida's Core Support to the Documentation Centre Cambodia (DC-CAM)" (Stockholm: Nordic Consulting Group, 2010), www.d.dccam.org/Abouts/Annual/pdf/Sida_Evaluation_June_2010.pdf.

CSOs working on TJ, we see a marked difference: civil society actors have received less than 10 percent of all TJ-related funds, even though the ECCC has only run for part of the period (i.e., from 2006 to 2012).[18] The main funders of CSOs for TJ activities have been the US government (through its support of DCCam), Sweden (also through support of DCCam), and GIZ and other branches of the German government. Other funders include the EU (only between 2007 and 2010), the Open Society Foundations (2003–13),[19] and the UK government (2009–12). Smaller amounts have been given on and off to various organizations from the governments of Belgium, Canada, France, the Netherlands, New Zealand, Norway, Sweden, and Switzerland.

However, as the donor cited earlier pointed out, such funding for CSO activities was largely haphazard in Cambodia: small bits of CSO funding were eked out of foreign ministry budgets, from development budgets, or from special solicitations. For example, a large EU grant for international justice mechanisms including the ICC and the Rome Statute provided $2 million to ADHOC over three years from 2007 to 2010 for monitoring, advocacy, outreach, and support to victim (civil party) participation. Similarly, a United States Agency for International Development (USAID) collaborative grant was awarded under a global request for proposals from its Office of Conflict Management and Mitigation in 2012, and another in 2015.

The other main TJ initiatives have received long-term funding, initially from GIZ's Civil Peace Service (CPS) (to work with a variety of local CSOs) and later from Germany's Federal Ministry for Economic Cooperation and Development, which supported the VSS – though some funding has been discontinued and funding amounts have gradually decreased.[20] France has funded the Bophana Centre's work on memorialization and documentation.[21] The OHCHR and the UN Development Programme (UNDP) have both been supporting actors in the TJ process, in different ways. The UN Trust Fund to End Violence against Women and the UN Trust Fund for Victims of Torture have funded projects related to gender and mental health, respectively.

All interviewees remarked upon the decline of assistance over the years, and the difficulty of seeking funding in the current climate, affected by the global financial crisis and changing priorities toward Myanmar/Burma or other countries or regions. The decline of assistance relates to the ECCC's problems with delays, corruption, etc., and has led some donors to encourage CSOs to shift emphasis away from the ECCC as reported by this civil society actor: "There has been a balance between the

18 Contributions to the ECCC through 2012 amounted to $170,308,046. See "ECCC Financial Outlook: October 2012," ECCC, accessed February 18, 2017, www.eccc.gov.kh/sites/default/files/Financial%20Outlook%20-%2031%20October%202012.pdf.

19 www.opensocietyfoundations.org

20 GIZ does not identify itself as a traditional donor; rather, as one interviewee said, "Our approach is different because our main mandate is to provide expertise; the money we give compared to other's funding is rather small. Our contribution per year is maximum $40,000 for each partner, and includes salary for local staff and some project activities, making life easier for our advisors involved."

21 Complete data on funding of all CSOs was not available.

ECCC and CSO activities – we have gone full circle now. There was a period when we couldn't run a [TJ] project unless it was connected with the ECCC. But now, over the last couple of years civil society donors are increasingly funding [projects] *not* [related to the] ECCC, and now we have to dress [the projects] up; it's a legacy project now."

However, Sweden, Germany, and the OHCHR have remained engaged, perhaps due to their longer-term planning and, in the case of the OHCHR, its clear mandate. Both Sweden and Germany from 2014 started focusing on links between the ECCC and select rule of law institutions, on fair trial rights, and on a few other key topics. As Germany has provided substantial funding to the ECCC over many years, the legacy work seems to be merely a shift of labels from outreach and advocacy, but still under the TJ umbrella.

Germany steered CHRAC's current projects toward engagement with legal educational institutions on ECCC legacy. The OHCHR has also remained engaged with the judiciary and others such as the Cambodian Bar and legal education institutions on human rights and ECCC legacy issues. Though their aid has decreased, both the Japanese and French have continued their long-term and sustained inputs on civil and criminal codes and procedures (respectively) for many years.

Challenges Facing Donors: Political Realism, Donor Fatigue, and a Lack of Resources

While donors highlighted the challenges of working in an environment of ongoing impunity, they have at the same time been unwilling or unable to stop it. One particular challenge all interviewees highlighted was the failure of the Cambodian government to make any significant progress in the areas of assistance to the judiciary, legal and judicial reform, and access to justice. This has resulted in the majority of donors, many of whom had been providing significant funding (including the United States, the EU, UNDP, Denmark, and others), entirely pulling out of assistance to that sector. One donor remarked:

> As donors, we focus on combating impunity that exists as well as bringing justice for what has happened in the past. The difficulty with my role as a project manager in trying to ensure that we meet these objectives is that it is easy on a superficial level in that Duch was convicted but, otherwise, most funding to legal and judicial reform has been completely given up, and there is no fertile ground for links with rule of law.

This lack of government progress on rule of law, as well as on administrative reforms and democratic governance, has required a subtle balancing act from donors. Several CSO interviewees felt that the donors were complicit in allowing impunity to continue, as most donors had accepted the status quo until a 1997 coup d'état (otherwise known as the "events" of 1997) forced their hand. The powerful Cambodian People's Party – housing many former KR – targeted the leadership and military of the opposition political parties, most of whom fled the country, and a few of whom were killed. After these events, US funding was withdrawn from the RGC, including a massive education project. Several other donors also temporarily halted funding. However, within a year of these events, most donors gradually resumed some funding – this required overlooking corruption and continuing human rights abuses. Generally though, donors (especially those from the West) have a strained relationship with the RGC, especially due to the lack of recent progress on democratic and judicial reforms. While China provides billions in aid, often without any pesky ties requiring Cambodia to comply with international standards, Western governments require more stringent controls.[22]

Donor fatigue around the ECCC is partly related to these factors, but is also linked to the initial funding mechanism of the court, based on voluntary contributions. Several donors (as well as some ECCC and CSO interviewees) stated a different mechanism should have been created (and should be created in future TJ mechanisms) to avoid the yearly struggle over funding that was causing various problems, including conflict between the national and international sides of the court over funding, strikes by (national) court staff due to several month-long delays in salary payments, and frequent change of staff due to job insecurity. All of these problems have resulted in inconsistent progress on cases. This directly impacted CSO support, because donors were so focused on obtaining sufficient funding for the court itself that there was little energy left over to fund CSOs and other TJ activities.

Donors (especially the foreign offices of the large embassies that often fund TJ, as well as the smaller embassies) were plagued by a lack of staff to fully evaluate and monitor grants and to attend all the coordination meetings that occur. Staff may not have the expertise or background for following all the various TJ mechanisms (and they are often covering a very wide variety of issues), and there are frequently gaps between political and development functions and communications (where TJ mechanisms often lie). "One challenge, especially in headquarters," one donor noted, "is that there is a limited understanding of these TJ issues among donors, also . . . understanding varies greatly within donor communities, and rule of law is different than TJ, peacebuilding, or conflict work. There are different boundaries, but it is very murky programming and this affects how requests for proposals are written."

Similarly, the majority of donor interviewees had trouble identifying long-term TJ goals, or how TJ goals related to general human rights, democracy, and governance goals. Some donor interviewees did not know what the term "transitional justice" meant. While most donor interviewees were familiar with funding to the ECCC, several donors had to refer to documents to provide any reference to TJ.

22 China historically supported the KR.

Opaque and Uncoordinated? Decision-Making of International Actors and Strategies for Better Engagement

An Absence of Strategy

Only a minority of interviewees could articulate a set of TJ goals or strategies. For example, although the Belgians did not have a specific TJ strategy, TJ was indirectly included under a conflict management and peacebuilding strategy; by contrast, New Zealand's TJ assistance was under rule of law programming. Various parts of the US strategy were considered under the State Department's Bureaus of Political Affairs; Conflict and Stabilization Operations; and Democracy, Human Rights, and Labor; as well as USAID's Office of Conflict Management and Mitigation. Sweden's TJ strategy was under human security; the United Kingdom's under fighting impunity and genocide prevention (and linked to the Foreign Secretary's 2014 championing prevention of sexual violence during conflict); and Germany's under governance and/or peacebuilding. While Germany and Sweden have thought about long-term goals related to human rights and good governance linked to the ECCC, insufficient information about other donors' overall goals was available to draw any conclusions.

Several donors expressed frustrations in carrying out their mandates, and the lack of institutional memory and ability to maintain long-term goals around TJ initiatives (such as the ECCC). They also observed that TJ initiatives were given various and fluctuating degrees of attention by decision-makers, who change frequently. In addition, many donors (and the majority of CSOs) mentioned the difficulties in maintaining a long-term focus on TJ when donor governments, and thus their priorities, change every four to five years, initially causing delays and then sometimes changes of policy, resulting in difficulties obtaining consistent funding.

Specifically related to funding for the ECCC and civil society activities, many donors observed that their strategy and commitment were damaged by their own internal processes, and that this resulted in a lack of sufficient or long-term funding of TJ activities: "How can you take decisions without knowing where money will come from?" Many interviewees spoke about the need for longer-term funding strategies: Sweden and Germany were the only ones who had actively implemented this long-term approach, which was widely appreciated by CSO interviewees and admired by other donors.

Internal Decision-Making – Ad Hoc, Disjointed, and Unspecific

Several interviewees spoke about the tension, if not competition, between the branches of governments providing funding – foreign ministry headquarters, foreign embassies, UN missions for the ECCC, and development cooperation units. Decisions related to the ECCC were often made in home offices, while CSO funding was implemented through separate tracks, and sometimes through development agencies. Decision-making by foreign ministries and/or their embassies versus their development agencies was reported as being fundamentally different in timing, priorities, planning, frameworks, and length of support.

When funding did exist, there was an urgent need to spend it, and this negatively impacted donor ability to contribute to bottom-up peacebuilding. Several donors complained about a lack of time to adequately consult: "I think we should do things more slowly … We have, like everyone else, disbursement pressures to commit funds. Ideally we would need another six months to dialogue, but it's just not possible, if we don't disburse the funds, we don't get them; it is a public administration Catch-22." CSOs also lack capacity or time to review lengthy consultation documents, as one donor noted:

> Consultations are very limited, we are always forced to do consultations, and we never have the means or time to include what was consulted on. For example, we just did a joint strategy for future support and consulted with civil society, but the final document was sixty pages, and a summary was twenty pages. But CSOs were not able to go through this in detail; mostly this was related to development organizations, but it is the same for TJ and governance – they don't have time to read our documents and really think about what we (and they) are doing.

When asked more specifically about their decision-making processes, no decision-making related to TJ was available from any interviewee. Many decisions are reportedly made on an ad hoc basis, and sometimes made too rapidly in response to crises and without sufficient consultations. In addition, sometimes there is fighting between various departments within donor agencies, complicating decision-making. Some decisions are made haphazardly when government officials or politicians visit certain countries and then for various reasons make public pronouncements or promises. As discussed by Skelcher and Smith in their work on administrative reform, donors with multiple departments and multiple goals must relate to their "institutional constituencies." This compartmentalization results in contradictory and fractured strategies that are inconsistent between offices. At the same time, friction occurs internally as donors may not want to admit these inconsistencies, instead attempting to project a coherent message.[23]

Decisions may also be made depending upon individuals' personal experiences. For example, one interviewee who had been involved in funding both the Sierra Leone and Cambodian tribunals had learned lessons that resulted in this donor's provision of sustained support for not just the ECCC, but also for continuing support for significant CSO and court outreach activities.

In the case of the ECCC, decision-making about funding, as well as for related CSO TJ activities, was further complicated because the primary funding decisions

[23] Chris Skelcher and Steven Rathgeb-Smith, "Theorizing Hybridity: Institutional Logics, Complex Organizations, and Actor Identities: The Case of Nonprofits," *Public Administration* 93, no. 2 (2015): 433–48.

were made at donors' headquarters and New York (at the UN missions) and were often managed by political entities – foreign embassies' legal officers who were less aware about development work and CSO activities and more focused on tribunals. Thus, disconnects sometimes occurred between headquarters, New York, and Phnom Penh. This type of disjointed, ad hoc decision-making further contributes to the tendency of donors to make top-down decisions, rather than focusing on hybrid solutions built from the bottom-up (or at the very least, by consulting with local partners).

One donor stated that the decision to decrease funding to civil society work on TJ was due to a decreased demand from TJ civil society actors in contrast to an overwhelming demand from general human rights defenders, especially with respect to land issues. This view was not shared by CSOs involved in TJ, all of which stated that they had been actively seeking funds for TJ but that donors had changed their priorities and funds were either less available or not available at all.

Donor Coordination

Donor coordination affects all three aspects of this research: the relationships between donors and CSOs; the factors that affect decision-making; and the impact of international aid on civil society. Almost every interviewee lamented the lack of transparency and coordination among donors. Several groups coordinate donor funding for the ECCC, including the "Friends of the ECCC" based in Phnom Penh and Bangkok and the Principal Donors Group (PDG) to the ECCC based at the UN in New York City, as well as some informal groups of like-minded donors – but the fact that a management committee was not created at the beginning of the ECCC was mentioned by several interviewees as being regrettable. The PDG includes Australia, France, Germany, Japan, Sweden, the United Kingdom, and the United States, with the EU as observer. The group meets regularly, or sometimes bilaterally as needed, and reviews progress on the ECCC.[24] The Friends Group is made up of ambassadors from donor countries, is cochaired by Japan and France, and meets regularly in Cambodia. A few interviewees commented that the Friends Group did not promote truly open or rigorous discussions; rather it focused instead on success stories and completion strategies.

Two donors interviewed who attended the Friends Group meeting stated that CSO assistance was not discussed at this meeting, but only funds to the ECCC itself. One long-term TJ civil society interviewee noted, "I was never able to meet the Group of Friends in Phnom Penh, they didn't seem to meet very often, were notoriously closed, and both France and Japan, who chaired it, had no interest in fostering relationships [with CSOs]." Although in theory relationships between donors and CSOs could have been enhanced through donor coordination, in reality

24 "Statement by the Principal Donors Group for the Extraordinary Chambers in the Courts of Cambodia," ECCC, June 27, 2014, www.eccc.gov.kh/en/articles/statement-principal-donors-group-extraordinary-chambers-courts-cambodia.

the secretive Friends Group actually worsened CSO–donor relationships. Because of the trend set by France and Japan, the other more open and accepting donors (such as the United States, Canada, Germany, and the United Kingdom) were inhibited from sharing information and having open discussions outside of the Friends Group. On the other hand, in the development sector a more coordinated approach was taken: a donor technical working group for rule of law included two civil society representatives. It was chaired by the OHCHR, and included legacy issues around the ECCC. At the same time, however, this group had been relatively inactive in the prior few years due to the lack of government cooperation with judicial reform.

Both donors and CSOs alike spoke about a lack of donor coordination. For example, regarding the recent downturn in funding, most CSOs felt that the donors had not discussed the fact that all of them (except USAID/US government) had simultaneously decreased their funding to this sector, or discussed how CSOs continuing with TJ work would cope. One donor with a long-term presence felt profoundly discouraged about donor coordination: "We will never have coordination strategies between donors. I used to have this dream ... but our agendas are different, there is a lot of turnover, the time frames are very different, and the mechanisms for disbursement and monitoring are so different." Another donor lamented that "the various donors that support the ECCC – we're not quite sure that they talk to each other, especially in terms of legacy. There are a lot of rumors and misunderstanding about what the focus is of each donor."

On the other hand, some interviewees did have some hope for positive donor coordination. Informal donor coordination between key donors, at least partly through the intervention of international CSOs that organized coordination meetings, did occur, which hopefully served to reduce duplication and close gaps.

Better Models of Engagement: The Participatory, Long-Term Model Donor

As mentioned earlier, GIZ's CPS has been one of the few bilateral actors to engage on a long-term basis with Cambodian civilian society working on TJ. Indeed, CPS was often mentioned as a positive model of engagement, and is a rare example of a focused and determined effort to increase the bottom-up and reduce the top-down approach. The program began in 2008 and is projected to end in 2020, with a budget that will exceed $10 million over the period. A (German) CPS coordinator has been posted in country full-time, providing support and coordination services to the CSOs receiving funding from GIZ, as well as to the seven CPS advisors placed in the major organizations conducting TJ activities.[25] The CPS advisors included psychologists, lawyers, and organization development specialists, chosen through

[25] It has advisors placed in several of the CSOs that are key players in TJ and, in particular, with those working with civil parties: ADHOC, CDP, CHRAC, TPO, Youth for Peace, and Kdei Karuna, among others.

a participatory process between GIZ and the CSO. The CSO was also given a small grant that could be changed over the year, which allowed flexible programming. The infusion of funds (about $35,000 USD recently, but up to $60,000 in past years) *along with* the GIZ advisors was seen as extremely important to allow the CSOs to build local capacity in management/organizational development, proposal writing, and fundraising.

The majority of interviewees widely praised GIZ as being particularly open to CSO participation in decision-making, due to its mandate and approach, and especially due to its investment in a CPS coordinator and the extensive network of CSO advisors. Regular meetings of grantees, CPS advisors, and the CPS coordinator occurred, focusing on various topics, including review of projects and specific overall goals of the GIZ projects. In the case of a developing country such as Cambodia (especially one with a decimated educated population), several interviewees spoke about the importance of this intensive approach, needed in order to help build the capacity of CSOs and to increase their sustainability. In addition, GIZ had another related program, "InVent," which brought civil society actors on exchange visits to Germany and provided local internships at the ECCC. These were also widely reported as being very successful at building civil society actors' capacity, as well as improving their informal networks.

The building of networks in civil society is recognized as an important measure of social capital and, indeed, of the success and sustainability of TJ mechanisms.[26] In the field of reparations, the network of GIZ advisors was intimately involved in working with victim and civil party groups to identify reparation projects, to coordinate the prioritization of those projects, and to seek funding for them. Decision-making about the projects was said to have been done by the lawyers representing the civil parties,[27] though there were several meetings and consultations to obtain feedback from others, including government officials, mental health professionals, and civil society actors involved with TJ. Formal (collective and symbolic) reparations was seen as a new concept in Cambodia, though the idea of reparations (as repair or compensation for harm done) was found in various surveys to be an important means of recovery from trauma by Cambodians from all walks of life.[28]

One successful strategy to expand networks from CSOs toward government and increase awareness of the Cambodian population, CSOs, and the international community was related to mental health programs linked to TJ processes. Here,

26 Pablo de Greiff and Roger Duthie, *Transitional Justice and Development: Making Connections* (New York: Social Science Research Council, 2009).

27 See "Meaningful Reparations for Victims of the Khmer Rouge," ECCC, February 25, 2014, www.eccc.gov.kh/en/articles/meaningful-reparation-khmer-rouge-victims.

28 See, for example, the following surveys: Suzannah Linton, "Reconciliation in Cambodia" (Phnom Penh: Documentation Center of Cambodia, 2004) and Laura McGrew, "Cambodian Civil Society and the Tribunal: The Survey: Results and Recommendations (Issue 9)," *On the Record*, The Advocacy Project, August 10, 2000, www.advocacynet.org/resource/424.

GIZ had funded both direct psychosocial services at the ECCC and dialogue and memorialization projects, but had also funded the Royal University of Phnom Penh's psychological training program, which included projects with government ministries – and linked them through networks. This approach, creating more links with government, should also improve sustainability. In addition, the power dynamics between the relatively weak CSOs and the various authoritarian, top-down government ministries could change with an increase in legitimacy of the CSOs provided by donor support in this comprehensive, long-term approach.

Struggles and Opportunities around Capacity Building

Several donors commented on their responsibility not just to support CSOs, but also to build capacity. However, not all donors had sufficient time, staff, and resources to do so. Furthermore, capacity building often focused more on individuals than the CSO, resulting in isolated effects, with impact lost as individuals changed jobs. Several interviewees brought up the point that without the GIZ and other advisors, CSOs would not have been successful with any of the complicated proposals for fundraising, and that in some cases, the advisors were also crucial in facilitating networking.

A joint project funded by the UN Trust Fund to End Violence against Women, awarded to the VSS, CDP, and TPO, was also mentioned as a successful capacity-building model. The three-year, $632,000 project, called "Promoting gender equality and improving access to justice for female and GBV survivors under the Khmer Rouge regime," ran from 2011 to 2014. Joint CSO participatory project design, implementation, and monitoring were largely described as a positive experience. Interviewees described monthly participatory management meetings as useful to build ties and collaborative action.[29]

Capacity-building opportunities can also be structured around proposal writing. Requests for proposals can be written in ways to ensure collaboration between partners, and which encourage positive and real cooperation, including mandatory joint proposals, monitoring, and evaluations. These may also include stipulations to encourage donor coordination. They can also address broader issues of integration of TJ activities into sustainable development practices. USAID's grouping TJ grantees, and conducting joint grantee meetings was considered valuable. USAID also included funding for one organization (TPO) to provide psychological counseling services to other cooperating organizations (YFP and ADHOC). This collaboration was written into agreements, so costs were covered and competition between organizations less likely.

[29] The project was renewed for a "Phase II" in 2015. The final evaluation of the first phase of the project is on the joint project web site, GBV under the Khmer Rouge web platform (gbvkr.org). See Julian Poluda, "Promoting Gender Equality and Improving Access to Justice for Female Survivors and Victims of Gender-Based Violence under the Khmer Rouge Regime: Final Evaluation Report" (February 2015), http://gbvkr.org/wp-content/uploads/2015/05/264-final-evaluation-report.pdf.

The Swedish donors Diakonia (not interviewed for this study, nor funding TJ) and ForumSyd were mentioned by several interviewees as examples of strong capacity building, as their approach is to give flexible long-term (ten year) funding to create CSOs that are able to change depending upon the needs of their grassroots populations, and mobilize to work directly with local populations on advocacy and awareness-raising. Scandinavian, especially Swedish, and German funding sources were also cited as being flexible in that changes in direction of projects could be made as lessons were learned in the field, which was seen as much more productive and sustainable than being strictly tied to inflexible outputs (as required by USAID) which are not able to take into consideration changing contexts.[30] These two Scandinavian donors (Diakonia and ForumSyd) were also mentioned by several interviewees as being able to work with small, less structured groups who may have innovative ideas they can implement with relatively small amounts of funding, yet are not able to manage complicated proposals or financial accounting. This flexible, small-project approach could be very useful in TJ projects of CSOs, for example such as TPO's mental health self-help groups, or support for minority or victim groups that lack structure.

Taken together, these efforts form the backbone of initiatives that have shifted CSOs along the power continuum toward true hybrid peacebuilding.

CIVIL SOCIETY – RISING FROM THE ASHES, WITH A LITTLE HELP FROM FRIENDS

Reduced donor funding over time, a lack of donor strategy, and the broader context of an authoritarian government often acting with impunity has affected civil society's ability to deeply engage in its work, particularly to maintain focus on victims and recovery. However, the outlook is not all bleak. CSOs have been able to overcome some of these challenges, in large part due to the consistent support of a few international donors and international CSOs. The majority of the CSOs involved in TJ have been supported by GIZ, and this support has facilitated a bottom-up approach for all CSOs in the field. GIZ's capacity-building components have been crucial in creating several organizations with much stronger structures. Three specific examples of this international support are discussed: first, the creation of CSO networks supported by international actors; second, the ECCC work on gender; and third, CSOs working with minorities.

Context

Cambodia is described as a post-conflict country, with a plethora of CSOs, most created after UNTAC's establishment: while some sources estimate the existence of some 3,500

30 Other funders such as Danida, the EU, and the UK may also demonstrate positive learning examples, but as some of these projects are no longer ongoing, detailed interviews were not possible with all donors and aid recipients.

NGOs, the RGC Council for Development in Cambodia reported as registered approximately 200 international NGOs, 400 local CSOs, and 600 associations, and the main umbrella organization for CSOs counts 1,350.[31] Most of the CSOs working on TJ activities have come from the human rights field, and as outlined earlier, human rights CSOs have long had an antagonistic relationship with the government.

Before the KR regime, some vestigial associations were related to the Buddhist temples and farming cooperatives, and between 1979 and 1991 (under the PRK and the State of Cambodia) there were strong state-sponsored associations (women's, youths', farmers', among others). A more open civil society did not begin, however, until the early 1990s with the arrival of UNTAC. CSOs are now notoriously aid-dependent, with very few of them able to develop revenue-producing approaches, and the populations with little experience or interest in paying membership fees. The aid dependency is also affected by traditional patron–client relationships in Cambodia, as this quote from a civil society actor shows:

> The patron–client relationships impact development partners and civil society relationships, and those between the international community and the people. Donors are seen as patrons for CSOs, and it is very difficult to break out of that model, framed and implemented now for a long time. How long can it take to see a stimulus of grassroots initiatives really coming from those people rather than being driven from outside?

CSOs in Cambodia are also notoriously personality driven, and many have been unsuccessful in implementing a sustainable organizational plan to develop middle management and plans for succession – this is partly due to the poor education system and dearth of educated middle-aged Cambodians due to the population and institutional losses during the KR period and many years of civil war. Recently, a higher number of younger people have benefited from improved standards of education at a handful of more reputable universities in Cambodia, or through obtaining advanced degrees or certificates outside the country.[32] There is thus much hope in the next generations.

CSOs working on TJ have operated in a difficult political climate, particularly at the beginning stages of the ECCC and TJ activities. Several interviewees stated that issues related to the KR were sensitive and should be avoided. This was partially due

[31] See, in relative order: "Helena Domashneva, NGOs in Cambodia: It's Complicated," *The Diplomat*, December 3, 2013, thediplomat.com/2013/12/ngos-in-cambodia-its-complicated; "III. General NGO Information," RGC Council for Development in Cambodia (no date), www.cdc-crdb.gov.kh/cdc/ngo_statement/general_ngo_information.htm; Louise Coventry, Menh Navy, and Alison Hillis, "Assessment of the Enabling Environment for Civil Society" (Phnom Penh: Cooperation Committee for Cambodia, 2013), www.ccc-cambodia.org/downloads/publications/EENA_report_FINAL-CCC-CIVICUS_EN.pdf.

[32] DCCam has been particularly successful in finding master's and PhD programs for its staff, now claiming to have sixty graduated or close to graduation. GIZ has also included training and higher education funding in its long-term TJ funding, which has increased the capacity of several key CSO staff members.

to the fact that several former KR serve in the current government, and two interviewees spoke of situations when civil society actors were questioned by authorities, and their activities had to be cancelled. One interviewee reported that a request to the government for support related to KR issues resulted in threatening phone calls to local staff members. This same interviewee also reported that KR-related CSO activities in communities with former KR in positions of power had resulted in threats to the individuals involved at the community level. A few civil society interviewees also mentioned resistance to including projects to address the KR past in more general programs related to women's affairs and mental health.

TJ activities, especially at the grassroots level, are also affected by the perception that any development work may be seen as sensitive, especially in the context of elections in July 2013, after which there were large-scale demonstrations on land and labor rights, as well as ongoing political unrest. While most TJ CSOs have requested permission at the village, commune, district, and/or provincial levels for their activities, the underlying tension between CSOs and government persists, as does fear that the government may shut down CSOs (which has happened in the past, and has increased in 2016 and 2017). Up until 2014, few TJ CSOs had worked on projects directly with the government at the central level, except for the psychosocial support organization TPO, and for DCCam, which works closely with the state-run Tuol Sleng Museum and with the Ministry of Culture and Fine Arts.[33] In any case, it is clear that CSOs operate in Cambodia under significant threat – both to their organizations and at a personal level.

Civil Society Networks – Influenced by International Actors

The TJ field remains dominated by DCCam, which unfortunately has maintained distance from the rest of the CSOs. DCCam's networks have been maintained for decades, but they are internal, first consisting of civil parties, victims, and perpetrators in the country, and second consisting of volunteers and advisors from outside the country. Nonetheless, several other TJ actors developed their own networks, through formal and informal meetings of organizations working on common issues, which have served various purposes. GIZ's CPS has fostered networks through its multiyear work with CSOs, as discussed earlier. Other CSOs have also worked jointly, for example CHRAC, which maintained an ECCC subgroup since well before the start of the ECCC. In addition, OSJI began the first multilevel, multidisciplinary, multi-partnered network as the ECCC was being created in 2004, which the ECCC took over once the PAS and the VSS became functional. However, while CSOs appreciated the ECCC's coordination efforts, there were also times when CSO advocacy was in contradiction to the ECCC's (government) interests, so separate CSO meetings were still seen as necessary.

[33] However, with the implementation of several reparations projects through the ECCC's VSS, greater engagement with the Tuol Sleng Museum and other state bodies was beginning.

This experience can be a model for other international and hybrid courts, whereby CSOs begin coordination before formal proceedings, then the court takes over – yet CSOs continue their own coordination networks separately. These networks could be further enhanced and sustained by effective and competent local leadership, by developing supportive structures, and through the use of modern technologies (cell phones and Facebook, for example). These civil society TJ networks have been longer-lasting and more effective in Cambodia when there has been committed leadership such as the initial CHRAC network in the early years of enthusiasm around the newly forming ECCC. In addition, the networks have proved more effective when they have had sufficient mandates, personnel, and funding to organize the meetings, rent meeting rooms, provide refreshments, and assist with follow-up (such as CHRAC, OSJI, and ECCC networks).

The presence of international CSOs (such as the International Center for Transitional Justice [ICTJ] and OSJI) focusing on TJ was remarked upon by both CSOs and donors as being helpful in providing technical assistance to local CSOs, and strengthening civil society networks. Furthermore, important inroads have been made in improving the strained relationships between human rights organizations and the government, through the existence of these joint projects, some of which are with the quasi-governmental VSS. The CSOs and the ECCC employees hired by the government started working together more often and have been building relationships that had been previously characterized by deep mistrust. Although the CSO networks have ebbed and flowed over time, a core group of actors has remained relatively consistent, especially those supported by steady international actors. However, the reductions in overall TJ and human rights funding have threatened the existence of some CSOs, so the networks have been changing as various CSOs become weaker. The tensions within and between the various CSOs, and between them and the organs of the ECCC have required multiple negotiations, and resulted in changing dynamics of these fungible networks.

In spite of these fluctuations and tensions, relationships between individuals working in the TJ field have generally been strengthened over time (and at least partly due to the presence of the various networks as well as to the presence of international CSOs and donor funding, and may continue to improve. The individuals from local CSOs have now worked together in multiple networks and projects, and many have developed close relationships (notwithstanding the common phenomenon of imploding CSOs over funding or personal disputes). Social media has enhanced these relationships, as the majority of Cambodians communicate frequently via Facebook or other Web-based forums.

GENDER ISSUES: MARGINALIZED IN CAMBODIA, BUT CHAMPIONED BY INTERNATIONAL VOICES AT THE EXTRAORDINARY CHAMBERS IN THE COURTS OF CAMBODIA

Frictions between the local and international interactions on gender have resulted in a prominent place for SGBV around the KR past in Cambodia. These frictions are particularly evident when cultural views of women expressed by especially some older CSO and ECCC personnel come into direct conflict with the human rights norms related to gender. The inclusion of SGBV issues in the ECCC is also reflected in the clash between local over international (bottom-up) approaches, versus the donor over local (top-down) approaches of most international assistance. Those most opposed to these changing norms within Cambodian society seem to ignore the new standards, continuing to publicly express traditional views with a blind eye to the contradictions, or by vigorously defending their views through the cultural relativity argument.

Gender issues at the ECCC have mainly been raised by international actors (including donors, court staff, and international CSOs), who have been focusing on general awareness-raising of SGBV under the KR (and in society today); the inclusion of SGBV (particularly forced marriage) as a crime in the ECCC; and the need for increased gender awareness at the ECCC. The grant mentioned earlier to the VSS, CDP, and TPO from the UN Trust Fund to End Violence against Women has provided support for the inclusion of SGBV and gender awareness, and some training on gender has been provided to the ECCC and some CSOs by OSJI and ICTJ. Several key international advisors led a coordinated strategy on gender issues to instigate the "Women's Hearings" – held in 2011, 2012, and 2013 in Cambodia[34] – and then to advocate for the inclusion of SGBV as crimes in the ECCC, in addition to other advocacy and awareness-raising campaigns. The first hearing was focused on SGBV during the KR, the second hearing expanded testimony about SGBV regionally, and the target group for the third was the post-violence generation in Cambodia. These hearings have been widely praised as breaking the silence about SGBV in Cambodia – during the KR period as well as in society today. Attended by more than 1,000 participants, the three hearings have enabled individuals who testified to have their suffering and courage acknowledged and to express their demands.[35]

34 See Cambodian Defenders Project, "Report on the Proceedings of the 2011 Women's Hearing on Sexual Violence under the Khmer Rouge Regime" (Phnom Penh: Cambodian Defenders Project, 2011), gbvkr.org/wp-content/uploads/2013/01/Report-on-2011-Womens-Hearing_Phnom-Penh.pdf; and Theresa de Langis, "Asia-Pacific Regional Women's Hearing on Gender-Based Violence in Conflict" (Phnom Penh: Cambodian Defenders Project, 2012), gbvkr.org/wp-content/uploads/2013/01/Asia-Pacific-Regional-Womens-Hearing-on-GBV-in-Conflict-2012-Report.pdf.

35 Beini Ye, "Transitional Justice through the Cambodian Women's Hearings," *Cambodia Law and Policy Journal* 2 (2014): 23–38, cambodialpj.org/wp-content/uploads/2014/05/DCCAM_CLPJ_Ye.pdf.

WORKING WITH MINORITIES: A RESULT OF THE EXTRAORDINARY CHAMBERS IN THE COURTS OF CAMBODIA?

There is a strong, historical, visceral racism by Cambodians against Vietnamese, which since the 1990s has been whipped up by the opposition parties (first the Sam Rainsy Party and then the coalition Cambodia National Rescue Party), using racism as a platform to gain popularity. While the larger human rights groups have worked toward the rights of the Vietnamese minority, these actions were not always viewed positively by the population (or by many of their own staff members). Part of this popular negative reaction to Vietnam is related to the government's close relationship to the country, and the perception that Cambodia's borders are being impinged upon. The racism against Vietnamese has also affected TJ activities, as, for example, the Vietnamese (and to a lesser degree the Khmer Krom)[36] minority civil parties at the ECCC claiming reparations against the KR leaders for acts of genocide are not widely supported by the majority Khmer civil parties, their lawyers, or some of the CSOs. As a result, only a handful of CSOs have started working over the past few years with minority Vietnamese in Cambodia.

Although the main Khmer Krom CSO is headed by a person of Khmer Krom ethnicity who has strong personal feelings about advocating for the group, the other main CSO working on both TJ issues and Vietnamese issues has, in taking on this sensitive topic, likely been influenced first by international actors in the peacebuilding field, and more recently, by the inclusion of the charges of genocide against ethnic Vietnamese as a minority group within the context of the ECCC. Taken in a vacuum, most Cambodians on their own (investigators, prosecutors, and CSO staff) would probably not have chosen to prosecute the issue of the Vietnamese minority at the ECCC, and the inclusion of this issue may be attributed to international influence. Legal experts concluded that the victim participation of ethnic Vietnamese in the ECCC had opened broader discussions about minority human rights issues, including ethnic Vietnamese access to Cambodian nationality and their request for collective and moral reparations.[37]

CONCLUSION

Thirty years passed between the end of the KR regime in early 1979 and the start of ECCC trials in 2008. This long time lapse in which memories faded, witnesses died,

[36] Kampuchea Krom or Khmer Krom people are ethnic Cambodians who were or are living in southwestern Vietnam, in the Mekong Delta area. The area used to be part of the Khmer Empire until the early eighteenth century, and Khmer Krom speak the Cambodian (Khmer) language, though the government of Vietnam does not recognize their minority group status.

[37] Lyma Nguyen and Christoph Sperfeldt, "Victim Participation and Minorities in Internationalised Criminal Trials: Ethnic Vietnamese Civil Parties at the Extraordinary Chambers in the Courts of Cambodia," *Macquarie Law Journal* 14 (2014): 97–126.

and desire for justice decreased among some, has made the justice component of TJ a challenge to administer. At the same time, those thirty years allowed for a UN peace process, the burgeoning of civil society, and the development of TJ norms and processes, thus creating an environment in Cambodia for the ECCC and complementary TJ memory and reconciliation processes to occur. However, the origin of the majority of the TJ CSOs in the human rights world with the support of the Western democracies has created friction (if not a clash) with the powerful, conservative, rent-seeking Cambodian government. International assistance and CSOs have had to carefully negotiate their way around these tensions.

This chapter has shown that international assistance to TJ in Cambodia has had mixed results. It has been hampered by the voluntary structure of contributions to the ECCC, donor personnel's lack of knowledge of TJ principles and processes, the separation of funding streams for the ECCC versus related CSO TJ activities, the dwarfing of funds to CSOs in comparison to the ECCC, a lack of knowledge *within* donor agencies of what different departments are funding and monitoring, and donor fatigue.

Nonetheless, international assistance has provided important inputs to TJ mechanisms for civil society, and the ECCC itself would never have happened without donors taking initiative. Direct assistance to CHRAC provided as the ECCC was being established (first by the National Endowment for Democracy and then by other donors), assisted in network support and relationship building between civil society actors, and between civil society and the ECCC. It was also crucial for advocacy and monitoring of the ECCC in its development stages and through its initial trial. Additional support to the CHRAC network provided by international CSOs (OSJI and ICTJ) provided important technical support to CHRAC and its partners, which significantly enhanced knowledge and capacity in the field of TJ.

While some donors have been significantly lacking in strategy, others, notably GIZ, have worked quietly and over a long period to build the capacity of its grantees. Its CPS-led TJ strategy – which integrated various aspects of TJ writ large (in this case, reconciliation, youth/elder dialogue, the arts, victim support, mental health, media, and journalism), together with a bottom-up approach of relating closely to local CSOs – is an ideal example of productive engagements. However, this effective and high-impact model may be impossible to duplicate elsewhere because of the long time commitment required.

International assistance has also, to an extent, enhanced civil society actors' leverage with respect to the ECCC. For example, international actors promoting the inclusion of gender aspects/SGBV in the ECCC and the rights of the Vietnamese ethnic minorities are proof of this leveraged power in creating new engagements. As a result of these interventions, various populations (such as SGBV survivors and Vietnamese minorities) allied with more powerful CSO actors have been able to claim the social and political space that opened up to achieve greater access to their rights[38] – a complex network of CSOs has been able to effect change, but this has been possible only because of support from a few engaged international actors.

On a more general note, this chapter shows how frictions across time (French colonial history, the US war in Vietnam, the Lon Nol period, the Eastern Bloc versus Western Bloc competition, the UNTAC period, and decades of foreign assistance since 1992) and across cultures (US, French, British, German, Japanese, Vietnamese, and others versus Cambodian) have contributed to the development of new interconnections. The most significant of these is the presence of civil parties at the ECCC – the first in history and acclaimed by many as an important positive judicial development (though far less ambitious than initially conceptualized, and not without its problems).[39] The origins of the Cambodian legal system in the French system have allowed a greater voice for victims in this TJ process; this has been cited as a model for the ICC. In addition, the presence of international actors has resulted in significant improvements in technical skills of younger Cambodian ECCC personnel.[40] As the Cambodian court staff and CSOs were able to see the longer hours, the greater attention to detail, the sophisticated computer use, the forward-thinking problem-solving, and other skills of the foreign staff, greater efficiencies have been achieved. The foreign staff have also been indelibly marked by their participation in Cambodia, seeing the perseverance and resilience of the Cambodians in the face of their horrific past.

All this said, the ECCC was and remains donors' main focal point for TJ in Cambodia – with the result that (the relatively little) donor interest in funding civil society actors working on TJ has ebbed and flowed with the performance of the ECCC. As the ECCC became bogged down in problems of funding, political interference, and corruption allegations, support for CSOs and TJ networks correspondingly declined, and the aid-dependent CSOs found difficulties mobilizing new sources of funding (except for some new funding streams from the United States). CSOs have also not maintained previous levels of cooperation between themselves as their activities have decreased. Since the guilty verdict announced by the ECCC on August 7, 2014, Case 002/02 created a steady of stream of news reports up until the evidentiary hearings ended in January 2017. Meanwhile, reports about

38 It is notable that a particular group in Cambodia – victims – has not been able to rise up and claim space as victims have in many other countries. This is probably due to the fact that almost every Cambodian can be named a victim, and the coalescing of such a large group was too difficult – especially in the context of the authoritarian RGC.

39 Eric Stover, Mychelle Balthazard, and Alexa Koenig, "Confronting Duch: Civil Party Participation in Case 001 at the Extraordinary Chambers in the Courts of Cambodia," *International Review of the Red Cross* 93, no. 882 (2011): 503–46.

40 Open Society Justice Initiative, "Performance and Perception: The Impact of the Extraordinary Chambers in the Courts of Cambodia" (New York: Open Society Justice Initiative. 2011), www.opensocietyfoundations.org/sites/default/files/performance-perception-eccc-20160211.pdf.

the controversial Cases 003 and 004 created occasional news blips. Finding funding for TJ activities remains challenging for both donors and CSOs.

With the lessons of history, both CSOs and donors would do well to take time to consider strategies of TJ and its relationship to impunity and the rule of law. The human rights situation now in 2017 is arguably the worst it has been since 1997. And in spite of international assistance to TJ, the links between impunity in the past and the present have not been made, as the government continues to trample citizens' rights.

PART II

Conceptualizing the Connections

6

Reframing Friction

A Four-Lens Framework for Explaining Shifts, Fractures, and Gaps in Transitional Justice

Christalla Yakinthou

Transitional justice (TJ) is a field based on the premise that violent legacies of conflict or authoritarianism must be held up to the light, understood, and to the largest extent possible repaired in order to rebuild trust between citizens, and between citizens and their institutions of state. Advocates argue that if this is not done, the past, and its physical, structural, social, and/or economic manifestations of violence, will continue to undermine a society's efforts to construct a democratic, inclusive, just society. It is a field given increasing salience in peacebuilding processes, and one that requires, for its success, interaction between stakeholders and supporters from across the spectrum, including international actors who fund TJ work; technical experts and specialists; domestic governments at multiple levels; various professions, including security sectors, the judiciary, the civil service, and education; civil society groups both international and those from within a society; survivors and victims (both aligned and unaligned to civil society and activist groups); the media in its various forms; historians; activists; political parties; and the list goes on. The process itself is now heavily professionalised. It is guided by various best practice formats that encourage inclusion of multiple voices, particularly at the planning and early stages of TJ, where the harms, and the methods for addressing these harms, are usually decided. While the engagements that shape the choice (and longer-term success) of TJ "tools" are infrequently transparent, the TJ mechanisms that are chosen, and their outcomes, are often presented as self-evident.

The introduction of this book has outlined why we have chosen to focus on the interactions between international actors – specifically bilateral and multilateral donors – and civil society. This chapter posits that for a field so deeply based (in theory) on collaboration, inclusion, and victim-centred justice, the relationships, tensions, and processes that guide or undermine key decisions over priorities and strategies for engagement and sustainability of those efforts are understudied and

My thanks to Paige Arthur, Nicolas Lemay-Hebert, Nicholas Wheeler, and Stefan Wolff for their (often multiple) readings of and reflections on this chapter, and to Paige Arthur, Laura McGrew, Anita Isaacs, and Rachel Schwartz for their comments and thoughtful reflections on my interpretation of their case studies.

underappreciated. In fact, few theoretical frameworks can bring light to the complex interrelationships between the TJ norms of right to justice, truth, repair, and non-repetition and their implementation in the world.

ALL TRANSITIONAL JUSTICE IS HYBRID (SO NOW WHAT?)

Hybridity is one of the few theories that looks to understand the role of power, agency, and change in TJ, and it is a conceptual tool that is undergoing a great deal of revision in the literatures through which it has travelled. Its central focus is describing and explaining the circulation of power between constituent actors; in this regard, the lines between hybridity and friction (discussed later in this chapter) are often blurred. Richmond and Mitchell understand the study of hybridity to involve "a range of practices, responses and agencies – including plural forms of acceptance and appropriation, resistance and the exertion of autonomy."[1] The term, its analytical relevance, and its evolution have been the subject of vast debates;[2] characterised by Marwan Kraidy as an "academic stampede,"[3] and used, sometimes interchangeably, as both a *descriptive* and *prescriptive* term.[4] The concept itself came out of postcolonial theory and race and cultural studies,[5] and it arose in part to escape unhelpful binaries and to encourage thinking about "the multiplicity of outcomes that might occur when two entities meet and interact."[6]

While hybridity is a theory that to some extent has become trapped in its own contradictions, the problems it seeks to foreground are pertinent to our work. The liberal peacebuilding paradigm has created an arguably false dichotomy of interactions and actors; most relevant to this book are the dichotomies between the

1 Oliver Richmond and Audra Mitchell, "Towards a Post-liberal Peace: Exploring Hybridity via Everyday Forms of Resistance, Agency and Autonomy," in *Hybrid Forms of Peace: From Everyday Agency to Post-Liberalism*, ed. Oliver Richmond and Audra Mitchell (London: Palgrave, 2012), 1.

2 See Oliver Richmond, "Becoming Liberal, Unbecoming Liberalism: Liberal-Local Hybridity via the Everyday as a Response to the Paradoxes of Liberal Peacebuilding," in *Rethinking the Liberal Peace: External Models and Local Alternatives*, ed. Sharnbanou Tadjbakhsh (London: Routledge, 2011); Edward Newman, "Liberal Peacebuilding Debates," in *New Perspectives on Liberal Peacebuilding*, ed. Edward Newman, Roland Paris, and Oliver Richmond (New York: United Nations University Press, 2009); and Anne Brown, Volker Boege, Kevin Clemens, and Anna Nolan, "Challenging State Building as Peacebuilding: Working with Hybrid Political Orders to Build Peace," in *Palgrave Advances in Peacebuilding: Critical Developments and Approaches*, ed. Oliver Richmond (London: Palgrave, 2010).

3 Marwan M. Kraidy, *Hybridity, or the Cultural Logic of Globalization* (Philadelphia. PA: Temple University Press, 2005), 2.

4 Gearoid Millar, "Disaggregating Hybridity: Why Hybrid Institutions Do Not Produce Predictable Experiences of Peace," *Journal of Peace Research*, 51, no. 4 (2014): 501–14.

5 As a key author of the term, see the work of Homi K. Bhabha, *The Location of Culture* (Abingdon: Routledge, 2004).

6 See Jenny H. Peterson, "A Conceptual Unpacking of Hybridity: Accounting for Notions of Power, Politics and Progress in Analyses of Aid-Driven Interfaces," *Journal of Peacebuilding and Development*, 7, no. 2 (2012): 12; Millar, "Disaggregating Hybridity"; and Kraidy, *Hybridity*.

"international" and "local," and (sometimes synonymously) "modern" and "traditional," or "top-down" and "bottom-up":

> As Goodale has observed, outside of the academic and policy literature, there is no place called "local" or "global" – any more than there is an "international plane," an "international community," or places called "on the ground" and "in the field," yet these concepts are often spoken of as if they actually existed. The global-local binary is also problematic insofar as it implies that there are only two levels at which social processes emerge or unfold, and insofar as it implicitly invokes a normative hierarchy and teleology. Thus, both categories tend to essentialize and depoliticize sets of actors that are neither ideologically monolithic nor politically homogenous.[7]

Most important for us is the recognition that while binary categories are largely artificial constructs and have limited conceptual resonance beyond the borders of policy and academia, the flattening of landscapes in such ways as those illustrated earlier has real implications for peacebuilding (and TJ) programming and goals. Donor funding structures and preferences themselves tend to replicate these simplified and depoliticised notions.[8]

It is, broadly speaking, out of these struggles that the concept of hybridity arose. The literature that has developed in response to these binary notions has gone in two primary directions: the first is to refocus on the agency of the "local" and to interrogate the broad spectrum of interactions between different levels of cultural, legal, and institutional legitimacy;[9] the second orients towards theories that focus on a broader landscape of social orders beyond this binary.[10] While the case studies in this book generally focus on two binary categories of actors, we are looking at the working *in* and *between* specific spaces (both geographical and contextual). In this book, we work within the confines of a language that has a recognised tendency to flatten the landscape of understanding we hold about the actors, actions, interactions, and consequences. We are aware, however, that this does not and indeed

[7] Dustin Sharp, "Transitional Justice and Liberal Post-Conflict Governance: Synergies and Symmetries, Frictions and Contradictions," *Grotius Centre for International Legal Studies* (PhD diss., Leiden University, 2016), 52.

[8] See Thania Paffenholz, "Civil Society," in *Post-Conflict Peacebuilding: A Lexicon*, ed. Vincent Chetail (Oxford: Oxford University Press, 2009); and Willemijn Verkoren and Mathijs van Leeuwen, "Civil Society in Peacebuilding: Global Discourse, Local Reality," *International Peacekeeping*, 20, no. 2 (2013): 159–72.

[9] Nicolas Lemay-Herbert and Rosa Freedman, "Critical Hybridity: Exploring Cultural, Legal and Political Pluralism," in *Hybridity: Law, Culture and Development*, ed. Nicolas Lemay-Herbert and Rosa Freedman (Abingdon: Routledge, 2017), 320. See also Francesco Colona and Rivke Jaffe "Hybrid Governance Arrangements," *European Journal of Development Research* 28, no. 2 (2016): 175–83; and Richmond and Mitchell, "Towards a Post-liberal Peace."

[10] Lemay-Herbert and Freedman, "Critical Hybridity," 320. See also David Roberts, "Hybrid Polities and Indigenous Pluralities: Advanced Lessons in Statebuilding from Cambodia," *Journal of Intervention and Statebuilding* 2, no. 1 (2008): 63–86; Peter Albrecht and Louise Wiuff Moe, "The Simultaneity of Authority in Hybrid Orders," *Peacebuilding* 3, no. 1 (2015): 1–16.

cannot capture the full picture. It is in these efforts to describe dynamics beyond the binary that the concepts of hybridity and friction intervene.

Hybridity theory moved into the orbit of TJ as particular events precipitated the introduction of mixed approaches to (especially, but not only) criminal prosecutions processes. Over the early 2000s, TJ actors began to incorporate international and domestic legal norms, as well as mixing staff members within those mechanisms. Thus, mixed mechanisms became known as hybrid.[11] While in TJ terms we understand hybridity to refer to mixed approaches to programming or TJ mechanisms (hybrid courts, hybrid approaches to justice, hybrid structures of governance, etc.), the literature is developing along two axes: understanding hybridity as both a noun (actors and institutions),[12] and a verb (a behaviour).[13] Increasingly, the term is being used to analyse not only the *products* of power and legitimacy, but also, importantly, the *processes* – seeking to highlight some of the mostly invisible power differentials at a country's domestic level, and between different kinds of actors seeking to engage the support of international actors. In this regard, those who link the study of TJ and hybridity are also following broader trends in the literature on hybridity.

However, this debate within TJ is moot for a number of reasons. First, if one looks at its evolution over time, TJ was "born" hybrid. To this end (though speaking of globalisation), Naomi Roht-Arriaza notes that:

> From country to country ... a process of diffusion of experiences and ideas followed. Chileans advised the South Africans on their TRC; the South Africans inspired the idea of confession in exchange for amnesty or leniency in a number of places. Forensic scientists multiplied exhumation and forensic teams, using newly minted techniques around the world. The peace agreement drafters designed the Guatemalan Historical Clarification Commission to *not* mimic aspects of the earlier Salvadoran Truth Commission.[14]

Indeed, the field itself is characterised by "a range of practices, responses and agencies – including plural forms of acceptance and appropriation, resistance and the exertion of autonomy,"[15] and in the ten years since this statement was written, such cross-learning has only become more embedded. What if, then, we were to

11 See, for example, Marieke Wierda and Caitlin Reiger, *"The Serious Crimes Process in Timor-Leste: In Retrospect"* (New York: International Center for Transitional Justice, 2006); and Tom Perriello and Marieke Wierda, *"Lessons from the Deployment of International Judges and Prosecutors in Kosovo"* (New York: International Center for Transitional Justice, 2006).

12 See, for example, the work of Chandra Sriram, "Post-Conflict Justice and Hybridity in Peacebuilding: Resistance or Cooptation?" in *Hybrid Forms of Peace*. Also see Phil Clark, "Hybridity, Holism, and 'Traditional Justice': The Case of the *Gacaca* Courts in Post-genocide Rwanda," *The George Washington International Law Review*, 39, no. 4 (2007): 765–837.

13 See, for example, Millar, "Disaggregating Hybridity"; Dustin Sharp, "Addressing Dilemmas of the Global and the Local in Transitional Justice," *Emory International Law Review* 29 (2014): 71–117.

14 Naomi Roht-Arriaza, "The New Landscape of Transitional Justice," in *Transitional Justice in the Twenty-First Century: Beyond Truth versus Justice*, ed. Naomi Roht-Arriaza and Javier Mariezcurrena (New York: Cambridge University Press, 2006), 5.

15 Richmond and Mitchell, "Towards a Post-liberal Peace," 1.

simply say that the development of the normative architecture of the field, as well as the structural factors that underpin it such as international aid and reliance on expert practitioners to "build the capacity" of domestic (usually human rights) actors, pushes us towards an acknowledgement that this field has hybridity in its DNA?[16]

And if this is so, if we can claim that *all TJ is hybrid* – and by this I mean its core concepts, its institutions, the way it is evolving over time, and the way it is funded and practiced – then we are freed to concentrate attention on what emerges. The existence – and embedding – of hybridity suggests that a process of engagement occurs between actors across all levels, and that a continuous negotiation is taking place. This reflection (though not new) is important, because it brings us back from assumptions about linear power relationships between "international" (or global) and "local" actors, and to thinking about how relationships between international actors and civil society create unexpected results, both regarding the outcomes of TJ processes and regarding the way we think about TJ's core concepts.

This brings us to the second reason for arguing that hybridity is not an adequate analytical framework for TJ interactions: while it has been argued that hybridity gives space to "understanding the active role aid participants play in the implementation and progress of programming,"[17] it cannot explain how that space comes about, how changes occur to the norms themselves, or the reasons that norms are implemented in particular ways. Hybridity explains the *context* of TJ, but it is unequipped to reveal the spectrum of outcomes that result from the (unequal) relationships between actors. It is here that the perspectives provided by the concept of friction – with its ability to focus on the *moments of interaction* between ideas and actors, and their outcomes – become important. In other words, friction can explain the ways in which hybridity manifests itself, and what those outcomes are.

Essentially, I see the difference as follows: the concept of hybridity aims for clarity of description (though this is not always managed), while that of friction aims to make the connections, engagements, and transformations transparent. Thus, I begin from the position that TJ is *by its nature a hybrid field*, but that hybridity cannot make the connections, engagements, and transformations within TJ transparent. As a result, this chapter uses the relational concept of friction to create a novel analytical framework to understand the data that has emerged from the five country studies of this book. More broadly, the framework is offered as a new way of revealing and interpreting relationships between international actors (in this case, donors) and civil society actors who do the work of TJ, and, importantly, the outcomes of those relationships.

This chapter is broken into two parts. Within *part one*, Anna Tsing's concept of friction is explained, and her work is used to build the theoretical framework for understanding the relationships between donor agencies funding TJ and civil society

16 My thanks to Paige Arthur for the discussion precipitating this claim.
17 Peterson, "A Conceptual Unpacking of Hybridity," 12.

actors on the receiving end of support. It draws out four themes resonant to TJ from Tsing's work: engaged universals and travelling packages; purification of conceptual and historical spaces; gatekeepers and the illusion of universals; and collaborations, shifts, and (co)imagining the universal ideal. *Part two* applies each of these four themes to the data that has emerged from the case studies in this book to explain how and why goals or institutions were pursued, redirected, and abandoned, and how, in this process, hierarchies of power were created and recreated and the consequences of such re/creations. In doing this, it offers a new way of thinking for donors, practitioners, and activists around TJ interactions, and a novel analytical framework for reflecting on many of the submerged and therefore opaque processes of engagement between actors in TJ, and the way the frictions between these processes and actors change both the TJ engagements in each context and the TJ norms themselves.

PART ONE: THEORETICAL LENS

Friction

In 2005, anthropologist Anna Tsing's field-shaping work on the co-production of cultures was published. In it, she contested the "clash of cultures" thesis of globalisation, instead using the decade of struggle around the commodification and reconstruction/destruction of the rainforests of Indonesia to argue that there are not "fixed" interactions that produce particular outcomes between solid groups of interested parties. Instead, she uses the term "friction," which she describes as "the awkward, unequal, unstable, and creative qualities of interconnection across difference"[18] to explain how inter/actions, misunderstandings, performances, and engagements lead in unpredictable ways to cycles of erasure and re/creation of knowledge, which both shape and are shaped by larger processes of cultural and economic change. The root of Tsing's work is to understand how culture and power are made and remade, in order to create room for possibilities of engagement for social and political change. One of the ways she illustrates this is through articulating in close detail the relationship(s) between universal ideals (think of freedom or democracy as examples) and their *in situ* application. Here, she speaks of the necessarily imperfect transfer of universal concepts; what she describes as "travelling packages." These travelling packages find their meaning in localised understandings, but the process of adoption changes both the understanding and the universal. Thus the universal, for Tsing, is itself a construct and a result of specific contexts.

In other words, Tsing uses the concept of friction to show the multiple and interrelated ways that "global trajectories come into being through specific histories of engagement and encounter."[19] Her focus is on undoing the notion that power is

[18] Tsing, *Friction*, 4. [19] Ibid., 6.

unidirectional and linear, and that universals are untouched or implementable as "virgin-born" ideals. Friction, here, can also be understood as an analytical or forensic tool: its purpose is to challenge the concept that ideas or results are stratified, one layer sitting cleanly above another. Instead, Tsing means for friction to show the full spectrum of movement and dis/engagement over time – between and within universals and their application, as well as between and within the various communities of people engaging with those universals and their enabling acts and movements.

Friction and Transitional Justice: Operationalising the Concepts

Our motivation for this book is, in part, to understand how TJ engagements or encounters between international actors and a country's civil society actors produce the results that they do. Underpinning this is the search for better ways of engaging, which gets us perhaps closer to the goal/s of creating more trustful, engaged, and safe societies after conflict or authoritarian rule. Thus, this section concentrates on setting out the core themes, drawn from Tsing's ideas, that are relevant to our work.

Tsing situates friction as a factor necessary to globalisation, something "required to keep global power in motion."[20] While most have focused on her idea of friction as the tool that shows "where the rubber meets the road," fewer have given attention to the second half of this description: "Roads create pathways that make motion easier and more efficient, but in doing so they limit where we go. The ease of travel they facilitate is also a structure of confinement. Friction inflects historical trajectories, enabling, excluding, and particularizing."[21] For us, and this book, friction is useful because it reveals *both* what is facilitated and what is constrained and rerouted. To this end, four threads of Tsing's work are of interest for understanding relationships between donors and civil society in TJ contexts. They are outlined directly in what follows, and used in part two to explain the findings of our case studies.

Engaged Universals and Travelling Packages: The Transfer of Transitional Justice

First, and most broadly speaking, Tsing's use of friction to reflect on the tension of universals and the way those universals "travel" through geographies and time are relevant to a field based on the transfer of four very clear universals: the core rights to truth, justice, repair, and non-recurrence upon which TJ is based. It is worth elaborating here on her articulation of knowledge and claims of universality. She argues:

> Universals are effective within particular historical conjunctures that give them content and force. We might specify this conjunctural feature of universals by speaking of engagement. Engaged universals travel across difference and are charged and changed by their travels. Through friction, universals become practically effective. Yet they can never fulfil their promise of universality. Even in

[20] Ibid., 6. [21] Ibid., 6.

> transcending localities, they do not take over the world. They are limited by the practical necessity of mobilizing adherents ... *All* universals are engaged when considered as practical projects accomplished in a heterogeneous world.[22]

The struggle between the universal and the engagement of that universal is one that has particular resonance in the TJ context. Think, for example, about the translation of the right to truth into truth commissions, or the right to justice into criminal prosecution programmes. And think also of the comprehensive criticism of the translation of those universals into what has been variously described as "toolkit TJ,"[23] as well as criticisms that TJ, as it is formulated, "steals the pain of victims."[24] The flattening of interconnected (temporal and geographic) landscapes before, during, and after conflict, and the self-conscious need in TJ to recover submerged truths is a more specific example of a "travelling package"; having arrived from traditionally post-authoritarian (mostly Latin American) contexts of widespread suppression of a particular group of people by a government, and transferred to post-conflict contexts, which often entail a quite different mishandling of truths.

Tsing's concern with the continuous relationship(s) between interactions and shifted interpretations of the universal is also relevant here, as understandings of reform are sometimes reframed or at least rearticulated within a TJ framework, even when they originate and define themselves independently of that framework, or even when the framework may not be relevant.[25] In these cases, the universal absorbs work under other guises, but in that absorption, the universal itself is altered.

Purifying Conceptual and Historical Spaces: Transitional Justice's Selective Focuses

Tsing's work uses the multiplicity of interdependent living spaces in the Meratus rainforests to dwell on the ways in which interconnected landscapes are flattened, imagined, and (re)cast as unidimensional to legitimise an industry of logging for profit. Much of the book is founded on explaining how, in order for the Indonesian government to create a context where Japanese and Indonesian loggers could legitimately harvest "'uninhabited' forest landscapes," there needed to be a reimagining of the landscape as a "pure stand ... [emptying] the forest, conceptually, of human residents," as well as of the diverse species that exist alongside the loggable dipterocarps (the source of plywood), "since the fruit orchards, rattans, and other human-tended plants of

22 Ibid., 6.

23 See, for example, Habib Nassar, "Transitional Justice in the Wake of the Arab Uprisings: Between Complexity and Standardization," in *Transitional Justice and the Arab Spring*, ed. Kirsten J. Fisher and Robert Stewart (Abingdon: Routledge, 2014).

24 Tshepo Madlingozi, "On Transitional Justice Entrepreneurs and the Production of Victims," *Journal of Human Rights Practice* 2, no. 2 (2010): 12.

25 See, for example, Christalla Yakinthou and Sky Croeser, "Transforming Tunisia: Transitional Justice and Internet Governance in a Post-revolutionary Society," *International Journal of Transitional Justice* 10, no. 2 (2016): 230–49.

forest dwellers were now mere waste."[26] This purification, or recasting, of space has a specific result that Tsing is concerned with: its cleansing for profit and the legitimisation of profit-making endeavours.

In a similar way, there is a connection between the reimagining of space – be that legal, historical, or geographic – and diagnosing a conflict-related problem while sidestepping colonial legacies and postcolonial (re)constructions and/or domestic and foreign policy needs. For example, the pursuit of mechanisms such as hybrid courts, truth commissions, and other "ad hoc" spaces sit uncomfortably alongside (or on top of) indigenous means of making sense of harms, often writing over the existing landscape. This, in turn, forces a need for multiple parties to create new understandings of the original event/s, their interpretation/s, and the mechanisms that can best address these harms. Donors, for example, may need to tell a story to their constituents or stakeholders about why a truth commission is needed, and subsequently why it appears to exist in a bubble without impact in communities. Victim-survivors – such as those about whom Rosalind Shaw writes in her work on Sierra Leone[27] – will try to fit the truth commission into cultural understandings of the value of silence or of catharsis, or/and integrate its meaning into a need for social assistance (for example).

More generally, before TJ approaches are determined, it is likely that a collection of international and domestic actors will participate in a struggle over defining the cause and legacy priorities of the conflict.[28] The process of designing TJ priorities in a country is itself part of the "forest clearing": for example, it is international best practice to hold national consultations before a TJ process begins.[29] Almost invariably, these consultations draw significantly from the travelling packages outlined earlier for their framing, and on international experts for their implementation. A recent example of national consultations processes heavily shaping TJ endeavours can be found in Tunisia, where the process itself has been suggested, framed, advised, and funded by international agencies. Consultations, while largely inclusive, were also framed in heavily technical language and conducted in a format that excluded those victims the process was set up to address. Any serious discussion of accountability for international actors who helped keep Ben Ali in place, and corporations that funded his surveillance machinery, has also been definitively off the table.[30] Here, the universals are in formation, and their politics are hidden.

[26] Tsing, *Friction*, 15.

[27] Rosalind Shaw, "Memory Frictions: Localizing the TRC in Sierra Leone," *International Journal of Transitional Justice* 1 (2007): 183–207.

[28] This usually happens directly after transition (though in more recent contexts such as Syria, the struggle over what should be prioritised is well under way).

[29] See, for example, Office of the High Commissioner for Human Rights, "*Rule of Law Tools for Post-conflict States: National Consultations on Transitional Justice*" (New York and Geneva: Office of the High Commissioner for Human Rights), 14–17, accessible at www.ohchr.org/Documents/Publications/NationalConsultationsTJ_EN.pdf.

[30] For support, see Yakinthou and Croeser, "Transforming Tunisia"; Arnaud Kurze, Christopher Lamont, and Simon Robins, "Contested Spaces of Transitional Justice: Legal Empowerment in Global Post-conflict Contexts Revisited," *The International Journal of Human*

In foregrounding the roles of colonialism, postcolonialism, and neocolonialism, Tsing dwells on the interplay between the creation of the universal and the denial of that process of construction; what I term the "virgin birth" notion. This aspect of friction speaks to critiques of how the practice of TJ is stripped of its political genesis, and especially how history is often smoothed over in order to ignore both the deeper legacies that embedded the seeds of violence and the wider structural violations of communal and economic rights.

Gatekeepers and the Illusion of Universals: Donors, Experts, and the Mutations of Applied Transitional Justice

But what we also hear in Tsing's work is a critique relevant to the gatekeepers of TJ, and particularly the practice of TJ.[31] Gatekeeping can be understood as "the process by which an individual or group controls access to goods and services but particularly to information and people with power."[32] It is important to note here that I also see donors as gatekeepers, particularly because they directly control access to resources. In reflecting on this tension between the universal and the particular, Tsing argues that "those who claim to be in touch with the universal are notoriously bad at seeing the limits and exclusions of their knowledge."[33] In other words, she foregrounds a disconnect between the architects of the universal and the travelling of that universal. This, we will see in what follows, may also be relevant to the analysis of our country case studies. Taking this idea further, Tsing highlights the importance of "contingent and botched encounters in shaping both business-as-usual and its radical refusals."[34] These encounters, while different to the intention, undergo unnoticed mutations, which both "forge ... new gaps" and create spaces for productive collaborations.[35]

Tshepo Madlingozi's work on TJ entrepreneurs and the reproduction and disempowerment of victims may provide us with an easy translation from Tsing to relationships between international assistance and civil society. Though not focused on friction, Madlingozi highlights how human rights or TJ non-governmental organisation (NGO) and international actors speak on behalf of victims, thus essentially cashing in professionally and economically on the "value" of victim and survivor narratives. International actors or NGOs decide the priority and amount of support for victims and survivors, who do not speak for themselves to

Rights 19 (2015): 260–76; Domenica Preysing, *Transitional Justice in Post-revolutionary Tunisia: How the Past Shapes the Future* (Berlin: Springer VS, 2015).

[31] Limited work exists on gatekeepers in TJ; however, the term is familiar in the human rights literature. See, for example, Bob Clifford, "New Human Rights Issues: Understanding Their Contentious Rise," *Colombia Internacional* 69 (2009): 14–35; Martti Koskenniemi, "Human Rights Mainstreaming as a Strategy for Institutional Power," *Humanity* 1, no. 1 (2010): 47–58; Lars Waldorf, "Getting the Gunpowder Out of Their Heads: The Limits of Rights-Based DDR," *Human Rights Quarterly* 35, no. 3 (2013): 701–19.

[32] "Gatekeeping," *Open Education Sociology Dictionary*, available at http://sociologydictionary.org/gatekeeping/.

[33] Tsing, *Friction*, 6. [34] Ibid., 272. [35] Ibid.

those in power. In other words, TJ gatekeepers "substitute emancipatory politics based on active citizenship with ... politics of demobilization and passivity reliant on 'state-delivery' or delivery by other institutions like NGOs whose mode of operation is, despite rhetoric to the contrary, overwhelmingly top-down."[36] Here we see that the botched encounter of TJ efforts to speak on behalf of victims, to block or regulate access of particular groups to those in power, and of TJ mechanisms like the South African Truth and Reconciliation Commission, created a gap that has been entered into by groups such as the South African victim- and survivor-led activist Khulumani Support Group. Khulumani has made active efforts to reshape the power asymmetries represented by gatekeepers such as experts and donors.[37]

Collaborations, Shifts, and (Co)imagining the Universal Ideal: Creating Alliances with "Mini-Me" Civil Society Organisations, and Disconnected Funding Frameworks

Tsing focuses on the process of friction creating collaborations that may not share common goals, and that may create new interests, but not necessarily with commensurate benefits for all parties involved:

> In transnational collaborations, overlapping but discrepant forms of cosmopolitanism may inform contributors, allowing them to converse – but across difference. Attention to collaboration moves discussion beyond the eternal standoff between opposing interest groups (e.g., the south and the north; the rich and the poor), but not because it assumes that compromise is always imminent ... In standardizing global knowledge, for example, truths that are incompatible are suppressed. Globally circulating knowledge creates new gaps even as it grows through the frictions of encounter.

This has both more and less productive possibilities. On the productive side, Tsing's work carefully describes the collaborations across power dynamics where groups come together to work in very different ways towards (sometimes accidentally) shared goals. Friction between ideas, interactions, and differing goals creates a process where, along the way towards the goal/s – in this case an end to logging – the collaborators influence and reshape one another's thinking and activism.

The work of Willemijn Verkoren and Mathijs van Leeuwen is instructive when considering the less productive side of such collaborations, particularly the privileging of particular voices.[38] In their work on peacebuilding and civil society, they note that while international expectations of civil society might not fit the context, implementing actors remain unwilling to let go of their expectations, causing frictional encounters. They offer descriptions of international actors attempting to

36 Madlingozi, "On Transitional Justice Entrepreneurs and the Production of Victims," 213.

37 Ibid.

38 The work of Thania Paffenholz is also important in this regard. Paffenholz discusses the phenomenon of donors privileging middle-class NGOs staffed by people with professional backgrounds: essentially, people who most closely resemble themselves. See Paffenholz, "Civil Society."

"tame" NGOs, particularly arguing that "donors are reluctant to support more politically oriented activities, which may jeopardize the 'neutrality' of NGOs and the relationships donors have with host governments";[39] thus depoliticising NGO work, reshaping it into something "uncritical of structural issues and power imbalances, whether domestically or internationally."[40] They argue that in the absence of a functional bureaucracy and trustworthy state, an unrealistic international expectation remains that NGOs that orient towards "global values" are necessarily the same NGOs that hold significant public legitimacy. Thus, there is a structural inability to work with "uncivil" NGOs that do not reject violence or harbour values such as inclusion, tolerance, equality, and so on. They highlight that while:

> intervening actors are increasingly aware of this tension ... they find themselves unable to compromise on their values. In practice, this means when faced with the choice between international and local legitimacy, they tend to choose the former ... [preferring] to work with organizations that resemble themselves, even if these have little local backing – as is often the case with local NGOs created in response to the availability of donor funds.[41]

As we will see in section two, a large part of this dilemma resonates with some of our case studies, where both donors and civil society representatives highlighted the artificiality and counter-productiveness of this form of support, but also the possibilities for productive collaboration across difference.

PART TWO: INTERPRETING THE DATA

Friction allows us to reframe the analysis beyond the "post-conflict" or "post-regime," to consider the in-between state of living, and to include in our understanding of TJ and how its priorities are set and implemented the messy engagements of colonial, hegemonic, and liberal paradigms.

This section therefore aims to reveal the interactions in the case studies that caused shifts, reformulated universals, and changed relationships. To this end, the four core ideas that come out of Tsing's work on friction will be used as analytical points for the case study analysis. That is, I will look to understand the data through the following four themes. The first, "engaged universals and travelling packages; the transfer of transitional justice," looks at the struggle between TJ universals of the rights to truth, justice, reparation, and non-repetition and the interactions and spaces of negotiation that result from the transportation of TJ mechanisms between geographies. The second, "purifying conceptual and historical spaces: transitional justice's selective focuses," foregrounds the political interests and historical factors that shape the choices and dimensions of TJ mechanisms, and reveals the stories that are shrunk and/or expanded to serve these goals. It also looks for factors that push against this selective spotlighting of narratives or time. The third, "gatekeepers and

39 Verkoren and Van Leeuwen, "Civil Society in Peacebuilding," 161. 40 Ibid. 41 Ibid., 164.

the illusion of universals: donors, experts, and the mutations of applied transitional justice," seeks to understand whether particular predispositions of gatekeepers shape particular TJ choices for the context they are advising or funding, and the extent to which these preferences are transparent. It focuses on what happens when these interventions are implemented and resisted, and how universal principles are reshaped through that process. The fourth, "collaborations, shifts, and (co)imagining the universal ideal: creating alliances with 'mini-me' CSOs, and disconnected funding frameworks," foregrounds the consequences of supporting particular civil society organisations (CSOs) and not others, and what results of forced collaborations of both CSOs and more generally. It also looks at how actors utilise particular universals and collaborations.

Engaged Universals and Travelling Packages: The Transfer of Transitional Justice

The concept of engaged universals and travelling packages may help explain why TJ mechanisms often create such large gaps between their articulation and their implementation, and help redirect our attention to the relationships and engagements that shape the outcomes we see. By way of an illustration drawn from the broader literature, Rosalind Shaw's work on truth commissions and Sierra Leone helps illustrate the travelling universal in the real world. Shaw offers an instructive analysis of the inter-rubbing of spaces:

> Just as "universals" never fully succeed in being universal, interventions are never fully realized as they were intended: when engaged in particular places with particular histories, they are invariably driven in unexpected directions ... Geopolitical and regional inequalities are changed but not neutralized through the local appropriation of globalizing and universalizing interventions.[42]

Shaw's work reflects on the interactions that shape Tsing's engaged universal, and draws down further to remind the reader how implementation of this engaged universal "can dissolve, unmake, and remake what 'transitional justice' actually *is* and how it works."[43] Using victim and survivor responses to the Sierra Leonean Truth and Reconciliation Commission (TRC), she shows the friction inherent in the remaking of narratives around the travelling universal of truth, and the engagement of the truth commission as an ideal-type redemptive tool across time and context. When this ideal and the surrounding narrative of "cleansing truth" were transferred to Sierra Leone, "the friction between local arts of forgetting and the TRC's transnational techniques of truth-telling was in some ways productive, creating new forms of remembering and forgetting";[44] here, "truth-telling became a new technique of forgetting."[45] At the same time, however, that productivity was limited, in that the TRC's ability to respond to the needs of victims remained extremely

[42] Shaw, "Memory Frictions," 186–87. [43] Ibid., 187. [44] Ibid., 207. [45] Ibid.

constrained, regardless of its transformation, and victims largely did not see it as having achieved its goal of providing justice or reconciliation.

In interesting ways, Uganda, Morocco, Guatemala, and Cambodia, and each reveal the political challenges of engaging universals in a context where genuine commitment from political leaderships is limited. In all of these cases, the struggle to mobilise adherents, to line them up on what the universal looks like in reality, and to agree on which of the collection of universals should have priority, has been characterised by struggle, disengagement, and contradiction – both between domestic political and international actors, and between grantees and donors.

Tania Bernath's chapter on Uganda demonstrates how universals do not always travel well together, particularly in complex environments and without real transitions. Bernath's explanation of the lifespans of Uganda's TJ policy process – between 2006, when it began, across 2013, when the draft National Transitional Justice Policy was submitted to the cabinet for consideration, to today, where it continues to languish un-adopted and hanging in limbo – takes us across the various frictions required to "create" TJ engagements. By describing the various blocks, shortfalls, clashing universals, insufficient donor attention spans, and a CSO community stuck on repeat, this chapter also draws a portrait of the struggle between the universals and their engagement in complex contexts; a situation Millar describes as "compound friction."[46]

Bernath reflects on how commitments made to TJ universals during the Juba peace negotiations – primarily justice and reconciliation – began the frictional encounter. It engaged international actors, which in turn brought "various funding mechanisms and allocations that contributed to an increased focus on TJ." Those engagements also shifted international funding focuses away from humanitarian aid, particularly in the north, where the Amnesty Commission had been working with communities to reintegrate those who had been abducted and became combatants during the conflict.

The clash between the International Criminal Court (ICC) process and ongoing support in conflict-affected areas for the protection of amnesty laws also prompts us to think about the struggle *between* universals: the frictions between justice and reconciliation (couched as amnesty) in Uganda can be seen as a focused example of this. In early peacemaking, the provision of amnesty for war crimes, crimes against humanity, and genocide was considered a necessary package of a smooth post-conflict or post-authoritarian transition. However, as customary international law has evolved, immunity from prosecution for large-scale systematic crimes such as these is increasingly prohibited, primarily on the basis that it embeds impunity.

The Amnesty Act of 2000 was enacted in part to encourage reconciliation at the community and national levels and to restore national cohesion. Since its

[46] Gearoid Millar, "Respecting Complexity: Compound Friction and Unpredictability in Peacebuilding," in *Peacekeeping and Friction*, ed. Annika Bjorkdahl et al. (London: Routledge, 2016), 55.

enactment, some 27,000 people have received amnesty; the overwhelming number have returned to their former communities, and many have been accepted and reintegrated after integration ceremonies. A considerable portion of the affected communities in northern Uganda and many CSOs had supported the amnesty, in part because "it encouraged the reintegration of formerly abducted people, especially children." But in 2012 a government-led TJ working group launched a review of the Amnesty Act, off the back of a general consensus that it could not continue as it was, because it endorsed impunity, undermined accountability mechanisms, and interfered with prosecution processes. The issue deeply divided actors within government and civil society.

Here we see the friction created not just when the rubber meets the road, but when two universals are in contest. In this case, the amnesty was reaffirmed in 2013 after religious and TJ CSO leaders from the northern communities petitioned the parliament for its continuation. However, the interaction between the two engaged universals led to a reframing of the law, leaving some perpetrators protected and others sitting outside the amnesty in an awkward compromise. This struggle between criminal justice and amnesty (the expressions of the universals) has led to renewed debate both in the TJ literature and internally within Uganda over the balance between the universals themselves: justice and reconciliation. It has also increased mutual mistrust between CSOs across the country, between CSOs and the state, and between regions more and less vulnerable to the conflict's resurgence.

As the universals travel and are reinterpreted, they are both changing (What does justice mean, and does it mean the same thing across a society? What does reconciliation look like?) and creating changes within society. These frictions have caused changes to laws, to CSOs, to shifting and fracturing pro- or anti-amnesty alliances that also respond to donor pressure/incentives to avoid amnesty, to perpetrators and victims who respond to the instability, and to the conflict itself.

This points to a larger issue, mentioned earlier: without a clear regime change and genuine political commitment to reform, chosen universals stall, precipitating unexpected outcomes. Because there has been so little genuine domestic political will for addressing the legacy of violence and redressing societal inequities, and because Uganda is considered relatively stable within an unstable region, donor support has moved towards establishing and strengthening the justice system and complementarity via the International Crimes Division of the Ugandan High Court, governance and infrastructure, and confronting government corruption. But this has particular ramifications, which Bernath outlines. Donors may have invested heavily in complementarity, but amnesty blocks real progress on prosecutions. However, they keep pushing the principle forward. One donor noted: "We want to push [the] ICD to bring a case . . . we feel there is some scope there." But without the requisite political support and overturning of the amnesty law, prosecutions are prevented from progressing. Things remain in limbo. The universal stalls.

In Morocco, Paige Arthur highlights the articulation of the universal – the right to remedy – into a format that was beyond, and subsequently shifted, international understandings of how the right worked. The Moroccan Equity and Reconciliation Commission (Instance d'Équité et Réconciliation, IER) recommended in its 2005 findings both individual and community reparations programmes. This was acknowledgement of the fact that during the "Years of Lead" under King Hassan II, entire regions had been punished and continued to suffer under the legacy of that violence. The idea of a collective programme, recommended by the IER and supported by the Moroccan government, can be understood as an expression of Tsing's engaged universal; one that redefined the universal, in that reparations are generally understood as rights belonging to individuals and related to individual harm suffered.

At the same time, the accepted format through which the universal is engaged was also shifted: the right to remedy is twinned with the state responsibility to provide that remedy, as an indication of will to repair, and to break with the past. But Morocco's community reparations programme was co-funded by the state and an external actor, the European Union (EU). This was a practical necessity: key human rights actors realised that the state would not prioritise this funding, and so sought support elsewhere. But this engagement of the universal, as a "practical project accomplished in a heterogeneous world," shifted the relationship between state responsibility and compensation. It also blurred Moroccans' perception of the state's role in the reparations programme, as a result of EU requirements that projects it co-funded be branded as EU projects with its logos and messaging.

This concept of engaged universals and travelling packages helps us see the (necessary) distance between the universal and its implementation. Engagement causes and requires change, as it also causes dislocation and creativity in the space between the universal and its engagement. Perhaps the exposure of these restrictions and their flow-on effects also points out the space for opportunities, for different ways of practically applying the universals, and for seeing the limitations of actors instrumental in the engagement of the universal.

Purifying Conceptual and Historical Spaces: Transitional Justice's Selective Focuses

The very real and very political process(es) of choosing which TJ universals to engage and how to bring them to life, as well as (sometimes by default) which universals to ignore, are far from transparent in periods of (and preceding) TJ design. Space, in the form of geographic and institutional focuses, history, in the form of time periods and perspectives included, and legal frameworks all set boundaries of inclusion and exclusion and shape legitimate and non-legitimate victimhood. This matters both because it frames understanding of what the problem leading to conflict was, but also the question of how to solve it.

The cleansing of historical space is a symptom of a field that is already predisposed to particular approaches. For example, one of TJ's largely unchallenged and frequently applied assumptions is that of the value of singular, "shared" truths. Correspondingly, TJ has not dealt particularly well with the idea of multiplicity of truths – truth commissions, for example, focus on the creation of "shared narratives" – and the field has had a tendency towards the clumsy reinterpretation of violence, which has sometimes resulted, usually accidentally, in the stripping away of the complexity of truth, victims' and survivors' stories, or the past more generally. The post-conflict world is littered with projects aimed at "shared histories" that lead to fixed interpretations and exclude vast swathes of populations who simply do not see the past this way. In other cases, and sometimes interrelatedly, the narrative is preset by the vehicles that shape it: for example, victim narratives are shaped by the rules of criminal tribunals, which in turn shape the "shared" narratives of history that come out of court records. In such cases truths of value to victims and witnesses, but not of value to tribunals, are excluded from "official" accountings.

Laura McGrew's work in Cambodia, in this regard, intersects with Tsing's reflections on this formation and shaping of the universals. While the TJ agenda may not have been framed by a carefully crafted consultation process, as we see happening with newer TJ engagements like Tunisia, the priorities *were* carefully shaped. McGrew explains how early TJ decisions by international donors about appropriate mechanisms to support TJ were related to:

> France's colonial history in Cambodia, Japan's role as a regional power, Germany's historical experience with the Holocaust, and the United States' history in the war in Vietnam. Each of these actors, we see, has had its own role in the court. In addition, because of the imprisonment, torture, and killing of nationals (notably of the United States, the United Kingdom, Australia, New Zealand, and France) by the KR during the KR period, as well as some attacks during the 1990s, these key international players were particularly insistent on prosecutions in an international court.

None of this was made visible in the international discussions around the priorities for TJ programming. However, these and other frictional engagements led to the coalescence of international and domestic elites in the late 1990s on an agenda of retributive justice. Very little value was placed on the work of CSOs focused on memory, trauma healing, outreach, or dialogue.

What does this mean? In Cambodia, the Extraordinary Chambers in the Courts of Cambodia (ECCC) was an effort to purify a historical as well as a legal space. It was framed by international actors as the clearest way of "healing" the past, and the quickest way to create a post-historical Cambodia. McGrew notes that "after the years of war between Eastern Bloc and Western Bloc proxies, both sides were eager to be finished with Cambodia, as the Western-style criminal prosecutions through the ECCC were originally envisioned to finish in three years. As a result, donors' (and the [Cambodian government's]) desire to close the chapter of the KR past dominated assistance decisions focusing on the large, flashy, and unique ECCC." The needs of the Cambodian population at the time were largely disregarded.

Such decisions hold particular implications. If the most appropriate response to the legacy of violence is to be a criminal prosecutions mandate with little other accompanying work, the landscape of history needs to be shrunk, and legacies of conflict related directly to colonialism discarded. Second, there are stability implications in a context where domestic perpetrators of violence or their party affiliates still hold power, perhaps accounting for a shared international and domestic political preference for "quick justice." The Cambodian government of the period seized the opportunity to sidestep accountability for those still in power, as well as to identify the potential for profit that a court like the ECCC might bring (though this was largely an unspoken goal). Such a process, and particularly its sharing of power between international and Cambodian staff members, would also bring the government legitimacy, as it is seen to be dealing with its past. Cambodian and international NGOs supported the initiative, in the hope that it would help dislodge the culture of impunity and bring perpetrators of violence to justice. Allies with very different goals lined up under the universal.

The colonial and postcolonial "forest clearing" was channelled into the ECCC process and mandate: the many years of negotiations between the United Nations (UN), the Royal Government of Cambodia, and US Ambassador-at-Large for War Crimes Issues David Scheffer over the court's jurisdiction ensured that there was to be no inclusion of the 1970s US bombings of Cambodia, no inclusion of Henry Kissinger's role in those bombings and their relationship to the rise of the KR's power,[47] and no inclusion of the post-KR civil war period.[48]

In engaging the justice universal in Cambodia, political power hierarchies – both international and domestic – pushed against one another. This shaped the ECCC's structure, rules, physical location, and visible and invisible agents – demonstrated through the mixed use of civil and common law practices through the court, the inclusion of French as an ECCC official language at France's insistence (in addition to English and Khmer), and the early and continuous negotiation between the Cambodian government, the UN, and donor countries for the staffing of certain prestigious positions within the court. It shaped the emphasis of the court's legacy and the function and location of the court's archives after its end. The division of responsibilities between national and international staff, the silent (passive-aggressive) power wielded by domestic actors, and the oversight role played by international actors was also an invisible source of struggle. In her chapter, McGrew argues that:

47 Although the defence teams brought up these issues throughout the trials.

48 My thanks to Laura McGrew for these points, which were not all in her chapter but were drawn out in subsequent discussions.

> The court's rules are themselves a mishmash of colonial and donor interests and legacies. The choice of legal system was related to Cambodia's [French] colonial past, and its later alignment with the United States and development assistance from other countries ... Part of civil law culture incorporates civil parties in criminal cases (as well as a system of investigating judges). Thus the ECCC was developed using primary elements of the French-influenced Cambodian civil law system. However, this was again adapted, including many unique aspects that marked the hybrid nature of the court – such as panels of judges with a majority of Cambodian and minority of foreign judges, with complicated rules necessitating agreement of at least one foreign judge in all decisions.

McGrew outlines how donors also became participants in the day-to-day of the ECCC: "The largest donors (Japan, France, the United States) routinely have had the presence of at least one judge or prosecutor among the ECCC personnel. They and the United Kingdom, Australia, Canada, New Zealand, and Germany have all had significant inputs into the court, including staff appointments." In other words, the politics underpinning the choice of TJ strategy, the shaping of the actual TJ mechanism, and the spectrum of exclusions that result are hidden from sight, part of the "forest clearing" necessary for the ECCC to take the legal, historical, and conceptual space it needs. This engagement has significantly steered the court towards international norms, resulting in the ECCC with all the characteristics, and all the weaknesses, that we see today.

Clearing the forest, and universalising norms, also provide space for growth. McGrew shares three points at which international victim-survivor, minority, and gender advocates utilised the friction caused by the engaged universal of justice to create spaces within and alongside the court in which victim and survivor voices would be more present; because of the nature of this influence, it resulted in a court focused more practically on non-repetition and repair. The first is, as McGrew highlights, civil party inclusion in the ECCC and the broader engagement of victims in the ECCC process. This provision was not initially included, but was an adaptation after the court had begun work. The admission of victims and civil parties was a response to concerns raised about the prior exclusion of civil society, and was made practically viable by funding from Germany. This change to the ECCC's understanding of inclusion of victims as civil parties in prosecution processes also caused a shift in the universal more broadly; as an expansion of victims' rights developed by the ICC's system of victim participation, it has also been celebrated as one of the ECCC's positive legacies.

Second, the additional focus on sexual and gender-based violence at the ECCC's later hearings is perhaps an example of how engaged universals can also *depurify* spaces. In this case, friction caused by the interaction between imported and domestic gender justice priorities at the court became part of, and perhaps also accelerated, the "changing norms within Cambodian society" on gender issues, and particularly in foregrounding the sexual and gender-based violations suffered by women. An international adviser, funded by the German Corporation for Development Cooperation, working with the Cambodian CSO, the Cambodian Defenders' Project, found and harnessed the frictional interactions to initiate a separate set of Women's Hearings that ran parallel to the ECCC.

Because friction creates shifts across society, the ECCC created space for suppressed narratives of marginalised groups to be heard and acknowledged. In addition to the notes presented earlier on the Women's Hearings, victimisation of ethnic Vietnamese was also unexpectedly foregrounded. McGrew writes that "most Cambodians on their own (investigators, prosecutors, and CSOs) would probably not have chosen the issue of the Vietnamese minority at the ECCC, and the inclusion of this issue may be attributed to international influence." She also notes that this brought changes further along the line: "Victim participation of ethnic Vietnamese had opened broader discussions about minority human rights issues, including ethnic Vietnamese access to Cambodian nationality and their request for collective and moral reparations."

The selective focus on particular universals is not a transparent process, but one that results from struggle. Cambodia has shown us how, in defining aspects of a conflict worthy of attention and the mechanisms to pursue this accounting, the spaces of exclusion are also defined. In order to justify this particular prosecutorial mandate, the legacies of various actors that engaged with or preceded the KR were compressed or disappeared. But in the creation of that focus, and the struggles to interpret the universal of justice, some marginalised voices emerged from a process that had been constructed largely without them in mind. And the engaged universal itself changed its form, as the notion of criminal prosecutions interacted with the Cambodian context and global power politics at a particular historical juncture to produce something new: hybrid courts drawing from mixed legal cultures, and a unique role for victims as civil parties.

Both Morocco and Cambodia show us the frictions created when international actors bring their own cultural specifics to contexts at the limits of their knowledge, as well as the interplay of botched and contingent encounters expanding the space for change. In explaining the reasons that EU donors funded memory and culture projects in Morocco, Paige Arthur finds that in part this relates to EU member states seeing similarities between Moroccan TJ processes and TJ in Germany, Northern Ireland/Britain, and Spain: "For them, learning from their own history had been important in the road to peace, and so they may have gravitated towards activities in the cultural domain such as archives, history, and memory projects as an important means of assisting a country to take ownership of its own past." It is interesting to note that the Germans carried this legacy into Cambodia also. But in Morocco, this created a "natural" (and less politically risky) choice over more meaningful – or more political – reform processes, which the Moroccan government was deeply disinclined to pursue. So in this case, donors framed the universal of dealing with the legacy of violence through their own internal cultural dialogues around the importance of archives, history, and memory projects for peacebuilding (though their actual motivation may have been more complex). In addition, and as with Cambodia, the domestic politics of donor states was important: "For some donors, such as the Dutch Embassy, support for TJ was part of a general commitment to human rights issues, and also motivated by the fact of a large Moroccan diaspora in the Netherlands." The lineage of these claims, however, was unlikely to have been particularly transparent.

But the choice of what universal to focus on also shapes – in very practical ways – subsequent choices around the extent to which we focus on the rest of the universals, as well as the kinds of institutions considered legitimate in delivering on the chosen universal – such as hybrid courts. For example, a choice to prioritise the universal of justice, in the form of an international or hybrid criminal prosecutions programme, will require a multi-year, multimillion-dollar commitment by engaged international actors. This will affect choices about how (and the extent to which it will be possible) to fund and prioritise other aspects of TJ, including and especially truth-seeking and reparations. The engagement of the universal also sets the boundaries of what is financially and practically feasible, and what is not, as well as the format of the universal's engagement in the world.

Gatekeepers and the Illusion of Universals: Donors, Experts, and the Mutations of Applied Transitional Justice

The idea of TJ as a "top-down," elite-driven process removed from the needs of those most affected by conflict is not new, and is the subject of much critical literature.[49] As we have seen, TJ processes are often heavily moderated by the foreign policy legacies and interests of donors and by the internal legacies of domestic political elites. However, they are also moderated by the domestic cultural specifics of international actors, and by international experts including international NGOs, who help frame these engagements. All this, as well as very real financial and capacity restrictions attached to the prioritising of particular universals (especially justice), affects the boundaries of what is feasible, what gets done, and whose voices are heard.

The Moroccan case highlights a number of these aspects. The series of frictional engagements described in Arthur's chapter resulted in the development of collective reparations, and also created several unintended consequences. The EU co-funded the work, but a state body, the Consultative Council of

[49] See, for example, Kieran McEvoy, "Beyond Legalism: Towards a Thicker Understanding of Transitional Justice," *Journal of Law and Sociology* 34, no. 4: 411–40; Patricia Lundy and Mark McGovern, "Whose Justice? Rethinking Transitional Justice from the Bottom Up," *Journal of Law and Society* 35, no. 2 (2008): 265–92; Argyro Kartsonaki, Christalla Yakinthou, Stefan Wolff, and Dawn Walsh, "Political Agreements in Intra-state Conflicts: Negotiating Power-Sharing and Transitional Justice," forthcoming.

Human Rights (later the National Council of Human Rights, CNDH), implemented it. This action meant that civil society was bypassed, and today's disengaged and disempowered civil society described in Arthur's chapter is one consequence of this decision. Second, the EU is a donor not usually associated with the term "flexibility" or "ease of access." Though a central objective was "to recognize and empower victims and victim groups as civic actors," Arthur outlines the many ways in which the EU's overly bureaucratic process excluded those very actors it sought to empower. This included the administering of grants through a competitive request for proposals process (which presupposed an ability to write professional grant applications), submission in French, when some of the most affected areas being targeted not only did not speak or write French, but also did not speak or write Arabic to a sufficient level, instead having Amazigh as their first language. In this, literacy was also presupposed. Finally, a certain percentage of co-funding was expected from the grantee, which simply would have closed the most affected and marginalised groups out of such opportunities to receive this form of reparations. Here, the universal travelled and was reinterpreted in innovative ways that have opened up conversations and opportunities around reparation, but at the same time the actors themselves and the norms they held about engagement limited the initiative's depth.

Further, the empowerment of a state agency (the CNDH) as a gatekeeper of TJ initiatives had its own flow-ons. Arthur points out that this has contributed to the lack of a strong civil society as a galvanising or effective actor against a state well known for its limited engagement around human rights reform:

> While some of the money that the EU has granted to the CNDH has subsequently passed through to civil society organizations, there has not been a corresponding donor focus on supporting the main civil society and victims' organizations active on TJ, which have been critical of the CNDH's approach. As a result, civil society efforts to act as a counterweight to the state on TJ have suffered. Indeed ... there has been a general decline in civil society action and collaboration on TJ since the close of the Moroccan Equity and Reconciliation Commission (Instance d'Équité et Réconciliation, IER) in 2006. After this point, responsibility for TJ shifted from civil society to the state, and donor money followed this trajectory, mainly from the EU. While international assistance did not cause this shift, it has contributed to it.

Reflecting on the TJ-related interactions between the EU, the state, and civil society, Arthur foregrounds the marginalising of civil society voices. She argues that civil society actors "saw the EU funds as a matter between the EU and the Moroccan state; civil society actors were not really involved." Further, a 2007 civil society-led evaluation of the EU-Morocco Action Plan stated that the Action Plan "was elaborated and negotiated without consultation with nor even information from CSOs.

This is contrary to all the engagements that express support for civil society participation in democratization processes."[50] There is a direct link between a strong and empowered civil society and the achievement of the TJ universals in societies that seek to overcome legacies of conflict and authoritarianism.[51] But here, the gatekeepers largely excluded civil society from the process, and their limited engagement in TJ after the IER's end bear witness to the impact of unreflective gatekeeping.

Gatekeeping also frequently occurs in relation to victim and survivor organisations, whose involvement in TJ processes and access to power are usually heavily mediated by mechanisms that constrain their input, such as criminal prosecutions processes, or by actors, such as international NGOs, that, as Madlingozi notes, appropriate victim and survivor voices. This occurred in Morocco, where Arthur notes that one of the most remarkable features of the community reparations programme, "given the fact that its intention was to benefit victims – is how little it appeared to work directly with victims' organizations." Some of Arthur's interviewees noted that "the program would have funded more relevant projects had it worked directly with victim organizations." This was also a characteristic of relationships between donors and victims' associations in Bosnia and Herzegovina (BiH), where some victims and survivors complained in interviews that their access to justice, to reparations, or generally to projects that represented their interests or needs was heavily mediated by other NGOs, which functioned as gatekeepers *to* donors. They stated that "NGOs often profit from false associations with the group, claiming to have cooperation with them to gain project support from donors." One victim-survivor from civil society argued that victims were not seen as part of the solution towards peace, but instead "we are seen as part of the problem."

One of the less-researched areas of TJ – and a core contribution of this book – is analysis of (or any kind of accounting for) where TJ funding goes, and the relationships between choice of TJ mechanism and impact on funding and support for other aspects of TJ. Gatekeepers – donors at the top, and key international NGOs and NGOs lower down the funding hierarchy – play a central role in those allocations; however, they are not necessarily best placed to make these (or at least *all* of these) decisions. As we saw in Uganda, donor-gatekeeper preferences for particular universals impact the viability of other TJ agendas. As Bernath's source notes: "Many funders chose to prioritize particular aspects of the peace agreements, with many opting to fund prosecutorial initiatives. Getting funding for

50 The report explicitly took the Action Plan to task for ignoring most of the IER's recommendations on institutional reforms, and it is based on workshops that included representatives of AMDH and OMDH, among others. Moroccan Euromediterranean NGO Network, "Évaluation du Plan d'Action Maroc/U.E. Dans le Cadre de la PEV" (report of a conference held in Rabat, October 25–26, 2007): 24; available at www.fes.org.ma/common/pdf/publications_pdf/PEV/PEV.pdf.

51 Laura Arriaza and Naomi Roht-Arriaza, "Social Reconstruction as a Local Process," *International Journal of Transitional Justice* 2, no. 2 (2008): 152–72.

other TJ mechanisms – including truth-seeking, reconciliation, and other measures – has proven difficult."[52] In her chapter, Bernath shows the gap between the knowledge of donors and international NGOs who were pressing for criminal prosecutions, and the urgent needs of affected communities and victims and survivors, as well as insufficient thinking about to address legacies of the conflict with the available resources.

This is important because particular kinds of gatekeeping, out of touch with the needs of survivors, have a direct and often detrimental impact on those who are supposedly beneficiaries. The most striking of these examples is the work of CSOs focusing on projects aimed at female survivors of the conflict who need multiple surgeries to address the physical impact of sexual violence, but that have funding only for the initial surgery. Bernath notes that "the biggest problem has not been that the issue has not been recognized, but that many of the programs geared towards trying to address these complex set of needs have been insufficient, inappropriate, or of poor quality, meaning women continue to suffer." One interviewee from civil society reflected: "Sometimes the focus of the [funded] project is to address one of these requirements, and when other [unfunded] needs arise, there is no flexibility within the project itself to be able to address them more holistically ... Without a little flexibility, I sometimes wonder if we are helping someone at all just by addressing that one need." In this instance, gatekeeping blocks the ability to better address harm.

Gatekeepers play an important, and often positive role in TJ processes. But in cases – like many in this book – where donors do not have a clear strategy for TJ or for helping CSOs develop into strong societal actors, and civil society itself is fractured and competitive, gatekeeping can undermine TJ goals. In BiH, CSO gatekeepers "spoke for" victims' and survivors' associations, to the detriment of the work being done. In Uganda, gatekeepers failed to see the limits of their knowledge when it came both to broader strategies of TJ engagement and to the needs of victims and survivors.

Collaborations, Shifts, and (Co)imagining the Universal Ideal: Creating Alliances with "Mini-Me" Civil Society Organisations, and Disconnected Funding Frameworks

International assistance generally, and donors in our case studies specifically, have been accused of supporting domestic civil society groups that fit into their conceptual frameworks for "good" civil society actors, as well as their professional requirements for engagement, leaving out vast swathes of relevant actors who do not or

[52] Oola, "The Coalition for Reconciliation in Uganda (CORU): Important Lessons for Proactive Civil Society Engagement in Catalysing Transitional Justice Discourse" (paper presented at the African Transitional Justice Research Network Workshop – Advocating Justice: Civil Society and Transitional Justice in Africa, Johannesburg, South Africa, August 30, 2010), 10.

cannot fit into their frameworks. The engaged universal, when it is chosen, when it is shaped, and as it moulds itself around gatekeeper knowledge, both causes and embodies change. In some cases, as we will see in Guatemala, engagements create productive collaborations over time: between donors, between donors and civil society, and between civil society groups. But those interactions, while adhering to a shared universal such as justice or reconciliation, can also hide differences in the way that universal is imagined. In some cases, co-imagining a universal is really a simulation of the act. As we will see, BiH shows us how civil society groups, aware of donor priorities, can co-opt an ostensibly shared universal to achieve political aims. In other cases, such as Guatemala, co-imagined universals can be abandoned by donors, leaving civil society partners to reorient or go it alone.

Guatemala shows us what happens when the universal's orbit changes, how, when donors disengage from the pursuit of this collaborative engagement of the universal, civil society organisations can find themselves disconnected and needing to shape-shift in order to continue doing their work. In so doing, however, all actors also participate in reconfiguring the universal itself. In their chapter on Guatemala, Anita Isaacs and Rachel Schwartz describe a civil society sector that had been deeply internally fractured, a result of the brutal civil war, and where institutional jealousies, class, ideological, and racial divisions all continue to colour the landscape of interactions between civil society actors, particularly among the left. At the time of the peace process, civil society was particularly damaged and mistrustful. None of this is surprising, given that, as the authors point out, "thirty-six years of armed conflict shredded the social fabric."

This frictional engagement between inclusion and an aggressive political landscape led to the development of coalition politics across a very broad spectrum of actors who would not have otherwise aligned, and soon an umbrella association, the Assembly for Civil Society (ASC), was created. It is noteworthy that this engagement was not sought by – but instead imposed upon – the peace process and, to some extent, upon the ASC members. But as CSOs interacted, their relationships developed, and this contributed significantly to pushing civil society beyond its internal divisions.

Isaacs and Schwartz explain how the collaboration between ASC members "forced its members to begin to listen to one another, to recognize each other's expertise, and to learn how to seek compromise"; it created a (temporary) common goal and an awareness of how to leverage transnational cosmopolitan values to pursue their demands for an accounting for past abuses – to "converse across difference," in Tsing's language. The engagements were both horizontal – between CSOs – and vertical – with political elites negotiating the peace agreement and with international actors.

Out of them grew organisations such as REMHI (Recovery of Historical Memory) – the Catholic Church–led truth-seeking initiative written by and for Guatemalans documenting the landscape of atrocities during the conflict.

The growth of victim support actions during the Historical Clarification Commission (CEH) process, and more generally the development of a Guatemalan civil society "battle-tested [and] politically savvy" can also be understood as an unintended consequence; the frictional encounters of the peace process helped civil society build strategies for community engagement and increasing trust among victims in official processes like the CEH (which also drew from REMHI's work) and criminal prosecutions.

However, wartime fractures were not erased, and in the new realities of the post–peace process period, divergent meanings emerged beneath the co-imagined language of collaboration. Here, we are reminded of Tsing's note that "coalition politics is essential. Yet what does it mean to work in coalition? The twentieth-century class-based solidarity model asks coalition allies to line up as parallel equivalents. Allies rarely line up that well. Without even intending to break the line, they push in new directions. Their friction changes everyone's trajectory."[53] International donors and agencies buttressed the new paradigms they co-created, legitimising and supporting TJ processes; the wheels turned, and victim and survivor groups and broader truth, justice, and reform-focused CSOs led work across a spectrum of priorities, supported for a decade by MINUGUA and by the OHCHR, USAID, and European donors. But the shared language held only so long.

Without a vehicle to implement civil society recommendations post-negotiations, each sector worked for its own reforms to the exclusion of others, "creating a social vacuum incapable of formulating or promoting an overall peace agenda."[54] This further weakened the ability of civil society to push for reform, creating a larger vacuum. And as politics in the country has taken a turn to the right with two successive governments closely tied to the military, donors have shifted away from TJ and towards strengthening the rule of law, unintentionally redirecting the programming of some formerly TJ CSOs towards non-TJ work in order to sustain their existence.

In other words, changing international priorities with respect to TJ reshaped civil society aims in ways that were unintended. As a consequence, some CSOs have argued that there is no space left for TJ. The executive arm of government pushes back the progress of previous years and civil society does not have the resources to counteract the backsliding on its own. The international community remains a critical actor to keeping the peace agenda a part of the national conversation, but its focus has shifted; it has changed its commitment to the universal.

In recent years, this unravelling of the co-imagined universal has also altered the terms of the collaboration between donors and civil society working on TJ, transposing the entire funding framework into (predominantly) rule of law and security-

53 Tsing, *Friction*, 13–14.

54 Enrique Alvarez and Tania Palencia Prado, "Guatemala's Peace Process: Context, Analysis and Evaluation," in *Owning the Process: Public Participation in Peacemaking*, Accord Series no. 13 (London: Conciliation Resources, 2002), 43.

focused work. As a result, victims' organisations are confronting a crisis, and decreased funding for TJ-focused work has created a "cutthroat funding environment," which has deepened fragmentation within and between CSOs; the ability to look beyond divisions faltered as new frictions were created. Those who continued to gain funds spoke of being "sellers of dreams" and learning how to camouflage their goals within the language of rule of law or other shifting priorities of international assistance. But as they do that, distance is also created between the centre and the peripheries of the country, and between people at the peripheries, where hierarchies of the centre are recreated, and as a consequence, divisions fragment and deepen again. And as that happens, the donor community grows increasingly fatigued with a less and less impactful civil society. Organisations that have managed to adapt to this climate also grow further away from their original mandates, while those that have not grow increasingly marginalised. Isaacs and Schwartz observe that:

> GAM [Mutual Support Group of Relatives of the Disappeared], for instance, has procured USAID funding for a project on crime prevention; CAFCA [the Center of Forensic Analysis and Applied Sciences] has nearly abandoned its work on exhumations to develop expertise in criminal investigation techniques; the FAFG [Guatemalan Forensic Anthropology Foundation] is seeking support for a project on disappeared migrants; and CONAVIGUA [National Coordinator of Widows of Guatemala] has been forced to set aside much of its work with widows and orphans of the armed conflict to focus on topical issues such as domestic violence because, in the words of one leader, "no one wants to fund projects that deal with the past anymore."

As this shift occurs, the options for reform in rule of law and security area open, but those for reform in areas such as TJ appear to be closing, leaving a great deal of work undone, particularly with victims of the conflict and their families. These shifts to funding frameworks also disconnect them (and grantees) from communities. In Tsing's terms, they define the space that is accessible and the space that is not.

In the wake of the Dayton Agreement, the international donor community engaged with TJ in BiH primarily under the universals of the right to justice, interpreted as the International Criminal Tribunal for the Former Yugoslavia (ICTY), and the right to truth, in the work of the International Commission on Missing Persons and its efforts to identify and return the remains of the approximately 30,000 missing and disappeared in the country. The universal of justice as it was articulated by the tribunal, it was thought, would also fill the cup of the rights to truth and reparation, as well as bringing reconciliation, in ways that were never clearly articulated. Important work is being funded – but it is not the same important work identified as a need by the broader society, or even as most urgent by many interviewees. The approximately 2.4 billion USD spent over two decades for the ICTY did not magically spill over into adequate victim reparation programmes and psychosocial support for victims and survivors, or bring Bosniaks, Bosnian Serbs, and

Bosnian Croats closer together as a result of hearing the historical record set right. In fact, the political context has grown more tense, victim reparation is problematic, and support for medical and psychosocial needs of victims and survivors has dwindled. In BiH, over the past two decades of international engagement in and support of TJ, we have seen a disconnect between CSOs and the greater public, growing distance between Sarajevo-based CSOs and those (especially service-provision) CSOs based outside the capital and therefore away from a direct line of communication with donors, and a deepening public suspicion of the capital-based TJ CSOs, who have been strikingly nicknamed "the NGO mafia."

This is not a condition exclusive to BiH: in Guatemala, we also see that the disparities between human rights organisations based in Guatemala City and victims'/survivors' associations in rural areas is vast. While there is genuine interest among international donors to support some of the under-resourced groups who do not usually receive funding, donors are impeded by their own stringent criteria related to technical and administrative capacity of the grantee organisation, and shifting funding landscapes. This also has the effect of preventing younger or smaller CSOs from the margins to build the necessary capacity.

Unable and unwilling to break free of clearly dysfunctional structural constraints, donors in Guatemala and BiH ended up continuing to support "mini-me" CSOs: capital-based, easy-to-access organisations that fit their requirements, funding profiles, and understandings of norms of professionalisation and resource allocation. CSOs, on the other hand, learn to divide their logic so that they present as groups "relatable" to donors, while managing to quietly keep their often activist-driven mandate; entirely remake themselves as "professional" CSOs, shaped by donor demands;[55] or find alternative (and often less successful) methods of survival. In all cases, this precipitates a divisive and competitive environment between CSOs across the spectrum. As a result, both the larger donors and the CSOs they support have arguably lost their legitimacy at the domestic public level.

But a broader political context also underpins the support of "mini-me" CSOs, and the disconnection of funding frameworks from actual public need. Especially in BiH, donors have worried about funding groups that are too political, which might disturb the fragile balance of peace that existed post-Dayton Accord. I outline in the chapter on BiH that both CSO and donor interviewees:

> emphasized that donor agendas and fear of "rocking the boat" in the early post-Dayton period were responsible for the emergence of a civil society unwilling to tackle tough political issues: "A political civil society was muted by the international community, which was cautious about funding projects that would exacerbate political polarization or politically charged work."

55 Chris Skelcher and Steven Rathgeb Smith, "Theorizing Hybridity: Institutional Logics, Complex Organizations, and Actor Identities: The Case of Nonprofits," *Public Administration* 93, no. 2 (2015): 441.

In other words, donors have not just gravitated towards mini-me CSOs, they also created them, both out of inhibitively structured funding frameworks, and (especially) a fear of supporting politically oriented activities and groups. In BiH, in Guatemala, and in Uganda, one cannot speak meaningfully of ineffectual TJ CSOs without understanding the funding contexts that create, shape, and ultimately undermine them, and the frictions that unravelled or blocked their ability to affect social change.

On a different note, BiH also shows us how civil society actors can sometimes co-opt purportedly shared understandings of the universal and usurp their power. In the travelling package of liberal peacebuilding, one particular victim and survivor group has usurped the package and language of human rights to both create a memorial centre that functions to "take back" a symbolically important site of genocide from the community in whose territory the land resides,[56] and to impugn the international community for its hypocrisy. Here, the Movement of the Mothers of Srebrenica and Zepa Enclaves is simultaneously marginalised – especially financially – and powerful (or savvy) enough to have actively created conditions such that the Office of the High Representative, BiH's international peacebuilding power, forced a strongly opposed state to accept a memorial to the victims of the Srebrenica genocide in the territory of Republica Srpska (RS), whose soldiers committed the crimes, in fact on the site of the genocide.

In this frictional encounter, the grassroots organisation redefined the boundaries of state and interventionist power, holding open the space for tension between the universals of justice and reconciliation; making use of and then rejecting the language of one to call for the other. Taking advantage of a high intervention period by the Office of the High Representative (OHR), the Movement's route to its goals was enabled by the friction created in the application of the OHR's Bonn Powers to override domestic political stonewalling. Most interestingly, the OHR's reason for intervening was to promote reconciliation between the two communities, particularly in light of Bosniak refugees' return to their homes in the RS after their forced displacement. Here the frictions of the peacebuilding and TJ paradigms led to the creation of a memorial to acknowledge victims and promote healing both within and between communities. However, the Srebrenica Memorial is (at best) ignored by the Bosnian Serb community in the area, and utilised by the Movement as a platform to advocate for justice for the families of the missing and murdered. From this platform, the Movement has relentlessly reminded the international community – and specifically the UN and the Dutch peacekeepers who failed to protect civilians in the safe zone during the war – of its failure to adhere to its own human rights universals.

[56] Johanna Mannergren Selimovic, "Frictional Commemoration: Local Agency and Cosmopolitan Politics at Memorial Sites in Bosnia-Herzegovina and Rwanda," in *Peacekeeping and Friction*, 64.

Its approach shows the results of these frictions; the Movement has used legal, political, and media strategies to enhance its own agency, and from there to advocate its message that there can be no reconciliation without rights and acknowledgment from both the RS and the international community.[57] In these ways, it has resisted a hidden violence of power hierarchies expressed through incompatible universals by refusing to allow their demands for justice and accountability to be submerged under a template of reconciliation. In other words, it utilised a vertical collaboration and the language of one shared universal to create a platform from which to lobby for another.

Both Guatemala and BiH have shown, in different ways, what happens when donors and civil society disengage from the collaborative engagement of the universal, and how frequently this disengagement leads to fractures, competition, and marginalisation, as well as opportunities for transformation in other areas. Finally, the engagement of administrative universals – expressed as transparency, political neutrality, fiscal responsibility, time frames and deliverables – also creates shifts in relationships between donors that provide international assistance and civil society grantees (the phenomenon of the "mini-me" CSO), as well as between CSOs; these are their own engaged universals, and are an unintended, and largely unacknowledged result of donor frameworks taken from a largely post-enlightenment, stable, Western bureaucratic context, and transferred, with a spectrum of implications and impacts, to contexts of post-conflict and post-authoritarian societies. In paying attention to the weaving and unweaving of collaborations in both BiH and Guatemala, we see how the frictional engagements create changes, both expected and unexpected.

CONCLUSION

This chapter has suggested that an adaptation of Anna Tsing's theory of friction enables us to recreate a three-dimensional understanding of actors, actions, interactions, and consequences of TJ engagements, and specifically the interactions between external donors and a country's civil society. It has used the four interrelated themes of engaged universals and travelling packages, purifying conceptual and historical spaces, gatekeepers and the illusion of universals, and collaborations, shifts, and (co)imagining the universal ideal to push us to think beyond normalised TJ engagements and their outcomes, to understand what they are and how and why they come about.

This framework is valuable for two primary reasons. First, as TJ universals have circled the globe and best practice has been built around their interpretation(s), their interaction has created the gaps, mutations, and innovations that are apparent throughout the pages of this book. While the language of cosmopolitanism provides a common vocabulary through which actors can each express very different ideas in ways that allow (some level of, or a simulacrum of) conversation across boundaries,

57 Author interviews with Movement of Mothers of Srebrenica and Zepa Enclaves, April 25, 2014.

this frictional engagement with the universal runs the risk of transforming the route through which social change is achieved, as well as reshaping the change sought. At the same time, some of our cases also point to the friction that exists in collaborations *between* international actors in TJ contexts; and these have both limited and created new pathways. This is to say that pursuit of (often different) understandings of specific universals does encourage collaborations between actors that can spur positive social change. But the collaborations and the pursuit of multiple understandings under what is ostensibly the same universal creates shifts, fractures, new gaps, and also new opportunities across the entire spectrum of actors engaged in or touched by this pursuit.

The conceptual framework offered in this chapter encourages us to think of interrelated (if asymmetrical) levels of influence both over a process and over the shaping of a universal norm, and allows us to capture these shifts, fractures, and gaps. It helps us see more clearly into the harms and potentialities that exist around such encounters. Here, Dustin Sharp's reflections provide a focus for such potentialities:

> It is thought-provoking to imagine, for example, what a transitional justice process might look like that did not privilege international "expertise" at the expense of local agency; national or capital-based justice at the expense of community and rural-based justice; largely western legal modes of justice at the expense of "traditional" or "local" modalities of justice; the prosecution of the so-called "big fish" at the expense of a focus on reparations and community needs; and physical violence and civil and political rights at the expense of economic violence and economic and social rights.[58]

By drawing on the book's case studies to elaborate this chapter's framework, we were able to look beyond the local-global binary to see and explain what happens during TJ processes, and more importantly, why.

Second, and as a result, this framework is useful for policy formation. If we apply Susanne Buckley-Zistel's work to lessons to take from these case studies, friction's exposure of the participation of actors in interpreting and embodying the universal "[opens] windows for a more conscious and empowered agency."[59] That is, she points out the most hopeful aspects of Tsing's *Friction*. What if, for example, instead of creating policies that front-load community engagement into predesigned packages of "inclusion" into already-set processes, possibilities can be created when space is actively shared with "resistance, contestation and argument as a natural part of a process, in which such policy designs can grow out from such interaction between the various parties"?[60] Given the fundamental tension outlined

58 Sharp, "Transitional Justice and Liberal Post-conflict Governance," 167.

59 Susanne Buckley-Zistel, "Frictional Spaces: Transitional Justice between the Global and the Local," in *Peacekeeping and Friction*, 39.

60 Chris Skelcher, "What Do We Mean When We Talk about 'Hybrids' and 'Hybridity' in Public Management and Governance?" Working Paper, Institute of Local Government Studies (Birmingham: University of Birmingham, 2012), 18.

throughout this chapter between a universal and its engagement, what would happen if international actors were simply to accept that friction happens? To observe it, and to realise that frictional engagements will produce both productive outcomes, and profoundly unproductive ones.

To be conscious to the existence of frictional engagements, and watchful of them, also allows an acknowledgment that projects will not necessarily lead to their anticipated outcomes, but that instead they may lead to a more meaningful social engagement as things shift and change. This shift can reveal valuable possibilities that were not previously apparent. This is particularly resonant for questions of how to re-see and overcome rigid institutional boundaries often put in place by international assistance in TJ contexts. One may not be able to design a just TJ process, in this context of living and often shifting injustices, but friction is so valuable because it allows one to explain how things are often unpredictable, and how, when different spaces of actors and ideas interact, we may not get what we set out to get. But as this chapter shows, nor should we.

At the same time, there are some hard questions. We need to think more carefully about a field that is set up to require funding from donor entities that are often the same actors who also did not intervene (or at least waited a considerable duration) in a conflict, maintained an authoritarian regime, were directly involved in colonial-era atrocities, or helped craft the fragile peace agreements that TJ is often seen to threaten. Questions exist about how we reconcile donor foreign policy and domestic interests with the demands of supporting TJ processes that may disturb these interests or legacies. And how can we reconcile both of these with the requirement that for TJ processes to be successful, they really do need to be integrated, inclusive, strategic, long-term engagements? Friction and this framework allow us to consider those interventions that are more harmful and those that are less harmful, and to consider accordingly.

7

Why Do Donors Choose to Fund Transitional Justice?

Paige Arthur

There is no shortage in the literature on transitional justice (TJ) of discussion of the role of international norms in shaping the practice of TJ. Researchers and observers have written incisively about "reconciling" global norms and local agency, how such norms are "negotiated" by local actors "on the ground," the importance of TJ "from below" led by "grassroots activists," "localizing" TJ, and "dilemmas of the global and local."[1] But what about the role of international assistance in TJ, and in particular, financial aid from governments? The challenges in addressing the issue are substantial: there is a dearth of data on such financial flows; donor agencies may offer little public insight into their decision-making; qualitative research among donors faces practical and political difficulties, simply in terms of identifying the right people and getting them to agree to an interview; and, finally, the sheer range of actors involved would be daunting to any researcher.

These challenges notwithstanding, this chapter tackles the issue of donor decision-making to fund TJ. The issue is important since, as Christalla Yakinthou argues, TJ initiatives have been increasingly hybridized through the adaptation of local to international norms (and vice versa), as well as through support from international actors: donors (whether governments or private foundations), multilaterals like the United Nations Development Programme (UNDP), and international nongovernmental organizations (INGOs) like the International Center for Transitional Justice

I thank Christalla Yakinthou, Riva Kantowitz, and Elena Baylis for insights that helped to improve this chapter.

[1] Notably, but not exhaustively, see Ruti Teitel, *Globalizing Transitional Justice* (New York: Oxford University Press, 2014); Alana Tiemessen, "The International Normative Structure of Transitional Justice," PhD thesis, University of British Columbia (2011); Diane Orentlicher, "'Settling Accounts' Revisited: Reconciling Global Norms with Local Agency," *International Journal of Transitional Justice* 1, no. 1 (2007): 10–22; Alex Laban Hinton, ed., *Transitional Justice: Global Mechanisms and Local Realities after Genocide and Mass Violence* (New Brunswick, NJ: Rutgers University Press, 2010); Kieran McEvoy and Lorna McGregor, eds., Transitional Justice from Below: Grassroots Activism and the Struggle for Change (Oxford: Hart Publishing, 2008); Rosalind Shaw and Lars Waldorf, eds., *Localizing Transitional Justice* (Stanford, CA: Stanford University Press, 2010); Dustin Sharp, "Addressing Dilemmas of the Global and the Local in Transitional Justice," *Emory International Law Review* 29 (2014): 71–117.

(ICTJ). Such hybridization has taken place to the extent that the division between "local" and "international" approaches to TJ has broken down; while not nonsensical, such distinctions are less and less analytically helpful. It is more fruitful instead to conceive of TJ at this point in time as ineluctably hybrid, and to use different analytical tools (such as the "frictions" framework) to help us assess the potential for such initiatives – always both global and local, to use that language – to address or provide justice for victims of human rights violations.[2]

This chapter develops a framework of decision-making specifically related to donor funding for TJ, based on our five case studies as well as a review of the (rather sparse) literature on international assistance to TJ. It begins, in part one, by situating the reader in the broader context of debates on international assistance (relating to the purposes, types, and effectiveness of aid). In part two, I take a constructivist approach to describing the ways in which decision-making on aid to TJ works, drawing on an analytical framework for understanding foreign assistance from international relations scholarship. This framework looks at the ideas, interests, and institutions that shape assistance to TJ.[3] Here, I add a fourth "I" – information – in order to adapt this framework for TJ, since decisions on TJ are often made in contexts with little information. I also address the question of how these four factors relate to support for (or lack of support for) civil society engagement in TJ. In part three, I draw conclusions about how donors fund TJ, and offer some reflections on how the factors shaping donor decision-making have had consequences for the way TJ has been conceptualized and implemented.

TRANSITIONAL JUSTICE AND DEBATES ON INTERNATIONAL DEVELOPMENT ASSISTANCE

Much has already been written about international development assistance by both its supporters and critics. Books like William Easterly's *White Man's Burden: Why the West's Efforts to Aid the Rest Have Done So Much Ill and So Little Good* (2006) and Jeffrey Sachs's *The End of Poverty: Economic Possibilities for Our Time* (2005) catapulted the debate over international development aid far beyond professional circles. Easterly's trenchant critique not only questioned whether the massive aid flows of recent decades had helped poor people, but suggested that, on balance, it may have actually harmed them. Sachs, by contrast, argued that the West should be spending far more on aid than it has been, albeit in a more careful way.

TJ does not fit particularly well in these debates relating to economic development, as it does not relate to traditional development or antipoverty interventions. Instead, TJ fits with the more "political" goals of democracy and human rights,

[2] See Chapter 6 in this volume.

[3] See, e.g., Carol Lancaster, *Foreign Aid: Diplomacy, Development, Domestic Politics* (Chicago, IL: University of Chicago Press, 2007).

support for which among donors has increased in prominence since the 1990s. "After decades of avoiding talking about or acting on political issues," Thomas Carothers and Diane de Gramont write, "in the early 1990s mainstream aid organizations suddenly changed tack. They began repeatedly emphasizing a close connection between political and economic development."[4] Key agencies, such as USAID and the Swedish International Development Cooperation Agency (Sida), added democracy to their agendas and developed programs that became a "standard template" of democracy aid, and they supported democracy as an intrinsic value connected to socioeconomic goals.[5] The shift took place in spite of the fact that little evidence existed to support the view that democracies perform better economically than other sorts of regimes. Indeed, the idea "emerged essentially whole cloth in the exuberant, triumphalist spirit of the early 1990s – when both liberal democracy and market economies appeared to be the clear winners in the global ideological contest of the previous decades. It was a kind of axiomatic conclusion in which correlation and cause blurred."[6]

The response to this shift varied. As Carothers and de Gramont note, and as our own case studies suggest, some "aid agencies did not put into place the organizational changes needed to support the full integration of democracy and rights perspectives into their traditional areas of socioeconomic focus." Those agencies that did develop special expertise and structures to address these new "development" issues tended to hive them off in specialized areas, rather than treating them as crosscutting issues to be integrated into broader development approaches. Some aid agencies supported a "depoliticized" approach to such assistance that focused on "governance" – following the World Bank's neutral definition of the term.[7]

In general, assistance to TJ has not typically been seen through the lens of development, strictly speaking, even when development agencies (such as Sida, USAID, UNDP) have funded it. Researchers have tried to elaborate the links between TJ and development in recent years, and even this approach suggests that there is not much sense to be made of the idea of TJ as a development initiative – instead, TJ is seen as a set of separate and potentially mutually reinforcing actions alongside development interventions.[8] One recent effort to argue for the salience of TJ to development is the 2011 *World Development Report, Conflict, Security and Development*, in which TJ is referred to as a "core tool" for restoring confidence in the wake of conflict.[9]

4 Thomas Carothers and Diane de Gramont, *Development Aid Confronts Politics: The Almost Revolution* (Washington, DC: Carnegie Endowment for International Peace, 2013), 55.

5 Ibid., 64. 6 Ibid., 65. 7 Ibid., 67–68.

8 See Pablo de Greiff and Roger Duthie, eds., *Transitional Justice and Development: Making Connections* (New York: Social Science Research Council, 2009).

9 See World Bank, *World Development Report 2011: Conflict, Security, and Development* (Washington, DC: World Bank, 2011), 251.

So where does that leave TJ in respect to the existing literature on development assistance? I see three ways that assistance to TJ fits: first, in relation to the purposes of assistance; second, in relation to the types of assistance; and, third, in relation to the effectiveness of assistance.

Purposes of Assistance

It is well known that the purposes of assistance have evolved since the 1950s, when it was primarily focused on diplomacy, commercial interests, humanitarian relief, and economic development (defined narrowly). As mentioned earlier, starting in the 1990s, the inherently political character of assistance was increasingly recognized. Indeed, the turn to supporting aid with purposes related to human rights, democracy, governance, and so forth was new at that time.[10]

It is difficult to imagine TJ initiatives – which relate to human rights, governance, democracy, and peacebuilding – receiving much attention from agencies delivering international assistance prior to the 1990s, during the Cold War. Starting in the 1990s, however, international donors began to take an interest in such initiatives. For example, two now-paradigmatic TJ initiatives that took place in the 1990s received international funding. South Africa's Truth and Reconciliation Commission (TRC) operated for two and a half years (1995–97) with an annual budget of at least $30 million.[11] This sum included a combination of state funding and international donations. International donors contributed approximately $9.6 million, including $1.4 million from USAID.[12] Guatemala's Historical Clarification Commission had a budget of $9.5 million to $11 million from 1997 to 1999, which was administered by the United Nations (UN). Roughly $1 million came from the Guatemalan government, while the rest came from international donors.[13]

Other shifts have heightened the relevance of TJ to donor paradigms related to political development. Most notably, support for anti-impunity initiatives and norms seen as linked variably to the purposes of human rights, democratization, rule of law,

[10] See Lancaster, *Foreign Aid*, 13–16. She argues that there were four new purposes, starting roughly in the 1990s: promoting social and economic transitions in the former socialist countries; promoting democracy in Africa, Asia, and Latin America; addressing global issues (like climate change or public health); and mitigating conflicts and managing post-conflict transitions.

[11] *Truth and Reconciliation Commission Report of South Africa*, Vol. I (1998), 95–96, available at www.justice.gov.za/trc/report/finalreport/Volume%201.pdf. Figure calculated by adding budgets for the 1994–95 and 1996–97 fiscal years, and then converting to USD at rate of 0.22, which is an average exchange rate for 1997 (see Oanda.com). The costs are higher – up to $50 million or more – if ongoing operations up to 2002 are included. See Priscilla Hayner, *Unspeakable Truths: Confronting State Terror and Atrocity*, 2nd edn. (New York: Routledge, 2010), 269.

[12] Ibid., 317–18. Donations totaled 45,808,228 ZAR, in addition to the $1.4 million from USAID; total dollar amount calculated at conversion rate of 0.22 USD to ZAR.

[13] Hayner quotes $11 million in a 2003 report coauthored with Mark Freeman, and $9.5 million in the updated version of her book *Unspeakable Truths*. See Hayner, *Unspeakable Truths*, 270; and Daniel Rothenberg, "Introduction," in *Memory of Silence: The Guatemalan Truth Commission Report*, ed. Daniel Rothenberg (Palgrave Macmillan, 2012), xxxvi.

and/or peacebuilding grew substantially during this period, starting with the international criminal tribunals for the former Yugoslavia and for Rwanda. Even more recently, such purposes have been influenced by the emergence of the fragile state paradigm and concomitant security threats linked to "lawless" spaces.[14] Some observers have referred to the "securitization" of development assistance, a phenomenon that saw a sharp uptick after 9/11.[15] TJ has also been pulled into this "security-development nexus"[16] – particularly in post-conflict states where reintegration of ex-combatants into communities where they may have committed abuses is a live issue, but also in other ways. Indeed, as of 2015, the European Union (EU) has developed an official policy on TJ, one of whose "guiding principles" is: "Situate transitional justice within the security-development nexus paradigm."[17] The inclusion of TJ in *World Development Report 2011: Conflict, Security and Development* is another indicator of this shift.

This political turn in development assistance has also been marked by a new way of thinking about the respective roles of recipient states and civil societies in achieving development aims, which we have already described in our introduction. Marina Ottaway and Thomas Carothers argue that a new focus on civil society in international assistance circles was brought in around the mid-1990s – that is, after the initial turn toward democracy, which focused on elections and then reforms of institutions such as judiciaries and parliaments.[18] It thus coincides with the early years of the TJ field.

At a more general level, there are also debates concerning whether the real purpose of aid is to help poor countries, or rather to make them more dependent on wealthy countries on the one hand, or replicas of liberal states on the other. The first concerns well-known dependency theories from the 1970s that argued that not only was capitalism generating such dependency but the expenditures of wealthy countries in the South were part and parcel of it. The second relates more specifically to TJ and the political turn in development assistance. Critiques of liberal peacebuilding or the neoliberal character of governance and democracy assistance are inescapable now in the broader literature. In regard to TJ, scholars like Chandra Lekha Sriram, Dustin Sharp, and Sara Kendall have picked up these critiques, albeit

14 On donor approaches to TJ in fragile states, see Elena Baylis, "Transitional Justice and Development Assistance to Fragile and Conflict-Affected States," in *Justice Mosaics: How Context Shapes Transitional Justice in Fractured Societies*, ed. Roger Duthie and Paul Seils (New York: International Center for Transitional Justice), 386–90.

15 See Stephen Brown and Jörn Grävingholt, eds., *The Securitization of Foreign Aid* (London: Palgrave Macmillan, 2016).

16 Lars Buur, Stefan Jensen, and Finn Stepputat, eds., *The Security-Development Nexus: Expressions of Sovereignty and Securitization in Southern Africa* (Uppsala and Cape Town: Nordiska Afrikainstitutet and HSRC, 2007).

17 Council of the European Union, "The EU's Policy Framework on Transitional Justice," Ares(2015) 6003265 – 22/12/2015: 12.

18 Marina Ottaway and Thomas Carothers, eds., "Introduction," in *Funding Virtue: Civil Society Aid and Democracy Promotion* (Washington, DC: Carnegie Endowment for International Peace, 2000), 6.

in different ways. Sharp has expertly explored TJ as a liberal peacebuilding model, and Kendall has written about the ways that the "neoliberal" language of the market has suffused international criminal justice efforts, as these are necessarily supported by international assistance.[19]

Types of Assistance

The literature also notes many types of assistance. Traditionally, development assistance has consisted of a mix of technical and financial assistance. Technical assistance, or technical "cooperation" as it is often called, has as its core mission the development of local capacity. According to one source, technical assistance amounts to roughly one quarter of all development assistance.[20] The object of capacity-building efforts varies – it can include both state agencies and local communities. In many cases, consultants, NGOs, and other entities may be engaged to deliver this kind of assistance. Financial assistance relates, as the term suggests, to financial transfers. Financial aid can be tied or untied; "tied" funds require that goods and services needed to implement activities for a grant should be purchased from the country giving the grant, in line with using development assistance to contribute to the commercial interests of the granting country. Untied funds have no such requirements. In recent years, tied aid has become less common than it once was.[21] TJ initiatives have benefited from all of these types of assistance, including tied aid.

Technical assistance has played an important role, given the fact that specific expertise required to implement TJ according to international standards may not exist among national actors, as the country has likely never had experience with TJ before. Therefore, such expertise must be developed, through bringing in outside actors and drawing on regional and international examples. This expertise can be critical to highly technical endeavors such as criminal prosecutions of international crimes, but is also significant for state-run administrative reparations programs, formal (state-run) truth-telling initiatives, and TJ-related institutional reforms.

Financial assistance – usually untied aid – has also been the lifeblood of many TJ initiatives, especially in low-income countries such as Liberia, Sierra Leone, the Democratic Republic of Congo, Uganda, Cambodia, Timor-Leste, and elsewhere. Note that in middle income countries – such as South Africa, Morocco, Colombia, and Guatemala – there is much greater prospect for state contribution, and even

19 Chandra Lekha Sriram, "Justice as Peace? Liberal Peacebuilding and Strategies of Transitional Justice," *Global Society* 21, no. 4 (2007): 579–91; Dustin Sharp, "Emancipating Transitional Justice from the Bonds of Paradigmatic Transition," *International Journal of Transitional Justice* 9, no. 1 (2015): 150–69; Sara Kendall, "Donors' Justice: Recasting International Criminal Accountability," *Leiden Journal of International Law* 24, no. 3 (2011): 585–606.

20 Arjan de Haan, *How the Aid Industry Works: Introduction to International Development* (West Hartford, CT: Kumarian Press, 2014), 94.

21 Roger C. Riddell, *Does Foreign Aid Really Work?* (Oxford: Oxford University Press, 2007), 99–101.

significant contribution, to TJ efforts.[22] We do not currently have a clear picture on the extent to which aid to TJ has been tied (although it seems rare). This said, we do know of one recent instance from our case studies: EU aid to TJ in Morocco was tied to the purchase of EU goods and services.

Effectiveness of Assistance

Finally, TJ is relevant in relation to current debates on effectiveness. The works by Easterly and Sachs mentioned earlier, among many others, are touchstones in general discussions of effectiveness of development assistance. Issues raised in relation to the effectiveness of assistance for "political" change include the fact that such initiatives are typically funded at a much smaller scale than other development projects; they still tend to operate in isolation from larger development agendas; they suffer from a proliferation of donors and concomitant fragmentation of approaches; they are not locally "owned"; and they are not as well suited to clear definitions of measurement and results as other types of development projects.[23] All of these issues hold true for TJ – with the exception of large-scale funding for international and ad hoc tribunals. As we will see, however, most funding for TJ is small scale, it typically is not integrated into development strategies, and issues of measurement and results remain a challenge for the field as a whole.

DECISION-MAKING ON ASSISTANCE TO TRANSITIONAL JUSTICE: A FRAMEWORK

International relations scholars going all the way back to Hans Morgenthau have understood the importance of interests in decision-making on international assistance. Interests may be geostrategic or commercial in nature, as primary examples. Over recent decades, the case has also been made for other important factors. These include the role of ideas – meaning world views or "moral visions."[24] These are the "principled beliefs" that define the "universe of possibilities for action" – particularly important as TJ has emerged as a field only in recent decades. It therefore represents a "new" universe of possibilities for action.[25] An additional factor relates to institutions, which we take in this chapter to refer to the domestic political institutions that

22 Classifications are based on: "World Bank Country and Lending Group," World Bank, accessed July 1, 2016, https://datahelpdesk.worldbank.org/knowledgebase/articles/906519-world-bank-country-and-lending-groups.

23 See Carothers and de Gramont, *Development Aid Confronts Politics*, 6; and Lancaster, *Foreign Aid*, 51.

24 See, e.g., David Halloran Lumsdaine, *Moral Vision in International Politics: The Foreign Aid Regime, 1949–1989* (Princeton, NJ: Princeton University Press, 1993); and Judith Goldstein and Robert O. Keohane, eds. *Ideas and Foreign Policy: Beliefs, Institutions, and Political Change* (Ithaca, NY: Cornell University Press, 1993).

25 Goldstein and Keohane, "Ideas and Foreign Policy: An Analytical Framework," in *Ideas and Foreign Policy*, ed. Goldstein and Keohane, 8. As they further explain, "John Ruggie has pointed out, 'fundamental modernist concepts such as market rationality, sovereignty, and personal privacy

TABLE 1 *Factors in donor decision-making on transitional justice*

FACTORS	MAXIMALIST	⟷	MINIMALIST
IDEAS	**Principled**: motivated by values and norms of TJ (e.g., truth, justice) as ends in themselves	⟷	**Causal**: motivated by desire to use TJ measures to achieve other ends, such as democracy, rule of law
INTERESTS	**Political**: linked to geostrategic or other interests	⟷	**Apolitical**: not linked to geostrategic or other political interests
INSTITUTIONS	**TJ ideas institutionalized**: linked to a strategy/ policy (TJ, development, peacebuilding, etc.) and positioned within an organizational structure	⟷	**TJ ideas not institutionalized**: not linked to a strategy or policy (TJ, development, peacebuilding, etc.) and positioned within an organizational structure
	Bureaucratic: no scope for application of individual reason	⟷	**Nonbureaucratic**: scope for application of individual reason
INFORMATION	**Informed**: application of theoretical and practical knowledge about TJ	⟷	**Uninformed**: no application of theoretical and practical knowledge about TJ

set policy, the multilateral institutions that do their own shaping, and the bureaucratic structures of assistance, from the embassy level on up. A final factor is information, which we have added as a result of our case study research, which suggests major information gaps in decision-making processes on TJ, especially in relation to the effectiveness of TJ measures.

A preview of the key factors relating to decision-making on TJ that I am proposing can be seen in Table 1. The table helps us to understand how aid to TJ can be multidimensional – motivated by ideals, for example, and also shaped by interests and institutions. Note that this rubric does not exhaust all the potential factors, but rather highlights the ones we have found most salient in our research. Also note that the intent is not to present "either-or" choices between maximalist or minimalist approaches, but instead to suggest a continuum between two poles. This approach fits strongly with our case study findings, which do not yield any general pattern or

would not have been comprehensible before the development of appropriate terms of social discourse.' These conceptions of possibility, or *world views*, are embedded in the symbolism of culture and deeply affect modes of thought and discourse. They are not purely normative, since they include views about cosmology and ontology as well as about ethics" (Ibid.).

model of donor assistance to TJ, which might lead to a general theory of such assistance. We find, in the case of TJ, a particularly contingent and often fragmented approach to how this kind of work gets funded.

Ideas

I have argued elsewhere that the field of TJ is animated by both principled and causal beliefs, looking mainly at the key actors and documents that began to shape the field starting in the late 1980s.[26] This current research on international assistance to TJ does not alter my perspective, but rather reinforces it. On the one hand, principled beliefs about the inalienability of human rights have become part and parcel of foreign policy for many countries (and a cornerstone for some, such as the Nordic states). The level of commitment to such beliefs as *legitimate or achievable foreign policy aims* clearly varies, even within governments and institutions, but it is still there nonetheless, and it is demonstrated in justifications that donors give for the decisions they make to fund TJ (which is itself a response to massive violations of human rights).

On the other hand, donor decisions are also animated by causal beliefs that link TJ to other ends (often themselves normative): democracy, peace, rule of law, and good governance, among others. In these cases, the rationale in supporting TJ may be led more by a belief that doing TJ will contribute meaningfully to these other goals, rather than by a belief in TJ as an end in itself. Of course, principled beliefs and causal beliefs need not be in conflict with one another; they can be mutually reinforcing. But these different types of beliefs both operate to varying degrees depending on the context and the donor as factors in making decisions to support TJ.

Indeed, it would be difficult to make sense of donor decisions to fund TJ at all, if we gave no weight to the power of ideas. Over the past twenty years, we have seen the creation of an international normative architecture for TJ, through soft law and through the standardization (for better or for worse) of norms and practices of TJ by the UN and by INGOs like ICTJ.[27] We have seen, similarly, the growth of a norm against impunity at the international level and in some regions, such as Latin America.[28] Accountability has become part of the universe of possible actions for donors in liberal countries in the post–Cold War era.

[26] Paige Arthur, "How 'Transitions' Reshaped Human Rights: A Conceptual History of Transitional Justice," *Human Rights Quarterly* 31 (2009): 321–67.

[27] UN Security Council, "Report of the Secretary-General: The Rule of Law and Transitional Justice in Conflict and Post-Conflict Societies," S/2004/616 (2004), and the updated version, S/2011/634 (2011); UN General Assembly, "Report of the Independent Expert to Update the Set of Principles to Combat Impunity," E/CN.4/2005/102 (2005); UN General Assembly resolution, "Basic Principles and Guidelines on the Right to a Remedy and Reparation for Victims of Gross Violations of International Human Rights Law and Serious Violations of International Humanitarian Law," A/RES/60/147 (2005); and UN, "Guidance Note of the Secretary-General: United Nations Approach to Transitional Justice" (New York: March 2010).

[28] See Kathryn Sikkink, *The Justice Cascade: How Human Rights Prosecutions Are Changing World Politics* (New York: W. W. Norton, 2012).

At a more granular level, our case studies support the view that ideas matter. In relation to principled beliefs, we saw that, in Morocco, the major donor to TJ – the EU – was partly motivated to support TJ owing to its own historical experience with dealing with legacies of mass atrocity after World War II. In Uganda and Guatemala, donors expressed support for TJ stemming from a belief that fundamental rights of victims should be recognized and upheld for their own sake. At the level of causal beliefs, in both Morocco and Guatemala, we heard TJ linked to democratization and, more specifically, to efforts to reinforce the citizenship and agency of victims of human rights abuse. In Uganda, through the Democratic Governance Facility (DGF) pooled fund, as well as assistance to the Justice, Law, and Order Sector (JLOS), TJ was linked to ideas on enhancing democracy, rule of law, and good governance. But assistance to TJ in Uganda was also clearly linked to peacebuilding aims; and in Bosnia and Herzegovina (BiH), we heard the clearest expression of an causal link between TJ and peacebuilding.

We had a particular interest, of course, in understanding donor beliefs on the relationship between TJ and strengthening civil society. The donors that we interviewed, all of whom worked on the political side of international assistance, affirmed the importance of civil society engagement in a general sense. These responses gave the impression that meaningful inclusion of civil society was indeed a principled belief – part of a core of democratic or liberal values underpinning their decisions. Additionally, some donors also saw the relationship in causal terms – albeit these were fewer in number. For them, TJ could only be successful, or lead to the intended democracy or governance outcomes, if it was undertaken in partnership with civil society. Indeed, some donors saw the lack of such civil society engagement as contributing to TJ's weakness in their countries. In BiH and Uganda, for example, some donors lamented what they saw as a lack of civic engagement on TJ, which they expressed in terms of not seeing people "in the streets" – perhaps not fully recognizing the Western or liberal bias in this perspective.

TJ is therefore playing a role (though perhaps as a bit player) in these world views that shape the "universe of possibilities for action" for donors. This said, the articulation made by donors of these principled and causal beliefs remains, in most cases, abstract and uncertain. And this is because most donors do not have any formal or official expressions of the role of TJ in their foreign policies or in their development, governance, or peacebuilding strategies. That is, the ideas have not become *institutionalized* in most cases (a fact that will be further explored under "Institutions" later in this chapter). The result is that we heard a rather confusing array of these types of world views, linking TJ to a variety of possible – and not necessarily mutually reinforcing – ends. Without commenting on the "rightness" of these world views, we observed that they were in many instances linked to the institutional positioning of the person making the statements. Someone working on peacebuilding or fragile states was likely to see the goals of TJ in that light; someone working on rule of law issues would see it in their light; someone in the development field would see it in their light; and so forth. The idea remained sufficiently malleable as to mean many things to many different people. That is, we see no evidence of a "norm" of TJ as the idea (or set of ideas) – for example, the growing body of norms at the international level around rights to truth, justice, and reparation – animating these decisions. Indeed, as the section on "Information" that follows will argue, donors sometimes do not know enough about TJ to take a meaningful view on what it is or whether it is a norm to which their funding should align.

This point brings me to an explanation of why the principled/causal distinction is important in the decision-making process on TJ. Principled beliefs are those that ideally should be upheld no matter the political context; in the maximalist sense, they are norms that are universally applicable. Our research suggests that most donors stop far short of seeing TJ in this light. Indeed, donors we spoke to were weighted toward the "causal" end of the continuum, primarily advancing instrumental reasons for whatever support they gave for TJ – peacebuilding, for example, or promoting democracy and rule of law. One or two even strongly recommended that TJ practitioners should reframe their work in development terms, if they really want to access funding. This finding should not be a surprise. Bilateral donors we spoke with were generally unfamiliar with normative advances on TJ within the UN architecture; their reference points for TJ were few and far between; and TJ was just one small piece of a larger set of issues that they typically work on. Moreover, the trend within the donor community is for stronger causal arguments to support funding. Donors primarily want to know, "What works?" – and secondarily (if at all), "What is right?"

As mentioned, there is debate in the TJ literature about whether we should see funding for TJ as a tool of dominant (liberal) states to exercise control and to replicate their own (liberal) values through a standardized "form" of TJ. There is no question that many liberal states are trying to support liberal values through these kinds of initiatives. I am skeptical, however, that donor institutions are sufficiently coherent in their approach to TJ, or that they support TJ strongly enough, to justify this critique. In fact, many donors are not *consistently* supportive of TJ, and what support there is appears to have weakened over the past ten years. One needs to look only at our case studies to see that inconsistency and/or weakening of support. If liberal states are trying to replicate liberal values through TJ in these cases, then by and large they are not succeeding. In fact, it seems that they may be giving up in all but a handful of countries, such as Colombia.

Interests

One reason why donors may be giving up on TJ (if they indeed are) relates to the dramatic shift in geopolitics since 9/11: the United States' global war on terror and the growing power of Russia and China as illiberal counterweights to the liberal West.

Here we are moving into the territory of interests and how they shape funding for TJ. In this section, I consider the role of political objectives in funding for TJ, by considering two types of interests: those related to constituencies, meaning internal and external lobbies for TJ; and those relating to the "traditional" interests of power, security, and commerce. Although interests obviously must shape decisions to fund TJ, the subject has rarely been written about in the literature. An exception is the recent work by Annie Bird on US foreign policy and TJ in Cambodia, Colombia, and Liberia.[29]

Theoretically, any funding decision should bear *some* relationship to interests – whether these are defined in terms of geopolitical interests, or in terms of interest groups and domestic lobbies. It is difficult to see how any such decision could be taken in a completely disinterested manner. In the case of TJ, however, it can sometimes be difficult to see a clear link to specific interests.

Starting with the concept of constituencies, TJ usually does not have a clear constituency in donor countries, in the sense of a public interest group advocating for allocating public funds for TJ (compare this to lobbying by the defense industry, agricultural interests, labor interests, etc.). What does exist are interests *within* government agencies – usually isolated departments and even individuals. It is hard to predict where these advocates will arise, although they are often legal professionals, as TJ can be grouped in with rule of law or international criminal justice work. In the US government, there are pockets of advocates in both USAID and the US State Department; there are some at the embassy level as well. But apart from the Swiss government – which has a dedicated department working on TJ issues – no other government has an internal, coordinated group of technical specialists or advocates to push for inclusion of TJ in various countries or agendas.

Outside of government, interest groups exist that take various positions for and against ratifying the Rome Statute and joining the International Criminal Court (ICC) – and, more generally, on support for criminal accountability mechanisms for international crimes (such as hybrid tribunals).[30] In the case of US support of accountability efforts in Cambodia, Bird describes the successful efforts of US-based advocates to gain government support for establishing a documentation center and, ultimately, war crimes trials.[31] Additionally, diaspora communities from places where TJ is an active possibility may exert political pressure on legislatures and other political institutions. Indeed, this may be one of the vectors by which civil society

29 Annie R. Bird, *US Foreign Policy on Transitional Justice* (New York: Oxford University Press, 2015).

30 For an account of the US government's foreign policy on TJ in Cambodia, Liberia, and Colombia, which includes an extensive discussion of the role of interests in that policy, see Bird, *U.S. Foreign Policy on Transitional Justice*. For a discussion of the US Congress's fraught relationship with the ICC, see "Congress and the ICC," American Non-governmental Organizations Coalition for the ICC, accessed February 20, 2017, www.amicc.org/usicc/congress. An inside account of the US government's "unsigning" of the Rome Statute can be found in John Bolton, *Surrender Is Not an Option: Defending America at the United Nations and Abroad* (New York: Threshold Editions, 2008).

31 Although, as Bird recounts, the United States did not initially provide funding for the ECCC. See Bird, *US Foreign Policy on Transitional Justice*, 58–61.

engagement links to interests. Examples include Cambodians, Liberians, and Guatemalans in the United States, Moroccans in the Netherlands, and so forth. More than any other, these are the pressure groups most likely to form a domestic lobby that might influence perceptions of interest. So, for example, we know from our case studies that there have been congressional earmarks in the United States to support the Documentation Center of Cambodia as well as forensic work in Guatemala. Similarly, the Dutch have supported TJ in Morocco partly because of the interests of the large Moroccan communities living in the Netherlands. The Armenian diaspora community has developed an effective lobby in several countries, including France and the United States, in order to enact legislation recognizing the Armenian genocide.[32]

Turning now to traditional interests relating to power and security, our case studies suggest a few findings. First, and unsurprisingly, donors are unlikely to fund TJ if it conflicts with important national interests. We rarely see the United States vigorously supporting TJ in countries that are key partners in the war on terror – such as Morocco, where US support for TJ Morocco has been completely absent. In the EU's most recent Action Plan for Morocco, TJ is nowhere to be found, in spite of the EU's previous support for it as the major TJ donor in that country. Morocco is one of the European Commission's (EC) biggest aid recipients globally (always among the top ten since at least 2003), and it is possible that the shifting political and security terrain after the Arab Spring may have played a role (among other factors) in discontinuing EU support for TJ.[33]

Similarly, if donors see a particular country as critical for stability (and security) in a region, their support for TJ may weaken if there is concern that TJ could contribute to instability. Our case study of Uganda surfaced this issue quite clearly, as donors were less and less willing to push the government on TJ issues, even as the government stalled on its never-ending National TJ Policy process. In Liberia as well, after the TRC named the sitting president, Ellen Johnson-Sirleaf, among people who should be barred from public office, donors like the United States expressed worry about the potentially destabilizing effect of the recommendation. Indeed, neither the Liberian government (which had provided the majority of the funds for the TRC) nor donors took significant steps to help implement the TRC report's recommendations.[34]

32 Tony Cross, "France's Armenian Genocide Bill – Who? What? When? Where? Why?" Radio France Internationale, January 1, 2012, http://en.rfi.fr/europe/20120125-frances-armenian-genocide-bill-who-what-where-why.

33 On the top ten EC aid recipients, and the importance of the Arab Spring in EU policy, see Mark Furness and Stefan Gänzle, "The European Union's Development Policy," in Stephen Brown and Jörn Grävingholt, eds., *The Securitization of Foreign Aid* (Palgrave, 2016): 144–53. For a helpful analysis of EU policy on justice in "liberal peace" versus "war-on-terror" contexts, see Iavor Rangelov, Marika Theros, and Nataša Kandić, "EU Approaches to Justice in Conflict and Transition" (London: Security in Transition, 2016), www.securityintransition.org/wp-content/uploads/2016/02/WP09_Justice_FinalEditedVersion.pdf.

34 On the Liberia issues, see Bird, *US Foreign Policy on Transitional Justice*, 109–12.

Second, there are rare cases where support to TJ *does* align with national security interests – or, at least, it is not perceived to be in undue conflict with them. US support for TJ in Colombia is a case in point.

Third, there are also instances where donors use assistance to TJ in support of advancing "soft" power. For Japan, support to Cambodia's Extraordinary Chambers in the Court of Cambodia (ECCC) was partly motivated by its wish to project its power regionally. Japan's contributions to the ECCC are notable given the fact that it is not a big contributor to TJ anywhere else in the world. Both France and Belgium have provided some funds for TJ in their former colonies (as one example, I participated in a conference in 2006 cosponsored by the French and Swiss governments to explore and promote TJ in *la Francophonie*[35]). The Netherlands also has a unique relationship with INGOs and international institutions in The Hague working on international criminal justice – raising the profile of the Netherlands as a key interlocutor on these issues. Finally, Bird has argued effectively that the US government has used its support for TJ partly as a symbolic gesture to advance its soft power in her case studies of Liberia, Cambodia, and Colombia.

Similarly, there are also cases in which a donor state may use assistance to TJ to burnish its image internationally, after having been negatively implicated in atrocity: Dutch funding for TJ initiatives in BiH, including the memorial for victims of Srebrenica, appears to have been partly motivated by this interest; US complicity in Guatemala's genocide or in Cambodia's atrocities are additional instances. Along similar lines, states may support TJ as a kind of recompense for failing to intervene – for example, during the genocide in Rwanda.[36]

Finally, we have not observed clear links between TJ and commercial interests – although this would be a very interesting area for further exploration. For example, we have not found significant amounts of tied aid in relation to TJ – although some of the EU funding for TJ in Morocco was tied to purchase of EU goods and services as well as partnership with EU institutions. There does not seem to be any obvious fit between TJ and commercial interests, and it is rare to hear of them mentioned in the same discussion. Where the link is sometimes made – in a negative way – is in relation to corporate accountability for human rights abuse. We have not turned up evidence, however, that donors are interested in this angle, and indeed it may run counter to their interests.[37] Perhaps the

35 The report of the conference proceedings is: Mô Bleecker and Carol Mottet, eds., *La justice transitionnelle dans le monde francophone: état des lieux* (Political Affairs Division IV, Swiss Federal Department of Foreign Affairs, 2007), available at www.cedhd.org/wp-content/uploads/2015/06/12-ei.pdf.

36 Thanks to Elena Baylis for suggesting this point.

37 See, e.g., Sabine Michalowski, ed., *Corporate Accountability in the Context of Transitional Justice* (New York: Routledge, 2013).

link could also be made through the angle of state corruption, which has been a rising issue for TJ in recent years.[38]

A last note on the ambiguity of interests: in a recent article, Sarah Kendall has argued incisively that international and ad hoc criminal tribunals, which are overwhelmingly donor-funded, serve the interests of donors more than they do the interests of justice. Looking at funding for the Special Court for Sierra Leone (SCSL), she argues that its general prosecutorial direction – focus on a small number of those "most responsible" – and its operations were predicated on donor support.[39] This is a welcome viewpoint, as Kendall explores the link between donor support for the tribunals and their political objectives in furthering a regime of rule of law and accountability at both the national and international levels. But here, I would argue that ideas and interests are blurred. While Kendall is right to highlight the role of donor interests in funding decisions, my view is that these decisions are multifaceted and defy monocausal explanations.[40] In fact, it is difficult to see how, for a country like the United States, funding an international or ad hoc tribunal of any kind is not problematic from the perspective of interests, given the fact that the United States resists signing the Rome Statute primarily on national security grounds. In a sense, by funding these courts, the United States is promoting norms from which it is simultaneously struggling to escape.

In sum, it would be surprising to find any donor decision-making on TJ to be completely disinterested – motivated purely by ideals or principled beliefs – and we do see evidence of the political nature of these decisions. And donors have to make a strategic calculation about whether to expend valuable political capital on TJ in countries where other priorities are in play. Yet these scenarios can be difficult to tease out in some cases. In a sense, it might be easier to understand how interest plays a role in choosing *not to fund* TJ, rather than *to fund* TJ, mainly because we have not come across many clear expressions of how TJ fits into the political interests of donors. As such, when budgets for international assistance shrink, or when resources

38 In Tunisia, for example, corruption has been integrated into the TJ process. See International Crisis Group, "Tunisia: Transitional Justice and the Fight against Corruption" (Brussels: International Crisis Group, 2016); and "Laundering the Corrupt Is a National Priority? Tunisian Civil Society Again Opposes the National Reconciliation Law," International Center for Transitional Justice, April 25, 2017, www.ictj.org/news/tunisia-civil-society-reconciliation-bill.

39 Sarah Kendall, "Donors' Justice." This sentiment is echoed by another observer in relation to the work of the SCSL: "In one case, the accused argued that the funding arrangements created, 'a legitimate fear of interference in justice delivered by the Court through economic manipulation since . . . donor States could indicate their displeasure with any decision of the Court by withholding their contributions to the funds of the Court." See Bird, *US Foreign Policy on Transitional Justice*, 102.

40 Many of the interests that Kendall identifies as important in donor decision-making are better viewed as normative ideas – democracy, rule of law, etc. – rather than interests per se. I point this out not to quibble with Kendall, but rather to encourage the use of a broader range of analytical categories when developing explanations for donor decision-making. I would also point out that I disagree with the conflation of international criminal justice and TJ. To this point, my sense is that decisions about funding for the tribunals are different in process and kind to the many other donor decisions that are made about TJ.

are pulled in another direction (e.g., to the current refugee crisis in Europe), we should not be surprised if funds for TJ are among the areas receiving cuts.

Institutions

In this section, I describe the features of institutions (and institutional arrangements) that are most salient for donor decisions to fund TJ. Some scholars, such as Lancaster, focus their attention on the domestic political institutions that set policy and allocate funds, and others include discussion of the structure of aid organizations themselves. Our research on TJ funding suggests the relevance of three types of institutions: political institutions, government aid agencies, and multilateral "pooled" or other institutional arrangements.

Some of the discussion of institutions is general. But following Judith Goldstein and Robert Keohane, I emphasize the link between ideas and institutions in this section. To what extent have ideas about TJ become embedded in institutions? Answering this question is important since, as Goldstein and Keohane argue, "The use of ideas over time implies changes in existing rules and norms . . . The impact of some set of ideas may be mediated by the operation of institutions in which the ideas are embedded. Once ideas have influenced organizational design, their influence will be reflected in the incentives of those in the organization and all those whose interests are served by it."[41] As we will see, this sort of institutionalization of TJ among most donor agencies is quite minimal.

Domestic Political Institutions: Setting General Conditions for Funding to Transitional Justice

Starting with domestic political institutions, there clearly would be much to say about this on a country-by-country basis. It is beyond the scope of this project, unfortunately, to describe the myriad of ways that domestic political institutions impact assistance to TJ. What we can do here is point to some examples of this impact and hope that future researchers will pick up the threads. As mentioned in the previous section on "Interests," there are few domestic political lobbies that could influence particular institutions; nonetheless, there are instances where this has happened, such as the case of US congressional earmarks for specific TJ-related activities in Cambodia and Guatemala; or the way that domestic lobbies for adoption of the Rome Statute have worked in countries all over the world.

It is much more likely, however, that these political institutions have an indirect effect on TJ funding, since TJ is not something that is typically acted on at the level of political institutions (being such a small part of international assistance). The types of indirect influence that would merit further examination include how

41 Goldstein and Keohane, "Ideas and Foreign Policy: An Analytical Framework," in *Ideas and Foreign Policy*, ed. Goldstein and Keohane, 20.

budgets for assistance are generated and, importantly, who has the power to set priorities for allocating those budgets. In general, the level of priority given to TJ-related issues (human rights, accountability) is framed by overall government priorities – and these issues change as political power changes, which may have follow-on effects for TJ down the line.

Knowing more about these issues would shed light on the extent to which we might expect a coherent versus a fragmented approach to funding TJ. A comparison between USAID and the Department for International Development (DFID) suggests ways in which these differences might matter. With respect to USAID, the agency's power is quite limited given the fact that Congress controls allocations through earmarks and "mortgages" (long-term funding for countries like Israel and Egypt), as well as strong directives about how the money should be used.[42] Add to this the fact that several other agencies within the US government have managed to hive off significant pieces of official development assistance (ODA) from USAID's budget (alongside the fact that it was folded into the Department of State in 2006). As USAID has lost power in recent decades, DFID, by contrast, has seen its power grow: elevated to a cabinet-level position (outside of the Foreign and Commonwealth Office [FCO]) with the power to set development policy.[43] The United Kingdom has become a major proponent of the "whole of government" approach, and DFID strives to work in coordination with the FCO and the Ministry of Defense.

These kinds of institutional differences could be examined in relation to how they set the conditions for funding for TJ: while US political institutions may have encouraged fragmentation of approaches, UK political institutions may have encouraged more coherence; while US institutions have weakened the budgetary and decision-making power of its development agency, UK institutions have strengthened theirs. Observers are generally critical of the fragmented nature of donor approaches – rightly so, and we will discuss how fragmentation has negatively affected TJ in further detail in what follows. However, there is a way to see fragmentation in a positive light: in the US case, it has permitted a certain level of freedom to fund TJ, absent an express interest in TJ at the political level. Therefore, we observe pockets of USAID and the State Department supporting TJ initiatives on their own. Where approaches are more coherent – such as DFID's – there is more discipline. Therefore, when TJ became less prominent in DFID's approach to fragile and post-conflict states, especially after 2011, there was less likelihood that pockets of the institution would continue to fund TJ.[44]

42 Joanna Spear, "The Militarization of United States Foreign Aid," in *The Securitization of Foreign Aid*, ed. Brown and Grävingholt, 28.

43 Owen Barder, "Reforming Development Assistance: Lessons from the U.K. Experience," in *Security by Other Means: Foreign Assistance, Global Poverty, and American Leadership*, ed. Lael Brainerd (Brookings, 2007), 291–300.

44 Christoph Sperfeldt, "An Outlook on Transitional Justice: Mapping International Assistance" (Berlin: Deutsche Gesellschaft für Internationale Zusammenarbeit, 2013), 8–9.

The Structure of Aid Agencies: Where Is Transitional Justice Located Institutionally?

This point takes us to the second issue related to institutions: the structure of the donor agencies funding TJ. Here again, we face challenges in capturing diversity across all of the agencies engaged in funding TJ. Our case studies show that funding for TJ initiatives cuts across a range of donor categories. A 2013 mapping to assistance to TJ by Christoph Sperfeldt, commissioned by the Germany's Corporation for International Cooperation (GIZ), is the best piece of research to date on this state of affairs. It describes the ebbs and flows of donor agencies' engagement with TJ, as well as the variety of institutional locations and issue areas that TJ might be conceptualized under: peacebuilding, rule of law, governance, human rights, and so forth.[45] For example, Sida describes TJ in relation to its work on "conflict resolution, peace, and security."[46] For USAID, TJ has been slated under the Democracy, Human Rights, and Governance Section of its Office of Transition Initiatives; and for the US Department of State, it is considered part of the work of the Bureau of Democracy, Human Rights and Labor (DRL).[47] Furthermore, EU institutions have held competing views: whereas the Council has seen TJ as a short-term, post-conflict issue, the Commission has seen it in light of long-term reconciliation.[48]

Because of the variety of institutional locations for TJ, and the general lack of an overarching approach to TJ, decisions to fund TJ initiatives come from a wide range of actors within government agencies – in embassies, development agencies, and ministries of foreign affairs – often with little internal coordination. There can be tension, confusion, and even competition between the branches of government providing funding – foreign ministries and headquarters, UN missions, and development cooperation agencies. We commonly heard that there is a disconnect between legal offices (which typically do not have funds to allocate, but who may have knowledge about TJ) and program staff members (who typically do have funds, but have weak knowledge about TJ). Decisions related to high-level TJ institutions

45 Ibid. Elena Baylis briefly touches on institutional issues in Baylis, "Transitional Justice and Development Aid to Fragile and Conflict-Affected States," 377 and 384.

46 As of 2015, Sida includes ICTJ "among the global peace and security organisations that receive most of Sida's support," and it highlights its funding for TJ work in Guatemala and DRC. See "Our Fields of Work: Conflict Resolution, Peace, and Security," Sida, www.sida.se/English/how-we-work/our-fields-of-work/conflict-resolution-peace-and-security/.

47 Transitional justice figures in USAID's 2013 Strategy for Democracy, Human Rights, and Governance, as part of sub-objective 3.1: Support mechanisms for protection, mitigation and response to violations against human rights, in particular human rights violations affecting the most vulnerable. See USAID, "Strategy on Democracy, Human Rights, and Governance" (Washington, DC: USAID, 2013), 22, www.usaid.gov/sites/default/files/documents/1866/USAID%20DRG_%20final%20final%206–24%203%20%281%29.pdf.

48 Thomas Unger, "The European Union and Transitional Justice," CLEER Working Paper 2010/1 (The Hague: Centre for the Law of EU External Relations, 2010), 10. Rangelov, Theros, and Kandić describe the lack of coherence on TJ within EU institutions prior to the policy: Rangelov, Theros, and Kandić, "EU Approaches to Justice in Conflict and Transition," 4–5.

like hybrid tribunals have often been made in home offices, while civil society–related funding may be done along separate tracks, sometimes through embassies and sometimes through development agencies. Decision-making in each of these cases may be fundamentally different in timing, priorities, planning, frameworks, and length of support.

But all of these issues lead us to an important conclusion, which is that TJ has not been sufficiently institutionalized in these agencies to lead to a more coherent approach. Goldstein and Keohane remind us, "Ideas that become institutionalized play a role in generalizing rules and linking issue areas."[49] A good indicator that such institutionalization has not taken place is the complete lack of policies on TJ in most donor agencies. Apart from the Swiss government, no other bilateral donor has a policy on TJ (though the Netherlands was in the process of developing one).[50] While the German government does not have a TJ policy, it participates in a cross-sectoral platform, the Working Group on Peace and Development (FriEnt). FriEnt has tried to promote a more strategic approach to TJ across its partner entities for more than a decade, and it has released several briefing papers on the subject. In general, however, our case studies suggest that such general rules and links between issue areas exist in only the most informal way in most donor agencies. TJ continues to fit into existing institutional structures in a highly variable way, and it generally lacks policies or even dedicated focal points to guide decision-making and coordination.

The important exception to this picture is the Swiss Federal Department of Foreign Affairs (FDFA), which has had a dedicated Task Force on Dealing with the Past since 2003. Working within the Division of Human Security, the Task Force disposes of a small budget to support programmatic initiatives, but it also plays an important functional role within the Swiss government, collaborating with the Directorate for International Law, the Swiss Agency for Development and Cooperation (SDC/DEZA), and the multilateral division.[51] It acts as a standing resource for others in diplomatic positions. As an example, one of our interviewees said, "Since 2009, we have had an explicit TJ strategy, and since 2003 we have had programs focused exclusively on 'dealing with the past.' … The fact of having a regional 'dealing with the past' advisor – not really because he knows the context here, but because he can suggest some mechanisms or approaches – facilitates the work of diplomats working on this portfolio." A level of institutionalization therefore exists within the Swiss government that is unique among bilateral donors.

Multilateral Approaches to Transitional Justice: Creating Pooled Funds

This brings us to our third and final issue relating to institutions, which is in regard to multilateral institutions and how they address TJ. As of this writing, the EU had just

49 Goldstein and Keohane, "Ideas and Foreign Policy: An Analytical Framework," 23.
50 Council of the European Union, "The EU's Policy Framework on Transitional Justice."
51 See Sperfeldt, "An Outlook on Transitional Justice," 14–15.

developed a TJ policy (December 2015), which it is too soon to assess. The UN, by contrast, has a normative framework on TJ, solidified through soft law, the Secretary-General's 2004 report, *Rule of Law and Transitional Justice in Conflict and Post-conflict Societies*, and the creation of the Special Rapporteur on the Promotion of Truth, Justice, Reparation, and Guarantees of Non-recurrence. The institutionalization of TJ has taken place within several agencies, including UNDP and the Office of the High Commissioner for Human Rights (OHCHR), each of which has had dedicated staff at HQ working on TJ.

Our case studies analyzed two different types of approaches to institutionalizing TJ in funding mechanisms. The first type is a dedicated, pooled fund for TJ (in this case run by the UN), and the second type is a pooled fund that includes TJ among many other issues.

In Guatemala, a major shift in international funding for TJ initiatives occurred in 2010 with the creation of PAJUST (Transitional Justice Accompaniment Program), administered by UNDP. Through financing provided by USAID, Sweden, Canada, Denmark, the Netherlands, the Basque government, the Catalan government, and the UN Peacebuilding Fund totaling nearly $35.9 million for a five-year period, PAJUST has a specific strategy to support state institutions as they comply with their obligations to armed conflict victims under international law and civil society organizations that advocate on victims' behalf. PAJUST programming is oriented around TJ's key measures: truth, reparations, criminal justice, and guarantees of non-repetition. A fifth measure, "articulation," refers to efforts to promote greater cooperation and networks between state and civil society actors. According to our case study, representatives of donor governments explained the emergence of PAJUST to channel TJ funding as the result of three main factors. First, decreases in funding for international missions and the contraction of in-country staff in the late 2000s meant that embassies no longer had the human resources to administer their own aid programs. Second, international mission officials realized that, in some cases, they were duplicating efforts because of a lack of communication. Finally, channeling funds through UNDP and PAJUST has allowed donor governments to create some distance between themselves and TJ efforts, which have become more politically charged over the past several years, while still supporting important TJ work.

In Uganda, donors also created a pooled fund called the Democratic Governance Facility (DGF). As part of the peace and reconciliation stream of their engagement in Uganda, the governments of Austria, Denmark, the Netherlands, Norway, Sweden, the United Kingdom, and the European Union established the DGF in July 2011. Started up in 2012, the fund is not dedicated to TJ, although TJ was included under one of the DGF's three pillars, and its funding supported ongoing efforts to assist the government and civil society actors in developing a draft national TJ policy, among other things. Funds provided by the DGF are limited to use by Ugandan entities, with 80 percent of the funds targeting civil society organizations and 20 percent going to the government. In mid-2014, however, the DGF identified new areas of donor engagement, and TJ was not among them, owing to lack of progress on TJ by the Ugandan government and shifts in donor priorities. Although this decision only impacted new partnerships, not existing ones, the decision was an unexpected one for some civil society organizations that had expected to receive funding. As of January 2015, following some headway in the pursuit of Lord's Resistance Army perpetrators, the DGF switched course again and signaled a continued interest in TJ by identifying two new implementing partners. The DGF is an important model for other complex environments, and there may be advantages to including TJ as part of a wider funding strategy on governance. However, the lack of a specific strategy for TJ, and the possibility that it can be moved off the agenda as donor priorities change, suggest that the DGF may not be the most sustainable model for TJ funding. In deciding on how to best pool funds for TJ, donors should consider the advantages and disadvantages of these two models – PAJUST (dedicated pooled fund for TJ) and the DGF (TJ as part of larger pooled fund) – for the particular country context.

Bureaucratic versus Non-bureaucratic Approaches to Decision-Making

Our case studies shed light on the highly bureaucratic forms employed by the EU and the US government (especially USAID), which we could contrast with the less bureaucratic approaches of a number of bilateral donors (such as the Nordic countries). In the bureaucratic approach, institutional processes and forms limit the degree to which individuals within donor bureaucracies may exercise their reason and judgment. We observed, in the case of EU funding, this approach as characterized by a high degree of rules that are set in Europe and difficult to modify in relation to the context. Bureaucratic processes include stringent requirements for applying for and receiving funding, for monitoring and reporting, for spending funds (including tied aid, so that goods and services must be purchased from European vendors), and even requirements for branding (using the EU logo). Additional to these processes, which weigh heavily on aid recipients, is the bureaucratic nature of the decision-making process itself, characterized by large-scale, multiyear "action plans" where TJ is a footnote, if it appears at all, and where every step of the process goes through committees and multiple rounds of oversight.[52]

This bureaucratic approach was not only widely criticized in our interviews, but we also observed its negative effects in places like Morocco. EU funding for the

[52] Relatedly, we observed during our research in BiH how the EU accession process approaches TJ through a narrow lens: the main focus was on cooperation with the ICTY. Since the adoption of the new EU policy on TJ, which states that "EU considers transitional justice to be a priority for candidate countries and potential candidates," it is uncertain what if anything has changed. Council of the European Union, "The EU's Policy Framework on Transitional Justice," Art. V:7. For an overview of EU conditionality and TJ that predates the TJ policy, see Iavor Rangelov, "EU Conditionality and Transitional Justice in the Former Yugoslavia," *Croatian Yearbook of European Law and Policy* 2 (2006): 365–75.

community reparations program required that all proposals for these small-scale, local-level initiatives be submitted in French or English (not Arabic, for example), which de facto excluded most local-level groups outside of large population centers from applying for funds. The requirement that everything funded by the EU should include the EU logo caused people to question whether the community reparations program was really a Moroccan initiative. The reporting requirements for these – again, small-scale – initiatives were so burdensome that one recipient observed, only half-jokingly, that the main outcome of their project was that they learned how to run an EU grant.

By contrast, less bureaucratic approaches allow greater flexibility in applying individual judgment or reason to the decision-making process within the framework of applicable institutional rules. Of course, outcomes from less bureaucratic approaches can be both positive and negative. While there is no such thing as completely "un-bureaucratic" decision-making in donor agencies, we saw a number of instances of "ad hoc" decision-making, often by embassy staff members (e.g., in Morocco and Cambodia). Where embassies control distinct pots of money and feel pressure to spend down funds, there is more of an opportunity for individual staff members to support pet projects. And, indeed, individual ambassadors can play a key role in determining whether TJ gets supported in any particular country – including obstructing TJ initiatives pursued from home offices. Such decision-making, when it is not linked to a long-term strategy or objectives, seems unlikely to support meaningful or sustainable programs. Another model of less bureaucratic decision-making that seems better poised to support sustainable programs concerns the agencies that simply allow greater flexibility and that devolve some decision-making authority to people who are working in the country on a long-term basis. The Nordic countries were noted to be good models of this kind of decision-making. Sweden, for example, funds Diakonia, a faith-based organization that takes a deep, long-term approach to engagement at the local level. Interviewees in Guatemala, Cambodia, and Uganda viewed Diakonia as more flexible and devolutionary in its decision-making structures.

Summing Up: A Fragmented Patchwork of Institutional Approaches

In sum, the features of institutions or institutional arrangements salient to TJ are mainly characterized by fragmentation and lack of institutionalization, particularly among bilateral donors, except in one significant case (Switzerland). Decisions on funding TJ are taken in different parts of donor agencies, for a variety of reasons, and at varying levels of authority. There is a somewhat greater institutionalization of TJ at the multilateral level, specifically in some country contexts (although not in others), resulting in more strategic approaches like pooled funds. But there remains experimentation and a lack of clarity about how and where to include TJ within institutional structures at the multilateral level.

Additionally, while there was some variety in terms of donor strategies with regard to TJ, the majority of our interviewees told us that their decisions were not made with respect either to a specific strategy (including clearly defined goals) for TJ in that country or to a government-level TJ policy. It seems that where there was a strategy as such, this was around supporting a specific state/hybrid TJ institution – such as the ECCC, the ICTY, Uganda's JLOS, the Bosnian War Crimes Chamber – rather than a more multifaceted approach to TJ. The exception to this generalization is Guatemala, where donors have created a special pooled facility for TJ called PAJUST, administered by UNDP. Also notable here is the Swiss Department of Foreign Affairs' long-term program, "Dealing with the Past," which is the only state-level framework related to TJ that we found. One factor in this general lack of TJ strategies is that, at the grant level, TJ assistance tends to be part of a larger basket of funding for human rights, democracy building, rule of law, etc. Donors can therefore pick and choose TJ projects to fund without regard to whether they are strategically placed to build momentum for TJ.

One takeaway from these findings in relation to the impact on funding for civil society actors is that support for them may be inconstant and variable, depending on the donor. This is not to say that the institutions cannot support civil society action, but rather that there typically is little inherent in the way that TJ has been institutionalized to ensure that donors attend to the needs of civil society when they are making funding decisions. Indeed, we found consistently that the Swiss and the Nordic donors, as well as UNDP and the National Endowment for Democracy, were seen as highly connected to the context and understanding of civil society's particular challenges – especially the importance of long-term engagement and core support. They were seen to have a commitment to building capacity, not just to funding projects. We also found that, by contrast, this general commitment to civil society remains vague for many other donors; civil society actors may be more concerned with completing one-off projects and getting new grants than working toward social change. It should therefore not be surprising that we see instances where a very large amount of funds is directed to institutions, like courts, with comparatively little going to the civil society actors that are critical to supporting those institutions. Our case study in Cambodia demonstrates this point clearly. Decision-making on support to the court was disconnected from decision-making on other critical aspects of TJ.

Additionally, across all case studies, the lack of institutionalization and incoherence of donor approaches to TJ was consistently cited as a key frustration of civil society. This is not to say that civil society representatives criticized all donors in all cases. Many were grateful for the support they received and had positive relationships with donors. But in most cases, there was a sense that the assistance would have been improved had there been a more coherent, long-term, and articulated approach. One issue that we have noted is the small amounts of funding for civil society, compared with the amounts given to states or institutions. On the one hand, this is appropriate, as small organizations may have difficulty in absorbing and effectively using large amounts of funds, especially over the short term. On the other, there may be reason to doubt that programs of $100,000 to $500,000 per year can meaningfully contribute to the kinds of social changes that are actually required to support a TJ process. In this sense, USAID has recently developed a potentially game-changing approach in Colombia – $50 million to $55 million over four years for support to support both state and civil society–related initiatives on TJ, including outreach and communications campaigns as well as community-level reconciliation efforts.[53] This is a completely new approach and it will be interesting to see if this kind of massive financial commitment will yield results. One can only wonder what might have happened in Cambodia, Sierra Leone, or elsewhere if donors had matched their commitments to courts and state actors with funds on a larger scale for civic action. This said, as a middle-income country, Colombia provides a different context that may be more amenable to this level of funding than low-income countries.

It is hard to say whether we will continue to see progress in terms of institutionalization of TJ, and how this may affect meaningful support to civil society. For the two major donors (in relation to TJ) in the world, the United States and the EU, we note that the recent EU policy makes a strong call for incorporation of civil society in every aspect of TJ processes. How this policy will be institutionalized, however, remains unclear. Given the high degree of bureaucratization of decision-making in the EU, it is possible that, if the policy gets institutionalized, then we may see more (and more consistent) support for civil society on TJ. We also note a general uncertainty around the role of human rights in US foreign policy under the new president in the United States, Donald Trump – and therefore question whether there may be any further progress within the US government over the short term.

As a final observation, there is a tension between the tendency of "institutionalizing" TJ through policies, strategies, and guidance, and the tendency of "bureaucratizing" TJ through the creation of formal structures that limit individual reason and judgment in making decisions about how to fund TJ. Suffice it to say that, at the moment, there is so little of the former in donor agencies that there is not yet reason to be afraid of the latter.

Information

The final dimension of donor decision-making on TJ concerns access to and application of knowledge – whether empirical or theoretical. Our case studies yielded rich examples of the ways that donors do apply such knowledge, as well as of the information gaps that donors face (and that they acknowledge themselves).

Not surprisingly, donors that have more significant institutionalization of TJ, such as the Swiss government and the UN, are more likely to have access to practical and

[53] See USAID, "Reconciliation Activity: Notice of Funding Opportunity 514-15-000012," September 18, 2015.

theoretical knowledge on TJ. This may partly be because these institutions have dedicated staff members who themselves are experts on TJ – which is not the case in many bilateral government agencies. For example, even in an entity as large as the US government, there are only one or two specialists with dedicated expertise in TJ who also have programmatic (funding) responsibilities. Typically, program staff members have been pulled from neighboring fields, like rule of law or peacebuilding/reconciliation, and asked to develop TJ expertise in addition to their current skill set. By contrast, the Swiss government has a team of experts whose core focus is TJ. UNDP and OHCHR have global experts on TJ, as well as field staff with significant expertise. The German government has access to TJ expertise through FriEnt. There are other governments with pockets of expertise – such as the Netherlands, which currently has a TJ expert at HQ. What is critical is to have the expertise in an institutional location that is readily findable by other donor agency staff, as the Swiss government does.

We observe, nonetheless, general information deficits of several kinds. Many of our donor interviewees, particularly at the bilateral level, were frank in saying that they were not always sure what TJ meant, or how it was different from criminal justice initiatives. While many had a good grasp of the concept and felt relatively comfortable with it, others asked us (the interviewers) for information about it, or told us that they looked in their own files or online for information before the interview. This gap is related to the facts that many donors are funding TJ-related work without "naming" it as such, and that TJ fits under different rubrics in different institutions (rule of law, peacebuilding, democratization, etc.). This gap was acute for decision-makers at the embassy level, who seemed to have a particular need for more specific guidance on TJ, as many funding decisions are handled locally – by staff members who are under-resourced and often managing a heavy and varied portfolio, and particularly so with respect to TJ. In short, for many, there is an information gap on the most basic level: what is TJ? For those who do have some understanding of it, then the next information gap is: how does it relate to my objectives?

For most donors, it may be challenging to obtain information about TJ initiatives that their own government may be funding in other countries – let alone what other governments are funding. This gap relates to an institutional issue discussed earlier – the lack of particular policies, offices, or mechanisms tasked with dealing with TJ across agencies. Absent such an institutional focal point, it is difficult for time-strapped staff members to find relevant data, even to know, quite simply, whether their government has funded similar initiatives elsewhere and what the outcomes have been. Many interviewees lamented a lack of guidance on TJ, which they would have welcomed in making decisions, and some said that they did not know whom to ask for help, even within their own governments. Compounding these difficulties can be general problem of inadequate processes for capturing institutional memory, in order to maintain continuity as staff rotate in and out. In relation to information on what other governments were funding, we did note a number of instances where donors developed coordination mechanisms of some kind, in particular in Guatemala, Cambodia, and Uganda. Nonetheless, on the whole, most coordination is not specific to TJ – which should not be surprising, given the fact that TJ does not typically figure in donor strategies.

Does this mean that donors have been funding TJ without adequate information as to what they were funding and why? It is difficult to make a generalization on the issue. Many donor efforts have been well-informed and sensitive to the context, with a commitment to both state and civil society aspects of the process. The approach the PAJUST has taken in Guatemala is a good example. Another is GIZ's long-term (ten-year) support for civil society work on TJ in Cambodia, as discussed in the Cambodia case study. But, as many donors report, they are just too busy much of the time to develop the expertise they might wish to inform their decisions on TJ. There is an imperative to get funds out the door quickly, especially at the embassy level. Many donors expressed the view that they are just doing the best that they can.

Our civil society interviewees also recognize the challenges their donors face, especially the demands on their time. But they also directly experienced the consequences that result in cases where donors lack appropriate knowledge about TJ. These consequences can include things like donor fatigue, as donors may not have understood that TJ was a long-term social change process rather than a one-off institution like a set of trials or truth commission. It can include misrecognizing the fundamentally political nature of TJ, and treating it instead as a technical enterprise related to "fixing" institutions (e.g., the judiciary, the police) – a view that was expressed several times of the EU's approach in Morocco and BiH. It can include a lack of awareness of victims' groups or lack of interest in engaging with or working to strengthen them. It can include having to constantly "fit" TJ work into other categories (rule of law, peacebuilding, etc.) and to follow donor trends rather than to pursue their own strategy, as civil society actors in BiH described. To be clear, this is not to say that all of these consequences necessarily follow from information gaps, but rather that these are ones we have observed in certain cases, and they are possible.

Perhaps the biggest information gap in relation to TJ is whether it achieves the social change outcomes it sets out to achieve. That this gap remains so large is a puzzling issue. The donor community has poured billions of dollars into TJ efforts (including the international tribunals), but with almost no data upon which to base its funding decisions, and almost no interest in understanding the impact of its assistance. Based on my experience in the TJ field spanning the past ten years (and as the former head of evaluation at ICTJ), I have observed that the few evaluations that are undertaken are primarily focused on the project level – rather than the TJ intervention level (like a truth commission) – including even small projects with budgets of less than $200,000. Nearly a decade has passed since Oskar N. T. Thoms, James Ron, and Roland Paris published their working paper "The Effects of

Transitional Justice Mechanisms: A Summary of Empirical Research Findings and Implications for Analysts and Practitioners" – a paper people in the TJ field saw as throwing down the gauntlet concerning lack of evidence for the impact of TJ on strengthening peace or democracy.[54] What has happened since? Aside from a number of academic studies, not much.[55]

Since most donors do not have specific policies or guidance on TJ, and donors categorize TJ under very different "headings," perhaps it should not be such a surprise that we have not seen more donor investment in this area. That is, there may not yet exist the needed level of institutional coordination to make a significant investment – and the investment would need to be significant, and it would likely need to be sustained over a longer period of time (e.g., five, ten, or fifteen years) than the standard donor funding cycle.

Given, however, the current funding climate, which has been so strongly marked by the "what works" agenda, it is hard to see this as the sole factor. Another factor that may be at work in this gap has been addressed by Lant Pritchett, as part of his larger analysis of impact evaluation in development assistance. In his article "It Pays to Be Ignorant: A Simple Political Economy of Rigorous Program Evaluation," Pritchett sketches an analytical model to explain "why randomized evaluations are infrequent and when evaluations can be expected" in the broader development field, looking specifically at interventions funded by the World Bank, DFID, and others.[56] It is motivated by his observations, during his ten-plus years of experience at the World Bank, that "there was heated debate among advocates of various activities but very rarely any firm evidence presented and considered about the likely impact of the proposed actions. Certainly in my experience, there was never any definitive evidence that would inform decisions of funding one broad set of activities versus another (e.g., basic education versus road construction or vaccinations versus macroeconomic reform) or even funding one instrument versus another (e.g., vaccinations versus public education about hygiene . . .)."[57]

One could easily say something similar of advocates on either side of the debate regarding TJ. The TJ field is also characterized by a general lack of evidence and

54 The paper was commissioned by a donor (Canada's then-Department of Foreign Affairs and International Trade), and the paper made the rounds in both donor and practitioner circles. A revised version was subsequently published as Oskar N. T. Thoms, James Ron, and Roland Paris, "State-Level Effects of Transitional Justice: What Do We Know?" *International Journal of Transitional Justice* 4, no. 3 (2010): 1–26.

55 See, e.g., Tricia D. Olsen, Leigh A. Payne, and Andrew G. Reiter, eds. *Transitional Justice in Balance: Comparing Processes, Weighing Efficacy* (Washington, DC: United States Institute of Peace Press, 2010); and Hugo van der Merwe, Victoria Baxter, and Audrey Chapman, eds., *Assessing the Impact of Transitional Justice: Challenges for Empirical Research* (Washington, DC: United States Institute of Peace Press, 2009).

56 Lant Pritchett, "It Pays to Be Ignorant: A Simple Political Economy of Rigorous Program Evaluation," in *Reinventing Foreign Aid*, ed. William Easterly (Cambridge, MA: MIT Press, 2008), 123.

57 Ibid., 122.

evaluation – not just rigorous evaluation, which Pritchett defines as randomized control trials (RCTs) – but any form of evaluation. And there is no evidence to support decision-making when confronted with choices and trade-offs (truth commission versus courts versus reparations programs, etc.). Looking beyond RCTs, which may or may not be the most appropriate method for assessing the impact of TJ, in general there is a lack of evaluations that are independent, that use social scientific methodologies, and that have adequate human and financial resources to look past a short-term project level.[58]

So let us adapt Pritchett's argument in light of information for making decisions on funding for TJ. Pritchett's model is based on a set of four actors: On the one side, there is the advocate for the intervention – for example, an NGO working on TJ. On the other, there are three types of external supporters: core supporters who already believe the efficacy of the interventions; middle, "on the fence" supporters, who need some persuasion; and the "hard headed," whom he defines as economists, but who in the TJ context could simply be skeptics. The model, when adapted to TJ, looks like this:[59]

TABLE 2 *Information and types of external transitional justice supporters*

Description	Core supporters	"On the fence" supporters	Skeptics
Prior belief in the efficacy of TJ	High	Medium	Low
Persuadability – in the sense of responding to rhetoric on TJ, rather than to rigorous evidence	High	Medium	Zero

Pritchett uses his model to pose the question of under what conditions the advocates for the intervention (in this case, TJ advocates) will undertake an expensive, rigorous evaluation instead of less expensive "promotional" activities (trying to persuade people using rhetoric, rather than evidence). The first response is when they are certain that such rigorous evaluation will be positive. With a positive rigorous evaluation, the TJ advocate can maintain core supporters, pull "on the fence" supporters to their side, and even convince some of the skeptics (who would not be persuaded by promotional activities in any case). The result, presumably, would be enhanced funding for the intervention. In this scenario, it would be well

58 Elena Baylis makes the point that one reason for the lack of impact-level evaluations relates to the structure of accountability within organizations. Offices may be held more accountable for the outcomes of projects they fund rather than for the ultimate impact of TJ on its intended beneficiaries.

59 For the sake of brevity, I am using a version of Pritchett's model that excludes his analysis of the weighting of program gains against one's own consumption. This piece is central to his argument, and here I am simply accepting it as given, rather than reproducing it in its complexity. For the full argument, please see his article.

worth the investment required on the part of the TJ advocate to undertake the evaluation, as they would be rewarded with more money.

The problem, of course, is that there can be no such certainty about the outcome of a rigorous evaluation of TJ. Assessing the options, Pritchett concludes that the risk of evaluation is too high for advocates. Since the "core supporters" are already on board, and the "on the fence" group can be persuaded through less expensive and less risky rhetorical efforts, "the best approach is never to do an evaluation that would reveal the truth but rather maintain sufficient uncertainty about true program efficacy so that we can overstate program benefits sufficiently to garner middle group support."[60] Hence the title of his article: "It Pays to Be Ignorant."

This is a conclusion that may be relevant not just to TJ advocates in civil society, who have not been conducting rigorous evaluation, but also to TJ advocates within donor agencies, who have not been funding rigorous evaluation. Perhaps the conclusion – "it pays to be ignorant" – seems unduly harsh. After all, TJ is hardly the only social intervention that has not been sufficiently investigated. However, claims made by TJ advocates that their work is too complex and therefore "cannot be measured" (meaning assessed or judged) are simplistic and misleading and must be challenged. Pritchett's model gives us valuable food for thought (which I have not seen raised in the literature on TJ before) about the motivations that might be animating such claims. It is indeed possible to assess the impact of TJ – with the right level of resources, skills, and time commitment. In fact, the USAID project in Colombia that I discussed earlier, funded at more than $50 million, includes provision for just such an impact-level evaluation. Continuing to operate in the dark may benefit TJ advocates in the short term (keeping the core supporters and "on the fence" supporters on their side), but over the long term, operating in the dark is unlikely to be sustainable, as supporters start to drift to the "skeptics" camp in the current "what works" funding environment.

In sum, the information environment for making decisions on TJ faces numerous challenges. Most fundamental is that donors may not have sufficient theoretical or practical knowledge about TJ to make decisions about meaningful and sustainable support for TJ. Additionally, we have very little evidence on the impact of TJ; and as long as there are a sufficient number of "core supporters" who do not require evidence to allocate funds, there will be little incentive to fund expensive and time-consuming impact evaluations that are needed to enhance information for decision-making. Other challenges include the fact that there may be little TJ expertise in-house for most bilateral agencies, that such agencies struggle to maintain institutional memory, and that they do not have mechanisms for learning about what has been funded in the past.

60 Pritchett, "It Pays to Be Ignorant," 131.

Conclusion: Fragmentation of "Globalized" Transitional Justice?

TJ is not a matter of policy for most donor governments, although obviously all funding decisions must align at some level to the world view of the agencies in question. In her book *Foreign Aid*, Carol Lancaster asks, "What purposes did governments pursue with their aid? And why did they choose those purposes and not others?"[61] In the case of TJ, the answers to these questions are not always clear, precisely because decisions about TJ are not usually taken at the level of policy, but may often be ad hoc or seen in relation to "sister" policies on human rights, rule of law, governance, peacebuilding, and so forth. Even so, Lancaster's question is fitting: why indeed would governments choose to use their scarce public funding on TJ in other countries?

There is no simple answer to this question – nor should we expect one given the diversity of actors and contexts where TJ is being tried. We can, however, identify some of the conditions under which donors do give assistance, as well as when we might expect for donors to do it in such a way as to strengthen engagement of civil society actors on TJ. In this chapter, I have described four factors that contribute to donor decision-making on TJ: ideas, interests, institutions, and information. I argue that we should not assume that there are monocausal explanations for why TJ does or does not get funded in any particular instance. International assistance to TJ – like assistance to other interventions – is multifaceted and defies simplistic explanations. In most cases, it may be quite difficult to understand why any particular donor is supporting TJ in the way that it does, especially since there may be no clear articulation of that donor's objectives for TJ. My hope is that the framework provided in this chapter will be useful to those wishing to better understand the decisions that any particular donor has made in any particular context – including donors themselves.

At a more general level, the framework leads us to three conclusions about donor decision-making. The first, unsurprisingly, is that we should not expect to see donors supporting TJ when it conflicts with their strategic interests, in particular those relating to security – which is a way of saying that there is no purely "principled" application of TJ. Concomitantly, we should expect to see donors supporting TJ mainly in situations where the risk is low of either (allied) government instability or radicalized social movements. The second is that although ideas, especially causal ideas linking TJ to a variety of outcomes, have played a central role in expanding the possible universe of actions for donors, these ideas have not been given sufficient form and content through institutionalization and information gathering. The result is a donor decision-making process for TJ that is characterized by fragmentation, incoherence, and possibly ineffectiveness in many (not all) instances. The third is that the clearest idea with the most vocal and powerfully placed constituencies inside and outside of institutions – namely, the idea of the power of trials, advocated by influential lawyers – has garnered the most success among donors, measured in terms of funding.

61 Lancaster, *Foreign Aid*, ix.

These conclusions have several consequences for the way that TJ has been conceptualized and implemented over time. One is that TJ is often confused with international criminal justice, which is a related, but much more high-profile, field. Donor support to tribunals runs in the hundreds of millions (ECCC, SCSL) to billions of dollars (ICTY, ICTR). No other TJ initiative is funded at this scale – a distant second is the highly technical forensic work relating to identifying remains of missing persons (in the Balkans, to take one example, this work has cost nearly $200 million). There is an important difference in donor approaches to these tribunals, in the sense that donors need not consider funding to such courts as part of a larger TJ process; instead, since the advocates for the courts tend to be legal professionals, they are just as likely to be seen through the lens of strengthening international criminal justice norms and regimes. This difference can be reflected not just in the large sums allocated to such institutions but also in the decision-making processes: financing for the courts may go through different channels than financing of other TJ initiatives. Taking US financing for courts as an example, much of the funding needed to go through Congress (ECCC, where it was initially blocked, and the SCSL[62]). US funding for the TRC in Liberia, by contrast, came from USAID.[63] Over the past decade, however, partly in response to criticisms of how expensive and inefficient these tribunals have been, donors have shifted attention to building national capacity to prosecute international crimes ("complementarity"), as the donor community has tried to do with JLOS in Uganda. In short, however, the sums of money for these kinds of initiatives far outstrip funds spent on other types of TJ work. If levels of funding provide a clear signal of which ideas the international donor community most values, the support for criminal justice approaches continues to stand at the forefront – although now through the lens of complementarity.

Another consequence is that TJ is not always supported in cases where it may be relevant – mainly because security or other important interests are in play. This kind of behavior is a clear example of friction between the universal and the

62 As Annie Bird notes, "Funding [for the SCSL] initially came from the Africa Bureau at the State Department. As time passed and as support for the SCSL within the Bush administration diminished, SCSL officials began to directly lobby members of Congress for support. For most years, Congress appropriated funds for the court under the Economic Support Fund (ESF) in the Foreign Operations Budget . . . As a result of Congress directly appropriating funds to the court, the State Department was often left scrambling to find sufficient funds, resulting in the reallocation of funds that would have normally been allocated to USAID projects in Sierra Leone." Bird, *US Foreign Policy on Transitional Justice*, 101.

63 One result of this difference is that much of the funding for the courts is not reported as ODA – and therefore did not appear in our searches of the OECD grants data to create the TJ International Assistance database. For example, although we know that the United States contributed $83 million to the SCSL through 2012, we only found funds for the 2009 contribution ($7.5 million) reported as ODA. On US contributions, see "Remarks by Ambassador Jeffrey DeLaurentius, U.S. Alternate Representative of the United States for Special Political Affairs in the United Nations, at Security Council Briefing on Sierra Leone," United States Mission to the UN, New York, NY, October 9, 2012, https://2009-2017-usun.state.gov/remarks/5532; and Reports of the President of the Special Court for Sierra Leone 2002–2013, accessed on February 7, 2014, www.sc-sl.org/DOCUMENTS/tabid/176/Default.aspx.

particular – of which there are many such examples in the TJ field. There are obvious cases where a government like the United States will not support TJ in relation to an ally in the war on terror – this is granted. But there are less obvious instances where different entities within government come into conflict. There is an example of a major donor agency that recently published a request for proposals for TJ in Nepal, only to have to withdraw the request because of resistance from the local embassy to any discussion of such politically sensitive issues. This kind of friction – and concomitant mixed messages on TJ – can be constant where people in decision-making authority hold different views on what is a priority, and where there is no policy or guidance on TJ to support internal decision-making.

Not only is TJ not always supported in cases where it may be relevant, but in those instances where it is supported, it may not be so in the most relevant way. The combination of high-profile ideas but low institutionalization and information can easily lead risk-averse donors to fall into general patterns of donor behavior: preferring to invest in visible, finite "outputs" like commissions, courts, or memorial sites on the one hand, or in countable deliverables like expert trainings, small-scale community workshops, and research reports. They may resist supporting the more politically risky, long-term, and difficult-to-measure social change work that is actually at the core of meaningful TJ initiatives.[64] Highly bureaucratized processes, such as the EU's, exacerbate risk-averse decisions and a "technical" rather than "political" approach. Additionally, TJ advocates must find a way to fit TJ work into the relevant donor paradigms – to find the right pot of money – and this means adapting it to current discourses on "fragile states," the "security-development nexus," and so forth. The elasticity of the TJ concept (already quite elastic) has therefore gotten further stretched, as TJ actors have dived into work on atrocity prevention; security sector reform; demobilization, disarmament, and reintegration (DDR) programs; corruption; poverty reduction; countering violent extremism; and so forth.

Taking these two issues together – TJ not supported in all relevant cases and TJ not supported in a relevant way in the cases where it does receive attention from donors – we see the balance of power between the principled and causal beliefs animating TJ to be shifting decisively toward the causal side (if it ever was tilted to the principled side). And, more and more, donors require a plausible, causal narrative that links TJ to a growing list of possible outcomes, expanding from improved human rights or democratization, to stabilizing lawless regions or countering terrorism.[65] For their part, TJ advocates inside and outside donor agencies may be more than happy to

[64] Of course, similar observations might be made of support to other kinds of political development assistance – TJ is not alone.

[65] As two examples of this linkage being made in policy environments, see US Department of State, "Transitional Justice Overview" (May 16, 2016), 4, www.state.gov/documents/organization/257771.pdf; UN General Assembly, "Promoting Tolerance and Reconciliation: Fostering Peaceful, Inclusive Societies and Countering Violent Extremism," High-Level General Assembly Thematic Debate (April 21–22, 2015), 2, www.un.org/pga/wp-content/uploads/sites/3/2015/06/170615_HLTD-Promoting-Tolerance-Reconciliation-Summary.pdf.

make these links – without much evidence to support their arguments – to persuade their "core" and "on the fence" supporters.

It remains to be seen whether changes in ideas and interests currently under way – whether related to the post-9/11 environment, the Syrian refugee crisis, the shift in US foreign policy, or other trends – combined with insufficient institutionalization and information, may signal a softening of international assistance to TJ. Has the globalized period of TJ reached its apex and now started a downward trajectory? While the normative architecture will remain in place, the financial architecture supplied by the world's major donors may be undergoing changes that may simultaneously put TJ under pressure but also push it to evolve. There is thus the potential (at least) for a return of "the local" in TJ activism – an opening for civil society actors, spurring them to innovation and new strategies of collaboration on the national and international levels.[66] They may need to do more to build constituencies (and source funding) in their own countries or regions; to find resonances between TJ and other important social issues, especially those important to younger people and to socioeconomic development; and to develop new networks with a wider set of actors. The concern, however, is in this era where so many governments are taking actions to close public space and suppress civil society, that courageous people require powerful allies more than ever.

66 Returning to the debate between Easterly and Sachs, Easterly would say that donor withdrawal is likely to lead to creativity, whereas Sachs would say that if we only spent money more wisely, this inherent creativity could thrive.

Conclusion

Refocusing on Civil Society: How to Make – not Miss – Connections

Paige Arthur and Christalla Yakinthou

Transitional justice (TJ) is not, nor ever has been, a straightforward technical enterprise – or a set of one-off institutions sitting on top of and apart from society. As the chapters in this book show, many of the actors involved in bringing TJ to fruition are long on ambition, courage, and (sometimes) perseverance. But they are as caught up in asymmetrical power dynamics and frictional engagements as any other actors working on less "principled" endeavors, and they perhaps have even greater deficits in terms of strategy, information, and communication than their colleagues working in more established development fields. What we discovered over the course of working on this book is a deepened and strengthened appreciation for the central role of a robust civil society sector in pushing forward TJ initiatives – which are long term and highly political, and therefore subject to delay, backsliding, and even reversal.

The donors we were most concerned with in this book – bilateral and multilateral funders – often understand the importance of supporting civil society. The reality, however, is that funding for TJ focuses squarely on institutions, whether state-led or "hybrid" entities. This should not be surprising, since the case studies also show that there is too often a lack of strategic consideration of the fundamental roles of civil society, even in those instances where donors make a long-term and costly commitment to supporting a TJ institution, such as the Extraordinary Chambers in the Courts of Cambodia (ECCC), Morocco's collective reparations program, or Bosnia and Herzegovina's (BiH) War Crimes Chamber.

Donor support to civil society should not be seen as unproblematic, but rather through a frictional lens that can have both productive and unproductive outcomes – for the latter, we noted unintentional outcomes such as dependency, cooptation, the creation of a "professionalized" civil society organization (CSO) sphere disconnected from communities, among others; for the former, if thoughtfully crafted alongside official efforts, productive outcomes lead to positive changes, as we saw in Cambodia and Guatemala. Similarly, supporting state-led institutions in an imbalanced way can also have perverse effects. We have argued that, in Morocco, European Union (EU) support primarily for state actors in TJ has contributed to the diminution of a once-strong civil society sector in TJ, which no longer acts as a counterweight to the state. In Uganda, donors placed their faith in the capacity of the Justice, Law and Order Sector (JLOS) to produce a national TJ policy, which has been stuck in the gears of the Ugandan government for years, going nowhere. In the meantime, civil society in Uganda has strengthened, but not enough to take on the state, which has significantly closed down public space and has turned its attention to its future development – while playing down its past conflict, in spite of that conflict's continuing and tragic effects.

This is not at all to say that it is incumbent on donors to engineer solutions – it is, instead, to urge them to think more strategically and relationally about the choices they do make (including *not* intervening), and to ensure that civil society priorities, capacities, and positioning are factored into that strategic thinking. Indeed, our book's research goal was to make significant headway in describing *how* the relationships work between international assistance and civil society actors engaged with TJ, and *what factors influence* their behaviors. With this in mind, this conclusion is structured in four parts, each of which is designed to give civil society its due weight. In the first, we tease out what the case studies tell us about the general environment for TJ in which these actors are operating. In the second, we offer some reflections on the relationship between TJ and strengthening of civil society. In the third, we draw conclusions on five specific "missed connections" on international assistance to civil society. In the fourth, we develop five concomitant recommendations, directed mainly to donors, which are intended to strengthen the connections between these actors.

REFLECTIONS ON THE GENERAL ENVIRONMENT FOR TRANSITIONAL JUSTICE ACTORS

Three main aspects of the general environment are worth highlighting from our research. First, in almost all of the case studies, we noted growth – in some cases, like BiH, massive growth – in CSOs over the past two decades, related to the end of a period of conflict or repression. Yet it is important to note that this growth did not appear to be linked to greater levels of trust or cooperation in many cases. Indeed, we saw a generalized competition and mistrust among civil society actors, driven by a range of contextual issues: in some places, such as Morocco, civil society actors are closely aligned with political parties; in others, like BiH, they are almost completely divided along ethnoreligious lines. But overall, the competition for scarce resources to survive (as an organization) creates mistrust and hinders collaboration. Data on trust from the World Values Survey would seem to support our view, as there has been a lack of change or even negative change in standard "trust" measures in countries for which such data is available (for example, Morocco, Bosnia) over the past twenty years.

Second, we also noted that the governments in these five countries generally show weak commitment to TJ. If we think of civil society in the context of Risse, Ropp, and Sikkink's classic five-stage model of how national and international human rights networks influence state behavior, we would find all of these states hovering around the middle phases of making "tactical (but insincere) concessions" to human rights actors and a weak "prescriptive status" of laws that are on the books, but not well implemented or enforced – concessions that seem to be in name only, rather than an indication of the state's sincere intention to adhere to human rights norms.[1] This is important, because in these middle to later phases of influencing state behavior, national civil society actors become more critical: they can now operate more or less openly, they can make proposals, and they are often seen as legitimate interlocutors.[2] That said, international actors remain important in order to make sure that pressure is on the state to continue with reforms, rather than to slip back into a cycle of repression and denial. We found this model relevant in thinking through the relationship between the state and civil society in all five countries; while in all of our studies national civil society actors do engage with the state, there was certainly a variety of perceptions concerning how committed the state is to reform – in spite of its public pronouncements.

While Guatemala and Uganda especially highlighted a serious closing of public space in recent years, all five countries had limiting environmental factors that were hindering civil society efforts on TJ. The most grievous of these factors included state repression, characterized by issues such as detention and torture of civil society activists, as well as a culture of intimidation of human rights actors linked to state and non-state actors. Another factor consistently mentioned as related to this closing of space included limitations on or state influence over the media, as well as restrictions on or monitoring of CSOs themselves (including receipt of foreign funds).

Third, the shrinking pool of donor money since the 2008 financial crisis has had a number of its own impacts. Many donors in the countries we studied have cut assistance and even closed/consolidated their embassies. Civil society actors have keenly felt this pullback. Those who have not succeeded in maintaining a sufficient level of funds see themselves in a more combative and weak position in the funding "marketplace." The fact that international financial assistance typically runs on

[1] In Risse, Ropp, and Sikkink's model, states pass through five phases, starting at the worst phases of 1) "repression" and 2) "denial" of that repression, moving to 3) "tactical concessions" in the face of international pressure, then to 4) "prescriptive status" of human rights norms (i.e., norms enter into law, but with weak enforcement), finally to 5) "rule-consistent behavior," in which states both walk the walk and talk the talk of human rights. See Thomas Risse, Stephen C. Ropp, and Kathryn Sikkink, eds., *The Power of Human Rights: International Norms and Domestic Change* (New York: Cambridge University Press, 1999); and Thomas Risse, Stephen C. Ropp, and Kathryn Sikkink, *The Persistent Power of Human Rights: From Commitment to Compliance* (New York: Cambridge University Press, 2013).

[2] Obviously, in early phases of "repression" and "denial," civil society may be attacked by the state or by warring parties – the role of international actors in bringing attention to abuses is critical in these early phases when national civil society actors may be severely under threat, if they exist at all.

a request for proposals (RFP) process for individual organizations, and the lack of transparency around donor decision-making in supporting some actors over others, contributes to this sense of atomization and competition. As one important indicator of this shrinking pool of funds for TJ, consider the dramatic drop in funding to the International Center for Transitional Justice (ICTJ), which is the main CSO working on TJ at the global level. ICTJ's revenues have steadily dropped from a height of more than $20 million in 2008 to less than half of that in 2016.[3]

REFLECTIONS ON TRANSITIONAL JUSTICE AND THE STRENGTHENING OF CIVIL SOCIETY

In this book, we were interested, among other things, to understand the evolution of relationships or networks of civil society actors working on TJ. How do they get established? How do they change and why? Do they cease after the end of a TJ initiative, or do they transform and continue? How broad and how deep are these relationships – for example, do they regularly include other civil society actors, such as media, religious actors, etc.? What is the role of international assistance in these relationships?

On the international level, strong civil society actors on TJ often have links with international solidarity networks – whether these are donors, human rights international nongovernmental organizations (INGOs), transnational activist/political movements, religious actors like the Catholic or Anglican Churches, and so forth. These networks are highly important in countries where civil society is repressed and under threat, as national and international actors can work together to keep international pressure on the local government. They remain important in a transitional period, too, connecting national actors to peers in other countries with experience with TJ to share lessons learned. On the national level, in many cases human rights and victim organizations seem rather isolated. Many human rights organizations have networks mainly with other human rights CSOs. In some cases, these organizations and their professionalized staff might have tenuous links with victims or victim groups. Without creative coalitions that cut across social and professional boundaries, sustained social change is difficult to achieve.

The Concept and Practice of "Networks"

We made a number of observations in regard to network strengthening and creation – things that many donors, in our experience, seek to fund. We have seen that in

[3] See ICTJ's Form 990s using the "Nonprofit Explorer" on ProPublica's website: https://projects.propublica.org/nonprofits/. There has been a consistent downward trend since 2008, when ICTJ's Form 990 reported more than $21 million in revenues. For the most recent Form 990 in the public domain (2014), revenues are reported at a little over $10 million. Internal sources suggest, however, that the budget has been reduced further (and substantially) since 2015.

most cases, sustainability is best achieved when international collaboration supports emergent civil society-led initiatives, rather than being driven and developed by donors and other international actors. Although frictions and asymmetries of power are inevitable in these collaborations, positive outcomes appear more likely where the asymmetry favors the people who are most affected and implicated in the decisions. In both Guatemala and Morocco, for example, national (and international) organizations and victim-survivor groups banded together to push forward a jointly conceived agenda. In contexts such as these, international financial assistance played a small role in building coalitions, but international technical assistance and solidarity networks were more important to providing support to national agenda-setting. Indeed, we found no instances of independently sustained networks that were the creations of international actors/donors – in spite of the fact that many have tried. For example, the International Commission for Missing Persons (ICMP) has fostered a regional network of organizations representing the families of missing persons. Yet after years of work in bringing these organizations together to share information and to influence their governments to act on missing persons issues, the union remains highly fragile and would seem unlikely to survive without ICMP's involvement.

We noted attempts at such collaboration that were weak and some that ultimately failed. In Uganda, for example, there have been successive attempts to create a variety of formal civil society networks on TJ, most of which have been supported by international financial assistance. None, however, has been sustained, and it seems that none has had much success in influencing the blocked TJ agenda in Uganda, which is primarily driven by the state. This weakness resulted from a variety of factors, including lack of leadership, internal power struggles, and mistrust. In BiH, there was a limited engagement with the western Balkans-wide network pushing for a truth commission on the regional level, known as RECOM. This network also received both international financial and technical assistance and succeeded in undertaking deep consultations with the full range of communities. Yet it too was affected by internal politics, power dynamics, and mistrust, and ultimately has not made headway on its proposals.

We saw that where networks were created, their lifespan was potentially short: in some cases, like in Cambodia and Morocco, new relationships are developed and sustained in direct connection to a TJ measure. Once that connection is removed, however, the sustainability of the relationship may be in doubt. In the case of the ECCC in Cambodia, the Victims Support Section of the court has been one locus of relationship building among organizations that represent civil party victims. Whether these kinds of relationships will have any meaning or utility once the ECCC has finished its work is unclear. In Morocco, the community reparations program attempted to build relationships both between local civil society organizations and between civil society and local political actors. We did not find that many of these relationships were sustained past the program itself. Perhaps this is natural and proper: not all networks need to exist in perpetuity, and their resuscitation may be propping up a partnership between actors that could work better elsewhere. The wisdom, though, is in knowing the difference between networks whose continuation holds value beyond the measure to which it is aligned, and those whose life is being artificially inflated – and to be able to discern the types and extent of support needed for each.

In many instances, we saw international actors acting as "neutral brokers" – whether between civil society and state actors, or between divided or competitive civil society actors. There are some contexts in which international actors can play a critical role in building bridges both between organizations, and with the state – as mentioned, ICMP and the United Nations Development Programme (UNDP) in BiH have played this role in acting as a neutral broker among organizations divided along ethnoreligious lines, as well as with government actors.[4] As mentioned earlier, however, in our case study countries, these relationships have so far hinged on the continued involvement of the international actor. We recognize that this situation may evolve, and a sustainable, independent network may emerge, but that has not yet happened in the instances we observed.

"Bridging" and "Linking"

In addition to understanding general collaboration among civil society actors working on TJ, we also wanted to understand the degree to which such actors build "bridging" and "linking" capital with marginalized and vulnerable groups, especially victims. Bridging capital describes relationships between socially diverse actors; whereas linking capital describes the degree to which a social network provides individuals access to sources of social or political power. The idea behind these concepts is that not all networks are equal: we see this in practice, for example, when women's organizations have connections to one another, but do not have connections to state actors or others in positions of power; they therefore lack recognition and the ability to influence. What is of interest, then, is when groups from different social milieus and with different relationships to power forge relationships. In our research, we thus asked interviewees who they considered vulnerable or marginalized, and what kinds of relationships they have now or have had in the past with groups representing these people.

Starting with links between civil society and the state, we saw a wide variety of relationships, defying generalization. In some countries, TJ CSOs had developed relationships with state actors, like Morocco's National Council of Human Rights

[4] For more on neutral brokers' role in divided contexts, see Paige Arthur, "'Fear of the Future, Lived through the Past': Pursuing Transitional Justice in the Wake of Ethnic Conflict," in *Identities in Transition: Challenges for Transitional Justice in Divided Societies*, ed. Paige Arthur (New York: Cambridge University Press, 2010), 288–89.

(CNDH), BiH's War Crimes Chamber, or Uganda's JLOS. The spectrum of these relationships is broad: we saw some cross-pollination between CSOs and state institutions in Morocco and Guatemala, suggesting an evolving relationship. The perception of such cross-pollination is interesting: in Morocco, some saw this negatively as state "cooptation" of civil society actors, but others perceived it as positive engagement between the state and civil society. In Cambodia, those relationships were weaker. And in BiH, the deep polarization along ethnoreligious lines has created such political paralysis that civil society actors noted that they desired international actors to help them engage the state.

We saw that victims and survivors in general emerged as the most important crosscutting group of vulnerable people in our case studies. Yet we found a wide variety of relationships with victim-survivor groups. In Morocco, victims populate the leadership of the main human rights organizations, which all have links with the national umbrella organization of victims – although these links seem to have weakened over time. In Guatemala, national CSOs like the Forensic Anthropology Foundation of Guatemala and Bufete Jurídico have established extensive networks in victim communities – yet at the same time the major indigenous groups (which represent the majority of victims of the conflict) appear not to participate in national human rights networks. In Cambodia, victim organizations are weak and apparently mainly organize only around the ECCC civil party process. In BiH, some victim organizations in Republika Srpska are deeply tied to Bosnian Serb–dominated politicians, receiving large sums of money from the entity; elsewhere, they are marginal, easily manipulated by ethnic politics and small amounts of money from their municipalities – unless they have achieved some measure of independence as have, for example, the Mothers of Srebrenica and Zepa.

We found in many instances clear gaps between professionalized CSOs and victim-survivor or community-based organizations. In most places, professionalized CSOs receive the lion's share of international financial assistance. In some cases, they have deep roots in communities and sincere connections with victim-survivor groups (or they are victim-survivor groups themselves). For example, in Morocco, the Moroccan Forum for Truth and Justice, a national umbrella group of victims, has been the main recipient of international assistance to civil society working on TJ. In others, professionalized CSOs receive funding even in cases where their networks may be thin and the depth of their reach into victim-survivor communities may be in doubt, looping us back to the strategies of assistance to civil society, and to a comfortability in funding the "usual suspects." This has important consequences for a field purportedly focused on supporting and reintegrating victims and survivors. Beyond this frequent distance between professionalized CSOs and victim-survivor communities, funding approaches that privilege the same groups or the same types of activities appear to provide fewer incentives for professionalized CSOs to work together – beyond very basic relations of information sharing – given the fact that they are in competition for funding with one another, and livelihood issues were necessarily in play for their staff members. We did find that these CSOs tended to report having good relations with one another and a general sense of "working together." But people who work at these organizations may be drawn from similar social milieus, casting doubt over the extent to which this "working together" has the capacity to reach horizontally across social sectors and to build vertical socioeconomic links.

The relationship between victim groups and other civil society actors is an important one for TJ actors to gain some clarity on. There is a perception – sometimes justified, sometimes not – that many professionalized CSOs and INGOs conducting advocacy, research, or technical assistance use victim groups for "extractive" purposes, without any real relationship building: to extract information for research/advocacy/etc.; to use the name of a victim group on a proposal to get funding, for example. We observed these phenomena at times in our case studies and also in our own work as practitioners. Yet we find that this is a complicated and context-sensitive set of relationships. Obviously, it would be hard to argue for benefits of a purely "extractive" relationship. But to say that any relationship between "professionals" and victims is extractive (or instrumental) by definition is potentially to miss the complexity and frictions at play. For example, we could hypothesize that victims' interests are more likely to be pushed with state actors if victims actually populate and lead professionalized, national human rights organizations – as they do in Morocco – rather than simply being "represented" by these organizations. But some in Morocco would say that these victims have been "coopted" by the state, which they view as using TJ to polish its image internationally, while not implementing real reforms (including those to address ongoing impunity) at home.

Women (including women victims) were also discussed as a marginalized/vulnerable group in a number of case studies, although this did not come through as strongly as the category of "victims" in general did. In Morocco, TJ actors did attempt to engage national women's groups, without much success; they were no better at bringing a gender "lens" to TJ than other human rights actors, and ultimately this lens was brought through the actions of a few individuals working on the Equity and Reconciliation Commission as well as international actors. Yet this is a reflection of the invisibility of certain kinds of victimhood, particularly the marginalization of gender-based violence within mainstream narratives. In most of the cases, we found a high number of women who were direct or indirect victims; in BiH, for example, many of the leaders of victim organizations were women. Also in Uganda, there are highly active women's groups and community-based organizations working on sexual and gender-based violence issues from the conflict – one of these recently addressed the Uganda parliament, suggesting that some level of linking capital was being forged. On a positive note, we found that international assistance has made a difference in promoting gender-sensitive practices and insisting on the inclusion of the perspective of vulnerable groups. In the cases of Morocco and

Cambodia, for example, international actors and donors have been critical in this respect. However, we note that the formal inclusion of gender in a truth commission process or a reparations program (again in Morocco) does not necessarily translate into a strengthening of vulnerable groups: instead, this requires active cultivation. We did not generally find evidence of the growth of linking capital among groups representing women victims and actors in positions of power.

In reflecting on these issues, we would also like to note some things that surprised us, as they may spur further reflection. First, many interviewees resisted our questions on vulnerable/marginalized groups, which were designed to better understand linking capital. Some thought that so many people in their country were vulnerable/marginalized that the question seemed pointless – whether because they were victims of conflict/repression, or because they suffered from deep poverty, or for other reasons. Others bristled at the questions, seeming to suggest that they were tired of being asked (by internationals) about whether they work with the perhaps donor-driven category of "vulnerable/marginalized people."

Both of these reactions are valid, even if we accept the idea (and we do) that some people are more vulnerable than others in any community. The reactions suggest that the category of vulnerable/marginalized may not be fully recognized as relevant and legitimate in every context. This point is related to our second observation, which was the fact that few (if any) interviewees identified lesbian, gay, bisexual, transgender, and/or intersex (LGBTI) people as a particularly vulnerable group, and few identified youth as a vulnerable group – this is in spite of the fact that both of these groups are indeed quite vulnerable in most of these countries. (In fact, a number of interviewees criticized international donors' recent attention to promoting LGBTI rights in their countries.) The lack of findings on links to youth actors is particularly disturbing, since most of these countries are places where young people have completely disengaged from TJ and learn little about the past in schools. This also suggests that the emerging body of research on the relationship/s between education and TJ will be particularly important to understanding this distance between youth disengagement and TJ.

Relatedly, there was little evidence of strengthening of broader networks outside of human rights or TJ circles, except in cases where it was an organization's express purpose to engage with broader networks. For example, in BiH, the role of the Balkans Investigative Reporting Network is to engage with the media, and it therefore is in contact with those actors. But beyond such incentivized collaborations, we found civil society actors working on TJ rather insular, perhaps taking a technical and project-focused approach rather than a social mobilization approach to their work – an approach that may be "safer" and more desirable to many risk-averse donors, in any case. While this generalization is less true of civil society actors in Guatemala and Morocco, it is fair to note this broad pattern in BiH, Uganda, and Cambodia.

MISSED CONNECTIONS ON TRANSITIONAL JUSTICE, INTERNATIONAL ASSISTANCE, AND CIVIL SOCIETY

Missed Connection 1: Where Is the Strategy?

One of our most important findings is that there are infrequently clearly defined goals for TJ within a recipient country, or indeed any consistent approach to TJ within a donor's home country. Where a strategy does exist, it is usually linked to particular TJ measures, such as a criminal prosecutions process, for example. Since most governments do not have policies or guidance on TJ, it usually gets rolled into funding baskets on development, human rights, rule of law, or peacebuilding. While this is not necessarily a bad thing, since TJ is related to these broader issues, TJ also needs special attention as a distinct social process.[5]

When thinking about approaches that are more and less constructive, we identified several methods that are worth reflecting on. In Guatemala, for example, donors have created a special pooled facility called the TJ Accompaniment Program (PAJUST), which is administered by UNDP, and which integrates civil society and state actors as critical components. At the "home" level, the Swiss Department of Foreign Affairs has developed a long-term program, "Dealing with the Past," which also gives due weight to the role of civil society actors, and which is the only state-level framework related to TJ that we found. On the flipside, we see that where TJ strategies are absent, donors may pick and choose TJ projects to fit their own priorities, without regard to whether they are strategically placed to build momentum for TJ. Such actions contribute to the "projectitis" we observed in places like BiH, where CSOs focus more on completing deliverables to raise more funds than on meaningful social change objectives. When donors support projects rather than a strategy (or strategies), they incentivize civil society actors to focus on one-off actions and deliverables: completing tasks and spending down funds, rather than mobilizing for social change. They also incentivize competition between civil society actors, which may have the unintended consequence of reinforcing fragmentation and mistrust that is a remnant of the conflict or authoritarian period. RFP processes may unintentionally feed this dynamic, as they are naturally competitive practices that pit organizations against one another in a limited funding "marketplace." The focus on projects over strategy is a key challenge for donors – one they recognize themselves, as they struggle to work within short-term funding cycles, and often have no idea what their budgets may be from year to year.

[5] We note that this lack of strategy can be as deleterious for state or UN actors working on TJ as it can be for CSOs. Although this issue is not our focus, much has been written, for example, about the problems of voluntary funding structures for the ECCC and the Special Court for Sierra Leone, among others. See, e.g., Marieke Wierda and Anthony Triolo, "Resources" in *International Prosecutors*, ed. Luc Reydams, Jan Wouters, and Cedric Ryngaert (Oxford: Oxford University Press, 2012), 121–28.

Further, our findings suggest that it is rare for donors to consult civil society actors when thinking about TJ funding decisions, or setting a general funding strategy (when this exists). We saw a tension that held through many of our chapters – that some donors, the EU in particular, were prone to treating TJ primarily as a technical enterprise, underplaying its political and social aspects. This approach has implications at multiple levels: not just how CSOs can become part of or distanced from social change movements, but also and more broadly how CSOs can respond to difficult political environments. We saw the consequences of such a technical approach to TJ in both BiH and Morocco, where momentum has shifted away from CSOs as social change actors in TJ.

Missed Connection 2: Large Imbalances in Attention and Funding

Linked to the lack of strategies is the fact of lopsided funding outlays. Throughout the chapters, we tried to note the gaps and imbalances between funding for state-led TJ initiatives and for civil society working on TJ. But this is not the only imbalance our research found. Lopsided resourcing especially affects the support available to victims, survivors, and vulnerable groups, who are all too rarely the main interlocutors for donors. Instead, donors may rely on professional CSOs that can speak donor "language" and are usually based in the capitals.

Supporting the agency of people whose fundamental rights have been violated and need to be reaffirmed is a critical need in a transition and a core principle of TJ. Yet an overwhelming proportion of TJ funding goes to support criminal prosecutions, which focus mainly on perpetrators. While prosecutions are important to many victims, they are not the only things that matter. In Sierra Leone, for example, analysis of donor contributions shows that more than $268 million was spent on the Special Court versus less than $5 million for reparations for all of the war's victims. It is difficult to grasp that, for example, $100,000 in donor money could fund either one international lawyer's salary for a year, or reparations for 1,250 victims (roughly $80 per person). No one planned it this way (nor would they have, we assume), but because of a lack of clear TJ strategy, this was the result.

In fact, in all of our research, we were only able to find $11 million (so far) in donor funding to support reparations programs from 2002 to 2012 – mainly in Morocco (from the EU) and Sierra Leone (from the UN Peacebuilding Fund). Contrast this with billions spent on various international and ad hoc courts – in a 2008 paper, Rupert Skilbeck placed the cost per accused at the International Criminal Tribunals for Yugoslavia and Rwanda at between $10 million and $15 million.[6] We know that national governments resist funding reparations programs as much as they can (as they can be very expensive); should we be surprised that TJ donors offer similar resistance? Without a clear strategy for TJ in any given context, the real risk remains that the

[6] Rupert Skilbeck, "Funding Justice: The Price of War Crimes Trials," *Human Rights Brief* 15, no. 3 (2008): 6.

bulk of funding will be eaten up by large and high-profile initial engagements, such as, for example, criminal prosecutions programs, without any commensurate financial or intellectual investment in other measures that are equally important for creating sustained social change.

Missed Connection 3: Informational Black Holes

The lack of communication within governments – to the extent that people within a donor's development agencies, foreign ministries, and embassies do not have much (if any) knowledge of how their colleagues were or were not funding TJ – means that there is often disconnect between projects being funded by the same donor, a lack of learning across countries, and added burden and work for donor staff, who may not have expertise in TJ. Those at the embassy level seemed to have a particular need for more guidance on TJ, as many funding decisions are handled locally – by staff who are under-resourced and under-supported in general, particularly so with respect to TJ.

One result is that donors often do not have an idea of what their own government has supported in the past, or what colleagues are funding in other contexts. Coupled with a lack of communication within and between agencies, and very limited time to think about broader questions of effectiveness, we see some of the explanatory backbone for why the connections between CSOs working in TJ and the international agencies supporting them are so often of dubious depth. The general commitment to supporting civil society exists, but a clear-eyed strategy for how to support them may be lacking.

Moreover, there are few instances of donors using impact assessment, baseline studies, or meaningful society-level indicators to assess how well states are meeting their obligations on TJ, to judge (for example) whether civil society actors are playing positive social roles, or to understand how well TJ is meeting the needs of victim groups.

Missed Connection 4: Not Another One-Year-Long Transitional Justice Project!

Overcoming cycles of conflict and atrocity, or building rights-respecting state institutions, takes time and may suffer political setbacks. TJ processes require long-term commitments: documentation of mass crimes needs to be gathered or reconstructed; complex investigations of and trials for massive human rights violations take years to complete; support for victims, especially those with lingering health and psychological effects, spans decades; reparations are sometimes multigenerational; victims take a long time to come forward; and judicial and social services often have to be (re)built.

In spite of these long-term needs, donor agendas, sometimes set in capitals, may shift and leave civil society actors without support at crucial moments, or the wrong type of support/funds at the wrong times. One-year funding cycles in particular are enemies of the sustainability and predictability that is needed to support long-term change. Instead of committing to the ups and downs of a long-term social change process, our cases have repeatedly shown that international assistance to TJ incentivizes short-term projectitis. Specifically, it tends to fund "professional" CSO activities, like workshops, trainings, facilitation, and report writing, or service provision. While these activities may be relevant, focusing on them can induce shortsightedness: CSOs and donors alike can promote their work as a success, whether or not there has been real movement on TJ at the social or political level. Investing in (perhaps political) activities to build a social movement, like community-based outreach and mobilization, would be a more long-term and strategic move, as it requires bridge building with other social actors outside of professional CSO circles. We found in BiH and Morocco, for example, that significant social movements in recent years are relatively disconnected from TJ and TJ actors.

Here, process matters for both substance and outcomes. For example, much was said about the administrative difficulties of EU processes that essentially require an organization to be professionalized (and fluent in French and/or English) in order to even submit a proposal. These funds – very significant in contexts like BiH and Morocco – necessarily support professionalized CSOs that know how to "play the game" but that may not be doing the most relevant work and may not be representing the most vulnerable and marginalized groups, including victims. Further, many actors noted that donors' unwillingness to support core funding was a way of incentivizing CSOs to "chase" projects and to adapt their agendas to those of donors – a factor that is not conducive to collaborative strategy development among CSOs. This disconnect between the desire for supporting social change initiatives and the methods of that support poses significant problems for donors at both the institutional and political levels. But without shifting these approaches to supporting civil society, international assistance will amount to tinkering at the edges of change.

Missed Connection 5: Not Enough (or the Right) Encouragement to a Weak Civil Society Sector

One of the primary goals of TJ is to promote trust between state institutions and society (and, more specifically, victim-survivors), as well as between citizens.[7] Civil society actors in transitioning contexts play a key trust-building role, through their functions as investigators of abuse, monitors of state action, advocates for victims and communities, etc. But, as our research shows, in many cases, only a small proportion of all funds for TJ goes to civil society actors, sometimes as an afterthought in the wake of funding to large-scale institutions. This means that they can be drastically

7 See, e.g., General Assembly, "Report of the Special Rapporteur on the Promotion of Truth, Justice, Reparation and Guarantees of Non-Recurrence, Pablo de Greiff," A/HRC/71/567 (August 9, 2012): paras. 28–46.

under-resourced and in a weak position relative to the state. Additionally, in too many places, civil society is not acting as that driving social force pushing forward a TJ agenda – because they are repressed politically, they are fragmented, they lack links to civil society actors outside their own milieu, or some combination of these.

Here, the overwhelmingly one-way communications process – where donors give funding but do not seek input on how to do their own work better – shows itself. In almost all contexts, CSOs complained that the funding they received was always tied to projects: a lack of core funding inhibits an organization's ability to set its own agenda, to respond to changing political contexts, and to focus on capacity building. In very few cases did donors take the lead from civil society actors engaged in human rights, social change, and TJ as to what support was needed, and at what time.

But if civil society is a key vector of social change, then a closer knowledge of how to support is necessary, and is largely lacking. One interesting example of a donor positively developing civil society capacity can be taken from Germany's Agency for International Cooperation (Gesellschaft für Internationale Zusammenarbeit, GIZ) and its Civil Peace Service's work in Cambodia. The project is a decade-long, $10 million commitment to increasing the capacity of Cambodian CSOs from the bottom up, with an innovative combination of in situ advisors from a variety of professional backgrounds chosen by both GIZ and CSOs, a focus on knowledge sharing, and small, flexible grants that could be adapted as programming needs changed. Its work was roundly admired by CSOs and donors alike.

Generally, however, we found that "donor fatigue" tended to set in at exactly the juncture where CSOs needed support to keep an agenda on the table politically. Fatigue was also linked to a lack of TJ strategy: in Cambodia, for example, aside from funding for the Documentation Center of Cambodia, very little money was put aside from the beginning for outreach and public information to support the ECCC: CSOs doing that work were left to scrape together funds, and as a result the court was perceived as remote and disassociated from the lives of victims.

RECOMMENDATIONS FOR MAKING CONNECTIONS

Recommendation 1: Support Strategies, not Projects

While we encourage donor agencies to develop a policy or guidance noted on TJ to help staff make decisions (similar to the policy that the EU recently developed), it may be unrealistic to expect all donor agencies to have a TJ policy or even a TJ strategy for each country. Simpler steps can be made, however, to take a more strategic approach to funding TJ. Country-level staff can develop a brief concept note or country strategy on TJ, and revise it periodically. While there may be little time for such exercises, there can be a clear benefit in terms of "value for money" if donors have some sense of their own goals and strategy for TJ. Donors ask their grantees to articulate goals and strategies – why not do the same? Depending on the context, the task could be led by embassies or by a TJ focal point, for example.

Rather than "going it alone" with a concept note or country strategy, donor agencies can consider supporting a common strategy developed by a trusted multilateral partner by participating in pooled funds. Pooling funds may be one way for donors to contribute more strategic support for TJ – although pools created specifically for TJ (like PAJUST in Guatemala) may be better placed to achieve positive results than larger pools covering a range of donor priorities (which may shift, even over the short-term, such as the Democratic Governance Facility in Uganda).

Absent or in addition to developing their own strategies, donors can also rely on the TJ road maps developed during national consultation processes, which can give at least a preliminary sense for how donors can offer relevant multiyear support. Such initiatives, whose importance has recently been highlighted by the Special Rapporteur on the promotion of truth, justice, reparation, and guarantees of non-recurrence, are critical for decision-making both for national actors and donors, especially before the start of any TJ processes.[8] These road maps can also be used to track the progress of a TJ process against objectives set out through national dialogues, policies, or strategies on TJ: Are states making good on their promises to support specific TJ initiatives? Are they progressing in a timely way? Are there signals of backtracking that should set off a need for different kinds of support or engagement from donors?

Another point is that TJ should be included in long-term development assistance strategies. Because TJ processes are multigenerational and progress can slow or face reversals, "donor fatigue" frequently sets in. There are cases when donors have withdrawn all TJ funding – to both state and civil society actors – when the state shows a lack of commitment. This, however, is precisely the moment when civil society action is often most critical to keep pressure on the state to fulfill its responsibilities. A focus on strategy rather than projects can help mediate such responses.

Finally, and in line with all of these points, donors should also consider solidarity with civil society as a strategy. Donors have a level and quality of access to national and regional policymakers that civil society actors often do not have. They sometimes also have the power to offer or withhold incentives to a country's policymakers if they are out of step with human rights norms. During the recent human rights trials in Guatemala, for example, civil society representatives emphasized the symbolic political importance of having ambassadors from the US and other embassies, along with the Commissioner of the International Commission against Impunity in Guatemala, attend the hearings. In cases when donors are supporting civil society actors aiming to create policy- or national-level change, civil society actors would

[8] See UN General Assembly, "Report of the Special Rapporteur on the Promotion of Truth, Justice, Reparation and Guarantees of Non-Recurrence, Pablo de Greiff," A/71/567 (October 25, 2016).

welcome donors galvanizing their own political and strategic resources to help change along. This could range from hosting events where civil society actors can network with policymakers, teaching them how to lobby, using political leverage to create incentives for policymakers to support civil society strategies, to expressing solidarity through appearances at criminal trials (for example) and therefore reinforcing civil society demands before the state. Donors can also support institutional decision-making and oversight structures for TJ – such as joint steering committees and structured dialogues – that integrate state and civil society actors and ensure that civil society has a meaningful "seat at the table." At the same time, donors should actively take the lead from civil society actors on the kind of political support needed, as well as the timing and visibility of such support.

Recommendation 2: Correct Lopsided Funding

Rethinking funding ratios among different TJ initiatives, and also including civil society actors in donor and government priority and strategy setting from the beginning, are important ways to ensure that the needs of stakeholders and relevant communities are reflected in key national policies and TJ or donor-country strategies and that issues of proportionality and scale are addressed. These actions help build relationships early, enhancing connections between TJ initiatives and the people they are intended to serve. One easy step could be to use target percentages for civil society support as a proportion of total TJ funding (especially when supporting formal institutions like courts or truth commissions) – as some development agencies already do for other funding.

Donors should also ensure balanced and appropriately scaled support that does not focus solely on perpetrators. They should consider supporting reparations programs for victims alongside other TJ measures, and plan for these resources at the earliest discussion of a TJ process. In the end, what is important is to strike a balance and to ensure that victims are not left by the wayside in donor funding or engagement.

Recommendation 3: More Information, Please!

Given the deficits in internal coordination and information sharing (let alone external deficits), one change that could make a clear positive different to donor agencies is the creation of a TJ focal point – one person or unit with a global view of TJ-related funding by development agencies, embassies, and ministries of foreign affairs. Agencies could consider whether it would be useful to have a TJ focal point in each country or region with heavy TJ investment. It would be useful to think about what kind of technical expertise this position might need (including nonlegal expertise), and where such a position would best fit organizationally in order to have an impact at various levels (embassy, foreign ministry, development agency, etc.).

In order to maintain regular internal contact, TJ focal points could schedule periodic briefings or phone calls with relevant embassy, development, and foreign affairs personnel related to countries of intensive TJ activity. This position would also be a useful point of contact for people outside of the agency, including and especially civil society actors. In our experience, it was often difficult simply finding the right person to talk to on TJ within any particular agency.

At the country level, donors should invest in population surveys before the start of a TJ process, and then follow through with periodic surveys as a process unfolds. Such surveys could be developed through partnerships between civil society actors, social scientists, and TJ specialists – rather than solely through contracts with international researchers – in order to build capacity and ownership. Similarly, on the project level, they should invest money in meaningful baseline studies for longer-term civil society projects, and ensure that these studies are conducted in partnership with people who have relevant social scientific skills. Finally, it is important for donors to start to fund long-term impact assessments. They will be expensive and methodologically complicated, but it is hard to see the field continuing to grow without some answers to fundamental questions about what kinds of long-term benefits TJ has for victim populations specifically, but also for other TJ goals such as building trust.

Recommendation 4: Treat Civil Society as a Long-Term Partner (and Plan for a Long and Winding Road)

Fundamentally, donors should take specific actions to ensure that civil society is meaningfully included in high-level strategic discussions on TJ before TJ begins, during a TJ process, and after it has "concluded." The last issue is critical, since TJ does not end with the closing of formal institutions, and civil society actors may be the only ones continuing the work of TJ once a truth commission or a court has ceased operations.

In the early stages, donors should learn the CSO landscape, by mapping stakeholders and CSOs – and particularly note vulnerable groups – to understand who may be (further) marginalized by the process. Efforts should be made to build their capacity and ability to network before TJ processes begin. They should also conduct extensive, good-faith consultations and stakeholder analyses with civil society actors when developing a strategy for funding TJ initiatives. And donors should support national and subnational consultation processes to create TJ "road maps." Such initiatives are critical for decision-making for both national actors and donors, especially before the start of any TJ processes. In all of these actions, victims should be prioritized; indeed, donors could do much more to engage with victim, survivor, and vulnerable groups. Embassy staff should develop relationships with victim and vulnerable groups: meet with them, ask them what they need, and offer feedback on their proposals, even – and perhaps especially – if the proposals are rejected.

During a TJ process, donors can support large-scale communication initiatives through various types of media (radio, TV, web, etc.); they can support CSO monitoring of the transparency, efficiency, legality, and effectiveness of TJ initiatives; and they can encourage their civil society partners to collaborate with people working on other issues, for example, poverty reduction, religious freedom, women's rights, LGBTI rights, and so forth. Civil society monitoring of the state's continued commitment to TJ is just as critical after a formal TJ measure is over, including efforts to engage a variety of audiences: schools, religious communities, media, and other social institutions. Public and academic history can also contribute to deepening social understanding, especially in countries where there may be little existing or deeply divisive history writing about the recent past.[9]

Long-term support may require large budgets, so engaging the relevant development agency and ensuring that funds are overseas development assistance (ODA) compliant may help unlock funds from countries trying to meet their ODA targets. Second, donors should do more to provide core support that spans several years rather than yearly project support. Slow and steady is preferable to funding peaks and crashes; indeed, overall lower levels of continuous funding are preferable generally to large short-term spikes followed by troughs. Third, it is important to maintain support for civil society even when – perhaps especially when – frustrations are high with the state's commitment to TJ; in those moments, civil society mobilization on TJ is critical.

Recommendation 5: Encourage Cooperation among a Diverse Set of Civil Society Actors

TJ is a social process that requires more than the state and a small group of human rights CSOs to succeed; a wide range of social actors needs to be engaged for sustainable results. Building sustainable networks and social capital across borders and social sectors (not just CSOs) is therefore critical. Donors can encourage this cross-sectoral collaboration in their funding, but should keep in mind the limits of international influence. In particular, our research found no evidence of sustainable networks that were pure creations of donor funding. Instead of trying to create networks on TJ from scratch, a more sound approach is to support existing and emerging networks already working on TJ-related issues, which are more likely to have deep roots (and legitimacy) in communities. These include cross-border networks – especially regional networks and those with south–south connections.

Donors can use funding models that incentivize or even require cooperation between local civil society actors (such as joint proposals), rather than individualized

9 Many other suggestions for interventions in the "cultural" sphere can be found in Pablo de Greiff's report on guarantees of non-recurrence. See UN General Assembly, "Report of the Special Rapporteur on the Promotion of Truth, Justice, Reparation and Guarantees of Non-Recurrence, Pablo de Greiff," A/HRC/20/42 (September 7, 2015).

models that foster competition for scarce funds. Also, when RFP processes are used, they should take care to ensure that the design is more inclusive than exclusive. For example: donors could take steps to circulate RFPs widely in the appropriate languages and media; require CSOs to submit proposals as partners; and support networking and peer-to-peer learning activities. They can also look beyond the "usual suspects," seeking new and unlikely local civil society actors in TJ; it could even set aside a proportion of TJ funding for up-and-coming or riskier organizations. In divided contexts, support for neutral brokers (often international actors) to foster networks among CSOs, victim organizations, etc., is a helpful strategy, but make sure that these actors do not dominate the funding landscape.

In all of this, donors should not forget victims and survivors. Support for victims and survivors usually requires multiple channels: legal assistance, medical assistance, psychosocial assistance, witness support, fostering victim organizations/representation, etc. Therefore, donors should consider ways to support collaboration across these types of organizations, or at least coordinate with other donors to ensure that victim and survivor needs are being met through a variety of donor measures. One idea is to sponsor periodic national meetings that bring these groups together for networking. In a tough political context where TJ is too sensitive an issue to directly tackle, then, at a minimum, donors should channel and sustain support to CSOs that provide long-term medical and psychosocial support to victims.

WHERE TO FROM HERE FOR THE FIELD?

This book has examined the relationship between international assistance and civil society actors working in or alongside the field of TJ. Our motivation, in part, was to understand how TJ engagements or encounters between international actors and a country's civil society actors produce the results that they do. Underpinning our research is the search for better ways of engaging (or not engaging), which get us perhaps closer to the goal of creating more trustful, peaceful, and rights-respecting societies after conflict or authoritarian rule. This conclusion has focused largely on drawing out these relationships, and providing suggestions, based on what we have found in our case studies, for better donor support for civil society and for less lopsided engagements in TJ contexts. What this book has also found, however, is that there is a great deal of room for further research on the issues raised.

Our assumption, as outlined in our introduction, is that civil society actors often play critical roles (alongside the state) in achieving social change in TJ contexts. This book has described a number of inhibitive factors, some of which may be easier, and others harder, to address when seeking to confront the theoretical and practical weaknesses we have seen throughout this book. Empirical research on the relationship between civil society and the cultivation of social trust and social capital in societies rebuilding in the wake of conflict and authoritarianism needs a great deal more work. Relatedly, there is important work to be done (re)thinking CSOs as a driver of civic power in difficult political environments, and particularly in environments that cultivate or encourage their dependence on international actors.

For their part, the conceptual chapters in Part II of this book have taken two different approaches to understanding how decisions are taken, how and why relationships are cultivated (or not), and what their impacts are, both on the broader context of TJ and on the recipients. Each has created a new framework to provide deeper perspectives regarding why we are where we are in practice. Pointing out the absence of clear information about (and sense-making of) donor decision-making and financial flows in the literature on TJ, Paige Arthur's chapter (Chapter 7) develops a framework of decision-making that explains what drives international assistance to TJ. She shows how donors' ideas, interests, institutions, and information combine as multidimensional motivations, arguing that these motivations are traceable. Moving forward, her framework enables us to understand when TJ is likely to be supported, under which conditions, and where the fractures and "missed connections" are likely to lie.

Focusing on the "why" of fractures and connections missed and made, Christalla Yakinthou develops a frame drawn from anthropologist Anna Tsing's work on frictional engagements. In Chapter 6, Yakinthou shows that – despite how we treat them – our understandings of TJ's core principles and the interactions that result from their application are not fixed, but instead they both shape and are themselves reshaped by relationships between actors, and between actors, their goals, and their legacies. The frictions framework gives insight into how TJ priorities and specific mechanisms are being shaped by historical legacies, foreign policy, exclusions, inclusions and hierarchies, and collaborations often for different (and sometimes disconnected) ends. It can also provide more careful and transparent explanations of how the spaces and interactions we do not usually see affect both TJ engagements and their products, and give a more interconnected understanding of what happens over the course of TJ processes and why. Both of these chapters are efforts to make sense of what the case studies tell us about where connections are being missed in practice and in theory.

The salience of these reflections is related to the changing landscape in which TJ operates. Global efforts to support liberal democratic development in post-conflict and post-authoritarian contexts live side by side with a move toward insular nationalism or extremist movements in many countries where TJ is at stake. As one result of this frictional interaction, clear links are being developed between TJ and new fields, like countering or preventing violent extremism.[10] On the one hand, this linkage risks the securitization of TJ as it becomes caught up in flattened and essentialized narratives of good and evil; on the other, it opens space to work with those who see CVE as a way of thinking about the challenges of building more inclusive and less

[10] It is interesting to note that the field of TJ has grown alongside and in the shadow of the war on terror. Indeed, ICTJ was founded just before 9/11, and some of its staff members watched the towers of the World Trade Center burning from the windows of their downtown New York offices.

marginalizing societies. Both sides of this razor have implications for how relationships among civil society actors are supported, and especially for what kind of civil society efforts are rewarded or sidelined. As we have seen through the pages of this book, the possibility of change cuts both ways. Perhaps it will encourage thinking about who plays a role in democratic transformation – especially in TJ.[11]

We are eager to see how TJ will adapt to new circumstances. But in the end, we still hope to see civil society actors (including victims and their families) substantively engaged in any TJ process. Why? For both principled and instrumental reasons: because victims should have the justice that they want, and because we find it hard to imagine TJ "working" – however one defines that term – without a strong civil society engagement. As Pablo de Greiff has written in relation to Uruguay, "It is generally the victims, their family members and victims associations that have promoted and continue to promote, tirelessly and with admirable dedication, initiatives for truth, justice, reparation and guarantees of non-recurrence."[12] Beyond the arduous and sometimes physically threatening work of pushing the state to fulfill responsibilities, civil society acts as the communicator, the facilitator, the arbiter – indeed, the heart beating at the center of TJ.

[11] Challenges such as what is unfolding in Syria and Iraq, for example, and efforts among combatants, civilians, and civil society both in the diaspora and in-country to bring measures of justice and cooperation at the level of towns living through conflict, are likely to challenge Western donors' perceptions of how to support "civil" and "uncivil" society. For more, see Scott Lucas, Christalla Yakinthou, and Stefan Wolff, "Syria: Laying the Foundations for a Credible and Sustainable Transition," *RUSI* 161, no. 3 (2016): 22–32.

[12] UN General Assembly, "Report of the Special Rapporteur on the Promotion of Truth, Justice, Reparation and Guarantees of Non-recurrence, Pablo de Greiff, Mission to Uruguay," A/HRC/27/56/2014/Add.2 (August 28, 2014): 2.

Annex: Interview Guides

GUIDE FOR CIVIL SOCIETY ACTORS

Background

1. When was your organization founded? How long has your organization worked on TJ?
2. What are your current projects on TJ (if any)? What are your past projects on TJ (if any)?

The Social and Political Environment

1. Please tell us about the general social and political environment that you work in: for example, how much tolerance is there for different political views? How well do civil society actors work together? Do civil society actors trust one another? Is there much interaction and connection between a range of civil society actors (not just human rights groups)? Do civil society actors face legal challenges or lots of government regulations?
2. How does this general environment affect your own work on TJ? Are there specific ways that the environment has either provided opportunities for you to succeed in your TJ-related work or has prevented you from succeeding in your TJ-related work?

Networks and Relationships

1. How has your organization changed or grown since it was established?
2. Can you please think about your relationships and networks with other civil society actors?

3. What do you use these partnerships for? Have you collaborated on activities? Please tell me more about how they started and what you did or did not achieve.

   i. Follow up: Are the partnerships mainly for exchanging information, or does it go beyond that to coordinating tactics and/or joint mobilization on specific issues? Talk through specific examples of partnership on TJ.
   ii. Follow up: How has decision-making taken place in these partnerships? Have you reached common agreement about which goals you are trying to achieve? Again, please talk through some specific TJ examples.
   iii. Follow up: Could you please tell us who your most important partners are?

4. Do these groups include/do you work with organizations that are not necessarily human rights actors? What about other kinds of civil society actors?
5. Reflecting on these partnerships, how have they changed over time? When have partnerships ended and why? When have new partnerships started and why? Do you have more partners now than you did in the past, fewer, or roughly the same number?
6. Have international, national, or local TJ initiatives created opportunities for collective civil society action? Have specific TJ efforts created positive or negative conditions for civil society to collaborate and work together? Why or why not?
7. What is the role of international NGOs or other international actors in fostering (or preventing) collaboration among CSOs? For example, how has technical assistance – workshops, trainings, etc. – from international NGOs or actors like the UN helped or hindered collaboration?

   i. Follow up: Can you provide examples of positive outcomes of technical assistance, resulting in CSO collaboration? What was the impact and how long did it last? Also, do you know of examples of negative or NO outcomes from technical assistance?
   ii. Follow up: Do you have suggestions for improving the impact of international technical assistance on creating sustainable CSO relationships/collaboration?

8. Who do you consider vulnerable or marginalized groups in your community, with respect to TJ? To what degree does your organization try to create relationships with these groups? Have you created any such relationships – why or why not? Have you acted jointly with these groups, and if so, how? What is the current status of your relationship with vulnerable or marginalized people in your community?

   i. Follow up: Ask the person to name the groups with which they have relationships. These should not be general populations like "rape victims," but rather organized civil society actors, e.g., "Tuzla Women's Association."

9. How do you see your relationship with the government? How has this changed over time?
10. How would you like to see civil society actors' relationships change over the next three to five years? What specific issues would you like to see organizations working together on? What needs to change for civil society to collaborate more closely on these issues?

Perspectives on Donors and International Assistance to Transitional Justice

1. How familiar are you with international assistance to TJ in your country? Is this kind of assistance transparent – do you know who the main donor countries are, and what projects they are funding? Do you know how much money is being spent on TJ, in general?
2. Do you think that donors have clear goals for TJ in your country? That is, do they know what exactly they want to achieve by funding TJ efforts?
   i. Follow up: If the person says yes, then ask, what are these goals? Are they the same across donors, or are there differences?
   ii. Follow up: If the person says no, then please ask them to explain – what are their impressions of donors' goals?
3. What are your impressions of how donors make decisions about TJ funding? To what degree are national and local actors – including civil society actors – included in donor decision-making processes? Can you please give examples of inclusion or exclusion? Should there be more or less consultation in making these decisions?
   i. Follow up: How well do donors understand the national and local contexts in your country?
4. Are there cases where lack of donor knowledge has led to poor decisions – and if so, can you give an example?
5. Can you please tell us your impressions of donor interest in TJ in your country – has it remained consistent over time, or not? Why or why not?
6. Have you found it easy to fundraise for some projects, and harder for others? Can you give examples? More generally, outside of your own organization, have you noticed cases of important projects that are likely to have an important social or political impact that have not received funding? Examples? Alternatively, do some projects get too many resources?
7. Would you mind telling us which donors support your work? We can keep this information confidential if you wish.

GUIDE FOR DONORS

Donor Approaches to Transitional Justice Funding

1. Role of donors in national processes: How do you perceive your role as a donor (and the role of international actors in general) in national TJ processes? How do you see your agency as potentially having a positive impact on TJ processes?
2. Donor approaches to TJ: To what extent do you have short-, medium-, and/or long-term strategies to support specific national TJ initiatives?

   i. Follow up: Do you use any indicators to assess progress of TJ-related initiatives? How do you assess whether progress is being made?

3. Donor decision-making: How do you decide which TJ initiatives to fund? Are these decisions made in reference to local priorities (and, if so, whose), donor priorities, or a mix of the two? Who defines "local priorities" on TJ?
4. Donor coordination: When and how do you communicate about and coordinate your assistance with other actors in the donor community? What effects does such coordination have when it does take place, and when it does not take place?
5. Donor funding: What key TJ-related projects have you funded over the past two to three years? What proportion of these have been civil society-led projects? How have you made decisions about either ending funding or continuing funding for TJ-related projects? Have you ended funding for certain projects? Why or why not?

Donor Approaches to Civil Society

1. Donor approaches to civil society: How does your agency define "civil society," and do you have a specific framework for civil society engagement (whether for TJ or in general)?
2. Civil society perspectives on donor programming: What role do civil society actors, especially national actors, play in donor decision-making? How transparent and inclusive is the process? Do you think civil society actors are aware of and do they understand donor rules/constraints, for example, or donor strategies for funding TJ?
3. Enabling environment: How do you perceive the enabling/facilitating environment for civil society actors in the country, and has this affected your funding strategies?

Impact of International Assistance on Civil Society Actors and Networks

1. Social capital and trust: Have you noted changes in civil society actors' networks and capacity for collective action over time and, if so, what did you perceive to be the causes of these changes?

   i. Follow up: How deep are these changes in networks? Do they touch a broad base of groups and communities? Do they include the most vulnerable and marginalized people in the country? Please describe.

2. Type of action: What are your perspectives on the types of civil society-led initiatives/actions that have made the most difference to building relationships/social capital? For example: Have you perceived any distinctions between actions that are primarily service delivery (i.e., filling a gap in an official TJ institution, like psychosocial support to victims) versus other types of actions (e.g., advocacy, communication, coalition building)?
3. Scope of international assistance: To what degree do you think that the level and type of international assistance to a TJ process make a difference to a civil society actor's work – including its ability to establish network relationships and act collectively with others? Has there been too much/too little funding? Too much/too little technical assistance?
4. Direction of international assistance: To what degree is international assistance flowing to civil society actors who can make the most difference? To what degree is assistance flowing to those actors who are adept at facilitating networks and coordinating action?

   i. Follow up: Is there a difference in your TJ funding between professionalized NGOs and other types of civil society groups, e.g., membership-based organizations, victims groups, media actors, etc.? Do you have a special way of funding or supporting civil society organizations that are less professionalized?

5. Timing of international assistance: To what degree do you perceive that the timing of international assistance to TJ measures has positively or negatively influenced chances for building social capital and trust? Have civil society actors received funding at the moment they needed it to build networks and relationships? Have there been missed opportunities for building such networks around specific political opportunities or issues?
6. Other outcomes: Have you seen civil society actors working primarily on TJ using their networks/coalitions to address other political and social issues (development, women's rights, etc.)? Do they do this spontaneously, or is it because they are trying to fit into donors' funding priorities?

Index